# COMPETITION POLICY IN HEALTHCARE

# COMPETITION POLICY IN HEALTHCARE

## Frontiers in Insurance-based and Taxation-funded Systems

Mary Guy

intersentia
Cambridge – Antwerp – Chicago

Intersentia Ltd
Sheraton House | Castle Park
Cambridge | CB3 0AX | United Kingdom
Tel.: +44 1223 370 170 | Fax: +44 1223 370 169
Email: mail@intersentia.co.uk
www.intersentia.com | www.intersentia.co.uk

*Distribution for the UK and Ireland:*
NBN International
Airport Business Centre, 10 Thornbury Road
Plymouth, PL6 7PP
United Kingdom
Tel.: +44 1752 202 301 | Fax: +44 1752 202 331
Email: orders@nbninternational.com

*Distribution for Europe and all other countries:*
Intersentia Publishing nv
Groenstraat 31
2640 Mortsel
Belgium
Tel.: +32 3 680 15 50 | Fax: +32 3 658 71 21
Email: mail@intersentia.be

*Distribution for the USA and Canada:*
Independent Publishers Group
Order Department
814 North Franklin Street
Chicago, IL 60610
USA
Tel.: +1 800 888 4741 (toll free) | Fax: +1 312 337 5985
Email: orders@ipgbook.com

Competition Policy in Healthcare. Frontiers in Insurance-based and Taxation-funded Systems


ISBN 978-1-78068-649-3
D/2019/7849/2
NUR 828

British Library Cataloguing in Publication Data. A catalogue record for this book is available from the British Library.

# FOREWORD

In both the United Kingdom and the Netherlands, competition plays an important role in healthcare. Governments have made the provision of healthcare services subject to market forces. This policy has met with fierce opposition from some, while others consider it to be the Holy Grail for solving major problems, such as the increasing rise of healthcare costs. People tend to either oppose introducing competition in healthcare or to embrace this development. But what does introducing competition in healthcare mean? Healthcare is a broad field involving many actors, complex relationships and complicated legislation. In the same vein, competition law compromises a sophisticated set of rules geared towards fostering competition in a wide array of markets and towards balancing various objectives and interests. What are the ramifications of applying competition rules to the various healthcare operators? Mary Guy has explored with great care these ramifications by focusing on the essential characteristics of the healthcare systems of the United Kingdom and the Netherlands.

An important component of Mary Guy's study is that the rationale of the British and Dutch healthcare reforms is explained. It is an understatement to say that these reforms are complicated and hard to understand for an outsider. The insights offered in this book are very helpful to getting a better grasp of the effects of competition on healthcare and of the way that competition law is applied to healthcare cases. Of great interest is the interplay between the general competition rules and the healthcare specific competition provisions. It is illuminating to learn which difficulties are caused by this interplay in both the United Kingdom and the Netherlands.

A very important issue raised by Mary Guy is the aim of universal access. Is enhancing competition in healthcare an end in itself or does it serve another cause? In the European approach to healthcare it is commonly accepted that the policies adopted by the governments must aim at giving every citizen access to healthcare. Introducing competition must contribute to achieving this goal, which, of course, means that it is not an end in itself. This finding makes clear that applying competition law to healthcare also implies that the various interests at play must be balanced. It does not come as a surprise that in this study much attention is paid to the concept of Services of General Economic Interest. This concept is generally considered to be suitable for striking a balance between competition and the aim of universal access. The potential of Services of General Interest is explored and, of great interest, its meaning at the domestic level is examined. To date, when it comes to these services, many studies (written in English) focus on developments at the EU level, such as the case law of the Court of Justice of the EU and Commission actions. It is therefore very helpful that the present study discusses in which way Services of General Economic Interest can be incorporated into domestic healthcare systems. Lessons learned from this are not only beneficial for policy makers in healthcare but also for officials responsible for policies in other areas, where universal access is a significant value.

Although general themes and directions of travel in healthcare receive considerable attention in this book, the author has not shied away from analysing in great detail some important case law. Judgments delivered both by the Union courts and domestic courts are discussed. As a result, national case law in this specialised area is made available to many scholars and policy makers interested in healthcare and competition. It is very impressive that Mary Guy has managed to master the Dutch language, to study the Dutch healthcare laws and judgments and also to understand these (complicated) laws and judgments. The Dutch competition authority is very experienced in applying competition law to healthcare, which has also given rise to interesting judgments delivered by the competent courts in the Netherlands. It is of great value that this experience is mapped in a comprehensive way in this study. It should be noted that the discussion is not limited to the application of the general competition rules to healthcare but also concerns healthcare specific competition rules.

It goes without saying that European competition law is also of interest. The competition law systems of the United Kingdom and the Netherlands are modelled after the Treaty provisions on competition. The consequence of this is that the national rules of these systems must be interpreted in accordance with EU law. It is therefore pointed out by Mary Guy that European competition law provides an overarching framework for the healthcare policies of the national competition authorities. The room for manoeuvre for these authorities is delineated by the decisions taken by the Commission and judgments handed down by the Union courts. Then again, to date, the case law of these courts dealing with competition law and healthcare remains limited. This is not a surprise, as healthcare is not high on the agenda of the policy makers in Brussels, since this area belongs to the competences of the Member States. It is on this limited EU experience that the national competition authorities must base their interventions in healthcare. This is a very challenging task, as these authorities are confronted with complex and detailed issues and questions. Decisions and rulings adopted with regard to particular issues could be interfered with by subsequent judgments handed down by the Union courts, as is evidenced by cases such as *FENIN*.

Although the marketisation of healthcare started a long time ago, it is striking that many EU judgments still address whether or not competition law applies to entities operating in this sector. The 'gate to competition law' is constituted by the concept of undertaking. In many cases, the question has risen of whether a particular healthcare operator is an undertaking for the purposes of competition law. It remains very difficult to answer this fundamental question, which involves a sound analysis of the interests at play. One of them is, evidently, solidarity and in particular universal access. The research carried out by Mary Guy shows that many questions are left open and that issues are addressed on a case by case basis; in other words, the analysis to be carried out is based on a piecemeal approach. It cannot be excluded that the Union courts should reconsider their case law and further shape the concept of undertaking in order to do justice to the specific features of the healthcare sector. In this regard, it must be noted that to date every healthcare provider has been qualified as an undertaking. It is, however, clear from Mary Guy's study that the term 'healthcare provider' may be too wide as a category.

To a certain extent the uncertainties surrounding the concept of undertaking are exemplary for the questions resulting from the introduction of competition in healthcare. This introduction has led to much controversy and new interventions on the part of the national governments. It is apparent from the research carried out by Mary Guy that the organisation of the oversight of the competition process in healthcare is subject to a continuous process of restructuring. Mary Guy has been able to make the national measures regarding this process and the rationale underpinning them transparent. As a result, this book is a must-read for every policy maker who is somehow involved in matters related to healthcare and competition. The application of competition rules has become a sensitive issue, which requires permanent attention from the government. It is not the Holy Grail for solving problems resulting from, for example, the increasing costs of medical treatments. On the other hand, it would go too far to argue that the introduction of competition in healthcare is a failure. The present study has demonstrated that precise and accurate analysis of the effects and legal consequences of a (partly) competition driven healthcare system is required. Fine-tuning of the measures taken and close monitoring may enhance the success of a healthcare policy (partly) based on competition. In this regard, it should be noted that the concept of managed competition presupposes that regulation and competition should go hand in hand.

One of the common threads running through Mary Guy's study is the impact of EU law on national healthcare policies and competition rules. This will definitely change after Brexit. Consequently, it remains to be seen to what extent European competition law will continue to provide an overarching structure for UK oversight of competition in healthcare. Divergent approaches may occur, but then again British authorities could also decide to follow EU good practices. In other words, it remains of great importance to learn lessons from other jurisdictions, especially in a field such as healthcare, in which great interests are at stake. Similarly, the EU could learn lessons from the UK experience with healthcare and competition. Therefore, I express the wish that scholars working in both the UK and the EU, such as Mary Guy, continue to carry out comparative analyses of the various national systems on both sides of the North Sea. The lessons learned, the best practices exchanged and the knowledge gained in such analyses will be of imminent importance in the post-Brexit era.

Johan W. van de Gronden
Professor of European law
Radboud University Nijmegen, The Netherlands

# PREFACE

How a nation manages healthcare provision is a mark of its civilisation. Since resources are always finite, the best of intentions requires the management of processes and allocations. How best to proceed is a question that continues to receive varying answers and continual refinements in policy and legal frameworks. The development of competition policy is but one example of this.

An initial stimulus for my research in this area arose from the confidence evident in claims that competition policy could work in the English National Health Service (NHS) as in other sectors of the economy. Was it really that simple, was my first response. Many more questions followed. To what extent could such comparisons work, and what could they usefully prove? Are there complexities attached to the NHS (or healthcare generally) which need to be explored? If the devil is indeed in the detail, surely that is where we should look. How did we get to where we are? Could elucidation be found by examining the attempts being made to introduce competition policy into another healthcare system?

These last two questions seemed especially promising if we are to understand the issues of developing competition in healthcare and move beyond polarised claims of competition being exclusively "good" or "bad" for healthcare reform. Despite the obvious distinction between taxation-funded and insurance-based system models, the Netherlands provided an obvious comparison in view of the common features of the organising principle of solidarity and the underlying EU competition law framework (the development of Brexit notwithstanding).

What has emerged from my doctoral research and subsequent updates for this book is an understanding of the English reforms in light of the Dutch experience, and considerations for the development of competition policy in healthcare. This book therefore provides comprehensive insight into how the operation of general competition law, merger control and sectoral regulation has developed over the first years following the introduction of mandatory private health insurance in the Netherlands in 2006, and the restructuring of the English NHS by the Health and Social Care Act 2012. This contribution is intended to facilitate future discussion both within the Academy and beyond.

Over the course of writing this book, various agencies have undergone changes, including with regard to their name. The most significant of these is the incorporation of Monitor – initially established as the independent regulator of NHS Foundation Trusts and subsequently re-cast as the sectoral regulator for healthcare by the Health and Social Care Act 2012 (HSCA 2012) reforms – into NHS Improvement in April 2016, along with the NHS Trust Development Authority (NHS TDA), another oversight body established by the HSCA 2012. A consequence of this has been a dilemma of which name to use. In order to make the discussions of this book as up-to-date as possible, I decided to use 'NHS Improvement' throughout unless it was necessary to draw a distinction between Monitor and the NHS TDA, for example in connection with the discussions of sectoral regulation in Chapter 3 and merger assessment in Chapter 4. Associated literature is listed in the Bibliography according to the agency which published it, under 'Monitor', 'NHS Trust Development Authority' and 'NHS Improvement', accordingly.

Chapter 3 in particular is concerned with the relationship between competition authorities and sectoral regulators; thus, it has been necessary to engage with the specific concepts of 'concurrency' in respect of UK economic regulation and *samenloop* in the Netherlands. In many circumstances, it would be perfectly acceptable and accurate to translate *samenloop* as 'concurrent', particularly in view of the general definition of the latter in the Oxford English Dictionary as 'Existing, happening or done at the same time'. However, when discussing aspects of UK economic regulation, 'concurrency' takes on the meaning of the competition authority and the economic regulator applying the *same* rules (applying general competition law). This situation is arguably better described as the agencies being 'co-competent'.[1] As the English nomenclature proves problematic in this comparative analysis, *samenloop* has therefore been translated as 'overlap' throughout this book.

Mary Guy
Utrecht, 1 October 2018

1 A term used by Sánchez Graells to describe the relationship between Monitor and the Competition and Markets Authority (CMA). See A. Sánchez Graells, 'Monitor and the Competition and Markets Authority', (2014) *University of Leicester School of Law Research Paper*, 14(32).

# ACKNOWLEDGEMENTS

Over the course of writing this book, I was fortunate enough to be able to present to and discuss my research with a wide range of academics and practitioners in the UK and abroad. Of particular note have been discussions with the Authority for Consumers and Markets (ACM), the Dutch Healthcare Authority (NZa), and Monitor (now NHS Improvement). With regard to academic audiences, the following workshops in particular contributed significantly to the development of the research in this book: the 'Old Markets, New Markets: Health Law after the 2012 Act' workshop of the Health Law and Policy Research Group (Sheffield, June 2013), British Association of Comparative Law Postgraduate Workshops (Essex, April 2013 and UEA, April 2015), Competition Law and Economics European Network (CLEEN) workshops (UEA, June 2014 and Tilburg, May 2015), Social Justice workshop (LSE, August 2014), the Antitrust Law and Healthcare workshop (EUI Florence, November 2014), the Markets, Medicines and Morals workshop (University of Liverpool, May 2016) and the Competition Law Scholars Forum workshop (University of Amsterdam, September 2017).

Individual thanks are due to the following for various kinds of support and encouragement: my PhD supervisors and internal examiner at UEA Law School, Professors Michael Harker, Morten Hviid and Andreas Stephan; Professor Johan van de Gronden (Radboud University, Nijmegen) for acting as external examiner for my thesis, providing the Foreword to this book and for ongoing collaborations and discussions of EU competition law and healthcare which have helped shape Chapter 2; Professor Wolf Sauter (Authority for Consumers and Markets and Tilburg University) for encouragement and support in related projects, many illuminating discussions which have helped to develop Chapters 2–4, and for specific feedback on an early draft of what has become Chapter 3; and Andrew Taylor (Aldwych Partners) for discussions about NHS reform and for feedback on Chapter 4.

I am also very grateful to my colleagues at Lancaster Law School and to Ann-Christin Maak-Scherpe, Rebecca Moffat and Ahmed Hegazi at Intersentia for their ongoing support in the production of this book. I am also grateful to Intersentia for allowing material from Chapter 3 to appear in an article, "Competition and sectoral regulation in Dutch and English healthcare: factors shaping the competition focus of the new healthcare regulators and their relationship with the competition authorities", published by Ius Publicum in December 2017.

This book is dedicated to my family.

# CONTENTS

# LIST OF CASES

## 1. EUROPEAN UNION (EU)

### COURT OF JUSTICE OF THE EUROPEAN UNION (CJEU) CASES



### GENERAL COURT (GC) CASES

## ADVOCATE GENERAL'S OPINION



## 2. THE NETHERLANDS

### COURTS AND TRIBUNALS

*Rechtbank Rotterdam – Rotterdam District Court (Rb)*



*College van Beroep voor het Bedrijfsleven – Trade and Industry Appeals Tribunal (CBb)*



### *AUTORITEIT CONSUMENT EN MARKT* (AUTHORITY FOR CONSUMERS AND MARKETS (ACM))/*NEDERLANDSE MEDEDINGINGSAUTORITEIT* (DUTCH COMPETITION AUTHORITY (NMA)) – CASES AND INFORMAL OPINION

## *NEDERLANDSE ZORGAUTORITEIT* (DUTCH HEALTHCARE AUTHORITY (NZa)) – CASES, OPINIONS AND REGULATION



# 3. UNITED KINGDOM (ENGLAND)

## COURTS AND TRIBUNALS

## COMPETITION AND MARKETS AUTHORITY (CMA)



## COMPETITION COMMISSION (CC)



## MONITOR

## NHS COOPERATION AND COMPETITION PANEL (NHS CCP)



## NHS IMPROVEMENT



## NHS TRUST DEVELOPMENT AUTHORITY (NHS TDA)



## OFFICE OF FAIR TRADING (OFT)

# LIST OF LEGISLATION

## 1. EUROPEAN UNION (EU)



## 2. THE NETHERLANDS

## GOVERNMENT DECREES

## LEGISLATIVE PROPOSALS AND ASSOCIATED DOCUMENTATION

*Preceding the Dutch Health Insurance Act 2006 (Zvw):*



*Preceding the Dutch Healthcare (Market Regulation) Act 2006 (Wmg):*



*Subsequent amendments to the Wmg:*



*Current proposals to amend the Wmg to implement the transfer of competence from the NZa to the ACM:*



*Proposed amendments to the Wmg*

## POLICY RULES

## 3. UNITED KINGDOM

### PRIMARY LEGISLATION

## SECONDARY LEGISLATION

## BILLS AND ASSOCIATED DOCUMENTATION



### *Hansard*



### *Policy Documents*

# TABLE OF FIGURES

## Chapter 4



## Conclusions

# ABBREVIATIONS

| | |
|---|---|
| ACM | *Autoriteit Consument en Markt* (Dutch Authority for Consumers and Markets) |
| ACO | Accountable Care Organisation |
| AMC | *Academisch Medisch Centrum* (Academic Medical Centre of the University of Amsterdam) |
| AQP | Any Qualified Provider |
| AWP | Any Willing Provider |
| CA98 | Competition Act 1998 |
| CAT | Competition Appeals Tribunal |
| CBb | *College van Beroep voor het bedrijfsleven* (Dutch Trade and Industry Tribunal – upper appeal court for competition cases) |
| CC | Competition Commission |
| CCG | Clinical Commissioning Group |
| CJEU | Court of Justice of the European Union |
| CMA | Competition and Markets Authority |
| CQC | Care Quality Commission |
| CVZ | *College voor Zorgverzekeringen* (Dutch Healthcare Insurance Board) |
| DHA | District Health Authority |
| DNB | *De Nederlandsche Bank* (Dutch National Bank) |
| EA02 | Enterprise Act 2002 |
| ERRA 2013 | Enterprise and Regulatory Reform Act 2013 |
| EUMR | EU Merger Regulation |
| FFT | Friends and Family Test |
| GP | General Practitioner |
| HSCA 2012 | Health and Social Care Act 2012 |
| IGJ | *Inspectie voor de gezondheidszorg en jeugd* (Dutch Health and Youth Care Inspectorate – quality regulator) |
| ISTC | Independent Sector Treatment Centre |
| KNAW | *Koninklijke Nederlandse Akademie van Wetenschappen* (Royal Netherlands Academy of Arts and Sciences) |
| LHV | *Landelijke Huisartsen Vereniging* (Dutch GPs' Association) |
| LOCI | Logit Competition Index |
| LLP | Limited Liability Partnership |

| | |
|---|---|
| Mw | *Mededingingswet* (Dutch Competition Act 1998) |
| NCA | National Competition Authority |
| NHS | National Health Service |
| NHS CCP | NHS Cooperation and Competition Panel |
| NHS FYFV | NHS Five Year Forward View |
| NHS PRCC | NHS Principles and Rules for Competition and Cooperation |
| NHS TDA | NHS Trust Development Authority (now part of NHS Improvement) |
| NMa | *Nederlandse Mededingingsautoriteit* (Dutch Competition Authority) |
| NVP | *Nederlandse Vereniging van Participatiemaatschappijen* (Dutch Venture Capital Association) |
| NZa | *Nederlandse Zorgautoriteit* (Dutch Healthcare Authority) |
| ODM | Option Demand Method |
| OFT | Office of Fair Trading |
| OPTA | *Onafhankelijke Post en Telecommunicatie Autoriteit* (Dutch Independent Postal and Telecoms Regulator) |
| PCT | Primary Care Trust |
| PMI | Private Medical Insurance |
| PPU | Private Patient Unit |
| PSO | Public Service Obligation |
| Rb | *Rechtbank Rotterdam* (Rotterdam District Court – lower appeal court for competition cases) |
| RES | Risk Equalisation Scheme |
| SGI | Service of General Interest |
| SGEI(s) | Service(s) of General Economic Interest |
| SIEC | Significant Impediment to Effective Competition |
| SLC | Substantial Lessening of Competition |
| SMP | Significant Market Power |
| SSNIP | Small but Significant and Non-Transitory Increase in Price |
| STP | Sustainability and Transformation Partnership |
| TFEU | Treaty on the Functioning of the European Union |
| VUmc | *Vrije Universiteit Medisch Centrum* (Vrije Universiteit Medical Centre) |
| WBMV | *Wet op bijzondere medische verrichtingen* (Dutch Special Medical Procedures Act 1997) |
| Whc | *Wet handhaving consumentenbescherming* (Dutch Consumer Protection (Enforcement) Act 2006) |
| Wlz | *Wet langdurige zorg* (Dutch Long-Term Care Act 2015) |

| | |
|---|---|
| Wmg | *Wet marktordening gezondheidszorg* (Dutch Healthcare (Market Regulation) Act 2006) |
| Wmo | *Wet maatschappelijke ondersteuning* (Dutch Social Support Act 2015) |
| WTP | Willingness To Pay |
| ZBO | *Zelfsbestuursorgaan* (autonomous administrative agency) |
| Zvw | *Zorgverzekeringswet* (Dutch Health Insurance Act 2006) |

# INTRODUCTION

Competition in healthcare provision is a subject which attracts much controversy, with an obvious sensitivity being the tension between competition (with an inherent focus on 'winners' and 'losers') and solidarity (defined here[1] simply as the principle of organising healthcare provision to enable universal access).[2] This tension can be said to arise because 'we do not come to markets as equals'[3] and, fundamentally, because solidarity forms the 'ideational point' upon which EU Member State healthcare systems converge,[4] regardless of whether these are, broadly speaking, taxation-funded (such as the English[5] National Health Service (NHS)) or insurance-based (such as the Dutch system). An immediate contrast becomes evident with how competition has developed in US healthcare, where efficiency appears to be prioritised over equity.[6]

The issues become more complex when it is realised that the distinction between a taxation-funded system and an insurance-based system has

1 Although it is recognised that 'solidarity' as a principle within EU law may be understood in various ways according to context. See, for example, E. Küçük, 'Solidarity in EU Law – An Elusive Political Statement or a Legal Principle with Substance?' (2016) 26(3) *Maastricht Journal of European and Comparative Law* 965.

2 A related tension arises from perceptions of public and private sector delivery of services.

3 T. Prosser, *The Limits of Competition Law*, Oxford University Press, Oxford 2005, p. 29.

4 T.K. Hervey, 'Public Health Services and EU Law' in M. Cremona (ed.), *Market Integration and Public Services in the European Union*, Oxford University Press, Oxford 2011, p. 186.

5 It is to be noted that England has experimented with market reforms in its NHS in a way that other countries of the UK have not, hence the focus of this book is on England. Indeed, the NHS is organised in different ways across the four countries of the United Kingdom: for recent discussion, see, for example, N. Timmins, *The Four UK Health Systems: Learning from Each Other*, London: King's Fund 2013. Furthermore, the Introductory Text to the Health and Social Care Act 2012 provides that it is 'An Act to establish and make provision about a National Health Service Commissioning Board [now NHS England] and clinical commissioning groups and to make other provision about the National Health Service in England …'

6 See M. Gaynor, 'Competition in Hospital Services', OECD Directorate for Financial and Enterprise Affairs Competition Committee, Working Party No. 2 on Competition and Regulation, DAF/COMP/WP2(2012)3, 06.02.2012. T. Stoltzfus Jost, D. Dawson and A. Den Exter, 'The Role of Competition in Health Care: A Western European Perspective' (2006) 31(3) *Journal of Health Politics, Policy and Law* 687.

implications for the ways in which, and the extent to which, competition can be developed, regardless of a common starting-point of solidarity. This is because

> in a supply-driven, tax-based system, governments are likely to determine the precise levels of benefits, whereas governments that rely on a health insurance scheme are more likely to leave some room for demand-driven competition with regard to the benefits that the insured persons are entitled to (for instance, based on supplementary insurance).[7]

A further distinction arises between *competition*, and *competition policy*. Whereas the former may be wide-ranging (depending upon the scope for competition), the latter may appear more rigid: the underlying legal framework is characterised by binary questions of applicability and exceptions which may not provide the flexibility needed to experiment with competition as a form of healthcare system modernisation.[8] The underlying framework may also not offer much recognition, let alone accommodation, of (public interest) values inherent in healthcare provision, namely, accessibility, affordability and quality. Ultimately, competition reforms of healthcare provision appear to attract a degree of (political) sensitivity which does not attach to other sectors, or even to ancillary aspects of healthcare such as mergers of health insurers or pharmaceutical companies.

The aim of this book is to provide insight into the development of competition policy in healthcare in light of such distinctions and sensitivities and by reference to the implementation of recent reforms in Dutch and English healthcare – namely, the introduction of mandatory private health insurance in the Netherlands in 2006 and the reorganisation of the NHS in England[9] by the Health and Social Care Act 2012 (HSCA 2012).

Overall, the book adopts a comparative methodology,[10] but this is not framed in terms of making recommendations for a 'transplant' of the Dutch system into England, or vice versa. Rather, it is suggested that the common starting-point of solidarity, and the underlying EU law framework, facilitate a

7 L. Hancher and W. Sauter, *EU Competition and Internal Market Law in the Health Care Sector*, Oxford University Press, Oxford 2012, pp. 232–33.

8 See further on this point, W. Sauter, 'Services of general economic interest and universal service obligations as an EU law framework for curative health care', (2007) *TILEC Discussion Paper* 29, <https://www.tilburguniversity.edu/upload/23c6e429-7ff9-44cd-9844-407c0bf3dfaf_SGEI-USO.pdf> accessed 24.06.2018.

9 The organisation of the NHS across the four countries of the United Kingdom varies, and the market-based reforms have been concentrated in England. Furthermore, the Introductory Text to the HSCA 2012 explicitly references England. See n. 5 above.

10 Comparisons between countries are perhaps more often found in health economics and policy circles. See, for example, L. Siciliani, M. Chalkley and H. Gravelle, 'Competition policy in five European countries – What can be learned for health policy in England?' *The Health Foundation Working Paper Number 1*, July 2017.

comparison (even in the absence of harmonisation in healthcare) and highlight limitations of competition reforms which may prove instructive for other countries.

This Introduction considers what can be understood by 'competition' and 'competition policy' in healthcare in general terms, before setting out an overview of the competition reforms in Dutch and English healthcare and discussing two narratives which help us to understand the development of associated competition policy in these two countries.

## 1. COMPETITION IN HEALTHCARE

> Healthcare is not a single service, but an enormous variety of different services. There is therefore no presumption that the desirability or feasibility of competition will be the same for all types of healthcare in all situations.[11]

The above quote encapsulates neatly some of the key difficulties of developing competition in 'healthcare', a term which can be problematic given the myriad actors and relationships involved. This is particularly so in England, where 'healthcare' masks the distinction between the NHS, which provides the majority of healthcare services, and the smaller, supplementary private healthcare sector. The relationship between the two is fundamental to understanding the design of NHS competition reforms.

The focus of this book is primarily on healthcare *provision* and how this market interacts with markets for healthcare purchasing and health insurance (particularly with regard to the Netherlands, although some mention of the UK private insurance market is made).

'Healthcare provision' has been further disaggregated as comprising a range of aspects and ancillary activities, with the finding that conditions for effective competition are 'good' in connection with ancillary activities such as pharmacy distribution, patient transportation and laboratory tests, merely 'average' for hospital care, primary care and long-term nursing care, and 'unlikely to be met' with regard to emergency treatment and intensive care.[12] Indeed, consensus appears to build around the feasibility of competition for some treatments, such as elective hip-replacement operations, but not, or to a much lesser extent, for others, such as major trauma services.[13]

---

11 Office of Health Economics (OHE), *Competition in the NHS*, OHE, London 2012, p. 8.

12 European Commission Expert Panel on Effective Ways of Investing in Health (EXPH), 'Competition among health care providers in the European Union – Investigating Policy Options', 17.02.2015, Table 4: 'Propensity to fulfil conditions for effective competition in health systems', p. 72, <https://ec.europa.eu/health/expert_panel/sites/expertpanel/files/008_competition_healthcare_providers_en.pdf> accessed 24.06.2018.

13 OHE, above n. 11, p. 47.

However, it must be recognised that feasibility of competition in healthcare can be assessed in various ways, ranging from demand-side factors (such as the existence of multiple providers and transparent information) and supply-side factors (such as easy entry and exit, cost and technology issues) to institutional and political factors, which recognise different types of ownership (i.e. public/private/mixed), that a provider may be 'too important to fail', and the incumbent provider's reputation.[14] Feasibility can also be closely linked to desirability of competition, which necessitates an examination of diverse factors, with patient willingness (or not) to travel frequently being considered a key factor in assessing how much competition and regulation may be viable. For example, emergency services and elective services in very rural areas may retain elements of a natural monopoly, necessitating substantial additional regulation, whereas elective procedures in urban areas and non-elective procedures may benefit from plurality of providers, suggesting that only some, or even a minimum level of regulation may be needed.[15] Potential to profit from a particular healthcare service can also be considered a measure of feasibility of competition in healthcare. However, this implies that services which can be excluded from competition (and the application of competition law) are extremely limited: an example being smallpox immunisation because it may not be possible to provide immunisation from communicable diseases to those willing/able to pay without also providing vaccines to those unwilling/unable to pay.[16] However, the inclusion of some other aspects in feasibility assessments – such as patient willingness/ability to pay – would suggest that 'normative or ideological'[17] questions of desirability of competition/exclusion from competition remain valid considerations.

In addition to the feasibility of competition, *types* of competition come into play in discussing healthcare reforms. Whilst various types of competition in healthcare can be identified,[18] the most relevant to the discussions in this book is competition *in* the market, where patients play a direct role, although competition *for* the market (procurement activity) is also noted. Whereas the Dutch system can be considered to incorporate a greater degree of competition

---

14 Ibid., pp. 45–47.

15 Department of Health, 'Protecting and Promoting Patients' Interests: the role of Sector Regulation', Department of Health, London 01.12.2011, p. 19, <https://www.gov.uk/government/publications/protecting-and-promoting-patients-interests-the-role-of-sector-regulation> accessed 24.06.2018.

16 O. Odudu, 'Are State-owned healthcare providers undertakings subject to competition law?' (2011) 32(5) *European Competition Law Review* 231.

17 Ibid.

18 Including benchmarking/yardstick competition and patient choice. See EXPH, above n. 12, pp. 21–29.

*in* the market,[19] there is considered to be greater scope for competition *for* the market within the English NHS.[20]

Further, to supplement the complex picture emerging from considerations of feasibility, desirability and type of competition in healthcare, a conceptual 'healthcare structure' can assist our understanding in this area. This comprises three levels as follows:[21]

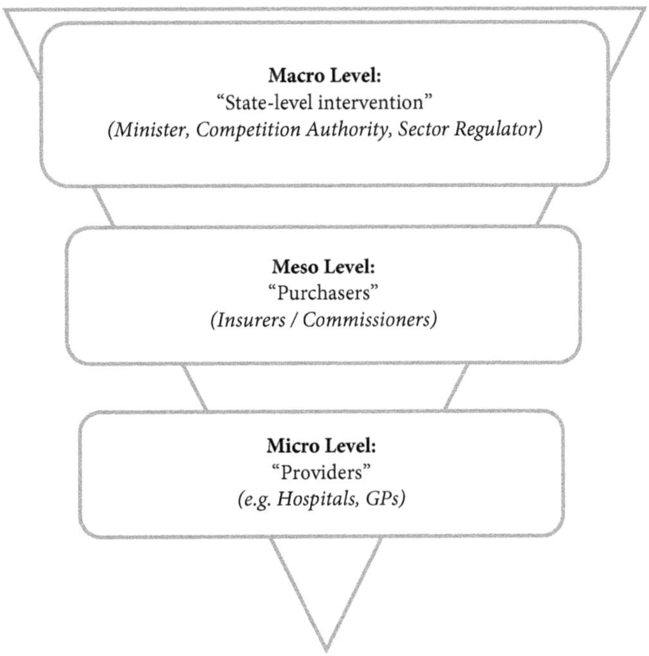


**Figure 1. Macro–Meso–Micro Healthcare Structure**

---

19 The scope for limited competition *in* the market in the English NHS is given effect by patient choice policies (for example, choice of provider in respect of a first outpatient appointment for certain elective services) which have latterly been enshrined by Regulations 11–13 of the National Health Service (Procurement, Patient Choice and Competition) Regulations (No. 2) 2013, SI 2013/500. These are considered further in Chapter 1 below.

20 OHE, above n. 11, p. 38.

21 This framework has been referenced by analogy with discussions of how healthcare is governed by K. Raptopoulou, *EU Law and Healthcare Services – Normative Approaches to Public Health Systems*, Kluwer Law International, Alphen aan den Rijn 2015, p. 153. It is derived from health law discussions of the organisation of healthcare provision. See, for example, descriptions of the structure of the NHS in C. Newdick, 'The Organisation of Healthcare' in A. Grubb (ed.), *Principles of Medical Law*, 2nd edn, Oxford University Press, Oxford 2004, pp. 3–38. See also, with regard to discussions of patient choice policies, M.K. Sheppard, 'Fallacy or Functionality: Law and Policy of Patient Treatment Choice in the NHS' (2016) 24 *Health Care Analysis* 279.

The above structure illustrates, in overview, a healthcare system, from state (government) intervention in system organisation and policy at one extreme (the macro level), to providers (ultimately the doctor–patient relationship) at the other (the micro level). The meso level serves to link the two and is populated by healthcare purchasers[22] (private health insurers in the Netherlands and NHS commissioners in England). The three levels help to give a more complete picture of 'competition' in healthcare, as well as providing a framework for discussing the applicability of competition law[23] and the development of competition policy.

Firstly, the macro level of state intervention is fundamental to any discussion of competition in healthcare, since whether or not to introduce competition is a question for national governments.[24] This level attracts a considerable degree of political sensitivity, since it is at the macro level that the difficulties in designing competition reforms in healthcare are most readily discernible. They include: 'unresolved tensions between a universalist model of health … emphasizing the principles of equal access and equal treatment of patients, and a market-driven model emphasizing efficiency, innovation, and patient choice.'[25]

These 'unresolved tensions' manifest themselves both in substantive law and institutional arrangements. The macro level may therefore be considered to be concerned with defining lines between where competition can take place and where regulation may be necessary, or at least desirable. This has implications for oversight, with the suggestion that where competition is possible, oversight will be exclusively by the competition authority, whereas where regulation is needed, this will be overseen by the sectoral regulator (possibly in conjunction with the government). In turn, this raises questions about accountability, with the HSCA 2012 reforms being considered to 'juridify' what was previously a matter of public policy (namely, the use of private providers to deliver NHS services).[26]

---

22 Also described as 'managing bodies' by, inter alia, J.W. van de Gronden, 'The Treaty Provisions on Competition and Health Care' in J.W. van de Gronden, E. Szyszczak, U. Neergaard and M. Krajewski (eds.), *Health Care and EU Law*, TMC Asser Press, The Hague 2011, pp. 265–94, in the context of discussions about EU competition law and healthcare.

23 The distinction between the meso and micro levels in particular is helpful for discussing the applicability of competition law (examined in Chapter 2 below) in view of divergent approaches taken to healthcare providers and managing bodies by the EU Commission and courts. For an overview, see, for example, J.W. van de Gronden and C.S. Rusu, 'EU competition law and policy and health systems' in T.K. Hervey, C.A. Young and L.E. Bishop (eds.), *Research Handbook on EU Health Law and Policy*, Edward Elgar, Cheltenham 2017, pp. 267–90.

24 Article 168(7) Treaty on the Functioning of the European Union (TFEU) effectively operates to reserve healthcare system organisation as a matter for Member States, so this is not a decision to be taken at EU level.

25 T. Prosser, above n. 3, p. 9.

26 For an excellent discussion, see A.C.L. Davies, 'This Time, It's For Real' (2013) 76(3) *Modern Law Review* 564.

Secondly, the meso level of purchasers or managing bodies in healthcare comprises NHS commissioners[27] in England and private health insurers in the Netherlands. The meso level – effectively the healthcare purchasing market – is useful for facilitating discussion of purchasing markets and the role of healthcare purchasers in stimulating competition among healthcare providers for contracts.

Thirdly, the micro level of healthcare providers – such as primary care providers (general practitioners (GPs)), hospitals or particular specialists – is significant, since at this level is found much of the above discussion regarding feasibility of competition and the clearest examples of competition from a patient's perspective. Thus, in England, competition may be seen to exist *between* an NHS provider and a private provider. In the Netherlands, patients' choice of provider may be constrained according to the type of insurance policy selected.[28]

What is difficult to incorporate explicitly within this framework, and what may initially appear missing from the above diagram, is patients. This is not a deliberate exclusion: patients, and particularly patient choice, form an important justification for competition-based reforms. Despite this, it is not possible to assign patients to just one level since they may be considered to feature (or at least be reflected) as a focus for the actors at each level: state, purchasers and providers.[29] Indeed, patients may also be deemed 'purchasers' of healthcare, operating at the meso level themselves. Examples of this would include patients who pay (particularly using their own resources rather than private medical insurance) to see private providers within the English system, and NHS patients with complex (typically long-term) conditions who receive a Personal Health Budget in England,[30] over which they can exert some control. However, such examples have not received much attention within the design of competition policy in healthcare thus far.[31]

Furthermore, to date, EU competition cases relating to healthcare have not considered the effects on patients deemed to be the 'end users', or 'ultimate

---

27 The Clinical Commissioning Groups (CCGs) and, in connection with specialist services, NHS England – both instituted by the HSCA 2012.

28 This is discussed further in Chapter 1 below.

29 See also M.K. Sheppard, above n. 21.

30 NHS England, 'Personal Health Budgets (PHBs)', <https://www.england.nhs.uk/personal-health-budgets/> accessed 24.06.2018. A parallel may be drawn with the *persoonsgebonden budget* (personal care budget) in the Netherlands. Zorgwijzer, *'Persoonsgebondenbudget'*, <https://www.zorgwijzer.nl/faq/hoe-kom-ik-aanmerking-voor-het-pgb> accessed 24.06.2018.

31 Although it has been noted that patients with Personal Health Budgets – who are effectively operating as NHS commissioners for their own care – are unlikely to be in breach of the National Health Service (Procurement, Patient Choice and Competition) (No. 2) Regulations 2013 provided that the services selected are clinically appropriate for the individual and have been suitably planned and agreed between the individual and the NHS team responsible for administering the personal health budget. See Monitor, 'Substantive Guidance on the Procurement, Patient Choice and Competition Regulations', London December 2013, p. 16.

consumers' of healthcare.[32] Whilst the reasons for this remain unclear, some explanation can perhaps be found in discussions of citizenship rights and public services,[33] and the 'dual identity' of individuals as 'patients' on the one hand, and 'taxpayers' (with regard to the English NHS) or 'insurance policyholders' (in the Dutch system) on the other.[34] Nevertheless, questions about the role of patients, and who the consumer (purchaser) of healthcare is, may well play a role in shaping competition policy.

## 2. COMPETITION POLICY IN HEALTHCARE – A STARTING-POINT

> [A] successful competition policy in this field is likely to be of central importance to the success of and/or support for liberalisation. This is because if, due to a lack of competition, the reforms fail to produce results, that is, improved health care performance in terms of quality, access, and affordability, the overall support for reform is likely to erode.[35]

It is difficult to disagree with this claim. However, it is to be noted that whilst multiple factors determine the *feasibility of competition* within healthcare, and different *types of competition* suggest a certain flexibility, the development of *competition policy* in healthcare is more rigid, offering binary distinctions between the applicability of competition law and narrowly-construed exclusions, or limited modifications. But before an examination of the issues, some clarification of 'competition policy' is in order.

In the wider context, 'competition policy' can be understood in terms of economic explanations of market activity.[36] However, it can also be considered a blanket term which covers general EU and/or national competition law (which may be understood as comprising several or all of the provisions governing anticompetitive agreements and abuse of dominance, merger control and state aid),[37] associated national-level, sector-specific regulatory rules and even

32 W. Sauter, 'The Impact of EU Competition Law on National Healthcare Systems' (2013) 38(4) *European Law Review* 457.

33 See, for example, T. Prosser, above n. 3, pp. 28–35.

34 This is discussed further in Chapter 3 below. See also, W. Sauter, 'Is the general consumer interest a source of legitimacy for healthcare regulation? An analysis of the Dutch experience' (2009) 2–3 *European Journal of Consumer Law* 419.

35 W. Sauter, 'Experiences from the Netherlands: The Application of Competition Rules in Health Care' in J.W. van de Gronden, E. Szyszczak, U. Neergaard and M. Krajewski (eds.), *Health Care and EU Law*, TMC Asser Press, The Hague 2011, p. 342.

36 For a notable example, see M. Motta, *Competition Policy – Theory and Practice*, Cambridge University Press, Cambridge 2004.

37 Which may simply be subsumed under the title of 'competition law', along with specific regimes, for example for the pharmaceuticals or media sectors, which may, respectively,

the relationships between, variously, the European Commission, National Competition Authorities (NCAs) and sectoral regulators.[38] 'Competition policy' can further be understood by reference to differing schools of competition theory,[39] and ongoing discussions of the purpose and delineating framework of competition law,[40] specifically the general focus on enhancing consumer welfare, which, although established, remains subject to questioning.[41]

'Competition policy in healthcare' is defined in this book as comprising two elements: general competition policy (the EU and national general competition/antitrust rules and merger control regimes); and the sector-specific competition policies which have developed in connection with both Dutch and English healthcare.[42] Each element has produced its own lines of discussion.

With regard to the general competition policy aspect, one notable focus has been the extent of the applicability of competition law, particularly in light of the tension outlined above between solidarity and competition, and the incorporation of the healthcare-specific values of affordability, accessibility and quality.[43] Other considerations include the use of exceptions, notably the

---

be overseen by either or both of the competition authority and the sectoral regulator. For an example of this wide-ranging definition of 'competition law', see J. Faull and A. Nikpay, *The EU Law of Competition*, 3rd edn, Oxford University Press, Oxford 2014.

38 The latter appear included within the Commission's definition of 'competition policy'. See European Commission, 'What is competition policy?', <http://ec.europa.eu/competition/consumers/what_en.html> accessed 24.06.2018.

39 It has been considered that current EU competition policy draws on all of ordoliberalism, the Harvard School and the Chicago School. S. Kingston, *Greening EU competition law and policy*, Cambridge University Press, Cambridge 2012, p. 10. Kingston analyses each school with regard to their assessment/accommodation of the role of environmental factors. Applying this to health, it might be considered that a similar integrated policy perspective as associated with the ordoliberal vision is needed.

40 For a comprehensive overview, see I. Lianos, 'Some reflections on the goals of EU competition law' in I. Lianos and D. Geradin (eds.), *Handbook in EU Competition Law: Substantive Aspects*, Edward Elgar, Cheltenham 2013, p. 1. W. Sauter, *Coherence in EU Competition Law*, Oxford University Press, Oxford 2016.

41 See V. Daskalova, 'Consumer Welfare in EU Competition Law: What Is It (Not) About?' (2015) 11(1) *Competition Law Review* 133. R. Claassen and A. Gerbrandy, 'Rethinking European Competition Law: From A Consumer Welfare to a Capability Approach' (2016) 12(1) *Utrecht Law Review* 1.

42 These legal provisions have also been discussed to a greater or lesser extent in analyses by health economists. See, for example, F.T. Schut and M. Varkevisser, 'Competition policy for health care provision in the Netherlands' (2017) 121(2) *Health Policy* 126. C. Propper, 'Competition in health care: lessons from the English experience' (May 2018) *Health Economics, Policy and Law* 1 (online). M. Sanderson, P. Allen and D. Osipovic, 'The regulation of competition in the National Health Service (NHS): what difference has the Health and Social Care Act 2012 made?' (2017) 12 *Health Economics, Policy and Law* 1.

43 See, for example, O. Odudu above n. 16; W. Sauter above n. 35; and J.W. van de Gronden and E. Szyszczak, 'Introducing Competition Principles Into Health Care Through EU Law and Policy: A Case Study of the Netherlands' (2014) 22(2) *Medical Law Review* 238.

classification of Services of General Economic Interest (SGEI),[44] but also the availability (and non-use) of ministerial intervention categories in UK merger control.[45] A further line of questions includes how competition authorities apply general competition law to the healthcare sector.[46]

With regard to the sector-specific competition policy aspect, examinations thus far include overall reviews of these by reference to other sectors,[47] and the compatibility of regulatory rules with EU law.[48]

A further aspect of competition policy in healthcare is apparent in competition law assessments. In particular, market definition in healthcare proves difficult because tools such as the 'Small but Significant and Non-Transitory Increase in Price' (SSNIP) test are limited in their ability to address issues such as the 'third party pays' principle, or patient insensitivity to bearing healthcare costs (these being borne primarily by health insurers in the Dutch system or NHS commissioners in England).

It is also to be noted that substitutability may vary according to different levels. For example, for patients there is little to no demand substitution for diagnosis (for example, hip replacement is not a useful substitute for heart surgery), but a limited degree of supply substitution may be possible (for example, an orthopaedic surgeon can operate on knees and shoulders alike).[49] An extra dimension is added in the English context by the coexistence of the NHS and private healthcare sector, as medical practitioners may treat both NHS

---

44 Article 106(2) Treaty on the Functioning of the European Union (TFEU). For a discussion of the potential significance of this within the context of the Dutch healthcare reforms, see W. Sauter, *'Diensten van algemeen economisch belang en universele dienstverplichtingen in de gezondheidszorg'* ('Services of General Economic Interest and Universal Service Obligations in Healthcare') (2008) *Markt & Mededinging*, 1, 4.

45 For example, the ability of the Secretary of State to intervene in certain 'public interest cases' within the UK merger control regime, under section 42 Enterprise Act 2002 (EA02). K. Desai, 'Public hospital mergers: a case for broader considerations than competition law?' (2013) 34(12) *European Competition Law Review* 646.

46 E.M.H. Loozen, 'Public healthcare interests require strict competition enforcement' (2015) 119(7) *Health Policy* 882.

47 See, for example, W. Sauter, *'Sectorspecifiek mededingingsrecht en fusietoetsing'* ('Sector-specific competition law and merger control') (2013) *RegelMaat*, (28)2, 77; and E.M.H. Loozen, *'Inrichting van meervoudig toezicht op marktwerking'* ('Introduction of multisector regulation of competition') (2013) *RegelMaat*, (28)2, 105. L. Stirton, 'Back to the Future? Lessons on the Pro-Competitive Regulation of Health Services' (2014) 22(2) *Medical Law Review* 180.

48 M. Wiggers, *De NMa en de NZa in de curatieve zorgsector – Een toetsing aan het Europees mededingingsrecht* (The NMa and the NZa in the curative healthcare sector – an assessment against EU competition law) Kluwer, Deventer 2013. A. Sánchez Graells, 'New rules for health care procurement in the UK: a critical assessment from the perspective of EU economic law' (2015) 1 *Public Procurement Law Review* 16; and A. Sánchez Graells, 'Monitor and the Competition and Markets Authority' (2014) *University of Leicester School of Law Research Paper*, No. 14-32.

49 W. Sauter, above n. 35, p. 345.

and private patients, and, subject to certain rules,[50] patients can opt to receive treatment on the NHS or privately.

## 3. OVERVIEW OF COMPETITION REFORMS IN DUTCH AND ENGLISH HEALTHCARE

In the Netherlands, 2006 saw the implementation of a system of mandatory private health insurance, designed along the lines of 'managed competition' conceptualised by the US health economist, Alain Enthoven. These reforms marked the culmination of an evolution of approximately 20 years, away from a bifurcated system of *ziekenfondsen* (state-run sickness funds) and private health insurance, and are enshrined in the *Zorgverzekeringswet* (Dutch Health Insurance Act 2006 (Zvw)). This system change is supported, inter alia, by the creation of the *Nederlandse Zorgautoriteit* (Dutch Healthcare Authority (NZa)) to work, inter alia, with the *Autoriteit Consument en Markt* (Authority for Consumers and Markets (ACM)).[51] It is further underpinned by a competition regulation framework, enshrined in the *Wet Marktordening Gezondheidszorg* (Dutch Healthcare (Market Regulation) Act 2006 (Wmg)), to operate alongside the general *Mededingingswet* (Dutch Competition Act 1998 (Mw)).

In England, the HSCA 2012 similarly marked the culmination of a period of developing market reforms in the English NHS. These started under the 1980s Conservative governments with the Enthoven-inspired 'NHS internal market', characterised primarily by the separation of purchasers and providers,[52] and continued, primarily with the expansion under New Labour of private sector delivery of NHS services, underpinned by patient choice policies. Although the HSCA 2012 reforms appear simply to formalise these developments, fundamental distinctions emerge. For example, explicit provision in statute is made for the first time – in varying ways – for the Competition and Markets Authority (CMA) to be involved in an NHS context with the application of UK and EU general competition law,[53] the UK market investigation regime[54]

---

50 Department of Health, 'Guidance on NHS patients who wish to pay for additional private care', 23.03.2009. NHS Commissioning Board (now NHS England), 'Commissioning Policy: Defining the boundaries between NHS and Private Healthcare', April 2013, Ref: NHSCB/CP/12.

51 Which has existed since 2013 and incorporates the former *Nederlandse Mededingingsautoriteit* (Dutch Competition Authority (NMa)).

52 However, the market reforms also included the conflation of purchasing and providing functions, which has latterly found reflection in the creation of Clinical Commissioning Groups (CCGs).

53 Section 72 Health and Social Care Act 2012 (HSCA 2012) with reference to the UK Competition Act 1998 (CA98) and Articles 101 and 102 of the Treaty on the Functioning of the European Union (TFEU).

54 Section 73 HSCA 2012 with reference to Part 4 EA02.

and the UK general merger-control regime.[55] In addition, the HSCA 2012 created a sectoral regulator – initially 'Monitor', now subsumed into NHS Improvement.[56]

The aforementioned competition–solidarity tension is evident to varying degrees in both sets of reforms. In the Netherlands, this has found reflection in recent and ongoing reforms to refocus competition with the recent transfer of most of the NZa's competition powers to the ACM,[57] and the 2017 *Regeerakkoord* (Government Agreement) considering the development of measures to minimise the negative effects of private insurance policies on a solidarity-based system.[58] In England, the competition–solidarity tension is characterised by the generic criticism of 'NHS privatisation' which relates mainly to the expansion of private sector delivery of NHS services, but also includes the development of NHS providers to function within the smaller, supplementary private healthcare market, typically by operating Private Patient Units (PPUs).[59] In view of this, it is difficult to overstate the controversies surrounding the enactment of the HSCA 2012,[60] and how these have shaped the resulting competition policy. This in turn appears to cast a shadow over subsequent wider NHS policy which emphasises integration[61] to the point that the Health and Social Care Select

---

55 Section 79 HSCA 2012 with reference to Part 3 EA02.

56 NHS Improvement encompasses Monitor, which was established by the HSCA 2012 as the sectoral regulator for healthcare. See in particular sections 61 and 62 HSCA 2012. NHS Improvement was established on 1 April 2016. NHS Improvement, 'Who We Are', <https://improvement.nhs.uk/about-us/who-we-are/> accessed 24.06.2018.

57 As set out in a legislative proposal which has been passing through the Second Chamber of the Dutch parliament since the 2015–16 Parliamentary Session. *Kamerstukken II, 2017–18, 34 445, Wijziging van de Wet marktordening gezondheidszorg en enkele andere wetten in verband met aanpassingen van de tarief- en prestatieregulering en het markttoezicht op het terrein van de gezondheidszorg* (Second Chamber documentation, Parliamentary Session 2017–18, 34 445, Amendments to the Wmg and other laws to apply tariff regulation and market regulation in healthcare).

58 VVD, CDA, D66 en ChristenUnie, *Regeerakkoord 2017–2021: 'Vertrouwen in de toekomst'* ('Trust in the Future'), 10.10.2017, p. 14, <file:///C:/Users/owner/AppData/Local/Packages/Microsoft.MicrosoftEdge_8wekyb3d8bbwe/TempState/Downloads/Regeerakkoord+2017-2021%20(2).pdf> accessed 24.06.2018.

59 A subject which polarises opinion. See, for example, A. Scott, T. Stevenson and V. Chua, 'The profitability of private patients', *Health Service Journal*, 27.09.2012. C. Leys, 'Treating private patients in NHS hospitals – benefit or cost?', *Health Service Journal*, 13.03.2018.

60 For the most comprehensive account thus far, see N. Timmins, *Never Again? The story of the Health and Social Care Act 2012 – A study in coalition government and policy making*, The King's Fund and Institute for Government, London 2012. For an overview, see The King's Fund, 'The Health and Social Care Act: the tale in a timeline', <http://www.kingsfund.org.uk/topics/nhs-reform/health-and-social-care-act-2012-timeline> accessed 24.06.2018.

61 Via the elaboration of the 'NHS Five Year Forward View', published in October 2014, and the current development of Sustainability and Transformation Partnerships. See, respectively, NHS England, 'Five Year Forward View', <https://www.england.nhs.uk/five-year-forward-view/>; and NHS England, 'Integrated Care', <https://www.england.nhs.uk/systemchange/> both accessed 24.06.2018.

Committee has recently called for legislative change regarding procurement and competition.[62]

What has also emerged during the implementation of the 2006 and HSCA 2012 reforms is a sense of ambivalence on the part of the competition authorities, which adds an interesting dimension to considerations of the future of competition and competition policy in healthcare. In the Netherlands, the ACM has been emphatic that its scope for intervention is limited: it can only intervene where competition law is breached, and this may be inconsistent with the Dutch government's ambitions for competition reforms.[63] In England, the CMA acknowledged the wider NHS policy context in the 2017 'Manchester Hospitals' merger, commenting that competition currently plays a limited role in the NHS and is not the basic organising principle for the provision of NHS services.[64]

There is clearly potential for ambivalence, if not outright inconsistency, in the development of competition policy in healthcare. It must be noted that, at a fundamental level, the distinction between an insurance-based healthcare system (the Netherlands) and a taxation-funded NHS (England) means that *competition* develops in different ways. In contrast, the development of competition *policy* in both systems is characterised by similarities which emerge from, perhaps most notably, the EU competition law framework (despite explicit harmonisation)[65] and national merger-control regimes.

Part of this ambivalence/inconsistency may be attributed to two narratives which have accompanied the development of competition policy in Dutch and English healthcare – these are now considered.

## 4. COMPETITION POLICY IN (DUTCH AND ENGLISH) HEALTHCARE – TWO NARRATIVES

> We did it in gas, we did it in power, we did it in telecoms. We've done it in rail, we've done it in water. So there is actually 20 years' experience of taking monopolistic,

62 House of Commons Health and Social Care Committee, *Integrated care: organisations, partnerships and systems*. Seventh Report of Session 2017–19, 11.06.2018, p. 7.

63 See, for example, Autoriteit Consument en Markt (ACM), *'Position Paper Autoriteit Consument en Markt Rondetafelgesprek "Kwaliteit loont"'* ('ACM Position Paper on the "Quality Pays" roundtable discussion'), 17.04.2015, <https://www.zorgkennis.net/downloads/kennisbank/ZK-kennisbank-Position-paper-AC&M-Kwalitieit-loont-3147.pdf> accessed 24.06.2018.

64 Competition and Markets Authority (CMA), *Central Manchester University Hospitals/University Hospital of South Manchester merger inquiry. Final Report*, 01.08.2017.

65 Concerns about differing approaches being taken to interpretation of EU competition rules have given rise to the concept of 'Euro-national competition rules for healthcare'. See further, J.W. van de Gronden above n. 22; and J.W. van de Gronden and E. Szyszczak, above n. 43.

> monolithic markets and providers and exposing them to economic regulation … [But] [i]t is too easy to say, 'How can you compare buying electricity with buying healthcare services?' Of course they are different. I would say … there are important similarities and that's what convinces me that choice and competition will work in the NHS as it did in those other sectors.[66]

> In general, all sectors and industries which we oversee take the view that the competition rules cannot really be applied to them. But healthcare really is a separate issue for me … I found 'healthcare and competition' the most difficult subject. First of all, of course, you have to learn how the healthcare market functions, but then you are confronted with issues which mean you cannot apply competition law without modification to mergers and cooperative agreements. You must always understand that there is much more going on: that on the one hand, a cooperative working agreement can contribute to quality, but on the other hand, it can also reduce price and accessibility.[67]

These two quotations – from the initial CEO of Monitor (now NHS Improvement) during the development and enactment of the HSCA 2012 reforms and the current CEO of the ACM – are separated by a few years, but reflect a shift in understanding about competition reforms and competition policy in healthcare. On the one hand, it is suggested not only that there is the pre-existing framework of the substantive general competition rules, but also that the experience of other liberalised sectors, such as energy and rail, can inform developments in healthcare. On the other hand, there is a realisation (if not immediate recognition) that developing competition in healthcare may entail its own considerations.

The juxtaposition of these two quotations raises the question of how one is to proceed in arguing for or against competition reform and competition policy in healthcare. It can also reveal two narratives underpinning the development of competition reforms, particularly the HSCA 2012 reforms in England, which merit consideration since they help explain some of the difficulty in implementing and developing the reforms. These narratives can be described as 'the comparative approach' and 'means-to-an-end or system change'.

## 4.1. NARRATIVE 1: THE COMPARATIVE APPROACH

The comparative approach is based around the question of whether healthcare is sufficiently similar to other liberalised sectors as not to merit special

---

66 Interview with David Bennett in C. Smyth, 'Gas and power markets are a model for the health service', *The Times*, 25.02.2011.

67 Interview with Chris Fonteijn cited in M.L. Louisse and M. Wiggers, Chapter 6 *'Toezicht'* ('Regulation') in M. Wiggers and W. Oostwouder, *Handboek compliance in de zorg* (Compliance in Healthcare Handbook), Uitgeverij Paris, Zutphen 2017, p. 134.

treatment. The foregoing quotes reference this to a greater and lesser extent. The logic is clear: competition law is fundamentally general in nature, with applicability determined by a functional definition which does not allow much room for consideration of claims that healthcare is somehow 'special'. The logic also suggests that doctors and patients behave in the same way as providers and consumers in other sectors: thus healthcare can be compared to automobile repair[68] on the basis that both involve relationships characterised by information asymmetry and principal–agent problems. The limitation of this approach is that it focuses too much on the individual patient (consumer),[69] and not on the collective, or systemic level,[70] as represented by the aforementioned 'healthcare structure', and which is necessary to shape competition reforms and ultimately competition policy.[71] The systemic level can be understood in terms of the institutional complexity surrounding the achievement of universal access and the requirement for broad political and societal support, which has been recognised in the context of Dutch private health insurance,[72] but applies equally to competition reforms in English healthcare. However, this is not to say that healthcare cannot, or should not, be compared with other sectors. It is simply suggested that comparison should be focused in terms of the systemic, rather than the individual level, or be less ambitious in its claims. A systemic focus might see parallels being drawn between healthcare and defence: 'Like National Defence, medical care involved issues of life and death, values, uncertainty, complex and changing technology, and professional cultures that were not much concerned about cost vs. benefit',[73] whereas an individual focus can successfully encompass more modest linkages, for example, between choosing Dutch health insurance policies and cable television packages on the basis that the more you pay, the greater your choice of provider.[74]

68 M. Gaynor, above n. 6.

69 For a discussion of the limitations of designating patients as consumers, see J. Tritter, M. Koivusalo, E. Ollila and P. Dorfman, *Globalisation, Markets and Health Policy – Redrawing the Patient as Consumer*, Routledge, Abingdon 2010.

70 'Individual' and 'systemic' being labels also used by Hervey and McHale to denote, respectively, 'consumerism' in healthcare and 'competition, solidarity, equality' within internal EU health law. T.K. Hervey and J.V. McHale, *European Union Health Law: Themes and Implications*, Cambridge University Press, Cambridge 2015.

71 Merely focusing on the individual, rather than the systemic level, enables myriad comparisons to be drawn since it fails to address the wider implications of competition reforms.

72 R.A.A. Vonk and F.T. Schut, 'Can universal access be achieved in a voluntary private health insurance market? Dutch private insurers caught between competing logics' (May 2018) *Health Economics, Policy and Law* 1 (online).

73 A. Enthoven, 'Introduction' in A. Enthoven, *Health Care, the Market and Consumer Choice*, Edward Elgar, Cheltenham 2012.

74 BN DeStem, *'Zorg en kabel-tv: ze lijken op elkaar'* ('healthcare and cable TV are similar'), Interview with Marcel Canoy and Wolf Sauter, 07.02.2009, <http://www.bndestem.nl/algemeen/economie/zorg-en-kabel-tv-ze-lijken-op-elkaar-1.371011> accessed 24.06.2018.

One implication of healthcare being sufficiently similar to other sectors as not to merit special treatment is that the same substantive law and institutional arrangements can be transposed. Indeed, this has influenced the thinking behind the respective 2006 and HSCA 2012 reforms insofar as Significant Market Power (SMP) – a concept developed in the context of EU telecommunications regulation – formed the basis for a competence of the NZa[75] and has now been transferred to the ACM. In England, this is evidenced most clearly by the adoption of 'concurrent powers'[76] – a longstanding feature of UK economic regulation[77] – as the model for the relationship between the CMA and NHS Improvement with regard to applying competition law and conducting market investigations.[78] Related implications arising from this approach are that all that is required is a 'strict' interpretation of competition law to deliver benefits, and that the critical focus should be on the competition authority's interpretation of competition law, rather than on any regulatory regime.[79]

I continue[80] to argue that using the model of other liberalised sectors as a template was too simplistic, building on other critiques at the time of the implementation of the HSCA 2012 reforms that lessons from other sectors are instructive,[81] but should be treated with caution.[82] The position that the experience of other sectors is of limited helpfulness can be supported by reference to solidarity and a recognition that the principle of universal access to healthcare may be predominant, and should not be relegated to the level of exceptions. Thus, in the English context of the relationship between the NHS and private healthcare, the NHS can be seen to act as a 'provider of last resort' relative to the private healthcare sector insofar as unplanned transfers of private patients to NHS hospitals occur.[83] However, this fails to engage with

---

75 Primarily Article 48 Wmg.

76 T. Prosser, 'Competition, Regulators and Public Service' in B. Rodger and A. MacCulloch (eds.), *The UK Competition Act – A New Era for UK Competition Law*, Hart Publishing, Oxford 2000.

77 The adoption of this style of relationship can perhaps also be connected with Andrew Lansley, former Secretary of State for Health and architect of the HSCA 2012 reforms, experiencing the liberalisation of utilities as a junior minister in the Conservative governments of the 1980s – a link which has been made elsewhere. See N. Timmins, *The Five Giants – A Biography of the Welfare State*, 3rd edn, William Collins, London 2017, pp. 682–83.

78 Sections 72 and 73 HSCA 2012, respectively.

79 For considerations of this, see in particular, E.M.H. Loozen, above n. 46 regarding the Dutch reforms; and A. Sánchez Graells (2014), above n. 48, in respect of the HSCA 2012 reforms.

80 M. Guy, 'Competition and sectoral regulation in Dutch and English healthcare: factors shaping the competition focus of the new healthcare regulators and their relationship with the competition authorities' (2017) 2 *Ius Publicum Network Review*, ISSN 2039 2540, <http://www.ius-publicum.com/pagina.php?lang=en&pag=fascicolo> accessed 24.06.2018.

81 A. Dixon, T. Harrison and C. Mundle, 'Economic regulation in healthcare – what can we learn from other regulators?', The King's Fund, London November 2011.

82 L. Stirton, above n. 47.

83 Indeed, this has been recognised as a criterion for private patients to assess private hospitals. CMA, Press Release, 'Better information for private patients moves closer', 01.12.2014.

the underlying fundamental aspect of solidarity, and to recognise that the NHS continues to provide the majority of healthcare in England.

Where questions of equity are considered subservient to efficiency (as acknowledged in the context of US healthcare),[84] an emphasis on individual patients/consumers and blanket comparisons may well be relevant. However, once solidarity is recognised as the organising principle for healthcare delivery, the game changes,[85] and certain issues become paramount. For example, public law considerations,[86] and how to deal with 'vulnerable consumers', which may initially have emerged as secondary concerns in competition reforms of sectors such as energy, are now assuming increasing importance and interest.[87] It is these issues which need to be considered alongside the development of competition – and competition policy – in healthcare.

## 4.2. NARRATIVE 2: MEANS TO AN END OR SYSTEM CHANGE?

A focus on the systemic level gives rise to a second narrative, developed around the question of whether or not competition is to be used as a means to an end (namely, modernising healthcare systems and dealing with increasing costs and demand) or an end in itself (namely, instituting a fundamental system change). It might be considered that what has emerged with the 2006 reforms in the Netherlands is that, whilst the original intention was a system change (from state-run sickness funds to private health insurance), current concerns about solidarity and the relative power of health insurers mean that there is an appetite to reframe competition as a means to an end. In contrast, whilst the controversies surrounding the implementation of the HSCA 2012 reforms in England were addressed to a certain extent by the refocusing of competition as a means to an end, concerns about an underlying system change – from a taxation-funded NHS to an insurance model – remain,[88] but are not explicitly articulated at

84 M. Gaynor, above n. 6.

85 Interpretations of US healthcare reform which involve extending insurance coverage, such as the Affordable Care Act, may be seen in this light – effectively as 'reverse engineering' aspects of solidarity into healthcare system design, as I have suggested elsewhere, see M. Guy, 'Book Review: The Affordable Care Act and Medicare in Comparative Context' (2017) 25(4) *Medical Law Review* 684.

86 T. Prosser, 'Public Service Law – Privatization's unexpected offspring' (2000) 63(4) *Law and Contemporary Problems* 63.

87 See, for example, M. Fernández-Gutiérrez, O. James and S. Jilke, 'Competition and switching in public service markets: Can they reduce inequalities?' (2017) 11 *Regulation and Governance* 41. See also, notably, the current distinct focus of the UK competition authority, CMA, 'News Story: CMA puts vulnerable consumers at the heart of its annual plan', 29.03.2018, <https://www.gov.uk/government/news/cma-puts-vulnerable-consumers-at-the-heart-of-its-annual-plan> accessed 24.06.2018.

88 In essence, the concern is that funding, and consequently support for the NHS, will wane, patients will increasingly turn to the private healthcare sector, and effectively an insurance

government policy level, and relate more to the underlying relationship between the NHS and private healthcare sector, rather than the HSCA 2012 reforms specifically.

## 5. STRUCTURE OF THE BOOK

The aim of this book is to provide a comprehensive insight into the development of competition policy by reference to the experience of the Dutch 2006 reforms and the English HSCA 2012 reforms.

Chapter 1 sets the scene for discussions of the substantive law and institutional relationships by outlining the development of the Dutch and English competition reforms in healthcare, and the evolution of competition policy by reference to legislation (notably the Zvw, Wmg and subsequent amendments in the Netherlands, and the various amendments necessary to secure enactment of the HSCA 2012 in England) and policy documentation (in particular, texts governing the relationship between the NZa and the ACM and the development of the 'NHS-specific' competition regime which preceded the HSCA 2012).

Chapter 2 examines the applicability and application of competition law in Dutch and English healthcare, demonstrating the significance of the EU law framework and how the two countries have had to transcend this and implement national provisions to give effect to their reforms.

Chapter 3 discusses the relatively new concept of sectoral regulation in healthcare in relation to both countries, specifically the relationship between the competition authorities (ACM in the Netherlands and CMA in England) and the sectoral regulators (NZa and NHS Improvement), regarding primarily the application of competition law.

Chapter 4 considers hospital mergers, perhaps the most conspicuous area of activity in terms of the number of cases in both countries. Alongside amendments to the general merger-control regime, the 'healthcare-specific' merger tests which have emerged in both countries are reviewed.

The Conclusion summarises the findings of the research underpinning the book and makes suggestions for future research and policy recommendations.

---

system will be created 'by the back door'. For an overview of the stages involved in the shift along the implied continuum between taxation-funded NHS and an insurance system in which the NHS is relegated to a safety net, see L. Reynolds and M. McKee, 'Opening the oyster: the 2010–11 NHS reforms in England' (2012) 12(2) *Clinical Medicine* 128.

# CHAPTER 1

# COMPETITION REFORMS IN DUTCH AND ENGLISH HEALTHCARE AND THE DEVELOPMENT OF COMPETITION POLICY

The Introduction to this book set out an overview of some of the general tensions and controversies which can arise in introducing competition reforms in healthcare. This chapter builds on that discussion by examining in more detail the Dutch and English competition reforms and the associated legislation and development of guidance which can be characterised as 'competition policy'.

Although there are differences in the ways in which competition develops within insurance-based and taxation-funded healthcare systems, a perhaps surprising common starting-point for the Netherlands and England is the influence of the 'managed competition' model developed by the US health economist, Alain Enthoven.[1] In essence, 'managed competition' comprises a purchasing strategy to obtain maximum value for consumers using rules for competition.[2] Originally launched in the late 1970s as a means to manage increasing costs and introduce more equity into healthcare access in the United States,[3] the 'managed competition' model was set out as a 'consumer-choice health plan' comprising two related parts: a financing system[4] and rules to create a socially desirable competition. Whilst both aspects can be considered

1 Although the work of Kenneth Arrow is also referenced with regard to competition reforms in both countries, specifically K. Arrow, 'Uncertainty and the Welfare Economics of Medical Care' (1963) 53 *American Economics Review* 941. See, inter alia, W. Sauter, 'Experiences from the Netherlands: The Application of Competition Rules in Health Care' in J.W. van de Gronden, E. Szyszczak, U. Neergaard, and M. Krajewski (eds), *Health Care and EU Law*, TMC Asser Press, The Hague 2011; and L. Stirton, 'Back to the Future? Lessons on the Pro-Competitive Regulation of Health Services' (2014) 22(2) *Medical Law Review* 180.

2 A.C. Enthoven, 'The History and Principles of Managed Competition' (1993) 12(1) *Health Affairs* 24.

3 A.C. Enthoven, 'Consumer-Choice Health Plan – Inflation and Inequity in Health Care Today: Alternatives for Cost Control and an Analysis of Proposals for National Health Insurance' (1978) 298(12) *New England Journal of Medicine* 650.

4 Which involved a shift away from fee-for-service payment models to physicians accepting responsibility for providing comprehensive healthcare services to defined populations, largely for a prospective per capita payment, or some other form of payment that rewards economical use of healthcare resources. See A.C. Enthoven, 'Consumer-Choice Health Plan – A National-Health-Insurance Proposal Based on Regulated Competition in the Private Sector' (1978) 298(13) *New England Journal of Medicine* 709.

to find reflection in the Dutch and English competition reforms,[5] this book is concerned primarily with the latter aspect because this underpins 'competition policy' in healthcare.

This chapter examines elements of the legacy of the influence of these ideas within Dutch and English healthcare. It takes each country in turn in order to facilitate understanding, and cross-references with subsequent discussions of the book regarding competition law, the relationship between sectoral regulator and competition authority, and merger control.

Section 1 examines the 2006 reforms of Dutch healthcare and considers how competition has developed in the context of introducing mandatory private health insurance, by reference to the overarching concept of the Dutch 'healthcare triangle'. This enables discussion of the two constituent elements of competition policy in Dutch healthcare. These are: first, relevant legislation underpinning the reforms, namely the *Zorgverzekeringswet* (Dutch Health Insurance Act 2006 (Zvw)), the *Wet marktordening gezondheidszorg* (Dutch Healthcare (Market Regulation) Act 2006 (Wmg)) and the ongoing legislative proposal to amend the latter; and second, the development of policy documentation by the *Autoriteit Consument en Markt* (Authority for Consumers and Markets (ACM)) and the *Nederlandse Zorgautoriteit* (Dutch Healthcare Authority (NZa)), namely the *Richtsnoeren voor de zorgsector* (Guidelines for the healthcare sector) and the *Samenwerkingsprotocollen* (Cooperation Protocols) of the two agencies.

Section 2 examines competition within English healthcare by reference to the underlying relationship between the NHS and the private healthcare sector to understand the overarching concept of the 'four categories of English healthcare'. This enables discussion of how competition policy has developed with regard to the English NHS, as well as the evolution of the controversial Health and Social Care Act (HSCA 2012) reforms and developments subsequent to this.

Section 3 concludes with an assessment of the current situation (as at June 2018), since it can be posited that competition in Dutch and English healthcare is at something of a crossroads following subsequent developments of the 2006 and HSCA 2012 reforms.

## 1. THE NETHERLANDS

### 1.1. COMPETITION IN DUTCH HEALTHCARE – THE 2006 REFORMS AND THE DUTCH 'HEALTHCARE TRIANGLE'

In the Netherlands, Enthoven's model of 'managed competition' found expression in the replacement of a bifurcated system of state-operated

---

5 Including, for example, 'Payment By Results' (PbR) in England. For a discussion, see Office of Health Economics (OHE), *Competition in the NHS*, OHE, London 2012, p. 17.

*ziekenfondsen* (sickness funds) and supplementary private health insurance with the development of a mandatory private health insurance scheme which grants patients varying degrees of choice of both health insurer and healthcare provider. This reform was proposed by the Dekker Committee[6] in the mid-1980s and developed incrementally before being ultimately implemented (primarily, for the purposes of the current discussion) by the Zvw and the Wmg. These reforms have been considered a 'living model of managed competition',[7] and even to provide a basis for possible further US healthcare reform.[8] They can also be illustrated by the interaction between patients (consumers), healthcare providers and health insurers and the associated respective markets within the Dutch 'healthcare triangle'[9] as follows:

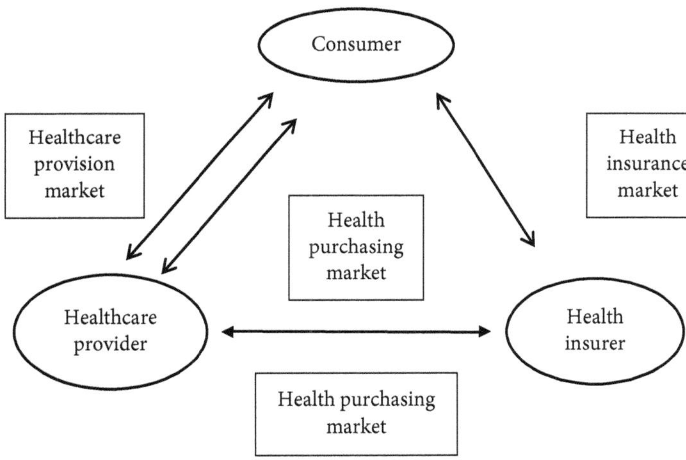


**Figure 2. The Dutch 'healthcare triangle'**

The logic behind the system can be summarised thus: by competing among and between themselves for patients (according to different types of insurance policy), healthcare providers and health insurers are spurred into more efficient behaviours. The system is underpinned by obligations under the Zvw

6 The name given to the *Commissie Structuur en Financiering van de Gezondheidszorg* (Committee on the Structure and Financing of Healthcare), which outlined the reforms in its report, *Bereidheid tot verandering* (Willingness to Change). For general discussions of the reforms, see, for example, H. Maarse, P. Jeurissen and D. Ruwaard, 'Results of the market-oriented reform in the Netherlands: a review' (2016) 11 *Health Economics, Policy and Law* 161.

7 A.C. Enthoven, 'A Living Model of Managed Competition: A Conversation with Dutch Health Minister Ab Klink' (2008) 27(3) *Health Affairs* 196.

8 A.C. Enthoven and W.P.M.M. van de Ven, 'Going Dutch? Managed Competition Health Insurance in the Netherlands' (2007) 357(24) *New England Journal of Medicine* 2421.

9 W. Sauter, 'Is the general consumer interest a source of legitimacy for healthcare regulation? An analysis of the Dutch experience' (2009) 2–3 *European Journal of Consumer Law* 419.

on all adults[10] living or working in the Netherlands to take out a *basispakket* (basic package) of health insurance. The contents of this basic package of health insurance are determined by the Minister for Health, Wellbeing and Sport and typically include GP care, hospitalisation, specialist mental health care and physiotherapy for people with chronic illnesses,[11] but has been expanded to include the first 12 sessions of exercise therapy for patients with arthrosis of the hip or knee joints and reimbursement of travel costs for cancer patients receiving immunotherapy.[12] The private health insurance companies in the Netherlands must offer the basic package of health insurance to all policyholders at the same premium, regardless of their age or state of health.[13] However, it has been noted that 2017 premiums for the basic package varied across health insurers, broadly between €99 and €120 per month, depending on the type of policy chosen.[14] Dutch patients typically choose between a *naturapolis* (benefits in kind policy), a *restitutiepolis* (reimbursement policy) or a *combinatiepolis* (combination policy). The benefits in kind policy is generally cheaper, but restricts the patient's choice of provider to those which have a contract with the insurer in question. Thus, patients with, for example, a Menzis policy may be restricted in their ability to opt for treatment from a Zilveren Kruis provider. The implications of this have been factored into the Zvw framework discussed below.

The basic package of health insurance is supplemented by two further expenses to patients, and the Dutch government has recently taken steps to address concerns about increasing costs. The first additional cost is an *eigen risico* (mandatory excess), which, following several increases, was frozen at €385 until 2021 following the 2017 Government Agreement.[15] Second, the basic package of health insurance is supported by patients making *eigen bijdrage*

---

10 Subject to limited exceptions. For an overview of the Dutch health insurance system, see Government of The Netherlands, 'Health Insurance', <https://www.government.nl/topics/health-insurance> accessed 24.06.2018.

11 See Ministry of Health, Wellbeing and Sport, 'Healthcare in the Netherlands', 09.02.2016, pp. 7–8, <https://www.government.nl/topics/health-insurance/documents/leaflets/2016/02/09/healthcare-in-the-netherlands> accessed 24.06.2018.

12 Rijksoverheid (Government of the Netherlands), *'Wat verandert er in het basispakket van de zorgverzekering in 2018?'* ('What's changing in the basic package of health insurance in 2018?') <https://www.rijksoverheid.nl/onderwerpen/zorgverzekering/vraag-en-antwoord/veranderingen-basispakket-zorgverzekering-2018> accessed 24.06.2018.

13 Government of The Netherlands, 'Standard Health Insurance', <https://www.government.nl/topics/health-insurance/contents/standard-health-insurance> accessed 24.06.2018.

14 Consumentenbond, *'Premieoverzicht basiszorgverzekeringen'*, 03.05.2018, <https://www.consumentenbond.nl/zorgverzekering/premieoverzicht-zorgverzekering> accessed 24.06.2018.

15 Rijksoverheid (Government of the Netherlands), *'Wat is het eigen risico van mijn zorgverzekerring en wanneer betaal ik dat?'* ('What is the mandatory excess in my health insurance and when do I pay it?'), <https://www.rijksoverheid.nl/onderwerpen/zorgverzekering/vraag-en-antwoord/eigen-risico-zorgverzekering> accessed 24.06.2018.

(personal contributions) to specific treatments, including hearing aids, contact lenses, wigs, hospital transport and medicines.[16] These contributions may represent a percentage of total costs and may vary according to age. Here, too, the 2017 Government Agreement has made provision for personal contributions to prescription charges to be capped at €250.[17]

The 'basic package' of health insurance relates primarily to general medical care (often described as the 'cure' sector) and this is where competition has been most developed thus far, and hence forms the focus of this book.[18] Supplementary insurance is available for medical treatment and services not included in the basic package – thus deemed to be of the patient's own responsibility. It is possible for patients to choose one health insurer for their basic package and a second insurer for any supplementary insurance.

In essence, the framework established by the Zvw underpins the development of a competitive health insurance market. From this, competition was intended to filter through to healthcare provision markets in the logic of insurers trying to gain competitive advantage by securing the best deal possible from healthcare providers, and consultants being put under pressure to provide high quality competitive services by provider combinations such as hospitals.[19]

Dutch healthcare provision markets broadly comprise practitioners and hospitals, with further distinctions being drawn between different categories of provision – typically between general medical care (the 'cure' sector) and long-term care (the 'care' sector).[20] The former *Nederlandse Mededingingsautoriteit*

---

16 Rijksoverheid (Government of the Netherlands), *'Wanneer betaal ik een eigen bijdrage voor zorg?'* ('When do I pay a personal contribution for healthcare?'), <https://www.rijksoverheid.nl/onderwerpen/zorgverzekering/vraag-en-antwoord/wanneer-eigen-bijdrage-zorgverzekering> accessed 24.06.2018.

17 VVD, CDA, D66 en ChristenUnie, *Regeerakkoord 2017–2021 'Vertrouwen in de toekomst'* ('Trust in the Future'), 10.10.2017, section 1.4, 'Healthcare', <https://www.rijksoverheid.nl/regering/regeerakkoord-vertrouwen-in-de-toekomst/1.-investeren-voor-iedereen/1.4-zorg> accessed 24.06.2018.

18 However, it should be noted that the Dutch health insurance market comprises two further elements: long-term care (the 'care' sector) which is not generally amenable to insurance in a competitive marketplace, and supplementary health insurance (over and above the mandatory basic package of health insurance) which is subject to competition, with patients having the option of choosing one health insurer for their basic package and a different health insurer for their supplementary insurance. For further discussion, see, for example, M. Wiggers, *De NMa en de NZa in de curatieve zorgsector – Een toetsing aan het Europees mededingingsrecht* (The NMa and the NZa in the curative healthcare sector – an assessment against EU competition law) Kluwer, Deventer 2013, pp. 322–26. Nevertheless, some attempts have been made to incorporate elements of long-term care, notably *'persoonsgebonden budgets'* ('personal health budgets'), within the scope of the Zvw 2006 regime.

19 W. Sauter, above n. 1, p. 339.

20 For example, in its 2015 Annual Report, the NZa distinguishes three categories of provision: specialist medical care (hospitals), curative mental health care and primary care. In 2015, specialist medical care comprised 81 general hospitals, 8 university medical centres, 65 non-affiliated hospitals (which typically treat specific categories of patient)

(Dutch Competition Authority (NMa)) distinguished between different professionals and types of care. For example, a physiotherapist is unable to exercise competitive pressure on a dentist due to the difference in services provided.[21] Examples of healthcare provision markets identified in NMa cases include care for people with learning difficulties,[22] mental health[23] and hospital care.[24] Subsequent to this, the ACM has examined cases regarding professional associations (discussed in Chapter 2) and focused recently[25] on mergers involving hospitals and pharmacists.

The Dutch healthcare purchasing market comprises most obviously pr ivate health insurers, but also patients (particularly in connection with long-term care). Under the Zvw, health insurers purchase care for policies where benefits may be delivered in kind. Thus, within healthcare purchasing markets, a further distinction can be drawn between, for example, the type of professional group (such as dentists, GPs or physiotherapists) or type of institution (such as hospitals or nursing homes).[26] Health insurers have a *zorgplicht* (duty of care)[27] to deliver healthcare or offer compensation. This has been interpreted as meaning, inter alia, that health insurers must pay attention to patient preferences – for example, for a healthcare provider located within a certain distance – and purchase healthcare accordingly.[28] Thus the NMa suggested that the purchasing market for GP care would be local on the basis that a patient in The Hague is unlikely to want to see a GP in Amsterdam.[29] It was envisaged that selective contracting in primary care by health insurers might spur competition, but the

---

and 198 independent treatment centres. Nederlandse Zorgautoriteit (NZa), *Stand van de zorgmarkten 2015* (NZa Annual Report 2015), <https://puc.overheid.nl/nza/doc/PUC_3352_22/1/> accessed 24.06.2018.

21 ACM, *Richtsnoeren voor de zorgsector* (Guidelines for the Healthcare Sector) March 2010, paragraph 82, p. 26.

22 Ibid, para. 85, p. 26.

23 Ibid, para. 86, p. 27.

24 Ibid, para. 87, p. 27. Den Exter and Guy also consider a further aspect of the 2016 reforms, namely the expanded scope for entry by providers to the Dutch hospital market in the context of the Dutch Health Facilities Admission Act 2007 (*Wet Toelating Zorginstellingen* (WTZi)). See A.P. Den Exter and M.J. Guy, 'Market Competition in Health Care Markets in The Netherlands: Some Lessons for England?' (2014) 22(2) *Medical Law Review* 255.

25 ACM, *Jaarverslag 2016* (ACM Annual Report 2016), <https://jaarverslag.acm.nl/jaarverslag-2016/concentratietoezicht> accessed 24.06.2018.

26 ACM, above n. 21, paragraph 80, p. 26.

27 Article 11 *Zorgverzekeringswet* (Dutch Health Insurance Act 2006 (Zvw)) places a duty of care on health insurers to ensure delivery and compensation of care as defined by Article 10 Zvw (including general medical care, dental care and pharmaceutical care). The NZa has interpreted the duty of care as meaning not only the content and extent of care, but also the quality, timely availability and accessibility of insured care. See NZa, *Beleidsregel TH/BR-018 Toezichtkader zorgplicht zorgverzekeraars Zvw* (Policy Rule TH/BR-018 Regulatory Framework for the Health Insurers' Duty of Care under the Zvw) December 2014, p. 5.

28 ACM, above n. 21, paragraph 81, p. 26.

29 Ibid.

NZa has acknowledged that this occurs to only a limited degree due to limited public insight into differences in quality.[30] In connection with mental health, selective contracting based on treatment effects does not occur because these are not yet sufficiently comparable.[31] However, health insurers are engaging with more selective contracting initiatives in connection with specialist medical care.[32] A further aspect of the healthcare purchasing market is seen in the distinction drawn between services which are subject to the tariff set by the NZa in conjunction with the Ministry for Health, Wellbeing and Sport ('A segment'), and those which have been liberalised, thus offering scope for competition ('B segment'),[33] by health insurers and healthcare providers agreeing a price for a treatment.[34]

By the end of 2015, approximately 70 per cent of hospital service prices in specialist medical care had been liberalised.[35] In 2015, prices were liberalised for physiotherapy, exercise therapy, diet advice, care pathways and pharmaceutical care[36] – with the NZa recommending to the Minister for Health, Wellbeing and Sport that prices for speech therapy be liberalised as they were below the tariff.[37] Subsequent to this, however, the NZa has acknowledged the extremes of *vaste tarieven* (fixed tariff prices) and *vrije tarieven* (liberalised prices) and suggested that a better approach may be to identify where which type of pricing is most beneficial and to consider where other problems with a given situation may arise, rather than seeking to change the rules.[38] In 2017, the NZa noted that new costing mechanisms were being devised for mental health care.[39]

With regard to the Dutch health insurance markets, two elements are of particular note when considering the development of competition.

Firstly, concerns have been raised in the light of substantial consolidation of insurers. Prior to liberalisation, there were around 100 hospitals and 30 independent health insurers; in 2014 there were about 85 hospitals and four large health insurers (with an amalgamate of smaller regional insurers acting as a fifth player in the health insurance market).[40] The four largest health insurers

---

30 NZa, above n. 20, p. 21.

31 Ibid.

32 Ibid.

33 See, for example, W. Sauter, above n. 1.

34 NZa, *Stand van de zorgmarkten 2016* (2016 Annual Report), p. 11, <https://puc.overheid.nl/nza/doc/PUC_3496_22/1/> accessed 24.06.2018.

35 Ibid, p. 50.

36 Ibid, p. 51.

37 NZa, above n. 20, pp. 11–12.

38 Ibid.

39 NZa, *Stand van de zorgmarkten 2017* (2017 Annual Report), <http://www.standvandezorgmarkten.nl/> accessed 24.06.2018.

40 W. Sauter, 'The balance between competition law and regulation in Dutch healthcare markets' (2014) *TILEC Discussion Paper*, DP 2014-041, <https://papers.ssrn.com/sol3/papers.cfm?abstract_id=2530356> accessed 24.06.2018.

had a combined market share of 88.8 per cent in 2015.[41] The 2017 Government Agreement has also highlighted wider concerns about health insurers and their role within the Dutch healthcare system.[42]

Secondly, patient movement between health insurers has highlighted another area of concern. Whilst it is possible for patients to switch insurers and policies on an annual basis, it has been noted that movement is small: in 2015, 7.3 per cent of patients did so,[43] in 2016, 70 per cent of patients did not.[44] The ACM noted in 2016 that whilst a 'lower premium' was the main motivation for switching,[45] 'healthcare coverage' was becoming an increasingly important factor for patients. A further limiting factor has been the restricted ability of insurers to distinguish themselves because of their need to comply with legislation regulating, for example, the obligation to accept patients, the risk equalisation scheme to enable universal access to healthcare, solvency requirements and the content of the basic package of insurance.[46]

The ACM has recently been active in monitoring competition in the health insurance market, concluding that there was scope to strengthen competition. To achieve this, the ACM proposed to focus on facilitating entry of new insurers to the market and patient switching behaviour.[47] In its 2017 Annual Report, the ACM identified barriers to health insurers entering the market as including regulatory uncertainty and the requirement to obtain a licence from *De Nederlandsche Bank* (Dutch National Bank, (DNB)).[48] Furthermore, the ACM and the NZa established that the large health insurers could distinguish themselves from each other most with regard to collective insurance packages and provision of services.[49] Following a joint consultation to investigate consumer choice in connection with the basic insurance package towards the

---

41 NZa, above n. 20, p. 20. This shows a slight decrease on 2014, where the market-share was 89.6%.

42 VVD et al., above n. 17.

43 An increase on 7% in 2014. NZa, above n. 20, p. 22.

44 ACM, *Jaarverslag 2016 – concurrentie zorgverzekeringsmarkt* (Annual Report 2016 – Competition in the health insurance market), <https://jaarverslag.acm.nl/jaarverslag-2016/concurrentie-zorgverzekeringsmarkt> accessed 24.06.2018.

45 The ACM has subsequently noted that an increased premium did not lead to more people switching insurer. ACM, *Jaarverslag 2017* (Annual Report 2017), section 3.1.3 *'Concurrentie op de zorgverzekeringsmarkt'* ('Competition in the health insurance market'), p. 47, <https://jaarverslag.acm.nl/sites/default/files/acm-jaarverslag-2017.pdf> accessed 24.06.2018.

46 The ACM commissioned Gupta Strategists to conduct an investigation into the health insurance market in 2015. Gupta Strategists, *'Het Bedrijfsmodel van zorgverzekeraars – Mogelijkheden om te concurreren'* ('Health insurer business model – options for competition'), Amsterdam 24.12.2015, <https://www.acm.nl/sites/default/files/old_publication/publicaties/15482_gupta-strategists-bedrijfsmodel-en-concurrentieel-onderscheid-zorgverzekeraars-2015-12-24.pdf> accessed 24.06.2018.

47 ACM, above n. 44.

48 ACM, above n. 45.

49 Ibid.

end of 2017,[50] the ACM and NZa published their findings in July 2018.[51] They established, inter alia, that 72 per cent of Dutch patients could have obtained a cheaper insurance policy and that distinctions between basic policies were less than first appeared.[52]

A further aspect of competition is in the provider market, with a focus on collaboration between healthcare providers and hospital mergers, considered in Chapter 4 below.

## 1.2. THE DEVELOPMENT OF COMPETITION POLICY IN DUTCH HEALTHCARE

### *1.2.1. Relevant Legislation*

The 2006 reforms and the development of competition policy in Dutch healthcare have been shaped primarily by the reach of the *Mededingingswet* (Dutch Competition Act 1998 (Mw)) and the development of sector-specific regulatory frameworks. However, the Dutch competition reforms may be viewed as a 'work-in-progress', particularly in view of the further reforms proposed by the 2017 Government Agreement which seem to heighten the tension between solidarity and competition. Although these have the potential to re-open questions about the extent of the applicability of the Mw to health insurers,[53] these are too new to be considered in detail in this book.

Whilst the 2006 reforms are wide-ranging, this book focuses on two aspects: the framework of mandatory health insurance as set out in the Zvw, which underpins the competition reforms, and the institutional framework of the competition reforms as elaborated by the Wmg. Both the Zvw and the Wmg, and specifically the functioning of the NZa, have been subject to independent review to consider, inter alia, whether they (continue to) achieve governmental ambitions regarding the development of a competition-based system in Dutch healthcare.

---

50 ACM, NZa, *'Echte keuze op de polismarkt?'* ('Real choice in the health insurance market?'), 01.12.2017, <https://www.acm.nl/nl/publicaties/consultatie-echte-keuze-op-de-polismarkt> accessed 25.08.2018.

51 ACM, NZa, *'Beter kiezen op de polismarkt'* ('Making better choices in the health insurance market'), 06.07.2018, <https://www.acm.nl/nl/publicaties/eindrapport-beter-kiezen-op-de-polismarkt> accessed 25.08.2018.

52 Ibid.

53 For further discussion, see L. Glas, A. Looijestijn and J.W. van de Gronden, *'Advies 2: Beoordeling van verschillende voorgenomen zorgmaatregelen in het licht van het EU-recht en het EVRM. Avies in opdracht van VGZ en Zilveren Kruis'.* ('Opinion 2: Assessment of different proposals for healthcare measures in light of EU law and the European Convention on Human Rights. Opinion commissioned by VGZ and Zilveren Kruis').

#### 1.2.1.1. Zvw

Competition within the system established by the Zvw 2006 and illustrated above by the Dutch 'healthcare triangle' is based on patient choice of insurer and/or provider, depending upon the type of policy chosen. As noted above, Dutch patients have a choice of policy type, but choice of provider may be restricted on the basis that the more you pay, the greater your choice of provider. Thus, patients selecting 'benefits in kind' policies have less choice of provider than those opting for a 'reimbursement' policy. Such restriction of choice can be mitigated by Article 13 Zvw, which provides that insurers are obliged to offer a certain amount of compensation to patients for treatment by providers with whom they have no contract. This might be considered to mean that a patient with a 'benefits in kind' policy is nevertheless entitled to exercise greater choice.

Although not considered in detail in this book, Article 13 Zvw is important for demonstrating the political sensitivity which attaches to access to healthcare. This was demonstrated by the 2014 'Christmas crisis'[54] of the then Dutch Labour/Liberal Coalition Government. This saw a near collapse of the government following opposition by Dutch Labour MPs to a proposal by the Liberal Minister for Health, Wellbeing and Sport to restrict the *vrije artsenkeuze* (free choice of provider) accorded to 'benefits in kind' policyholders. In other words, insurers would be permitted to offer a policy which restricted patient choice of provider to those with whom an insurer had a contract. Although this crisis was subsequently resolved to a certain extent within the wider refocusing of competition, it nevertheless provides an important illustration of the tension inherent in balancing healthcare values with the primarily economic concerns of a competition-based system.

The Zvw also contains an important provision from a competition law perspective. Article 122 Zvw provides that the Dutch health insurers are subject to Dutch competition law, which, at least at a national level, resolves the anomaly arising from the EU *AOK Bundesverband*[55] judgment regarding healthcare purchasers in an insurance-based system (considered further in Chapter 2).

A recent review of the Zvw[56] has led to the identification of changes which have occurred in the Dutch healthcare system, such as the further development of the risk equalisation scheme and an increased willingness of health insurers to bear risks. Such developments have significant effects for parties involved in

---

54 See EU Observer, 'Dutch PM misses EU summit to save coalition', 18.12.2014, <https://euobserver.com/news/126994> accessed 24.06.2018.

55 Joined cases C-264/01, C-306/01, C-354/01 and C-355/01, *AOK Bundesverband et al. v. Ichthyol-Gesellschaft Cordes et al.*, ECLI:EU:C:2004:150.

56 KPMG Plexus, *Evaluatie Zorgverzekeringswet – Eindrapportage* ('Evaluation of the Dutch Health Insurance Act 2006 – Final Report'), September 2014, <http://docplayer.nl/5145339-Evaluatie-zorgverzekeringswet-eindrapportage-september-2014.html> accessed 24.06.2018.

healthcare, their roles and their incentives, which have been considered recently by the Dutch government in deciding to retain lower turnover thresholds in the assessment of healthcare provider mergers.[57]

#### 1.2.1.2. Wmg

The Wmg supports the above system by establishing the NZa with ex ante competition powers relating to Significant Market Power (SMP) investigations (Article 48 Wmg) and contract terms (Article 45 Wmg), by defining the NZa's relationship with the ACM with its ex post powers to apply competition law (provisions governing anti-competitive agreements and abuse of dominance),[58] and with the quality regulator, the *Inspectie voor de gezondheidszorg en Jeugd* (Dutch Health and Youth Care Inspectorate (IGJ)[59]).[60] The Wmg also outlined the relationship between the NZa and the Minister for Health, Wellbeing and Sport by empowering the NZa to set tariffs and determine which hospital services can be opened up to price negotiation. The Wmg also elaborated on procedures involving merger control, although these were clarified further by soft law documentation such as the ACM–NZa Cooperation Protocols.

An initial 2009 review of the functioning of the NZa by the Boer & Croon consultancy agency[61] encompassed the initial issues of the NZa being created out of two previous agencies operating under the pre-2006 sickness funds scheme, its development in relation to this in view of the NZa's continued functions (such as tariff-setting) and its new role of *marktmeester* (market umpire) in respect of its competition functions under Article 45 Wmg (power to intervene in contracts) and Article 48 Wmg (power to conduct SMP investigations). Boer & Croon concluded that the NZa had made a good start in difficult circumstances, but suggested that more was needed to establish the NZa as a truly autonomous agency independent of government. Two subsequent

57 Staatsblad 2017 503, *Besluit van 13 december 2017, houdende wijziging van het Besluit van 6 december 2007, houdende tijdelijke verruiming van het toepassingsbereik van het concentratietoezicht op ondernemingen die zorg verlenen (Stb. 2007, 518) in verband met een verlenging van het besluit en de reikwijdte van het concentratietoezicht op aanbieders van maatschappelijke ondersteuning* (Bulletin of Acts and Decrees 2017 503, Decree of 13.12.2017 extending the Decree of 6 December 2007 instituting temporary measures regarding the applicability of merger control to undertakings providing care (Bulletin of Acts and Decrees (Stb) 2007, 518) in connection with extending the time period of operation of the Decree and the scope of merger control regarding providers of social care).

58 A relationship elaborated further via a series of Cooperation Protocols (*Samenwerkingsprotocollen*) in 2006, 2010 and 2014.

59 Formerly known as the *Inspectie voor gezondheidszorg* (Dutch Healthcare Inspectorate (IGZ)), which merged with the *Inspectie voor jeugzorg* (IJZ) (Dutch Youth Care Inspectorate) in 2018.

60 Article 19 Wmg requires the NZa to follow the guidance of the IGJ with regard to advice on quality.

61 Boer & Croon, *Evaluatie CVZ en NZa* (Assessment of the Dutch Healthcare Insurance Board (*College voor Zorgverzekeringen* (CVZ) and NZa), 25.09.2009.

reviews, in 2014 by Andersson Elffers Felix (AEF) of the Wmg and the NZa,[62] and by the Borstlap Committee of the internal operation of the NZa,[63] have contributed to the changes now discussed.

#### 1.2.1.3. Second Chamber Documentation, 34 445, Amendments to the Wmg (Parliamentary Sessions 2015–16, 2016–17, 2017–18)

The documentation in dossier 34 445 provides the basis for amendments to be made to the Wmg, enshrining the recent transfer to the ACM of the NZa's SMP competence and role in connection with the *zorgspecifieke fusietoets* (healthcare-specific merger test).

While the ACM will have oversight of the day-to-day implementation of these tools, policy decisions in respect of these will remain with the Minister for Health, Wellbeing and Sport.[64] These changes – and the implications for the relationship between the NZa and the ACM – are considered primarily in Chapters 3 and 4.

This transfer of competence emerges in part as a result of the two aforementioned independent reviews of the NZa conducted in 2014. These reviews prompted the Minister for Health, Wellbeing and Sport to propose changes to the Wmg, on the one hand to address concerns that the NZa is perceived to lack sufficient independence from the Ministry for Health, Wellbeing and Sport, and on the other to strengthen competition in the healthcare sector.[65] With regard to the latter, the government's concern was the apparent *fusiedrift* (merger mania) arising from the ACM's widespread approval

---

62 Andersson Elffers Felix (*in samenwerking met Radicand Economics and Tilburg Law and Economics Center (TILEC)*), *'Ordening en Toezicht in de zorg: Evaluatie van de Wet marktordening gezondheidszorg (Wmg) en de Nederlandse Zorgautoriteit (NZa)', September 2014* (AEF in cooperation with Radicand Economics and TILEC, 'Oversight and regulation in healthcare: Assessment of the Dutch Healthcare (Market Regulation) Act 2006 (Wmg) and the Dutch Healthcare Authority (NZa)') September 2014.

63 H. Borstlap, P.F.M. van der Meer Mohr and L.J.E. Smits, *'Het rapport van de onderzoekscommissie intern functioneren NZa'*, 02.09.2014 ('Report of the investigation committee on the internal operation of the NZa'), 02.09.2014. This independent report into the functioning of the NZa was prompted by the suicide of Arthur Gotlieb, an NZa employee, in 2014. The investigation encompassed how Gotlieb had been treated as well as concerns he had raised about aspects of the NZa's work and relationship with the Ministry for Health, Wellbeing and Sport. This review, conducted by the Borstlap Committee, was indeed wide-ranging, but the aspects relevant to this book focus on the relationship between the NZa and the Minister for Health, Wellbeing and Sport.

64 The ACM is accountable ultimately to the Minister for Economic Affairs. However, this arrangement – whereby the ACM has oversight of the practical implementation of specific tools, but policy decisions fall under the remit of the sector-specific Minister – is found elsewhere, for example, in connection with transport. A. Ottow, *Market & Competition Authorities – Good Agency Principles*, Oxford University Press, Oxford 2015, pp. 114–17.

65 E. Schippers, *'Kwaliteit loont'* ('Quality Pays'), Letter from the Minister for Health, Wellbeing and Sport to the Chairman of the Second Chamber, 06.02.2015.

of healthcare (hospital) mergers. The ACM's response has been to suggest that changes in practical terms have already taken place – for example, staff from the NZa were seconded to the ACM to create a temporary 'Healthcare Task Force',[66] but this has now been given a more permanent status as a *Directie* (Directorate) within the ACM.[67]

Although the Legislative Proposal passed through the *Tweede Kamer* (Second Chamber) during the 2015–16 Parliamentary Session, it has yet to reach the *Eerste Kamer* (First Chamber), and was delayed in part by the 2017 General Election, which led to it being deemed a 'controversial' matter to be dealt with by the new government. At the time of writing, it appears that further documents were anticipated in the first quarter of 2018,[68] and a plenary debate in the Second Chamber and technical briefing by the Ministry of Health, Wellbeing and Sport were scheduled for 18 and 20 June 2018, respectively.[69]

### *1.2.2. Documentation by the ACM and the NZa*

The development of what might be termed a 'competition policy' in Dutch healthcare by the competition authority (initially by the former NMa and subsequently the ACM) has evolved alongside the development of the 2006 reforms and is also shaped by the changes in approach by the Dutch government regarding competition in healthcare. Thus this 'competition policy' has evolved from a series of exemption requests in the initial application of the Mw in the late 1990s/early 2000s.[70] If the exemption requests can be considered to delineate a broad framework of operation of a 'competition policy' comprising what has

---

66 C. Fonteijn, 'Netherlands: Authority for Consumers and Markets', *The European, Middle Eastern and African Antitrust Review* 2017, 22.07.2016, <https://globalcompetitionreview.com/insight/the-european-middle-eastern-and-african-antitrust-review-2017/1067851/netherlands-authority-for-consumers-and-markets> accessed 24.06.2018.

67 ACM, 'Organogram', <https://www.acm.nl/nl/organisatie/organisatie/organogram> accessed 24.06.2018.

68 *Kamerstukken II, 2017–18, 34 445, 9 – Wijziging van de Wet marktordening gezondheidszorg en enkele andere wetten in verband met aanpassingen van de tarief- en prestatieregulering en het markttoezicht op het terrein van de gezondheidszorg. Nr. 9 Brief van de Minister voor Medische Zorg aan de Voorzitter van de Tweede Kamer der Staten-Generaal, Den Haag, 16 november 2017* (Second Chamber documentation, Parliamentary Session 2017–18, 34 445, 9 – Amendments to the Wmg and other laws to apply tariff regulation and market regulation in healthcare, Document No. 9 Letter from the Minister for Medical Care to the Chairman of the Second Chamber of the States-General, 16 November 2017).

69 *Tweede Kamer der Staten-Generaal* (Second Chamber of the States-General), '*Wetsvoorstel – Aanpassingen tarief- en prestatieregulering en markttoezicht op het terrein van de gezondheidszorg*', <https://www.tweedekamer.nl/kamerstukken/wetsvoorstellen/detail?cfg=wetsvoorsteldetails&qry=wetsvoorstel%3A34445#activity-2018a02393> accessed 24.06.2018.

70 With the healthcare sector submitting the highest number of exemption requests. J.W. van de Gronden, '*Richtsnoeren voor de zorgsector: codificatie van de NMa-beleidspraktijk*' ('Guidelines for the healthcare sector: codification of the NMa's policy practice') (2003) *Markt & Mededinging*, 2, 36.

become the ACM's approach, then further detail has arguably been provided, inter alia, by the former NMa clarifying its position on scrutinising hospital mergers.[71]

With regard to action taken in respect of the anticompetitive agreements provisions, ACM action has proved diverse, spanning the imposition of fines, the giving of opinions and clarifying safe havens. Indeed, this varied activity is regarded as being divisible into four periods:[72] a 'starting point' (1998–2002) characterised by the introduction of the Mw and how this could apply to the healthcare sector; a 'preliminary enforcement phase' (2003–06) distinguishable by the transition from a supply-driven to a demand-driven system with the 2006 reforms; a more active 'enforcement phase' (2007–11) marked by an acceptance of competition in healthcare; and a 'judicial scrutiny period' (2012–14) characterised by challenges of ACM decisions on an initial appeal to the *Rechtbank Rotterdam* (Rotterdam District Court (Rb)) and, in some cases, subsequently the *College van Beroep voor het bedrijfsleven* (Trade and Industry Appeals Tribunal (CBb)). Each phase has been accompanied by the issuing of guidance by the NMa and subsequently the ACM. The main guidance is considered in overview below.

If guidance by the NMa and ACM can be regarded as a statement of substantive law and policy regarding competition in healthcare, further insights emerge with the guidance which outlines the relationship between the competition authority (now ACM) and the sectoral regulator (NZa). This relationship is considered in detail in Chapter 3, but it is noted here how the relationship between the two agencies has developed over time, with lesser or greater degrees of cooperation. In some ways, the relationship was contextualised by the establishment of the NZa by the Wmg against the backdrop of the wider 2006 reforms, which effectively formalised a competition-based system. The guidance also clarified parameters of this, such as the applicability of the Mw.

Prior to the 2006 reforms, the coexistence of the NMa with a variety of healthcare regulators had been noted and questioned.[73] Further, prior to the 2013 establishment of the ACM – which incorporated the NMa, the former *Consumentenautoriteit* (Dutch Consumer Authority) and the former *Onafhankelijke Post en Telecommunicatie Autoriteit* (Dutch postal and telecoms regulator (OPTA)) – it had been suggested that the NZa should be

---

71 Nederlandse Mededingingsautoriteit (NMa), *'Concurrentie in de ziekenhuissector', Visiedocument 3128/55, Den Haag, januari 2004.* ('Competition in the hospital sector', Vision Document 3128/55, The Hague, January 2004).

72 M. Wiggers and J. Dibbits, *'Twintig jaar karteltoezicht in de zorg* – A bumpy ride' ('Twenty years of regulating anticompetitive agreements in healthcare – a bumpy ride') (2018) *Tijdschrift Zorg & Recht in Praktijk*, 1, 13.

73 J.W. van de Gronden, *'Toezichthouders in de zorg en de NMa: conflicterende bevoegdheden?'* ('Healthcare regulators and the NMa: conflicting competences?') [2002] *Tijdschrift voor Gezondheidsrecht*, 5, 323.

included in this amalgamation of regulators.[74] However, the creation of the ACM appears to have had surprisingly little bearing on the formal relationships which existed between the NMa and NZa, insofar as the relationship between the two agencies appeared to be subject to a mere substitution of the NMa for the ACM in the Wmg.[75] Nevertheless, whilst the change from the NMa to the ACM did not fundamentally modify the 'competition authority–sectoral regulator' relationship, the subsequent – and ongoing – changes to expand the ACM's competition 'armoury' regarding healthcare and associated reduction in the NZa's competition focus have done so.

#### 1.2.2.1. *Richtsnoeren voor de Zorgsector* (Guidelines for the Healthcare Sector)

The NMa produced successive 'Guidelines for the Healthcare Sector' in 2002, 2007 and 2010, which encompassed the developments prior to,[76] and arising from, the 2006 reforms. The 2002 edition comprised explanations of Dutch and EU competition law. It also highlighted horizontal agreements between healthcare providers or between health insurers; vertical agreements within the healthcare sector and abuse of a dominant position in the healthcare sector.[77] This edition has been described as 'codifying' NMa policy practice.[78]

The 2007 Guidelines expanded to include discussions of competition in the healthcare sector (following the 2006 reforms) and the role of the NMa, as well as cooperation between the NMa and NZa.[79] These Guidelines also included discussion of merger control, presumably, inter alia, to reflect the NMa's change in policy circa 2004 to examine hospital mergers.[80] However, the 2007 Guidelines make no mention of the reach of provision governing abuse of a dominant position – this has been regarded as surprising in light of regular appeals made regarding this provision at the time and the aim of the Guidelines to give a

74 Government proposal discussed in B. Baarsma and M. Snoep, '*Voeg toezichthouders NMa, OPTA, NZa en Consumentenautoriteit samen*' ('Merge the NMa, OPTA, NZa and the Consumer Authority'), *MeJudice – Economen in debat*, 22.10.2010, <http://www.mejudice.nl/artikelen/detail/voeg-toezichthouders-nma-opta-nza-en-consumentenautoriteit-samen> accessed 24.06.2018.

75 While some amendments are evident in the ACM-NZa Cooperation Protocol, these primarily reflect the ACM's adoption of the former Consumer Authority's interests, so are beyond the scope of this book.

76 For discussion of the Dutch healthcare sector prior to the 2006 reforms and competition law, see J.W. van de Gronden, 'Mededingingsrecht en gezondheidszorg' (2001) *Markt & Mededinging*, 8, 267.

77 Nederlandse Mededingingsautoriteit (NMa), *Richtsnoeren voor de zorgsector* (Guidelines for the Healthcare Sector), 2002.

78 J.W. van de Gronden, above n. 70.

79 Nederlandse Mededingingsautoriteit (NMa), *Richtsnoeren voor de zorgsector* (Guidelines for the Healthcare Sector), 2007.

80 NMa, above n. 71.

complete picture of competition law.[81] Nevertheless, these Guidelines do give an idea of where substantive exceptions may apply, for example regarding Services of General Economic Interest (SGEI).[82] The core of the 2007 Guidelines lies in the overview of cooperation and agreements in the healthcare sector.[83] With regard to facilitating understanding among the healthcare sector of the reach of the anticompetitive agreements provisions, the NMa drew distinctions between 'agreements between competitors' and 'agreements between non-competitors'.

Whilst the need to reflect the 2006 reforms explains the publication of the 2007 Guidelines, the reason for the publication of the subsequent 2010 Guidelines within a relatively short space of time is perhaps less obvious, although it is logical that clarification of a new and developing system would be needed sooner rather than later. Certainly the NMa justified the 2010 Guidelines on the basis that healthcare providers found themselves in a dilemma between calls for greater cooperation (such as different types of healthcare chains) by the Ministry for Health, Wellbeing and Sport on the one hand, and the limits imposed on cooperation by the Mw on the other.[84] Indeed this tension – between competition law and public interests in healthcare – has offered a perspective on the 2010 Guidelines. It has been noted that whilst the Dutch government defined 'public interests' in healthcare as tripartite, comprising accessibility, affordability and quality, the NMa focused on the latter two only.[85] Nevertheless, whilst traces of all three public interests can be found across the 2010 Guidelines, a more comprehensive overview is lacking, which has been viewed as regrettable in view of the uncertainty which contributed to the dilemma recognised by the NMa.[86] Whilst it was hoped that a subsequent edition of the Guidelines would clarify further the relationship between public interests and competition law, the codification character of the Guidelines appeared to preclude further elaboration of the NMa's approach.[87]

---

81 W.S. Geelhoed and F.J. Leeflang, '*NMa-richtsnoeren voor de zorgsector nader beschouwd*' ('A closer examination of the NMa Guidelines for the Healthcare Sector') (2008) *Markt & Mededinging*, 4, 115.

82 W.S. Geelhoed and F.J. Leeflang, ibid, suggest that the guidance is limited effectively to German examples in EU case law which may not extend, or translate, to the Dutch system. In a contemporaneous article, Sauter suggested that the SGEI concept would become increasingly pertinent within the context of the Dutch healthcare reforms, especially in the context of healthcare merger cases, with hospital markets providing an important example of a sector subject to strict regulation where the government was considering whether to allow more competition. W. Sauter, '*Diensten van algemeen economisch belang en universele dienstverplichtingen in de gezondheidszorg*' ('Services of General Economic Interest and Universal Service Obligations in Healthcare') (2008) *Markt & Mededinging*, 1, 4.

83 W.S. Geelhoed and F.J. Leeflang, above n. 81.

84 ACM, above n. 21, section 1.1. Introduction, paragraph 4, p. 5.

85 J.W. van de Gronden, '*Een upgrade van het zorgbeleid van de NMa: de derde versie van de Richtsnoeren voor de zorgsector*', ('Upgrade of the NMa's healthcare policy: the third edition of the Guidelines for the Healthcare Sector') (2010) *Markt & Mededinging*, 6, 195.

86 Ibid.

87 Ibid.

In addition to outlining the Dutch and EU competition law framework and 'codifying' its practice based on approaches taken in earlier cases, the successive sets of Guidelines have made reference to particular characteristics of Dutch healthcare and the 2006 reforms. These have included the means by which the NMa/ACM deal with aspects such as insurers' preference policies and how healthcare intermediaries are dealt with.

A *preferentiebeleid* (preference policy) is a policy where an insurer indicates that only one or certain products within a specific group of medicines will be covered by its basic health insurance.[88] These have been described as creating both horizontal and vertical relationships, and the relative scope for creating competition problems has been considered.[89]

A *zorgmakelaar* (healthcare intermediary) may be used by healthcare providers to negotiate with health insurers. This arrangement can be explained in terms of vertical relationships in healthcare,[90] and has led to concerns about coordination of market behaviour.[91]

In addition, the NMa produced separate guidance on specific aspects, notably the development of competition in the hospital sector,[92] and, in conjunction with the NZa, Guidelines regarding the concerns raised by *Zorggroepen* (care groups), including *Zorgketen* (healthcare chains).[93]

It perhaps seems curious that there has been no subsequent, fourth edition to follow the 2010 Guidelines. However, the ACM has continued to issue guidance, particularly regarding its approach to assessing mergers,[94] presumably in light of growing criticism of its widespread approval of hospital mergers (discussed in Chapter 4).

The ACM's approach of 'codifying' in guidance its practice developed in cases, is also evident in its 2015 guidance regarding primary care providers.[95] This appears to have been developed in light of evolving case law regarding the *Landelijke Huisartsen Vereniging* (Dutch GPs' Association (LHV)), discussed in Chapter 2. In this particular instance, specific guidance has prompted questions

---

88 Juridisch-Economisch Lexicon – The Legal and Economic Lexicon. Online edition. Wolters Kluwer.

89 See NMa, above n. 77, paras. 156–160, and ACM, above n. 21, section 6.3.3.6.

90 NMa, above n. 79, section 3.4.2.

91 ACM, above n. 21, section 6.3.3.

92 NMa, above n. 71.

93 Nederlandse Mededingingsautoriteit (NMa), Nederlandse Zorgautoriteit (NZa), *Richtsnoeren Zorggroepen* (Guidelines for Healthcare Groups), August 2010.

94 See, for example, Autoriteit Consument & Markt (ACM), '*Regierol zorgverzekeraar crucial bij toestaan ziekenhuisfusies*' ('Leading role of health insurers critical in approving hospital mergers'), 07.12.2012. ACM, '*ACM-lijn maatschappen en ziekenhuizen*' ('ACM Guidance on Partnerships and Hospitals'), 06.06.2013. ACM, 'Assessing mergers and collaborations in hospital care', 27.09.2013.

95 ACM, '*Uitgangspunten toezicht ACM op zorgaanbieders in de eerste lijn*' ('Starting points for ACM oversight of primary care providers'), 19.09.2015.

of whether a similar approach may be relevant in other sectors,[96] and whether the guidance actually has implications for (and intended application to) the wider healthcare sector, and not just primary providers.[97]

At the time of writing, the ACM's focus on 'healthcare' is explained by reference to healthcare providers, health insurers and patients (consumers).[98] In particular, reference is made to guidance regarding how to notify mergers and *samenwerking* (collaborative relationships) in healthcare.[99] With regard to collaborative relationships, particular guidance is given for *eerstelijnszorg* (primary care), *specialistiche zorg* (specialist care), *geboortezorg* (obstetrics), care delivered in connection with the *Wet maatschappelijke ondersteuning* (Social Support Act (WMO)), long-term care (*langdurige zorg*) and health insurers.[100]

#### 1.2.2.2. *Samenwerkingsprotocollen* (Cooperation Protocols)

The relationship initially between the NMa and NZa, and subsequently between the ACM and NZa, has been elaborated through a series of 'Cooperation Protocols' in 2006, 2010 and 2014. These build on the relationship between the agencies as defined in the Wmg[101] – for example, that in cases of possible *samenloop* (overlap) of competence between the two agencies, parties address the NZa first,[102] and that the NZa follows the definitions of competition law used by the NMa/ACM[103] – and discussed in the 2007 and 2010 Guidelines for the Healthcare Sector.[104]

---

96 M. Wiggers, R. Struijlaart and J. Ruigewaard, *'Landelijke Huisartsen Vereniging – Annotatie van de uitspraak van de Rechtbank Rotterdam van 17 december 2015'* ('Dutch GPs' Association – Case Comment on the Judgment of the Rotterdam District Court of 17 December 2015') (2016) *Markt en Mededinging*, 4, 160.

97 W. Verloren Van Themaat and M. Bosch, *'De uitgangspunten toezicht eerstelijnszorg in een context'* ('The starting-points of oversight of primary care providers in context') (2016) *Markt en Mededinging*, 1, 31.

98 It being recalled that the ACM incorporated the former Dutch Consumer Authority. Patients are directed to the ACM's *'Consuwijzer'* website for consumers. With regard to healthcare, specific reference is made to concerns regarding patient choice of health insurer and what patients should do if a family doctor (*huisarts*) refuses to treat them. See ACM, *'Denk mee met ACM in de zorg'* ('join the ACM's conversation about healthcare'), <https://denkmee.acm.nl/thema/gezonde-samenwerking-de-zorg-2016-2017?status=inactief> accessed 24.06.2018.

99 ACM, *'Wat doet de ACM in de zorgsector?'* ('What does the ACM do in the healthcare sector?'), <https://www.acm.nl/nl/onderwerpen/zorg/wat-doet-de-acm-in-de-zorgsector> accessed 24.06.2018.

100 ACM, *'Samenwerken in de zorg'* ('Collaboration in healthcare'), <https://www.acm.nl/nl/onderwerpen/zorg/samenwerking-in-de-zorg/samenwerking-in-de-zorg> accessed 24.06.2018.

101 Indeed, Article 17 Wmg makes provision for the NZa to enter into cooperation protocols with various agencies, including the NMa/ACM.

102 Article 18(1) Wmg.

103 Article 18(4) Wmg.

104 See NMa, above n. 79, section 2.3; and ACM, above n. 21, section 2.4.

Whilst the Cooperation Protocols can be seen primarily as 'putting the flesh on the bones' of the statutory framework for the relationship between the NZa and NMa/ACM, they also offer further elaboration, both in substantive and procedural terms. Thus, for example, the NZa's previous function to provide an Opinion in healthcare merger cases appeared to be underpinned by the Cooperation Protocols, not the Wmg. Furthermore, the Cooperation Protocols have developed a sense of how 'overlap' of competence operates between the NMa/ACM and NZa, which typically reflected the Article 18(2) Wmg definition of interaction between the ACM's abuse of dominance powers and the NZa's SMP competence.[105] Parallels between the anticompetitive agreements provisions and the NZa's contract intervention competence under Article 45 Wmg were also considered in the 2010 Cooperation Protocol, but attracted criticism.[106] This relationship between the NMa/ACM and NZa is examined in detail in Chapter 3 and comparisons and contrasts are drawn between 'overlap' within the Dutch system and 'concurrency' within UK sectoral regulation.[107]

Whilst the legal status of the Cooperation Protocols may be relatively unclear, it has been noted that healthcare clients need to be conscious that any information they share with the NZa could be seen by the ACM and vice versa.[108]

The 2014 Cooperation Protocol reflected the development of the healthcare-specific merger test (discussed in Chapter 4) to elaborate the NZa's procedural check of a proposed merger prior to the ACM's competition assessment. However, precisely how subsequent Cooperation Protocols will be developed in light of the transfer of competence under the aforementioned Amendments to the Wmg remains to be seen. For example, whilst the substantive distinction between SMP and abuse of dominance remains, it is now in the hands of a single agency, the ACM, to decide effectively between ex ante or ex post intervention. This avoids the additional previous dimension of which agency should take action. In other words, the focus shifts from 'who' should intervene to 'when' intervention should occur.

---

105 *'Samenloop'* can have a wider definition – broadly of using different rules to address the same conduct – which has developed in Dutch criminal law and Dutch administrative law. For a discussion of this, see E.M.H. Loozen, *'NMa en NZa: houd je bij je leest! Een analyse van de mededingingsbevoegdheden van beide toezichthouders aan de hand van het Samenwerkingsprotocol NMa-NZa 2010'* ('NMa and NZa, stick to what you're good at! An analysis of the competition powers of both agencies in light of the NMa–NZa Cooperation Protocol 2010') (2011) *Tijdschrift voor Toezicht* 4, 25.

106 Ibid.

107 For clarification of why *'samenloop'* has been translated as 'overlap' in this book, see the Preface.

108 A.P.E. van der Wolk, *'Nieuw samenwerkingsprotocol ACM & NZa' ('New ACM-NZa Cooperation Protocol'), Banning publicaties*, 16.01.2015, <https://Www.Banning.Nl/Publicaties/Nieuw-Samenwerkingsprotocol-Acm-Nza/> accessed 24.06.2018.

# 2. ENGLAND

## 2.1. COMPETITION IN THE NHS AND THE 'FOUR CATEGORIES OF ENGLISH HEALTHCARE'

Enthoven's conception of competition in healthcare was reflected in the English NHS by the separation of the purchasing and providing functions,[109] which found expression in the establishment of District Health Authorities (DHAs) (purchasers) and NHS Trusts (providers) in the context of the 'NHS internal market' arising from the National Health Service and Community Care Act 1990. However, competition within the English NHS has been shaped by other factors, so the approach may be described as more 'piecemeal' as it encompassed not only Enthoven's recommendation of separating purchasing and providing functions with regard primarily to secondary healthcare provision, but also the conflation of these in connection with primary care with the GP Fundholding Initiative, a voluntary scheme whereby GPs could become budget-holders, which was also set out in the 1990 Act.[110] Although Enthoven has been explicit that this was not his recommendation,[111] he acknowledged the potential benefits which could be offered by GP practices competing for patients. In the course of subsequent competition reforms under New Labour and the Coalition Governments, these fundamental characteristics were retained, even though the 'NHS internal market' terminology was swiftly abandoned by New Labour. However, the contemporaneous description of the NHS as a 'quasi-market' persists and remains relevant. A 'quasi-market' can share various common features with 'standard' markets (such as competition and the use of financial incentives,[112] and even include regulation), but can be distinguished on both the demand and supply sides.[113] For example, purchasers typically consist of the state via agents (NHS commissioners), rather than patients using their own resources, whilst providers may include not-for-profit, as well as for-profit, organisations.

---

109 A.C. Enthoven, 'Reflections on the management of the National Health Service – An American looks at incentives to efficiency in health services management in the UK', The Nuffield Trust, London 04.10.1985.

110 At sections 14–17, National Health Service and Community Care Act 1990.

111 A.C. Enthoven, 'Internal Market Reform of the British National Health Service' (1991) 10(3) *Health Affairs* 60. Indeed, the GP Fundholding Initiative was designed by Professor Alan Maynard. For an overview of Enthoven's and Maynard's different conceptions of competition, see D. Baines, 'Improvements suggested by Enthoven and Maynard' (2014) 25(12) *Prescriber* 33.

112 J. Le Grand, 'Quasi-Markets: the answer to market failure in health care?' in P. Day, D.M. Fox, R. Maxwell and E. Scrivens (eds.), *The State, Politics and Health: Essays for Rudolf Klein*, Blackwell, Oxford 1996.

113 W. Bartlett and J. Le Grand, 'The Theory of Quasi-Markets' in J. Le Grand and W. Bartlett (eds.), *Quasi-Markets and Social Policy*, Macmillan, London 1993.

A further, 'most controversial',[114] quasi-market reform under New Labour was the development of NHS Foundation Trusts[115] overseen by an independent regulator, Monitor.[116]

Following the HSCA 2012 reforms, elements of the GP Fundholding Initiative can be found in the mandatory system of Clinical Commissioning Groups (CCGs) developed by the HSCA 2012. The purchaser/provider separation found reflection in discussions of NHS commissioners (CCGs and NHS England in respect of specialist services) and successive government policies to 'upgrade' NHS Trusts to NHS Foundation Trust status following the introduction of the latter in 2003–04.[117] However, the introduction of the NHS Five Year Forward View in 2014 has emphasised integrated models of care and an emerging focus on localism. This is evident in the development of Sustainability and Transformation Partnerships.[118] The latter have been hailed as marking the end of the separation of purchasing and providing functions.[119] Nevertheless, Enthoven's concept of separating purchasing and providing functions can be viewed as contributing an additional dimension to what might be considered underlying competition between the NHS and the smaller, supplementary private healthcare sector which has been in existence since the inception of the NHS in 1948.[120] Within this wider, potentially competitive, relationship,[121] patients can move between the

---

114 T. Prosser, *The Limits of Competition Law*, Oxford University Press, Oxford 2005, p. 9.

115 By the Health and Social Care (Community and Health Standards) Act 2003 c.43. For an excellent discussion of the changes in organisational structure these represented at the time, see A.C.L. Davies, 'Foundation Hospitals: a new approach to accountability and autonomy in the public services?' [2004] *Public Law* 808.

116 For an excellent overview, see T. Prosser, 'Monitor, the Independent Regulator of NHS Foundation Trusts' in T. Prosser, *The Regulatory Enterprise – Government, Regulation and Legitimacy*, Oxford University Press, Oxford 2010, pp. 136–52.

117 As indicated in Department of Health, *A Guide to NHS Foundation Trusts, Department of Health*, London December 2002, Chapter 1. The Coalition Government articulated its wish for all NHS Trusts to achieve NHS Foundation Trust status by April 2014 in the White Paper which launched the HSCA 2012 reforms. Department of Health, 'Equity and Excellence: Liberating the NHS' (Cm 7881, July 2010), pp. 35–36. See further for an overview of the policy – National Audit Office, 'Department of Health – Achievement of Foundation Trust status by NHS hospital trusts', Report by the Comptroller and Auditor General, HC 1516, Session 2010–12, 13.10.2011. This process became known as the 'NHS Foundation Trust pipeline' and is discussed in Chapter 4.

118 See NHS England, 'Local Partnerships to Improve Health and Care – Sustainability and Transformation Partnerships (STPs) and Accountable Care Organisations (ACOs)', <https://www.england.nhs.uk/systemchange/> accessed 24.06.2018.

119 R. Thomas, D. West, 'STPs will end the purchaser-provider split, says Stevens', *Health Service Journal*, 27.02.2017.

120 The ability of patients to move between the NHS and private healthcare sector is governed by Department of Health guidance and latterly NHS England guidance. Department of Health, 'Guidance on NHS patients who wish to pay for additional private care', 23.03.2009. NHS Commissioning Board (now NHS England), 'Commissioning Policy: Defining the boundaries between NHS and Private Healthcare', April 2013, Ref: NHSCB/CP/12.

121 Although the relationship can also be interpreted as cooperative – with examples of private healthcare sector assistance to the NHS being in evidence since the inception of the NHS.

NHS and private healthcare sector, and healthcare practitioners can undertake work in both.[122] This is significant from a competition perspective for creating, however unintentionally, the basis for a framework of demand and supply-side substitution between the NHS and private healthcare sectors.

This distinction between NHS (public) and private healthcare, coupled with the separation of purchasers and providers, results in the 'four categories of English healthcare' as follows:[123]

| | | | |
|---|---|---|---|
| 1.<br>Public Purchaser<br>and<br>Public Provider | 2.<br>Public Purchaser<br>and<br>Private Provider | 3.<br>Private Purchaser<br>and<br>Public Provider | 4.<br>Private Purchaser<br>and<br>Private Provider |

**Figure 3. The 'four categories of English healthcare' – the relationship between the NHS and private healthcare sectors as demonstrated by the purchaser/provider separation**

The NHS purchasing market (categories 1 and 2) comprises primarily NHS commissioners, typically the new CCGs for most services, but also NHS England for specialist services. The private healthcare purchasing market (categories 3 and 4) comprises self-funding patients and patients with private medical insurance. Publicly-available data, collected in connection with the NHS Provider Licence introduced alongside the HSCA 2012 reforms, can help give an indication of the extent of the licensing regime across the NHS provision market (categories 1 and 2), currently comprising approximately 150 NHS Foundation Trusts with a licence and approximately 110 'other providers' (from the private or voluntary sectors) with a licence.[124]

The 'four categories of English healthcare' can be elaborated as follows.

---

For an overview, see NHS Partners Network/NHS Confederation, 'Working together since 1948: celebrating 70 years of partnership between the NHS and independent sector', June 2018.

122 Following provision made by section 5 National Health Service Act 1946, which enabled consultants to continue private practice alongside their NHS workload.

123 Adapted from the relationships as set out in Office of Fair Trading (OFT), Private Healthcare Market Study, OFT1396, p. 13; and O. Odudu, 'Competition Law and the National Health Service', *Competition Bulletin: Competition Law Views from Blackstone Chambers*, 08.10.12, <https://competitionbulletin.com/2012/10/08/competition-law-and-the-national-health-service/> accessed 24.06.2018.

124 See data available at NHS Improvement, 'NHS Foundation Trust Directory and Register of Licenced Healthcare Providers', <https://improvement.nhs.uk/resources/nhs-foundation-trust-directory-and-register-licensed-healthcare-providers/> accessed 24.06.2018. However, these are indicative only in view of limited data. Licences may be revoked at the request of the licence-holder pursuant to section 89(a) HSCA 2012, or providers may cease to exist following a merger. Further, it should be noted that the NHS provision market can be seen as much bigger: for example, data published by the NHS Confederation in July 2017 stated that there were 853 for-profit and not-for-profit independent sector organisations delivering services to

### 2.1.1. *Category 1 – Public Purchaser and Public Provider*

Category 1 can describe the scenario of an NHS patient receiving treatment at an NHS Trust or a Foundation Trust, thus combining public purchase of healthcare (via taxation) and public provision. NHS Trusts are secondary care institutions (typically hospitals) conceived as part of the NHS internal market model to offer some degree of provider competition. New Labour developed these to introduce NHS Foundation Trusts in 2004, which have a greater degree of financial autonomy from the Department of Health and have been overseen by an independent regulator ('Monitor', in its original conception). Although NHS Foundation Trusts have greater independence from government, their legal status is that of a public benefit corporation, so are to be distinguished from private providers and thus category 2.[125]

Category 1 also offers an illustration of competition as envisaged by the NHS internal market, whereby the then newly-constituted NHS Trusts (public providers) competed for NHS contracts with DHAs (public purchasers). In the intervening period, this arrangement has largely persisted, although additional providers have emerged in the form of NHS Foundation Trusts, and alternative purchasers have existed, such as Primary Care Trusts (PCTs), now superseded by CCGs.

The subsequent discussions in this book reference category 1 in various ways. For example, Chapter 2 engages with the applicability of general competition law to NHS Trusts and NHS Foundation Trusts. Chapter 3 discusses the different agencies involved in oversight of NHS Trusts and NHS Foundation Trusts. The distinction between NHS Trusts and NHS Foundation Trusts is most evident in considerations of merger control in Chapter 4, as section 79 HSCA 2012 confirms that the general merger control regime (of the Enterprise Act 2002 (EA02)) is applicable to mergers involving NHS Foundation Trusts.

### 2.1.2. *Category 2 – Public Purchaser and Private Provider*

Category 2 can potentially refer to any of the instances of private healthcare sector delivery of NHS care for NHS patients, facilitated by the Concordat signed by the NHS and the Independent Health Association in 2000 as part of New Labour's NHS Plan.[126] One example of such NHS/private healthcare

---

NHS patients. NHS Confederation, 'NHS statistics, facts and figures', 14.07.2017, <http://www.nhsconfed.org/resources/key-statistics-on-the-nhs> accessed 24.06.2018. This suggests that further research to understand the real reach of the licensing regime would be beneficial.

125 O. Odudu, above n. 123, similarly discusses NHS Foundation Trusts in the context of category 1.

126 Department of Health, *The NHS Plan – A Plan for Investment, A Plan for Reform*, 01.07.2000 (Cm 4818-I, July 2000).

arrangements saw the establishment of Independent Sector Treatment Centres (ISTCs)[127] as private clinics dedicated to treating NHS patients in order to reduce waiting lists. The Concordat thus paved the way for private providers to deliver NHS services (at the National Tariff) in connection with various types of healthcare. Between 2000 and 2015, arrangements under the Concordat expanded appreciably beyond the original intention (to harness private healthcare capacity to manage NHS waiting lists), to cover a wider range of healthcare provision in cooperation with the NHS. Whilst NHS providers continue to be involved in services as diverse as primary care, urgent and emergency care, mental healthcare, community care and wellbeing and prevention, a varied range of independent sector providers are also involved in different ways.[128] Whereas general practice can be considered to have long been delivered by independent sector providers insofar as GPs are self-employed, independent sector providers now also deliver specialist care, urgent care centres, mental health services and community care services.

Within category 2, the NHS represents a customer of the private healthcare sector, although there are distinctions to be drawn between different types of care. For example, in the hospital setting, non-NHS providers compete for NHS work under the fixed national tariff.[129] In contrast, there is no system of national pricing in community health and mental health services, so local commissioners determine the quality and price parameters of any contracting.[130]

As regards the substantive discussions of this book, category 2 is significant. For example, a category 2 relationship illustrates the tension arising out of the *FENIN*[131] judgment since it potentially involves private providers (which would be subject to competition law following, for example, *Pavlov*)[132] not being subject to competition law by virtue of their providing healthcare for the purposes of the NHS. The Competition and Markets Authority (CMA)

---

127 For an overview, see C. Naylor and S. Gregory, 'Briefing – Independent Sector Treatment Centres', The King's Fund, London October 2009, <https://www.kingsfund.org.uk/sites/default/files/Briefing-Independent-sector-treatment-centres-ISTC-Chris-Naylor-Sarah-Gregory-Kings-Fund-October-2009.pdf> accessed 24.06.2018. See also, variously, House of Commons Health Committee, *Independent Sector Treatment Centres, Fourth Report of Session 2005–2006* Volume I (<https://publications.parliament.uk/pa/cm200506/cmselect/cmhealth/934/934i.pdf> accessed 24.06.2018); and S. Player and C. Leys, *Confuse and Conceal: The NHS and Independent Sector Treatment Centres*, Merlin Press, London 2008.

128 NHS Partners Network/NHS Confederation, '15 Years of Concordat: reflection and renewal', June 2015. Figure 2.2: 'The NHS provider landscape and independent sector provision', p. 9.

129 S. Lafond, S. Arora, A. Charlesworth and A. Mckeon, 'Into the red? The state of the NHS' finances – An Analysis of NHS Expenditure between 2010 and 2014', Nuffield Trust Research Report, July 2014, p. 34.

130 Ibid.

131 Case C-205/03 P, *Federación Española de Empresas de Tecnología Sanitaria (FENIN) v. Commission of the European Communities*, ECLI:EU:C:2006:453.

132 Joined cases C-180/98 to C-184/98, *Pavel Pavlov and Others v. Stichting Pensioenfonds Medische Specialisten*, ECLI:EU:C:2000:428.

is explicit that its guidance on competition law for private providers does not extend to category 2 activities.[133] Category 2 relationships are, further, important to discussions in Chapter 3 of the relationship between the competition authority and the sectoral regulator since the HSCA 2012 makes several delineations where healthcare is provided for the purposes of the NHS, thus circumscribing the scope for oversight by the CMA, inter alia, under the Competition Act 1998 (Concurrency) Regulations 2014.[134] In relation to the Chapter 4 discussions of merger control, however, category 2 relationships involving a merger of private providers delivering services for the NHS appear to be subject to the general merger control regime of the EA02, not the modified version introduced by section 79 HSCA 2012. The latter requires the involvement of an NHS Foundation Trust.

### *2.1.3. Category 3 – Private Purchaser and Public Provider*

If category 2 can be regarded as including instances where private healthcare providers operate within the NHS, then category 3 offers a kind of mirror image, with NHS providers operating in the private healthcare sector, for example by means of NHS Foundation Trusts operating Private Patient Units (PPUs).[135]

It is *essential* to be clear about whether a given situation involves private healthcare providers operating in the NHS, or NHS providers operating in the private healthcare sector. This is necessary because different consequences – regarding applicability of competition law and oversight by NHS Improvement or the CMA – arise as a result of the HSCA 2012 reforms, as will be discussed in Chapters 2 and 3, respectively.

### *2.1.4. Category 4 – Private Purchaser and Private Provider*

Category 4 is mentioned here mainly for the sake of completeness as it refers exclusively to the private healthcare sector, and the HSCA 2012 reforms do not affect category 4 relationships or activities. However, it is important to note that in its guidance on competition law to private providers, the CMA emphasises that the advice relates to private healthcare sector activity (category 4), not NHS work (category 2).[136] This is considered further in the contexts of the applicability of competition law and the relationship between the CMA and NHS Improvement in Chapters 2 and 3.

---

133 CMA, '60-second summary – Private medical practitioners: information on competition law', 03.12.2015.

134 SI 2014 No. 536.

135 Other arrangements in this category might include public-private arrangements arising in the context of Private Finance Initiative (PFI) projects. O. Odudu, above n. 123, cites contracts to lease buildings and land by way of example.

136 CMA, above n. 133.

Competition policy in English healthcare can be regarded as shaped primarily by the reach of general competition law and the strict distinction drawn between the NHS and private healthcare sector (as exemplified by the CMA's guidance above). Despite the current and ongoing development of the private healthcare sector by the CMA following its 2014 Market Investigation,[137] there appears to remain little appetite to bridge the gap between the NHS and private healthcare sector as regards competition oversight.[138]

## 2.2. SETTING THE SCENE FOR THE HSCA 2012 REFORMS: COMPETITION POLICY IN THE NHS 'QUASI-MARKET'

A range of policy guidance regarding competition and the NHS 'quasi-market' exists but appears to have received comparatively little (academic) attention thus far. This section considers this guidance in overview by reference to three chronological stages of developing competition in the NHS: the NHS Internal Market (Conservative governments 1987–97), 'Choice and Competition' (New Labour governments 1997–2010) and 'Opening Up Public Services' (Liberal Democrat–Conservative Coalition Government, 2010–15).

### *2.2.1. NHS Internal Market (Conservative Governments 1987–97)*

Initial guidance regarding anticompetitive behaviour emerged in 1994 with the development of the NHS Internal Market and the separation of purchasing and providing functions. 'The Operation of the NHS Internal Market: Local Freedoms, National Responsibilities' offered, for the first time, 'a simple set of ground rules that everyone in the NHS can work by'.[139] This guidance set out not only the 'management relationship' between the NHS Executive (part of the Department of Health) and purchasers, and its oversight function vis-à-vis providers, but also made reference to the power of the Minister – for example, to approve mergers which required NHS Trusts to be dissolved.[140] The guide also clarified examples of what constitutes 'collusive behaviour', such as price-fixing,

---

137 CMA, *Private Healthcare Market Investigation*, last updated 28.04.2017, <https://www.gov.uk/cma-cases/private-healthcare-market-investigation> accessed 24.06.2018.

138 In contrast, there are currently developments afoot to align regulation of the NHS and the private healthcare sector by the quality regulator. See Care Quality Commission (CQC), 'CQC consults on plans to evolve regulation of independent healthcare services in England', 26.01.2018, <https://www.cqc.org.uk/news/releases/cqc-consults-plans-evolve-regulation-independent-healthcare-services-england> accessed 24.06.2018.

139 NHS Executive, 'The Operation of the NHS Internal Market: Local Freedoms, National Responsibilities', Department of Health, December 1994, paragraph 8, p. 4.

140 Ibid, paragraph 15, p. 6.

and criteria for assessing boundary adjustments and mergers (responsiveness and patient choice).[141] A distinction was drawn between cooperation and collusion.[142] This guidance can be seen to reflect the general competition law regime in operation at the time: thus the Restrictive Trade Practices Act 1976 and the Resale Prices Act 1976 are referenced explicitly in connection with collusion,[143] and it is suggested that contracts, for example between DHAs (purchasers) and NHS Trusts (providers) or private providers, may fall within the scope of the legislation.[144] Under the Restrictive Trade Practices Act 1976, a presumption existed that all agreements between companies containing restrictions of a kind likely to inhibit competition were against the public interest, although this could be rebutted if the agreements could pass through one of the rather broad 'gateways' of the Act.[145] This emphasis on the 'public interest' also provided a basis for assessing mergers[146] as well as more general intervention by the NHS Executive.[147] This emphasis finds reflection in the balancing of patient interests and anticompetitive behaviour within the HSCA 2012 reforms,[148] although the general competition regime now takes a very different approach.

The 1994 guidance has been criticised[149] – correctly – on broadly two grounds. Firstly, for the lack of independence of the NHS Executive in having oversight over NHS bodies (NHS Trusts on the provider side and DHAs on the purchaser side). Secondly, for imposing a competition policy designed for the private sector[150] on the public sector, with little regard for wider shortcomings of the general competition regime in operation at the time (most notably ministerial discretion as to what constituted anticompetitive behaviour). Despite subsequent developments under New Labour and the HSCA 2012 to establish an independent sectoral regulator and a more clearly-defined competition policy for the NHS, these criticisms arguably remain valid.

---

141 Ibid, paragraph 15, p. 6.

142 Ibid, paragraph 23, p. 8.

143 Ibid, paragraph 10, p. 46.

144 Ibid, paragraph 12, p. 47.

145 Ibid, paragraph 11, p. 46.

146 Ibid, paragraph 15, p. 6.

147 Ibid, paragraph 3, p. 1.

148 See, for example, NHS Improvement's duty under sections 62(1) and (3) HSCA 2012.

149 D. Dawson, 'Regulating competition in the NHS. The Department of Health guide on mergers and anti-competitive behaviour', *University of York Centre for Health Economics Discussion Paper 131*, March 1995.

150 Dawson identifies the relevant primary legislation as being the Fair Trading Act 1973 and the Competition Act 1980. She further notes that while the NHS Executive mentions the Restrictive Trade Practices Act 1976, it does not allow for the possibility of referring NHS Trusts to the Monopolies and Mergers Commission under the Competition Act 1980. Ibid, fn. 2, p. 4.

### 2.2.2. *'Choice and Competition' (New Labour Governments 1997–2010)*

With the landslide election of New Labour in 1997, the terminology of the 'NHS Internal Market' was abandoned, but the purchaser/provider separation was retained and reconfigured by the concept of 'quasi-markets' and an emphasis on using choice and competition as mechanisms to deliver reforms.[151] Thus, significant efforts[152] were made on the supply side to expand private sector delivery of NHS services, encourage NHS Trusts to achieve NHS Foundation Trust status and have greater autonomy from central government, including the creation of Monitor as independent regulator of NHS Foundation Trusts.[153] On the demand side, patient choice policies were promoted to support these developments. However, these developments started to raise questions about whether the NHS could indeed be open to challenge under general competition law or the public procurement rules.[154]

It is notable that this period (late 1990s–mid-2000s) also saw significant changes in the wider competition regime, both to the substantive law and in terms of oversight. The enactment of the Competition Act 1998 (CA98) not only transposed EU competition law (prohibitions on anticompetitive agreements and abuse of dominance) into UK law, but also created the Competition Commission (CC) to replace the Monopolies and Mergers Commission.[155] With regard to merger control, a new system of voluntary notification and a two-phase investigation of whether a 'relevant merger situation' gave rise to a 'substantial lessening of competition' was instituted by the EA02, which also established the Office of Fair Trading (OFT) to replace the former Director General of Fair Trading.[156] These developments marked a decisive end to the 'ministerial

---

151 For a thorough discussion, see J. Le Grand, *The Other Invisible Hand - Delivering Public Services through Choice and Competition*, Princeton University Press, Oxford 2007.

152 See, for example, Department of Health, above n. 126, which outlined not only scope for redeveloping the relationship between the NHS and private healthcare sector, but also made provision for patients to be offered a choice of GP and choice of time and location in respect of hospital appointments for some elective treatments (p. 89). For discussion of the patient choice policies, see A. Dixon and R. Robertson, 'Patient Choice of Hospital' in N. Mays, A. Dixon and L. Jones (eds.), *Understanding New Labour's Market Reforms of the English NHS*, The King's Fund, London 2011.

153 These latter being enshrined by the Health and Social Care (Community Health and Standards) Act 2003.

154 As noted, inter alia, by N. Timmins, *The Five Giants - A Biography of the Welfare State*, 3rd edn, William Collins, London 2017, p. 332.

155 See Chapter 4, Competition Act 1998. For further discussion of these changes, see T. Prosser, above n. 114. For discussion of changes to the Dutch general competition regime in the same period, see J.W. van de Gronden and S.A. De Vries, 'Independent competition authorities in the EU' (2006) 2(1) *Utrecht Law Review* 32.

156 See Part 1, EA02.

discretion' approach to applying competition law, which has had implications for the development of competition policy within the English NHS as questions of applicability became more objective.[157]

Whilst the 'Blair years' (1997–2007) of New Labour governments appeared concerned with changing the underlying framework for competition in the NHS, the 'Brown years' (2007–2010) saw a more comprehensive approach being taken to instituting an 'NHS-specific' competition regime to operate in parallel with the general competition law system. This included policy guidance in the form of the NHS Principles and Rules for Competition and Cooperation (NHS PRCC) in 2007[158] and 2010,[159] and subsequently a merger control regime[160] to facilitate the aforementioned successive government policies for NHS Trusts to achieve Foundation Trust status. This new system was overseen by the NHS Cooperation and Competition Panel (NHS CCP)[161] introduced in 2009; again associated with the Department of Health, but hailed as 'the NHS' own Competition Commission'.[162] The role of the NHS CCP was to provide advice on compliance with the NHS PRCC, including giving advice to the Secretary of State (regarding NHS Trusts) and Monitor (regarding NHS Foundation Trusts),[163] although it also appears to have been active in developing competition within the English NHS as evidenced by a range of guidance and working papers.[164]

The NHS PRCC comprised 10 principles underpinned by a rationale, rules and illustrative 'actions and behaviours' which covered matters as diverse as procurement (commissioning),[165] payment regimes,[166] cooperation between providers and commissioners,[167] promoting patient choice to give effect to the

157 See further the discussions in Chapter 2 of this book.

158 For an overview, see The Health Foundation, 'The Principles and Rules for Cooperation and Competition (2007)', *Policy Navigator*, <https://navigator.health.org.uk/content/principles-and-rules-cooperation-and-competition-prcc-2007> accessed 24.06.2018.

159 Department of Health, 'Principles and Rules for Cooperation and Competition', 30.07.2010, <https://www.gov.uk/government/publications/principles-and-rules-for-cooperation-and-competition> accessed 24.06.2018.

160 NHS Co-operation and Competition Panel (NHS CCP), *Merger Guidelines*, 25.10.2010, <http://www.ccpanel.org.uk/reports-and-guidance/index.html> accessed 24.06.2018.

161 For an overview, see <https://www.ccpanel.org.uk/> accessed 24.06.2018.

162 As described by Ben Bradshaw MP. HC Deb, 24.02.2009, Column 66WH.

163 Department of Health, above n. 159, p. 5.

164 See, for example, C. Pike, *NHS CCP Working Paper Series – Volume 1 Number 5* 'Inside the Black Box: How competition between hospitals improves quality and integration of services', July 2012. See also <http://ccpanel.org.uk/reports-and-guidance/guidance-documents.html> accessed 24.06.2018.

165 Department of Health, above n. 159, Principles 1 and 2.

166 Ibid, Principle 3.

167 Ibid, Principle 4.

'Any Willing Provider' policy,[168] promoting equal treatment of patients,[169] and encouraging appropriate promotional activity as long as it remained consistent with patients' best interests and the brand and reputation of the NHS.[170]

The NHS PRCC also had specific 'Principles' to address anticompetitive behaviour and assess mergers. Principles 6 and 7 reflected, to a greater or lesser extent, the provisions of general competition law governing anticompetitive agreements and abuse of dominance, but placed these within an NHS context which perhaps reflected a public interest criterion. Thus, commissioners and providers were not permitted to reach agreements,[171] and providers were not permitted to refuse to accept services or to supply essential services to commissioners,[172] 'where this restricts commissioner or patient choice against patients' and taxpayers' interests'. As will be seen in the discussions of competition law in Chapter 2 and the focus of the healthcare regulators in Chapter 3, this NHS-specific focus, which suggested that *both* NHS commissioners and (individual) NHS patients equated to the 'consumer' in need of protection from anticompetitive practices and acknowledged the 'dual identity' of patients and taxpayers, has taken on a different dimension with the HSCA 2012 reforms.

Although cases brought under the NHS PRCC and assessed by the NHS CCP did not include specific reference to Principles 6 and 7,[173] further guidance was developed regarding the forms that anticompetitive behaviour could take in the context of the English NHS. This examined the implications of competition rules for 'providers of NHS-funded services' (thus, categories 1 and 2), referencing both anticompetitive agreements[174] and abuse of dominance (unilateral conduct),[175] as well as emerging practice reforms such as the delivery of integrated care[176] and clinical networks.[177] This guidance was produced broadly during 2012

168 Ibid, Principle 5. The 'Any Willing Provider' policy was introduced for elective services in 2008 to give effect to patient choice policies whereby NHS patients would have a choice of private or NHS providers. This initiative was subsequently rebranded 'Any Qualified Provider' to highlight the requirement that certain service standards must be met and that the providers be open to regulation by the Care Quality Commission. See further, OHE, above n. 5, p. 17.

169 Department of Health, above n. 159, Principle 8.

170 Ibid, Principle 9.

171 Ibid, Principle 6.

172 Ibid, Principle 7.

173 At the time of writing, limited information remains publicly available about NHS CCP cases, but 'conduct cases' appear to have focused on Principles 1, 2 and 5. See <http://ccpanel.org.uk/cases/index.html> accessed 24.06.2018.

174 NHS CCP, 'The Implications of Competition Rules for Agreements Involving Providers of NHS-Funded Healthcare Services', 22.03.2013.

175 NHS CCP, 'The Implications of Competition Rules for the Unilateral Conduct of Providers of NHS-funded Services', 22.03.2013.

176 NHS CCP, 'The Implications of Competition Rules for the Delivery of Integrated Care', 14.12.2012.

177 NHS CCP, 'The Implications of Competition Rules for Clinical Networks', 22.03.2012.

and 2013, which coincided with the development of the Health and Social Care Bill and included reference to developments which have taken effect with the HSCA 2012 reforms, such as the 'Choice and Competition condition' of the NHS Provider Licence.[178]

Principle 10 of the NHS PRCC dealt with merger control within the context of the English NHS as follows:

> Mergers, including vertical integration, between providers are permissible when there remains sufficient choice and competition or where they are otherwise in patients' and taxpayers' interests, for example because they will deliver significant improvements in the quality of care.[179]

This was underpinned by 'Merger Guidelines'[180] which the NHS CCP used to assess mergers and which reflected the general merger control regime of the EA02 insofar as it comprised a voluntary regime and two-stage assessment process. This NHS-specific merger test is examined in Chapter 4, since it was not immediately discontinued with the implementation of the HSCA 2012.

Overall, the NHS PRCC have been viewed as a regime which operated in parallel to the general competition regime of the CA98 and the EA02, and have been described variously as comprising the principles of competition law[181] and representing an 'alternative source' of competition law.[182] What is more persuasive is the description of the NHS PRCC as offering a 'new style' of competition law for quasi-markets,[183] since this acknowledges the nature of the NHS and the complex interactions between NHS commissioners and NHS patients and taxpayers which need to be taken into consideration.

### *2.2.3. 'Opening Up Public Services' (Liberal Democrat–Conservative Coalition Government 2010–15)*

From the foregoing, it seems clear that the development of the NHS CCP guidance and practice coincided with the Coalition Government's proposed reforms of the White Paper[184] which subsequently formed the basis for the HSCA 2012. This reflected the Coalition Government's and New Labour's

178 Ibid, pp. 2–3.
179 Department of Health, above n. 159, Principle 10.
180 NHS CCP, above n. 160.
181 O. Odudu, 'Are State-owned healthcare providers undertakings subject to competition law?' (2011) 32(5) *European Competition Law Review* 231.
182 O. Odudu, above n. 123.
183 I. Lianos, 'Toward a Bureaucracy-Centred Theory of the Interaction between Competition Law and State Activities' in T.K. Cheng, I. Lianos, and D.D. Sokol (eds.), *Competition and the State*, Stanford University Press, Stanford 2014.
184 Department of Health (Cm 7881, July 2010), above n. 117.

differing conceptions of what competition in the NHS should be. On the one hand, the idea of a 'new style of competition law' may be inferred from the NHS CCP guidance with NHS-specific examples of anticompetitive behaviour. On the other hand, the development of the NHS Provider Licence provides a clear example of wholesale borrowing from other liberalised sectors, where licensing regimes were introduced as a form of regulation. Certainly the experience of the architect of the HSCA 2012 reforms, Andrew Lansley, as a junior Minister in the Conservative governments of the 1980s, has been considered influential for his conception of how competition could work within the NHS.[185]

A further aspect of Coalition Government policy which has had implications for the development of competition in the English NHS and the HSCA 2012 reforms is the wider project to open up public services, inter alia, by increasing choice and encouraging a diversity of providers (including from the private and voluntary sectors) to deliver public services.[186] Implications for the development of competition in the English NHS and the HSCA 2012 reforms can be identified in a range of OFT guidance,[187] but this appears to have developed quite independently of the evolution of the HSCA 2012, and independently, specifically, of subsequent NHS development with the NHS Five Year Forward View and focus on integrated care. Thus, what we see is the HSCA 2012 reforms affecting categories 1 and 2 specifically,[188] whereas the 'opening up public services' reforms appear directed towards NHS Foundation Trusts, whether with regard to their category 1 or their category 3 activities. The distinction between the two can be illustrated by the juxtaposition of the development of a

---

185 N. Timmins, above n. 154, pp. 680–90.

186 For an overview, see Cabinet Office, Press Release, 'Opening Up Public Services', 11.07.2011, <https://www.gov.uk/government/news/opening-up-public-services> accessed 24.06.2018. Also, HM Government, 'Open Public Services White Paper' (Cm 8145, July 2011).

187 See, for example, OFT, 'Developing public service markets – Insights for regulators, commissioners and policy makers', OFT1497; OFT, 'Orderly Exit – Designing continuity regimes in public markets', OFT1468, December 2012; OFT, The Competition Act 1998 and Public Bodies, Policy Note1/2004, OFT443, August 2004; OFT, 'Assessing the impact of public sector procurement on competition', OFT742a; OFT, 'Commissioning and Competition in the Public Sector', OFT1314; OFT, 'Guidance on how to assess the competition effects of subsidies', OFT829; OFT, 'Government in Markets – Why competition matters – a guide for policymakers', OFT1113; OFT, 'Choice and Competition in Public Services', OFT1214; OFT, 'Empowering Consumers of Public Services through Choice-Tools', OFT1321; OFT, 'Competition in Mixed Markets: Ensuring Competitive Neutrality', OFT1242; and OFT, 'Competition Law and Public Bodies', OFT1389. For a discussion of these developments, see O. Odudu, 'Why it matters – Selling competition law in the new frontier', *Competition Law Insight*, 10.12.2013.

188 Although the HSCA 2012 reforms may also be seen to affect category 3 activity of NHS providers treating private patients insofar as an expansion in Private Patient Units was intended by section 165 HSCA 2012.

'failure regime' for NHS Foundation Trusts,[189] and a 'success regime' for NHS Trusts,[190] on the basis that the latter is needed to ensure continuity of care.

## 2.3. THE DEVELOPMENT OF THE HSCA 2012 COMPETITION FRAMEWORK

As noted in the Introduction to this book, the passage of the HSCA 2012 was problematic and a 'pause' was called between April and June 2011 for a newly-constituted body, the NHS Future Forum, to review and address the increasing and widespread criticisms of the reforms.[191] The NHS Future Forum reported in June 2011, and its concerns regarding the development of competition[192] within the NHS have made a significant contribution to the subsequent development and implementation of the HSCA 2012 reforms.

It is useful to consider the development of the current 'competition policy' in English healthcare by reference to a series of chronological stages, namely pre- and post-NHS Future Forum examination, and subsequent developments which have emerged against a backdrop of increasing scepticism about competition and the NHS.

### *2.3.1. Pre-NHS Future Forum Examination*

In the White Paper preceding the HSCA 2012 reforms, Monitor was reconceptualised as an economic regulator (akin to OFCOM and OFGEM) with one of its three main functions being to promote competition and ensure its effective working in the interests of patients and taxpayers.[193] This included Monitor sharing concurrent powers with the OFT to apply competition law to prevent anticompetitive behaviour.[194] Provision was also envisaged for NHS Foundation Trusts to merge more easily and for all NHS Trusts to become NHS Foundation Trusts.[195] A new development was Monitor's licensing oversight

189 As referenced in OFT, OFT1468, above n. 187.

190 NHS England, 'Five Year Forward View – The Success Regime: A whole systems intervention', 03.06.2015.

191 Between April and June 2011. For the most thorough account thus far of the Health and Social Care Bill as a whole, see N. Timmins, *Never Again? The story of the Health and Social Care Act 2012 – A study in coalition government and policy making*, The King's Fund and Institute for Government, London 2012. For an overview, see The King's Fund, 'The Health and Social Care Act: the tale in a timeline', <http://www.kingsfund.org.uk/topics/nhs-reform/health-and-social-care-act-2012-timeline> accessed 24.06.2018.

192 NHS Future Forum, 'Choice and Competition – Delivering Real Choice. A report from the NHS Future Forum', June 2011.

193 Department of Health (2010), above n. 117, p. 38.

194 Ibid, p. 38.

195 Ibid, p. 36.

function, with a distinction being drawn between licensing, which would apply only to publicly-funded health services, and Monitor's powers to apply competition law, which would apply to both publicly- and privately-funded healthcare and to social care.[196]

As introduced to the House of Commons in January 2011, Part 3 of the Health and Social Care Bill included a regime of 'Economic Regulation' which, under Chapter 1 of the Bill, established Monitor with a general duty to protect and promote the interests of people who use healthcare services by promoting competition where appropriate and through regulation where necessary.[197]

Chapter 2 of the Bill, 'Competition', further set out what might be termed a 'competition policy' comprising:

- Application of general competition law (the provisions governing anticompetitive agreements and abuse of dominance under the CA98 and the Treaty on the Functioning of the European Union (TFEU)) by Monitor and the then OFT sharing concurrent powers;[198]
- Concurrent powers of Monitor and the OFT to conduct Market Investigations under Part 4, EA02;[199]
- Competence to institute regulations governing good procurement practice, protecting and promoting the right of patients to exercise choice in respect of healthcare providers, and promoting competition in the provision of healthcare services for the NHS;[200]
- Application of general merger control (Part 3, EA02) to mergers involving NHS Foundation Trusts;[201]
- An obligation for the then Competition Commission to review the development of competition in the provision of healthcare services for the NHS and Monitor's exercise of its functions.[202]

Chapter 4 of the Bill made provision for the licensing regime, including a remit for Monitor to set or modify licence conditions 'for the purpose of promoting competition in the provision of health care services for [the] purposes [of the NHS]'.[203]

---

196 Ibid, paragraph 4.29, p. 39.

197 Health and Social Care Bill 132 (HC Session 2010–11), as introduced 19.01.2011, Clause 52(1), <https://publications.parliament.uk/pa/cm201011/cmbills/132/11132.i-v.html>.

198 Ibid, Clauses 60, 62 and 68.

199 Ibid, Clauses 61, 62 and 68.

200 Ibid, Clauses 63 and 64.

201 Ibid, Clause 65.

202 Ibid, Clauses 66 and 67.

203 Ibid, Clause 89(2)(b).

These provisions remained intact following amendments in the Public Bill Committee,[204] but substantial changes began to appear in the draft Bill produced in July 2011, following the investigation by the NHS Future Forum during the pause in the passage of the legislation called by the Coalition Government to address the growing concerns about, and criticism of, the Health and Social Care Bill. In seeking information and feedback on Part 3 'Competition' of the Bill, the NHS Future Forum noted that '[t]he fact that the choice and competition issue received the most comments on the [Department of Health] website demonstrates the importance of this issue'.[205]

The NHS Future Forum proposed that competition be conceptualised as one of the tools to drive choice and efficiency,[206] acknowledging the concerns which had been advanced about the disruption of integrated care initiatives and cooperation, and about cherry-picking and profiteering.[207] It also saw competition and integration as a false dichotomy,[208] and considered that the former should drive the latter.

The NHS Future Forum acknowledged that it was making significant proposals in reframing competition: with parameters being set within a wider framework of a 'choice mandate' elaborated by NHS England[209] and to be enshrined in law, with obligations on Monitor and NHS England.[210] However, perhaps most significantly, the NHS Future Forum proposed that competition be refocused so that competition in itself is never the driving factor, clarifying that the best safeguards against misuse of competition would be effective commissioning and strong regulation.[211]

To this end, various safeguards were recommended, including the removal of the provision in the Health and Social Care Bill for Monitor to 'promote competition' and clarification that Monitor is sectoral regulator for health, not an 'economic regulator'.[212] Furthermore, Monitor's primary duty should be to protect and promote the interests of patients and citizens, as the NHS Future Forum opined that there needed to be an effective regulator that tackles abuses that are not in the interest of patients or the taxpayer.[213] This was reinforced in the proposal that Monitor's role should be clarified as supporting choice,

---

204 See Health and Social Care 177, 02.04.2011 (HC Session 2010–11), variously, Clauses 55, 64–75, and in respect of the competition-related licence condition, Clause 100(2)(b).
205 NHS Future Forum, above n. 192, p. 10.
206 Ibid, p. 4.
207 Ibid, p. 5.
208 Ibid, p. 6.
209 Ibid, p. 8.
210 Ibid, p. 11.
211 Ibid, p. 9.
212 Ibid, p. 9.
213 Ibid, p. 9.

competition and integrated care within the model of choice and competition set out by NHS England.[214]

Interestingly, the NHS Future Forum saw the granting of 'concurrent powers' to Monitor and the OFT in respect of applying competition law as a further safeguard against the disproportionate application of competition.[215] Further amendments to this relationship of 'concurrent powers' in respect of applying competition law were developed in the context of the Enterprise and Regulatory Reform Act 2013 and the wider revision of the UK concurrency regime, and elaborated in the Competition Act 1998 (Concurrency) Regulations 2014.[216] These are examined in detail in Chapter 3, but offer a useful reminder for the purposes of the present discussion that controversy surrounding the HSCA 2012 reforms regarding competition has not abated. However, it is notable that the amendments to concurrent powers relate to those in respect of applying competition law, but not conducting market investigations.[217]

Overall, however, it is to be noted that the NHS Future Forum did not see any reason to remove Part 3, 'Competition', from the Health and Social Care Bill; merely that it be significantly amended.[218]

### *2.3.2. Post-NHS Future Forum Examination*

The NHS Future Forum's recommendations found expression in subsequent drafts of the Health and Social Care Bill as follows. The proposal that Monitor be designated a sectoral regulator rather than an 'economic regulator' was reflected in the title of Part 3 being changed to 'Regulation of Health and Adult Social Care Services'[219] from 'Economic Regulation' in the draft Bill prior to the NHS Future Forum's report. Whilst Monitor's primary duty of protecting and promoting the interests of patients and citizens (implied in the wording of 'people who use healthcare services') remained,[220] the need for an effective

214 Ibid, p. 11.

215 Ibid, p. 30.

216 SI 2014 No. 536.

217 For further discussion, see M. Guy, 'Competition and sectoral regulation in Dutch and English healthcare: factors shaping the competition focus of the new healthcare regulators and their relationship with the competition authorities', (2017) 2 *Ius Publicum Network Review*, ISSN 2039 2540, <http://www.ius-publicum.com/pagina.php?lang=en&pag=fascicolo> accessed 24.06.2018.

218 NHS Future Forum, above n. 192, p. 9.

219 Health and Social Care Bill 221, 18.07.2011, Part 3. This wording was retained across subsequent drafts (HL Bill 92, 12.09.2011, HL Bill 119 2010–12 22.12.2011, HL Bill 132 2010–12 14.03.2012) and enshrined by the HSCA 2012.

220 Ibid, Clause 58(1). This wording was retained across subsequent drafts (HL Bill 92, 12.09.2011 Clause 59(1), HL Bill 119 2010–12 22.12.2011 Clause 60(1), HL Bill 132 2010–12 14.03.2012 Clause 62(1)) and enshrined by section 62(1) HSCA 2012.

regulator to tackle abuses which are not in patient or taxpayer interests was elaborated by reference to anticompetitive behaviour:[221] 'Monitor must exercise its functions with a view to preventing anti-competitive behaviour in the provision of healthcare services for the purposes of the NHS which is against the interests of people who use such services.'

Whilst the NHS Future Forum did not make specific mention of the NHS Provider Licence regime, these amendments – specifically the abandonment of emphasis on 'promoting competition' – subsequently found reflection in the wording of the Health and Social Care Bill and latterly the HSCA 2012, such that Monitor's role became to set or modify licence conditions 'for the purpose of preventing anti-competitive behaviour in the provision of healthcare services for those purposes [for the NHS] which is against the interest of people who use such services'.[222]

Furthermore, a definition of 'anticompetitive behaviour' was introduced in July 2011,[223] apparently by reference to the provisions governing anticompetitive agreements:

> 'Anti-competitive behaviour' means behaviour which would (or would be likely to) prevent, restrict or distort competition and a reference to preventing anti-competitive behaviour includes a reference to eliminating or reducing the effects (or potential effects) of the behaviour.

This apparent reference to balancing anticompetitive behaviour with patient and taxpayer interests found further reflection in subsequent Department of Health guidance elaborating the new, post-HSCA 2012 regime, which acknowledged that 'competition and regulation will always play an important role', whilst drawing distinctions between the natural monopoly elements of healthcare (such as emergency services in rural areas or specialised stroke services)

---

221 Ibid, Clause 58(3). This wording was retained across subsequent drafts (Health and Social Care Bill 92, 12.09.2011 (HL Session 2010–12), Clause 59(3); Health and Social Care Bill 119, 22.12.2011 (HL Session 2010–12), Clause 60(3); Health and Social Care Bill 132, 14.03.2012 (HL Session 2010–12), Clause 62(3)) and enshrined by section 62(3) HSCA 2012.

222 Ibid, Clause 103(2)(b). This wording was retained across subsequent drafts (Health and Social Care Bill 92, 12.09.2011 (HL Session 2010–12), Clause 95(2)(b); Health and Social Care Bill 119, 22.12.2011 (HL Session 2010–12), Clause 97(2)(b); Health and Social Care Bill 132, 14.03.2012 (HL Session 2010–12), Clause 96(2)(b)) and enshrined by section 96(2)(b) HSCA 2012.

223 Ibid, Clause 59(2). This wording was retained across subsequent drafts (Health and Social Care Bill 92, 12.09.2011 (HL Session 2010–12), Clause 60(2), Health and Social Care Bill 119, 22.12.2011 (HL Session 2010–12), Clause 62(2), Health and Social Care Bill 132, 14.03.2012 (HL Session 2010–12), Clause 64(2)) and enshrined by section 64(2) HSCA 2012.

and elements where varying degrees of competition may be possible (elective and non-elective procedures in rural and urban areas).[224]

Furthermore, in implementing the HSCA 2012 reforms, it was envisaged that commissioners would be responsible for deciding whether to use competition and the form this would take, which might be: competition in the market and accreditation; competition for the market and frameworks; or no competition – with recourse to reconfiguration, contract variations or contract extension.[225] In sum, the commissioner's decision would be on where choice and competition are in the best interests of patients, and the criteria considered for making this decision would include: Secretary of State regulations on procurement and competition, the standing rules on patient choice; NHS Commissioning Board (now NHS England) guidance; and the national tariff or rules on local pricing.[226] This approach distinguishes between the limited scope for competition *in* the market in the English NHS (activated by the 'any qualified provider' (AQP) policy,[227] enabling choice of accredited NHS, private or voluntary sector providers) and the greater range of competition *for* the market via procurement exercises. The option of choosing 'no competition' is significant for underscoring the refocusing of competition within the NHS by the NHS Future Forum, as noted previously.

The suggestion that competition – and by extension, competition law – is something which can be applied or not applied at will by NHS commissioners is controversial in view of the functional triggers for these laws and the potential for inconsistencies in approach. It suggests a shift in emphasis to the purpose of a competition policy vis-à-vis the NHS as simply designed to serve ends of advocacy and compliance, as much as actually offering a basis for active enforcement of competition law.[228] Experience from the Netherlands – where questions of whether competition law applies to private health insurers are considerably less controversial – suggests the former as the latter enforcement has been minimal, partly as a result of a detailed regulatory framework.[229]

224 Department of Health, 'Protecting and Promoting Patients' Interests: the role of Sector Regulation', Department of Health, London 01.12.2011, p. 19, <https://www.gov.uk/government/publications/protecting-and-promoting-patients-interests-the-role-of-sector-regulation> accessed 24.06.2018.

225 Department of Health, 'Sector Regulation – a short guide to the Health and Social Care Bill. What you need to know as a provider of NHS services', 23.02.2012, 'Figure 5', <https://www.gov.uk/government/publications/sector-regulation-a-short-guide-to-the-health-and-social-care-bill> accessed 24.06.2018.

226 Ibid.

227 For further information on AQP, see OHE, above n. 5, p. 17.

228 See further on this point, O. Odudu, above n. 181; and O. Odudu, 'Competition law and the welfare state' in J. Galloway (ed.), *Intersections of Antitrust: Policy and Regulations*, Oxford University Press, Oxford (forthcoming), <https://papers.ssrn.com/sol3/papers.cfm?abstract_id=3160784> accessed 24.06.2018.

229 On this point, see W. Sauter, above n. 40.

## 2.4. DEVELOPMENTS SUBSEQUENT TO THE HEALTH AND SOCIAL CARE BILL

Aside from the NHS Future Forum's recommendations to refocus the competition framework of the Health and Social Care Bill, other amendments need to be noted, as these helped shape the eventual regime which has been enshrined by the enactment of the HSCA 2012.

For example, in responding to the NHS Future Forum's report, the Coalition Government volunteered to put the pre-existing New Labour policy guidance (the NHS PRCC) on a statutory footing rather than design new rules governing procurement best practice.[230] This was intended to avoid further controversy, but the resulting National Health Service (Procurement, Patient Choice and Competition) Regulations 2013[231] required a second version[232] (still in force) in order to address concerns attaching to the prohibition on 'anticompetitive behaviour' by commissioners.[233]

A further important development was the inclusion of a role for Monitor in the assessment of mergers involving NHS Foundation Trusts. In light of the commitment in the White Paper to facilitating NHS Foundation Trust mergers, and certainly the controversy surrounding the passage of the HSCA 2012 and the consideration that the sectoral regulator would be best-placed to determine the appropriateness of competition vis-à-vis the NHS, it is perhaps surprising that this amendment found reflection in the terms of the Health and Social Bill relatively late in the legislative passage, namely in the final version debated by the House of Lords[234] prior to enactment of the HSCA 2012 in March 2012.[235]

---

230 Department of Health, 'Government response to the NHS Future Forum report', CM8113, 22.06.2011, paragraph 5.16, p. 44.

231 National Health Service (Procurement, Patient Choice and Competition) Regulations 2013, SI 2013/257.

232 National Health Service (Procurement, Patient Choice and Competition) (No. 2) Regulations 2013, SI 2013/500.

233 For a comprehensive discussion of the revisions, particularly regarding the procurement regulations, see S. Smith, E. Heard and D. Bevan, 'New procurement legislation for English healthcare bodies – the National Health Service (Procurement, Patient Choice and Competition) (No. 2) Regulations 2013' (2013) 4 *Public Procurement Law Review* 109.

234 Health and Social Care Bill 132, 14.03.2012 (HL Session 2010–12), Clauses 79(4) and (5).

235 Certainly, debates in the House of Lords considered questions of oversight and suggestions that the NHS PRCC and Secretary of State oversight be retained. See, for example, Baroness Thornton during HL Deb 13.12.2011 Column 1111 and Baroness Williams of Crosby during HL Deb 15.12.2011 Column 1448. However, the need for regulator input may also have become apparent from the OFT's Phase I scrutiny of the 'Dorset Hospitals' merger, which was notified on 29.11.2011, and which acknowledged the need for approval of the merger by Monitor and the Secretary of State for Health. OFT, *Anticipated merger between The Royal Bournemouth and Christchurch Hospitals NHS Foundation Trust and Poole Hospital NHS Foundation Trust*, Case reference ME/5351/12, 07.02.2013, paragraph 3. This merger was subsequently blocked at Phase II by the then Competition Commission – and is discussed further in Chapter 4.

From a substantive law perspective, it is also surprising that applying the general merger control regime and affording the sectoral regulator the opportunity to identify 'relevant customer benefits' (which have subsequently become known as 'relevant patient benefits') within this context was eventually included in the HSCA 2012, rather than actively and explicitly exploring the option of classifying NHS mergers as a Secretary of State public interest category,[236] thus exempting these from the reach of the EA02.[237]

Whilst the HSCA 2012 reforms concern primarily the NHS, section 165 HSCA 2012 makes provision for an expansion of the private healthcare sector involvement by removing the 'private patient income cap', namely the limit to the amount of money an NHS provider can make from private patients. The possibility for this to prompt an expansion in PPUs was recognised by the CMA in the course of its Private Healthcare Market Investigation.[238] In order to address perceived concerns about this – from the perspective of the private healthcare market only (categories 3 and 4) – the CMA proposed a new test to examine 'PPU arrangements'[239] since these had not previously met the thresholds of general merger control, so were not being scrutinised by the CMA. This is considered further in the context of healthcare-specific merger control in Chapter 4.

## 3. CONCLUSIONS

The Netherlands and England have arguably shared a common starting-point for their competition reforms, namely the 'managed competition' model and other ideas of the US health economist, Alain Enthoven. However, the development of a competition policy to support the evolving competition reforms has proved difficult. This is because it has combined engagement with general competition law with developing 'sector-specific' rules which are, to a greater or lesser extent, being shaped by governmental reforms which currently emphasise solidarity over competition.

This historical review of the evolving competition policies of Dutch and English healthcare serves to highlight where common themes emerge – notably the considerable scope for government or parliamentary intervention to shape competition policy in healthcare. This is perhaps most evident in the divergent

236 Under Part 3, Chapter 2, EA02.

237 See further on this point, K. Desai, 'Public hospital mergers: a case for broader considerations than competition law?' (2013) 34(12) *European Competition Law Review* 646.

238 CMA, *Private Healthcare Market Investigation Final Report*, CMA25, 02.04.2014, paragraph 11.249, pp. 11–58.

239 CMA, *Private Healthcare Market Investigation Final Order*, 01.10.2014, Part 2, pp. 5–6.

approaches to competition reform in the English NHS taken by the New Labour and Coalition Governments, although the ongoing refocusing of competition oversight by the ACM is also testament to this.

Ultimately, the chapter has provided a point of reference for, and contextual information underpinning, the following substantive discussions relating to the applicability of competition law, the relationship between the competition authority and healthcare regulator, and modifications to general merger control (Chapters 2–4). This is useful as the notable developments outlined here suggest that the 2006 and HSCA 2012 reforms may be taking on a different character from what was originally intended, such that ongoing flexibility is required.

# CHAPTER 2

# COMPETITION LAW

## Its Applicability and Application in Dutch and English Healthcare

## 1. INTRODUCTION

One of the controversial aspects of the Health and Social Care Act 2012 (HSCA 2012) was the apparent underscoring of the *applicability* of general competition law – the provisions governing anticompetitive agreements and abuse of dominance in the Competition Act 1998 (CA98)[1] and Articles 101 and 102 of the Treaty on the Functioning of the European Union (TFEU) – to the English NHS. There had been a growing consensus that competition law was indeed applicable, partly in consequence of the expansive requirement for an 'undertaking' which does not distinguish between public and private ownership,[2] and likely as a result of the expanding private provision of NHS services, and increased autonomy of NHS Foundation Trusts and their similarities with commercial entities.[3] Consequently, the enactment of the HSCA 2012 may be considered to mark a turning-point in terms of the consequences of making the applicability of competition law explicit.[4] This was in contrast to the 'new style of competition law'[5] formed by the New Labour policy rules, which have

1 Sections 2 and 18 Competition Act 1998 (CA98) (the 'Chapters I and II prohibitions').

2 O. Odudu, 'Are State-owned healthcare providers undertakings subject to competition law?' (2011) 32(5) *European Competition Law Review* 231.

3 Boeger and Prosser suggest that the radical changes introduced by New Labour may well have been enough for the NHS to have moved from a system organised on the basis of solidarity to one subject to competition law. See N. Boeger and T. Prosser, 'United Kingdom' in M. Krajewski, U. Neergaard, J.W. van de Gronden (eds.), *The Changing Legal Framework for Services of General Interest in Europe – Between Competition and Solidarity*, TMC Asser Press, The Hague 2009, p. 367. B. Collins, 'Procurement and Competition Rules – Can the NHS be exempted?', The King's Fund Briefing, London March 2015, <https://www.kingsfund.org.uk/sites/default/files/field/field_publication_file/procurement-competition-rules-kings-fund-mar-2015.pdf> accessed 24.06.2018.

4 See A.C.L. Davies, 'This Time, It's For Real' (2013) 76(3) *Modern Law Review* 564.

5 I. Lianos, 'Toward a Bureaucracy-Centred Theory of the Interaction between Competition Law and State Activities' in T.K. Cheng, I. Lianos and D.D. Sokol (eds.), *Competition and the State*, Stanford University Press, Stanford CA 2014. See also M. Sanderson, P. Allen

been described as competition law principles (as distinct from competition law)[6] and an alternative source of competition law.[7] What the HSCA 2012 could not do, however, was to change the underlying, fundamental nature of the NHS as a quasi-market, and so conceptions of a 'new style of competition law' may still be appropriate to describe the HSCA 2012 reforms. Certainly the total absence of cases assessed under the CA98 and the TFEU thus far can be attributed as much to confusion about the extent of the substantive law in this area (including what applying competition law can usefully achieve in healthcare reform) as to the complexity of the regulatory regime – the NHS Provider Licence and the National Health Service (Procurement, Patient Choice and Competition) (No. 2) Regulations 2013[8] (the 2013 Regulations) – implemented alongside and subsequent to the HSCA 2012 and the associated interaction between the Competition and Markets Authority (the CMA) and NHS Improvement. Indeed, the respective priorities of these two agencies, ongoing political sensitivity attached to the NHS and perhaps recognition that competition cases are problematic in terms of cost and complexity may also have played a part in recourse to regulatory rules emerging as a more proportionate response to potentially anticompetitive behaviour. Certainly, it has increasingly been suggested that recourse may not be had to general competition law in view of the development of the Competition Oversight condition of the NHS Provider Licence.[9] Such recourse has also been termed 'soft enforcement'.[10]

However, the applicability of competition law to healthcare more generally has also generated much discussion in light of the framework established by EU case law.[11] In general terms, a distinction has been drawn between providers

---

and D. Osipovic, 'The regulation of competition in the National Health Service (NHS): what difference has the Health and Social Care Act 2012 made?' (2017) 12 *Health Economics, Policy and Law* 1.

6 O. Odudu, above n. 2.

7 O. Odudu, 'Competition Law and the National Health Service', *Competition Bulletin: Competition Law Views from Blackstone Chambers*, 08.10.12, <https://competitionbulletin.com/2012/10/08/competition-law-and-the-national-health-service/> accessed 24.06.2018.

8 National Health Service (Procurement, Patient Choice and Competition) Regulations (No. 2) 2013, SI 2013/500.

9 See, for example, D. Sinclair, '"Undertakings" in competition law at the public-private interface – an unhealthy situation' (2014) 35(4) *European Competition Law Review* 167. C. Graham, 'UK: The Concurrent Enforcement by Regulators of Competition Law and Sector-Specific Regulation' (2016) 7(6) *Journal of European Competition Law & Practice* 407.

10 O. Odudu, 'Competition Law and the Welfare State' in J. Galloway (ed.), *Intersections of Antitrust: Policy and Regulations*, Oxford University Press, Oxford (forthcoming), <https://papers.ssrn.com/sol3/papers.cfm?abstract_id=3160784> accessed 24.06.2018.

11 See, for example, T. Prosser, 'EU competition law and public services' in E. Mossialos, G. Permanand, R. Baeten and T.K. Hervey (eds.), *Health Systems Governance in Europe: The Role of European Union Law and Policy*, Cambridge University Press, Cambridge 2010; J. Lear, E. Mossialos and B. Karl, 'EU competition law and health policy' in E. Mossialos, G. Permanand, R. Baeten and T.K. Hervey (eds.), *Health Systems*

and purchasers, whereby the former may be subject to EU competition law but the latter may not be. This has influenced how competition law is perceived at a national level, with the *AOK Bundesverband*[12] and *FENIN*[13] judgments proving particularly influential in, respectively, the Netherlands and England.

In the Netherlands, questions of the applicability of competition law were raised in connection with the move between *ziekenfondsen* (sickness funds) and private health insurers under the 2006 reforms.[14] This led to the enactment of Article 122 *Zorgverzekeringswet* (Dutch Health Insurance Act 2006 (Zvw)), which in essence clarified that the private health insurers were indeed 'undertakings' for the purposes of the *Mededingingswet* (Dutch Competition Act 1998 (Mw)), even if they are not so for the purposes of EU competition law. However, the recent proposals by the Dutch Government to emphasise solidarity in the functions of the health insurers have been viewed as having the potential to re-open the question of whether these are subject to competition law.[15] With regard to healthcare providers, the applicability of competition law appears not to be in doubt, but questions have been raised recently regarding how the *Autoriteit Consument en Markt* (Authority for Consumers and Markets (ACM)) has applied competition law to primary care providers.[16]

---

*Governance in Europe: The Role of European Union Law and Policy*, Cambridge University Press, Cambridge 2010; J.W. van de Gronden, 'The Treaty Provisions on Competition and Health Care' in J.W. van de Gronden, E. Szyszczak, U. Neergaard and M. Krajewski (eds.), *Health Care and EU Law*, TMC Asser Press, The Hague 2011, pp. 265–94; L. Hancher and W. Sauter, *EU Competition and Internal Market Law in the Health Care Sector*, Oxford University Press, Oxford 2012; and W. Sauter, 'The Impact of EU Competition Law on National Healthcare Systems' (2013) 38(4) *European Law Review* 457.

12 Joined cases C-264/01, C-306/01, C-354/01 and C-355/01, *AOK Bundesverband, Bundesverband der Betriebskrankenkassen (BKK) et al. v. Ichthyol-Gesellschaft Cordes et al.*, ECLI:EU:C:2004:150.

13 Case C-205/03 P, *Federación Española de Empresas de Tecnología Sanitaria (FENIN) v. Commission of the European Communities*, ECLI:EU:C:2006:453.

14 In essence, the former *ziekenfondsen* had been deemed subject to competition law, but this was reviewed in light of the *AOK Bundesverband* finding that German *Krankenkassen* (which shared similarities with Dutch *ziekenfondsen*) were not. See S. Belhaj and J.W. van de Gronden, 'Some room for competition does not make a sickness fund an undertaking. Is EC competition law applicable to the health care sector? (Joined cases C-264/01, C-306/01, C-453/01 and C-355/01 *AOK*)' (2004) 25(11) *European Competition Law Review* 682. J.W. van de Gronden, 'Purchasing care: economic activity or service of general (economic) interest?' (2004) 25(2) *European Competition Law Review* 87. J.W. van de Gronden and E. Szyszczak, 'Introducing Competition Principles Into Health Care Through EU Law and Policy: A Case Study of the Netherlands' (2014) 22(2) *Medical Law Review* 238.

15 See L. Glas, A. Looijestijn and J.W. van de Gronden, *'Advies 2: Beoordeling van verschillende voorgenomen zorgmaatregelen in het licht van het EU-recht en het EVRM. Avies in opdracht van VGZ en Zilveren Kruis'* ('Opinion 2: Assessment of different proposals for healthcare measures in light of EU law and the European Convention on Human Rights. Opinion commissioned by VGZ and Zilveren Kruis').

16 W. Verloren Van Themaat and M. Bosch, *'De uitgangspunten toezicht eerstelijnszorg in een context'* ('The starting-points of oversight of primary care providers in context') (2016)

In England, section 72 HSCA 2012 provides for NHS Improvement and the CMA to share concurrent powers to apply the UK and EU provisions governing anticompetitive agreements[17] and abuse of dominance in respect of the provision of healthcare services in England. This provision is examined in terms of its substantive content in this chapter and institutional oversight in Chapter 3. This chapter examines the framework established by EU case law and the Dutch and English responses to this, as well as national cases and guidance thus far, in order to understand what the effects of applying competition law in the context of healthcare provision may be in practical terms.

With the foregoing in mind, this chapter is structured as follows. Section 2 examines the EU competition law framework as defined by reference to the 'undertaking' concept. Section 3 considers the emergence of national frameworks affecting the application of competition law in Dutch and English healthcare cases. Section 4 elaborates how the provisions governing anticompetitive agreements and abuse of dominance can apply to healthcare provision and how these have been applied in Dutch and English healthcare cases. Section 5 concludes.

## 2. THE EU COMPETITION LAW FRAMEWORK AS DEFINED BY REFERENCE TO THE 'UNDERTAKING' CONCEPT

This chapter is concerned with clarifying the defining features of the *applicability* of competition law and how this is being translated into actual *application* in practice regarding Dutch and English healthcare via cases and guidance. Therefore, the focus of this section is on the 'undertaking' concept in view of the fact that other 'boundaries'[18] which may trigger the *applicability* of

---

*Markt en Mededinging*, 1, 31. M. Wiggers, R. Struijlaart and J. Ruigewaard, *'Landelijke Huisartsen Vereniging – Annotatie van de uitspraak van de Rechtbank Rotterdam van 17.12.2015'* ('Dutch GPs' Association – Case Comment on the Judgment of the Rotterdam District Court of 17.12.2015') (2016) *Markt en Mededinging*, 4, 160.

17 The choice of the more generic term, 'anticompetitive agreements', is chosen throughout this book since a range of agreements may be at issue – not only the most 'hard core' example of cartels. It is recognised that this is in contrast to Dutch and EU-related literature, which can reference the 'cartel prohibition' in relation both to Article 101 TFEU and Article 6 Mw. See for example, J.W. van de Gronden, above n. 11, and L. Hancher and W. Sauter, above n. 11, for an EU focus; and, with regard to the Netherlands, W. Sauter, 'The balance between competition law and regulation in Dutch healthcare markets' (2014) *TILEC Discussion Paper*, DP 2014-041, <https://papers.ssrn.com/sol3/papers.cfm?abstract_id=2530356> accessed 24.06.2018. W. Sauter, 'Experiences from the Netherlands: The Application of Competition Rules in Health Care' in J.W. van de Gronden, E. Szyszczak, U. Neergaard and M. Krajewski (eds.), *Health Care and EU Law*, TMC Asser Press, The Hague 2011.

18 By reference to Sauter's delineation of the framework of applicability of EU competition law to healthcare systems in terms of 'boundaries' and 'exceptions'. See W. Sauter, above n. 11.

EU competition law are very much in development.[19] Further, delineation of the *applicability* of EU competition law is limited to acknowledging the existence of the wider, related EU concepts of Services of General Interest (SGI),[20] and specifically Services of General Economic Interest (SGEI).[21] This is because these 'exceptions'[22] have not been engaged in connection with applying competition law to healthcare *provision* in England and only to a limited extent in the Netherlands.[23] However, this may form a fruitful area for future research in view of recent attempts to connect the English NHS with both the SGI[24] and SGEI[25] concepts.

---

19 For example, the state action doctrine. For a comprehensive discussion, see W. Sauter, above n. 11.

20 An extensive literature exists in this area which includes healthcare as a case study. Two notable examples are W. Sauter, *Public Services in EU Law*, Cambridge University Press, Cambridge 2015, and M. Krajewski, U. Neergaard, and J.W. van de Gronden (eds.), *The Changing Legal Framework for Services of General Interest in Europe – Between Competition and Solidarity*, TMC Asser Press, The Hague 2009.

21 The possibility that the SGEI exception may afford some degree of protection to healthcare systems in general, and the English NHS in particular, has been widely acknowledged. See, for example, O. Odudu, above n. 2; E. Szyszczak, 'Modernising Healthcare: Pilgrimage for the Holy Grail?' in M. Krajewski, U. Neergaard and J.W. van de Gronden (eds.), *The Changing Legal Framework for Services of General Interest in Europe – Between Competition and Solidarity*, TMC Asser Press, The Hague 2009; and A. Sánchez Graells, 'Monitor and the Competition and Markets Authority', (2014) *University of Leicester School of Law Research Paper*, No.14-32. In addition, the organisation of the English NHS has been regarded as meeting requirements the exception (notably an act of entrustment with an SGEI). See, for example, N. Boeger and T. Prosser, above n. 3; and T.K. Hervey, A. Stark, A. Dawson, J-L. Fernandez, T. Matosevic and D. McDaid, 'Long-term care for older people and EU Law: the position in England and Scotland' (2012) 34(1), *Journal of Social Welfare and Family Law* 105.

22 See W. Sauter, above n. 11.

23 For a discussion of how the SGEI exception could work in Dutch healthcare, see W. Sauter, *'Diensten van algemeen economisch belang en universele dienstverplichtingen in de gezondheidszorg'* ('Services of General Economic Interest and Universal Service Obligations in Healthcare') (2008) *Markt & Mededinging*, 1, 4.
A further example may be the classification of some activities of university hospitals as SGEI, which removes them from the reach of Dutch general merger control. See further the discussions of the AMC–VUmc merger in Chapter 4. However, the SGEI exception has been engaged in connection with the Risk Equalisation Scheme of the Dutch insurance systems regarding the State aid rules. See L. Hancher and W. Sauter, above n. 11, pp. 274–75.

24 The National Health Service Bill (HC Bill 51 2016–17) was sponsored by the Labour MP Margaret Greenwood and had been due to receive a Second Reading on 12.05.2017, but fell by the calling of the UK 2017 general election and no further action was taken. An earlier version had been tabled by the Green MP Caroline Lucas. Clause 1 of the Bill substitutes section 1 National Health Service Act 2006 regarding the duty of the Secretary of State vis-à-vis the English NHS as a comprehensive health service, and Clause 1(4)(a) clarifies that 'the 'comprehensive health service' is 'for the purposes of … Protocol (No. 26) to the Treaty on European Union (Services of General Interest), a non-economic service of general interest'.

25 The National Health Service (Amended Duties and Powers) Bill (HC Bill 18 2014–15) was tabled by the Labour MP Clive Efford and received significant support on its second reading in November 2014 (241 Ayes, 18 Noes). It was eventually abandoned at Committee stage in March 2015 following protracted and circular discussions of the concept of 'solidarity', led by

This section considers the 'undertaking' concept in overview before considering the relevance of solidarity and the *AOK Bundesverband* and *FENIN* judgments as these have proved influential in shaping national frameworks for applying competition law in, respectively, Dutch and English healthcare.

## 2.1. OVERVIEW OF THE 'UNDERTAKING' CONCEPT

It is well-established that the definition of an 'undertaking' is functional; that is, the legal status of an entity under national law is not determinative. To this end, the basic test of whether or not there is an 'economic activity' established in *Höfner v. Macrotron*[26] (clarified further as the offering of goods or services on a market by *Commission v. Italy*)[27] appears deceptively straightforward. Broadly speaking, there are at least two categories of activity which are typically not categorised as being 'undertakings'.[28] A first category involves the exercise of essential functions of the state; while a second category comprises those social security systems which are mainly based on the principle of solidarity. A third category comprises activities with a social dimension where these are totally or predominantly financed by the state for fulfilling a specific public purpose,[29] for example, religious educational activities in *CEPPB*.[30] The second category is clearly of most relevance to the discussions of this book, with the distinction drawn between implementing organisations which are not categorised as 'undertakings' within a social security system based on the principle of solidarity (which includes a pay-as-you-go system, tariffs set by legislation and a high degree of government oversight), and implementing organisations which are subject to competition law within a social insurance system based on a mix of solidarity and competition with less government oversight.[31]

---

the Conservative MP Jacob Rees-Mogg. Clause 1(2)(b) of the Bill sought to amend section 1 National Health Service Act 2006 regarding the Secretary of State's duty vis-à-vis the English NHS by imposing an obligation to 'ensure that the health service is a public service which delivers services of general economic interest and operates on the basis of social solidarity.'

26 Case C-41/90, *Klaus Höfner and Fritz Elser v. Macrotron GmbH*, ECLI:EU:C:1991:161.

27 Case C-35/96, *Commission of the European Communities v. Italy*, ECLI:EU:C:1998:303.

28 J.W. van de Gronden, *Mededingingsrecht in de EU en Nederland* (Competition Law in the EU and the Netherlands), Uitgeverij Paris, Zutphen 2017, pp. 28–30. J.W. van de Gronden, 'Services of General Interest and the Concept of Undertaking: Does EU Competition Law Apply?' (2018) 41(2) *World Competition* 197.

29 Ibid (2017), pp. 29–30. Van de Gronden acknowledges that further case law is needed to develop the category. However, the category may have relevance to healthcare insofar as distinctions can be drawn between 'economic' and 'non-economic' activities with regard to different treatments.

30 Case C-74/16, *Congregación de Escuelas Pías Provincia Betania v. Ayuntamiento de Getafe*, ECLI:EU:C:2017:496.

31 J.W. van de Gronden (2017), above n. 28, p. 29.

In practice, however, designation of an activity as 'economic' or 'non-economic' may be complicated as this is a problem of where to draw the dividing line and it is hard to tell where the market ends and social solidarity starts.[32] Furthermore, the *AOK Bundesverband* and *FENIN* judgments suggest that it is contingent upon a range of factors such as the potential for profit (as distinct from actual profit-making), the degree of competition within a healthcare system and the ultimate purpose of the activity,[33] thus distinguishing between upstream and downstream activities. However, as noted above, a distinction has been drawn between purchasers and providers by the EU courts.[34]

The applicability of competition law to healthcare *providers* has proven relatively uncontroversial and has relied on the functional approach of *Höfner*, as evidenced, for instance, by *Pavlov*[35] and *Ambulanz Glöckner*.[36] The *Pavlov* case established that an independent medical specialist who assumes financial risk and receives remuneration is an undertaking subject to competition law. *Ambulanz Glöckner*, a case which considered the distinction between emergency and standard patient transport, examined other criteria, such as public service obligations (PSOs), but linked these to the determination of an SGEI rather than the existence of an undertaking. The extent to which hospitals are subject to competition law appears to be influenced by the degree of state control, despite the fact that the TFEU does not discriminate between public and private ownership.[37] Although public hospitals which provide services for free and receive state financing can be distinguished from self-employed doctors,[38] these have nevertheless been recognised as undertakings by national competition authorities.[39] Further inconsistency has been noted between healthcare providers operating within insurance-based systems (where competition is considered more feasible) and those in taxation-funded systems.[40] In contrast to healthcare providers, the applicability of competition law to purchasers

---

32 For a discussion of this in the context of State aid in Commission decision 2015/248 concerning compulsory health insurance in Slovakia, see P. Nicolaides, 'Non-Economic Activities', Stateaidhub.eu blog, 10.03.2015, <http://stateaidhub.eu/blogs/stateaiduncovered/post/1707> accessed 24.06.2018.

33 For further discussion of this aspect within *FENIN*, see N. Dunne, 'Knowing when to see it: state activities, economic activities, and the concept of undertaking' (2010) 16(3) *Columbia Journal of European Law* 427.

34 The distinction has been described as an 'all too subtle difference' which results in a divergence from the way economic activity is defined in the context of the free movement rules. W. Sauter, above n. 20, p. 119.

35 Joined cases C-180/98 to C-184/98, *Pavel Pavlov and Others v. Stichting Pensioenfonds Medische Specialisten*, ECLI:EU:C:2000:428.

36 Case C-475/99, *Firma Ambulanz Glöckner v. Landkreis Südwestpfalz*, ECLI:EU:C:2001:577.

37 Article 345 TFEU.

38 J. Temple Lang, 'Privatisation of Social Welfare: EU Competition Law Rules' in M. Dougan and E. Spaventa (eds.), *Social Welfare and EU Law*, Hart Publishing, Oxford 2005, p. 65.

39 For a comprehensive overview, see O. Odudu, above n. 2.

40 J.W. van de Gronden, above n. 11.

has been questioned by connections being drawn between purchasing and solidarity – with distinctions emerging in cases such as *Poucet and Pistre*[41] and *Albany*.[42,43]

## 2.2. THE RELEVANCE OF SOLIDARITY IN A HEALTHCARE CONTEXT

### *2.2.1. Solidarity and Competition in Healthcare – General Considerations*

In a healthcare context, competition and solidarity have been described as 'two sides of the same coin',[44] albeit ones which appear in conflict. In general terms, social solidarity is the idea that the state has duties to ensure equal treatment of citizens irrespective of their economic resources.[45] However, this has been described as incompatible with a market-based view of citizenship as underlying the full application of competition law to public services.[46] It would therefore seem that competition – and the application of competition law – may serve to undermine long-standing systems based on solidarity. However, any transition from a solidarity-based system to a competition-based system is not straightforward. An example can be seen with long-term care in England, where the care home market is considered more responsive to competition than the English hospital sector,[47] yet the underpinning of solidarity complicates this. For example, concerns[48] have been raised that privately-funded residents in care homes are disadvantaged because they cross-subsidise residents who are eligible for funding from other sources, typically Local Authorities,[49] and competition law offers no obvious remedy.

---

41 Joined cases C-159/91 and C-160/91, *Christian Poucet v. Assurances Générales de France and Caisse Mutuelle Régionale du Languedoc-Roussillon*, and *Daniel Pistre v. Caisse Autonome Nationale de Compensation de l' Assurance Vieillesse des Artisans (Cancava)* ECLI:EU:C:1993:63.

42 Case C-67/94, *Albany International BV v. Stichting Bedrijfspensioenfonds Textielindustrie*, ECLI:EU:C:1999:430.

43 For further discussion of the distinctions between these lines of cases, see, for example, N. Boeger, 'Solidarity and EC competition law' (2007) 32 *European Law Review* 319. For a brief discussion of the English NHS context, see L. Goulding, 'Is the NHS subject to competition law?', eutopia law, 19.07.2013, <https://eutopialaw.com/tag/health/> accessed 24.06.2018.

44 S. Belhaj and J.W. van de Gronden, above n. 14.

45 T. Prosser, *The Limits of Competition Law, Oxford University Press*, Oxford 2005, p. 35.

46 Ibid.

47 A. Street, 'Overview' in A. Charlesworth and E. Kelly (eds.), *Competition in UK health care – Reflections from an expert workshop*, Nuffield Trust and IFS Research Report, London 2013.

48 M. Hviid, 'Procurement By Dominant Buyers', *CCP Research Bulletin*, May 2011, <http://competitionpolicy.ac.uk/documents/8158338/8193544/CCP-Research-Bulletin_May_2011.pdf/2b0743e2-db4d-49e8-9829-dddeb85002be> accessed 24.06.2018.

49 The distinction drawn here is further complicated by the existence of NHS funding – which in limited circumstances is available based on a patient's complex healthcare – as distinct from

The concept of solidarity in healthcare is significant as a feature which helps define where competition law can be applied. This has repercussions in terms of EU-level intervention – so solidarity as a defining feature needs to be balanced alongside Article 168(7) TFEU, which provides that healthcare system organisation is a matter for Member State competence. The latter suggests that the degree and extent of market-based reforms are left to the discretion of national governments,[50] but the consequences of deciding to experiment with, for example, greater private delivery of healthcare provision, can trigger the competition rules.[51] It might then be expected that once the competition rules have been found to be applicable, they will increasingly be applied,[52] although this has not been borne out, so far, in the English context. By examining the Dutch and English experience with their different models of competition against the backdrop of solidarity, it becomes possible to examine this expectation. Certainly it already appears possible to say that the application of competition law in practice is proving less straightforward than this theoretical framework of applicability may suggest.

In serving as a mechanism to determine the applicability of competition law, solidarity operates in various ways. Most obviously, it has been used to distinguish both an exemption from competition law and a partial exception by means of designating SGEIs, as noted above. The former can be seen in cases such as *Poucet & Pistre*, in which a system with a social aim was exempt from competition law, and the logic may also have influenced the ultimate non-applicability of competition law in *AOK Bundesverband* and *FENIN*. The latter can be seen in *Ambulanz Glöckner*, where solidarity was held to support the finding of an SGEI in respect of emergency ambulance services, but not general patient transport. In *AG2R*,[53] a supplementary insurance scheme was considered to be based on solidarity, and thus entrusted with an SGEI. These two aspects – which can be described as 'exemption' and 'exception' perspectives – are now examined in light of EU-level case law concerning healthcare purchasing and provision, which has had most impact on the Dutch and English reforms.

social care – needs, irrespective of their ability to pay. 'Healthcare needs' can be considered in general terms to be 'medical' in nature, whereas 'social care needs' are ancillary to this and include the provision of food, bathing etc. The distinction between the two can be unclear and was at issue in judicial review cases of NHS funding decisions prior to the Care Act 2014. See, for example, *R v. North and East Devon Health Authority, ex parte Coughlan* [2000] 2 WLR 622 and *R (on the application of Grogan) v. Bexley NHS Care Trust* [2006] EWHC 44 (Admin).

50 A. Andreangeli, 'Healthcare Services, the EU Single Market and Beyond: Meeting Local Needs in an Open Economy – How Much Market or How Little Market?' (2016) 43(2) *Legal Issues of Economic Integration* 145.

51 On this point see, inter alia, T. Prosser, above n. 11.

52 O. Odudu, above n. 2.

53 Case C-437/09, *AG2R Prévoyance v. Beaudout Père et Fils SARL*, ECLI:EU:C:2011:112.

### 2.2.2. *Solidarity and the 'Exemption' Perspective – Healthcare Purchasing (*AOK Bundesverband *and* FENIN*)*

In terms of solidarity operating as a mechanism to exempt the *applicability* of competition law, the approach taken in EU case law appears to have evolved from solidarity providing a complete exemption from the competition rules in *Poucet and Pistre*, via solidarity as a balancing mechanism to be weighed against competitive elements, such as we see in *AOK Bundesverband*, and supporting a solidarity-based system as the ultimate aim of a purchasing activity as in *FENIN*. However, it might be considered that solidarity has effectively come full circle and ceased to function as a means of exempting the applicability of competition law, as evidenced by a further permutation of 'internal' solidarity (between members of a scheme) apparently developed to allow the application of competition law in the UK *BetterCare* case.[54] This permutation reflects EU case law (such as *Albany*) relating primarily to pension and insurance funds, where the level of contributions can prove determinative of the applicability of competition law. Consequently, these cases may be considered to have greater relevance to an insurance-based healthcare system such as that of the Netherlands. The implications of these cases for a taxation-funded system are less clear, although as regards England, it is acknowledged that periodic suggestions to overhaul the NHS to deliver health and social care on a mutual basis,[55] if implemented, would render this line of cases more relevant. These cases have, however, been viewed as representing solidarity as a means of ensuring adequate distribution of a particular service which could not necessarily be achieved by the market.[56] These can usefully be distinguished from solidarity as a means of ensuring public-spiritedness, to protect certain values that may be compromised by competition reforms.[57] This latter category appears to encompass the fundamental principle of solidarity in EU healthcare systems and perhaps has particular relevance for England, in light of ongoing commitments to keeping the NHS as a system based on clinical need, not the ability to pay.[58] Although referenced in connection with

54 Case 1006/2/1/01 *BetterCare Group Limited v. Director General of Fair Trading* [2002] CAT 6, [2002] Comp.A.R. 229, paragraph 238.

55 L. Elliott, 'Run the NHS and social care like John Lewis, says Frank Field', *The Guardian*, 02.12.2016, <https://www.theguardian.com/society/2016/dec/02/run-the-nhs-and-social-care-like-john-lewis-says-frank-field> accessed 24.06.2018.

56 N. Boeger, above n. 43.

57 Ibid.

58 'Recommendation 15 – We strongly recommend that a tax-funded, free-at-the-point-of-use NHS should remain in place as the most appropriate model for delivery of sustainable health services both now and in the future (paragraph 170)': House of Lords Select Committee on the Long-Term Sustainability of the Nhs. Report of Session 2016–17, 'The Long-term Sustainability of the NHS and Adult Social Care', 05.04.2017. 'The Government is committed to providing for patients and the public the highest quality, most compassionate health and care service in the world, built on the guiding principles of the NHS: that access

adequate distribution as well, the *AOK Bundesverband* and *FENIN* cases provide clear examples of the latter protection of certain values, and have influenced the 2006 and HSCA 2012 reforms.

#### 2.2.2.1. *AOK Bundesverband*

The *AOK Bundesverband* case saw German sickness funds (*Krankenkassen*) exempted from competition law, as they fulfilled an exclusively social function based on their non-profit-making status and inability to influence the level of benefits or contributions paid. This finding, in an outcome considered hard to predict,[59] of the predominance of solidarity elements (i.e. a risk-equalisation scheme) over competition (on price via contribution rates and on management and organisation by offering different services to consumers), has been criticised for not giving greater significance to the possibility for price competition within the system,[60] and as a step backwards from previous cases.[61]

In using solidarity effectively as a reason for *not* applying competition law, it becomes a balancing mechanism and marks a departure from the functional approach. Instead of using the straightforward 'potential economic activity' test of *Höfner*, the *AOK* case established a 'potential for competition' criterion (considered by the CJEU as a consequence of, and by Advocate General Jacobs as a condition for, the finding of an economic activity).[62] This is more elaborate because it considers not only the nature of the activity, but also its aim and legal framework.

A potential consequence is that the existence of economic activities may be ruled out if the legislator has decided to exclude competition or to impose anticompetitive conduct in the general interest.[63]

#### 2.2.2.2. *FENIN*

In *FENIN*, the EU courts examined whether or not purchasing activities by managing bodies within taxation-funded NHS systems amounted to economic

---

to health care is based on need and not the ability to pay, and that services are comprehensive and available to all': Department of Health, 'The Government's Revised Mandate to NHS England for 2017–18', March 2018, para. 1.1. '[I]f the NHS is to continue to thrive as a universal health service, free at the point of delivery – something which Monitor is committed to': Monitor, 'Monitor's Strategy 2014–2017 – Helping to redesign healthcare provision in England', 10.04.2014, Summary.

59 L. Hancher and W. Sauter, above n. 11.

60 J.W. van de Gronden, above n. 11.

61 L. Nistor, *Public Services and the European Union: Healthcare, Health Insurance and Education Services*, TMC Asser Press, The Hague 2011, p. 167.

62 J. Baquero Cruz, 'Beyond Competition: Services of General Interest and European Community Law' in G. De Búrca (ed.), *EU Law and the Welfare State: In Search of Solidarity*, Oxford University Press, Oxford 2005, p. 184.

63 Ibid.

activities. This case involved claims that Spanish NHS bodies abused their dominant position by making systematic late payments for medical goods and equipment used in Spanish hospitals. What was ultimately determined in this case, however, was whether the managing bodies were undertakings for the purposes of competition law. Thus, a distinction was drawn between upstream and downstream activities so that the ultimate purpose for the purchased goods, i.e. to provide free medical treatment within a publicly-funded system, was determinative in concluding that the Spanish NHS managing bodies were not undertakings, and therefore not subject to competition law. This logic is useful for clarifying that bodies otherwise not regarded as undertakings are not subject to competition law 'by the back door' merely because they engage in purchasing activities with private providers.[64] However, *FENIN* has been swiftly dismissed as constituting merely an '*exceedingly narrow and non-functional (sub-)concept of "economic activity"*'.[65] This is unfortunate since it offers an important EU-level case-law framework (arguably the only one to date) suitable for analysing the English healthcare system, without needing to contort the complex relationship between the NHS and private healthcare sector into an analytical framework shaped by social insurance systems in a manner reminiscent of square pegs and round holes. More legitimate criticisms concern the limitations of the *FENIN* judgment in terms of what was not included: for example, consideration of the scope for competition between providers within a solidarity-based system,[66] and that the Court of Justice's failure to develop the (uncontested) solidarity argument leaves room for further clarification.[67]

The foregoing demonstrates the complexity of defining 'undertakings' in healthcare and suggests that further clarification – if not refinement – of when a healthcare purchaser or provider is likely to be subject to challenge under the competition rules would be beneficial. The recent General Court judgment in *DZP/UZP*,[68] a State aid case which confirms that Slovak state-owned insurance companies are indeed undertakings (thus annulling the Commission's initial finding), involved a surprising focus on profit-making, and is based in part on the existence of competition on quality, may serve to re-ignite discussion in this area,[69] subject to the outcome of a further appeal.

64 M. Krajewski and M. Farley, 'Non-economic activities in upstream and downstream markets and the scope of competition law after FENIN' (2007) 32(1) *European Law Review* 111.

65 A. Sánchez Graells, *Public Procurement and the EU Competition Rules*, 2nd edn, Hart Publishing, Oxford 2015, p. 140.

66 See N. Boeger and T. Prosser, above n. 3, p. 367.

67 L. Hancher and W. Sauter, above n. 11, paragraph 8.17, p. 230.

68 Case T-216/15, *Dôvera zdravotná poisťovňa, a.s. v. European Commission*, ECLI:EU:T:2018:64.

69 An early discussion being J.W. van de Gronden (2018), above n. 28.

Despite the criticism directed at both *AOK Bundesverband* and *FENIN*,[70] these have proved influential in shaping the national frameworks for competition in healthcare in both the Netherlands and England as discussed below.

### 2.2.3. *Solidarity and the 'Exception' Perspective – Healthcare Provision (*Ambulanz Glöckner*)*

As regards solidarity operating as a mechanism to activate the SGEI exception, this has been demonstrated in *Ambulanz Glöckner* as noted above. However, it should be noted that the extent to which healthcare *provision* can benefit from exceptions from competition law has been considered limited. Nevertheless, it has been recognised[71] that recourse to the SGEI exception offers greater potential than total exemption for healthcare as a Service of General Interest. However, here too, more is needed to clarify the scope of the exception vis-à-vis competition law – for example, it has been suggested that the EU needs to provide further guidance in order to identify a core of healthcare activities which are 'truly solidaristic'.[72] *Ambulanz Glöckner* demonstrated the possibility of separating different aspects of related activity (emergency ambulance services from general patient transport). Indeed, the identification of specific treatments would appear to offer one way of testing the extent of the SGEI exception – with disability and public health concerns being cited as potential candidates.[73] Whilst this suggestion has logic, it may prove difficult to implement in practice, with – in the worst case scenario – some conditions effectively being 'favoured' over others. Furthermore, it appears to suggest that competition is exclusively at the level of a particular treatment, which is not necessarily the case: a more obvious defining line may simply be whether treatment needs to be available to all (such as emergency ambulance services).

In the context of English healthcare, an interesting situation emerges whereby private healthcare providers offer extensive ranges of treatment which may also be available on the NHS, so differentiating by treatment type becomes problematic. The distinction therefore is simply between the private healthcare sector and the NHS (as universal access provider and provider of last resort relative to the private healthcare sector). Indeed, it has been suggested that legislation governing the NHS may amount to an 'act of entrustment' for the purposes of SGEI.[74] However, the NHS has not been formally categorised as

---

70 In the development of EU case law in this area, there has also been conceptualisation of the functional test of Höfner as an 'abstract' test and consideration of additional criteria in *AOK Bundesverband* and *FENIN* as a 'concrete' test. See J.W. van de Gronden, above n. 14.

71 O. Odudu, above n. 2, and E. Szyszczak and A. Sánchez Graells, both above n. 21, all make reference to the SGEI exception within their considerations of healthcare.

72 E. Szyszczak, above n. 21.

73 W. Sauter, above n. 23.

74 N. Boeger and T. Prosser, above n. 3; T.K. Hervey et al., above n. 21.

an SGEI, and questions may arise concerning the proportionality requirement inherent in the provider of the majority of healthcare services within a Member State being so classified.

The framework regarding the *applicability* of EU competition law outlined above has generated various issues regarding the application of EU competition law at a national level in the Netherlands and England. (This is a separate matter from the development of ex ante, regulatory rules which may amount to a 'healthcare-specific' competition regime at a national level.) Such issues comprise an EU dimension and a national dimension which are now considered.

## 2.3. THE EU COMPETITION LAW FRAMEWORK AND THE DUTCH AND ENGLISH HEALTHCARE SECTORS

The foregoing suggests a framework which may be limited in its ability to respond to the characteristics of individual Member States (where competition may depend as much upon purchasers as providers) and the increasing possibility that the EU rules may be triggered in view of healthcare providers in one Member State delivering services in another. This gives rise to concerns at both EU and national levels. Perhaps the most obvious concern in this regard from an EU perspective is the need to ensure consistent application of EU competition law across all Member States. This is complicated not only by variations of healthcare system models (even within the broad categories of insurance-based and taxation-funded systems), but also the extent to which Article 168(7) TFEU[75] may protect the delivery of healthcare provision as a matter of Member State competence.[76]

This has been questioned by the identification of a process of 'spontaneous harmonisation' taking place in the majority of Member States with regard to competition law, whereby national competition authorities (and courts) may be confronted with healthcare cases to which they will have to apply national

75 Article 168(7) TFEU provides: 'Union action shall respect the responsibilities of the Member States for the definition of their health policy and for the organisation and delivery of health services and medical care. The responsibilities of the Member States shall include the management of health services and medical care and the allocation of resources assigned to them.'

76 It has been suggested that while Article 168(7) TFEU may be capable of curtailing the effects that result from the CJEU's case law on competition, it may also expand the limits of the EU's role in public health relative to the previous Article 152 EC. See J.W. van de Gronden and E. Szyszczak, 'Conclusions: Constructing a "Solid" Multi-Layered Health Care Edifice' in J.W. van de Gronden, E. Szyszczak, U. Neergaard and M. Krajewski (eds.), *Health Care and EU Law*, TMC Asser Press, The Hague 2011.

competition rules shaped in accordance with Articles 101 and 102 TFEU.[77] These have been termed 'Euro-national competition rules' for healthcare.[78]

In terms of national perspectives on applying competition law at a national level, at least two concerns are evident in both the Netherlands and England. The first, and arguably of fundamental concern in both countries, is how to preserve the principle of solidarity (universal access) – whether via the exemption or the exception perspective – in applying competition law. Indeed, although this imperative has received surprisingly little attention in the literature thus far,[79] this should be the starting-point for designing a competition policy in healthcare. A second concern is whether, and if so how, to make use of competition law to underpin competition reforms in view of the broad exemptions implicit as a consequence of the *AOK Bundesverband* and *FENIN* cases. This may include how to ensure that equivalent standards are applied to both sides of an economic transaction; that is, to allow for the possibility of applying competition law to healthcare purchasers (whether Dutch health insurers or NHS commissioners), as well as to healthcare providers, in view of the inconsistent approach arising out of EU case law.

These two concerns are used to explore the emergence of frameworks – which comprise regulatory rules as well as general competition law – in the Netherlands and England to apply competition law in healthcare cases. A further but separate consideration is ensuring compliance with EU law in the development of national (regulatory) sector-specific competition rules in cases where parallel application may be an issue.

## 3. THE EMERGENCE OF NATIONAL FRAMEWORKS FOR APPLYING COMPETITION LAW IN NATIONAL HEALTHCARE CASES

### 3.1. THE NETHERLANDS

#### *3.1.1. Protecting the 'Fundamental Principle' of Universal Access*

In the 2006 reforms, as part of the mandatory private insurance scheme, a risk-equalisation scheme (RES) was developed to ensure universal coverage and avoid the market failure of adverse selection. This was given informal approval by correspondence in 2003 between Hans Hoogervorst (then Minister for Health, Wellbeing and Sport) and Frits Bolkestein (then Commissioner for the

77 J.W. van de Gronden, above n. 11.
78 Ibid. For further discussion of this, see J.W. van de Gronden and E. Szyszczak, above n. 14.
79 See E. Szyszczak, above n. 21.

Internal Market).[80] Although the legal status of Bolkestein's response was unclear, the RES was formally categorised as an SGEI by the Commission in a State aid case.[81] It might therefore be considered that – at least in part – competition in Dutch healthcare is constructed *around* this protected 'core'.

### *3.1.2. Treatment of Purchasers and Providers*

As noted in Chapter 1, the way competition works in the Dutch 'cure' sector since 2006 can be illustrated as a triangle.[82] Within this 'triangle', there was little doubt that healthcare providers were 'undertakings', but the status of the private health insurers was less clear in light of the *AOK Bundesverband* judgment. This prompted a re-evaluation as Dutch sickness funds (*ziekenfondsen*) in operation prior to the 2006 reforms had previously been deemed subject to Dutch competition law.[83]

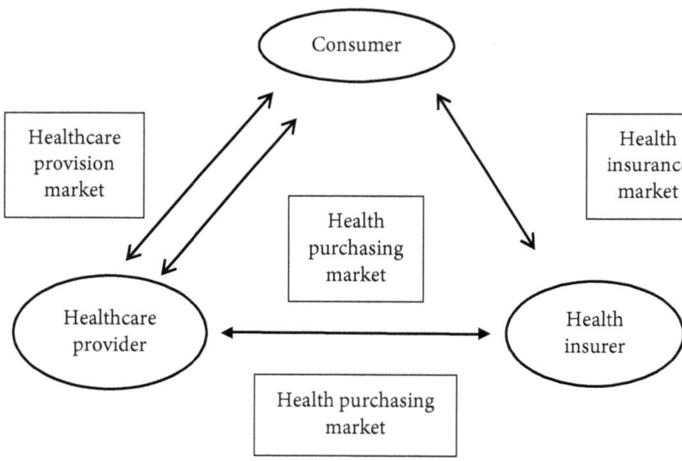


**Figure 2. The Dutch 'healthcare triangle'**

As noted above, enactment of Article 122 Zvw provided that even if the private health insurers are not 'undertakings' for the purposes of Article 101 TFEU, they

[80] The development of the Dutch private health insurance model is discussed in detail, particularly in connection with the Third Non-Life Insurance Directive, by S. Thomson and E. Mossialos, 'Private health insurance and the internal market' in E. Mossialos, G. Permanand, R. Baeten and T.K. Hervey (eds.), *Health Systems Governance in Europe: The Role of European Union Law and Policy*, Cambridge University Press, Cambridge 2010.

[81] For discussion of this decision, see inter alia L. Hancher and W. Sauter, above n. 11.

[82] Figure 2 in Chapter 1, above p. 21. See also W. Sauter, 'Is the general consumer interest a source of legitimacy for healthcare regulation? An analysis of the Dutch experience' (2009) 2–3 *European Journal of Consumer Law* 419.

[83] For a discussion of this, see J.W. van de Gronden, above n. 14.

are nevertheless regarded as 'undertakings' in the sense of Article 1 Mw.[84] The Explanatory Memorandum to the Zvw therefore drew a distinction between the 'not-for-profit' character of the German sickness funds performing their legal obligations in the *AOK Bundesverband* case and the system of mandatory private health insurance developed by the Zvw.[85] The Dutch government deemed the health insurers to be 'undertakings' because the Zvw may only be implemented by insurers, and also due to their 'for-profit' character.[86] However, the Dutch government acknowledged that its designation has no decisive influence on any finding by the European courts, which may decide otherwise in respect of the health insurers. Nevertheless, it considered that Article 122 Zvw offered a safety net to ensure adequate regulation of competition.[87] At least at a national level, Article 122 Zvw thus appears to enable equivalent standards to be applied, as both health insurers (purchasers) and healthcare providers are nominally subject to competition law. This would appear to be consistent with the intention that both insurers and providers compete for patients.

### *3.1.3. National Framework Resulting from Healthcare Reforms*

The foregoing suggests that the delineating framework provided by Article 122 Zvw and the SGEI classification of the RES therefore operate both to ensure universal coverage and to enable competition law to be applied to both insurers and providers, thus giving effect to the 'healthcare triangle' in line with the 2006 reforms. As noted in Chapter 1, the Dutch healthcare competition policy framework also comprises rules enshrined in the *Wet marktordening gezondheidszorg* (Dutch Healthcare (Market Regulation) Act 2006 (Wmg)) which permit the NZa to intervene with regard to the drafting of contracts (Article 45 Wmg), and initially the NZa, but now the ACM, to take action with regard to Significant Market Power (primarily Article 48 Wmg). These have been linked, respectively, to the provisions governing anticompetitive agreements[88] and abuse of dominance[89] and are considered further below.

---

84 Article 1(f) Mw provides that an 'undertaking' has the same meaning as 'undertaking' under Article 101 TFEU.

85 *Kamerstukken II, 2003–04, 29 763, 3 – Regeling van een sociale verzekering voor geneeskundige zorg ten behoeve van de gehele bevolking (Zorgverzekeringswet). Nr. 3, Memorie van Toelichting.* (Second Chamber documentation, Parliamentary Session 2003–04, 29 763, 3 (Explanatory Memorandum) – Regulation of social insurance for curative care for the whole population (Zvw)), p. 28.

86 Ibid.

87 Ibid.

88 J. Bijkerk and W. Sauter, *'Een nieuwe mededingingsbevoegdheid voor de NZa? Artikel 45 Wmg over ingrijpen in de voorwaarden en de wijze van totstandkomen van overeenkomsten met betrekking tot zorg of tarieven'*. ('A new competition power for the NZa? Article 45 Wmg and intervention in the conditions and formulation of agreements relating to healthcare or tariffs') (2010) *Markt en Mededinging*, 4, 145.

89 For discussions on this point, see W. Sauter (2014), above n. 17.

## 3.2. ENGLAND

In the context of English healthcare, the two concerns – protecting the 'core' of universal access and treatment of purchasers and providers – are best understood by reference to the 'four categories of English healthcare' introduced in Chapter 1 that demonstrate the purchaser/provider separation and the distinction between the NHS (categories 1 and 2) and the private healthcare sector (categories 3 and 4).[90]

| | | | |
|---|---|---|---|
| 1.<br>Public Purchaser<br>and<br>Public Provider | 2.<br>Public Purchaser<br>and<br>Private Provider | 3.<br>Private Purchaser<br>and<br>Public Provider | 4.<br>Private Purchaser<br>and<br>Private Provider |

**Figure 3. The 'four categories of English healthcare'**

### *3.2.1. Protecting the 'Fundamental Principle' of Universal Access*

Within English healthcare, the 'core' of universal access comprises the NHS (categories 1 and 2), which provides the majority of healthcare and can clearly be distinguished from the smaller, supplementary private healthcare market (categories 3 and 4). It is therefore essential to be clear about which sector is at issue: on the one hand, whether NHS providers are operating in the private healthcare sector (via Private Patient Units) or in the NHS; and on the other hand, whether private providers are operating in the private healthcare sector or in the NHS.[91] In overview, the *applicability* of competition law is uncontroversial in respect of the private healthcare sector, whether category 4

[90] Figure 3 in Chapter 1, above p. 40. Based on the classification in Office of Fair Trading (OFT), *Private Healthcare Market Study*, OFT1396, p. 13, and discussions in O. Odudu, above n. 7.

[91] It is to be noted that competition between the NHS and private healthcare sector (in the sense of NHS providers providing facilities to both NHS and Private Patients) can be attributed to a concession made by Aneurin Bevan in order to implement the NHS whereby consultants were allowed to continue private practice alongside their NHS workload (ultimately enshrined by section 5, National Health Service Act 1946). Bevan drew a further distinction between 'NHS pay-beds' (for private patients) and 'NHS amenity beds' (for NHS patients who wished to pay). See further on this point, A. Bevan, 'A Free Health Service' in A. Bevan, *In Place of Fear*, Quartet Books, London 1978, p. 115. It appears that 'amenity beds' still exist, but may be located in private wards within NHS hospitals. In contrast, private-sector provision of NHS services is a relatively recent phenomenon, and has been facilitated by reforms since the NHS internal market emerged and particularly by the Concordat under New Labour as discussed in Chapter 1 above.

or category 3 – arguably since this is not the 'core'.[92] This is evidenced by examples of enforcement activity in respect of NHS Foundation Trusts exchanging commercially sensitive information about their Private Patient Units in category 3,[93] and anticompetitive information exchange and pricing agreements in the private ophthalmology sector in category 4.[94]

By analogy with the Dutch system, competition which is constructed *around* the 'core' of NHS healthcare provision is thus evident in the private healthcare market (categories 3 and 4) among private providers, and particularly in the development of NHS providers to compete in the private healthcare sector. The latter is evidenced by the creation of NHS Foundation Trusts and particularly in the removal of the private patient income cap by section 165 HSCA 2012, which is viewed as paving the way for an expansion in NHS Private Patient Units.[95]

NHS competition reforms – from the purchaser/provider separation of the NHS internal market, via creation of NHS Foundation Trusts, to increasing private-sector delivery of NHS services – attract controversy and entail complications because they all involve this 'core' of universal access. So questions emerge regarding whether competition can be constructed *within* this 'core', as distinct from *between* the NHS and private healthcare sector (that is, *around* the 'core'), and if so, what any resulting competition policy would look like.

#### 3.2.1.1. Competition within the 'Core' of Universal Access in English Healthcare

It has already been noted that there is greater scope for competition within an insurance-based system than a taxation-funded system in view of the greater scope for demand-driven competition in the former as distinct from the supply-driven nature of the latter, where governments are likely to determine the precise levels of benefits.[96] What has emerged within the NHS is limited scope for patients to exercise choice of NHS or private provider in respect of certain elective treatments at the level of secondary care, although in terms

92 NHS providers are not exempt by virtue of their 'public', taxation-funded status. For a robust explanation, see O. Odudu, above n. 2.

93 OFT, 'OFT welcomes action by NHS trusts to ensure compliance with competition law', OFT Press Release 71/12, 16.08.2012.

94 CMA, Case Reference CE/9784-13, *Private Ophthalmology: investigation into anti-competitive information exchange and pricing agreements. Infringement decision*, 20.08.2015.

95 This prompted the CMA to propose a new test for PPUs in the context of its Private Healthcare Market Investigation, and is considered further in Chapter 4 below in connection with merger control.

96 L. Hancher and W. Sauter, above n. 11, para. 8.25, p. 232.

of primary care, there have been attempts to link patient choice of General Practitioner (GP) with competition.[97] Indeed, many of the wider competition developments discussed in Chapter 1 can be linked to this 'core'.

It is useful at this point to consider briefly the nature of the NHS and private healthcare markets in light of the view that 'there are markets and markets, some highly regulated and others operating more freely'.[98] The private healthcare market is notable in that it arguably represents a 'textbook' market in view of relative ease of entry and exit, but nevertheless represents an anomaly among (European) healthcare systems due to its supplementary nature,[99] and thus a lack of engagement with the concept of universal access. In contrast, the NHS has long been considered a 'quasi-market' in view of the limited scope for competition and difficulty surrounding provider exit given the fundamental principle of universal access.[100] It is therefore interesting to note divergent, even contradictory, approaches to competition being taken within the NHS: for example, failure regimes designed for NHS Foundation Trusts were recognised in the wider context of the CMA's project to open up the public sector to competition,[101] while NHS England conceived a 'success regime' to ensure sustainability of NHS providers.[102] The conception of the English NHS as a quasi-market would therefore appear to still be relevant, as the HSCA 2012 reforms cannot change this underlying characteristic. So the picture at present is complex: on the one hand, there is a demonstrable ongoing commitment by both the government and NHS Improvement[103] to maintaining the NHS as a system based on clinical need, not the ability to pay (suggesting a solidarity basis); but on the other hand,

---

97 Further on this point, see C. Pike, 'CCP Working Paper 2: An Empirical Analysis of the Effects of GP Competition' 2010. Monitor, 'Choice and competition toolkit: scenarios for GPs working together', 01.06.2015. However, asking patients to choose their GP is a long-standing aspect of exercising access to healthcare and can still be construed in terms of a collaborative relationship between GP and patient. See further, I. Greener, 'Towards a history of choice in UK health policy' (2009) 31(3) *Sociology of Health & Illness* 309.

98 T. Prosser, above n. 11, p. 324.

99 A characteristic which sets it apart from other health insurance schemes which are typically complementary or mandatory (such as we see in the Netherlands). For further discussion, see S. Thomson and E. Mossialos, above n. 80.

100 J. Le Grand, 'Quasi-Markets: the answer to market failure in health care?' in P. Day, D.M. Fox, R. Maxwell and E. Scrivens (eds.), *The State, Politics and Health: Essays for Rudolf Klein*, Blackwell, Oxford 1996; and J. Le Grand, *The Other Invisible Hand – Delivering Public Services through Choice and Competition*, Princeton University Press, Oxford 2007.

101 For example, OFT, 'Orderly Exit – Designing continuity regimes in public markets', OFT1468, December 2012. For a comprehensive overview of this CMA enterprise, see O. Odudu, 'Why it matters – Selling competition law in the new frontier', *Competition Law Insight*, 10.12.2013.

102 NHS England, 'Five Year Forward View – The Success Regime: A whole systems intervention', 03.06.2015.

103 See above n. 58.

there has been a dedication[104] to developing further the relationship between the private sector and the NHS, which might suggest greater movement towards a system based on competition. However, this has recently been linked with the current development of Sustainability and Transformation Partnerships,[105] and the CMA has recently suggested that in this policy context,[106] competition plays at best a limited role. This raises the question of whether it is possible to use competition to drive a solidarity-based system.

#### 3.2.1.2. Competition Policy within the 'Core' of Universal Access in English Healthcare

As regards competition policy for the 'core' of English healthcare, it might be considered that this is determined primarily by questions of the extent of *applicability* of competition law. This can be examined in terms of the perspectives of 'exemption' and the (SGEI) exception as follows.

*The 'Exemption' Perspective*

As regards the 'exemption' perspective, the legacy of *FENIN* appears to leave unresolved the question of the extent to which the NHS is subject to competition law. This has been deemed unsatisfactory in at least two ways.

Firstly, the distinction between upstream and downstream markets and the focus on considering the ultimate purpose of an activity have led to a proposed test whereby 'actual or potential' economic activity on a downstream market can determine the *applicability* of competition law to either providers or purchasers.[107] Whether this would succeed in clarifying the applicability of competition law to the English NHS is unclear. However, this test should be welcomed in view of the difficulty which can arise from separating purchasing and providing functions in healthcare.

Secondly, the lack of explicit consideration of the degree of competition between providers within a taxation-funded system was not ultimately pursued by the Court of Justice of the European Union (CJEU) in *FENIN*.[108] In view of the

---

104 'The government will encourage long-term partnerships between the NHS and the private sector to modernise buildings, equipment and services, and deliver efficiencies, especially where these partnerships support the upgrade of diagnostics capabilities and the development of new models of care, such as Accountable Care Organisations and hospital groups': HM Treasury, 'Spending Review and Autumn Statement 2015', Cm 9162, November 2015, para. 2.48, p. 94.

105 HM Treasury, 'Autumn Budget', HC 587, November 2017, pp. 65–66.

106 Competition and Markets Authority (CMA), *Central Manchester University Hospitals/ University Hospital of South Manchester merger inquiry. Final Report*, 01.08.2017.

107 D. Sinclair, above n. 9.

108 T. Prosser, above n. 11.

potential for competition between private and NHS providers of NHS services, such clarification might have proved sufficient to determine the applicability of competition law to the English NHS. In the absence of this clarification, we are left with no obvious recourse in a situation where, for example, a private provider in category 2 engages in anticompetitive activity regarding its NHS activities, but not its private healthcare activities in category 4, where competition law clearly applies.[109] The CMA has been explicit (emphasising in bold type) that its guidance on competition law relates to private providers operating in the private healthcare market (category 4), not their activities in connection with the NHS (category 2): 'This advice does not apply to work carried out under employment with the NHS in relation to NHS funded services.'[110] However, this position may also be attributed to changes in oversight following wider elaboration of the UK concurrency regime.[111]

*The 'Exception' Perspective*

Regarding the 'exception' perspective, it was noted previously that legislation governing the NHS may be sufficient to bring this within the scope of SGEI.[112] As noted above, proportionality requirements may suffice to explain why the provision of the majority of healthcare services in England has not been thus formally recognised. However, recent reforms maintain the separation of the NHS and private healthcare which may be inherent in SGEI categorisation, such as the distinction drawn within the HSCA 2012 between 'healthcare' and 'for the purposes of the NHS',[113] CMA guidance on competition law relating to a private provider's category 4, but not category 2, activities,[114] and the inference that the NHS is effectively a 'provider of last resort' relative to the private healthcare sector.[115]

It can be demonstrated that the NHS shares characteristics with the SGEI exception, even if not formally categorised as such. This has implications for

[109] It has been considered that category 1 activity – NHS Foundation Trusts and NHS Trusts delivering NHS services – falls outside the scope of competition law due to the nature of the relationships involved. See O. Odudu, above n. 7.

[110] CMA, '60-second summary – Private medical practitioners: information on competition law', 03.12.2015, <https://assets.publishing.service.gov.uk/government/uploads/system/uploads/attachment_data/file/481620/Private_medical_practitioners_-_information_on_competition_law.pdf> accessed 24.06.2018.

[111] Discussed in Chapter 3.

[112] N. Boeger and T. Prosser, above n.3; T.K. Hervey et al., above n. 21.

[113] See, for example, the qualifications which emerge between sections 62(1) and 62(3) HSCA 2012 in respect of NHS Improvement's general duties.

[114] CMA, above n. 110.

[115] Implicit in the metric of the proportion of private patients transferred back into NHS facilities being used as a metric for private patients to assess private hospitals. CMA Press Release, 'Better information for private patients moves closer', 01.12.2014.

NHS competition reforms, as these suggest that competition is being developed *within* the context of a category which would typically form the exception to the applicability of competition law. This represents a curious situation which might be read in at least two ways. Firstly, it might be construed as a misunderstanding of the EU competition law framework within healthcare, with a potentially wide scope for exceptions to apply. Secondly, it might suggest that the competition law framework and distinctions drawn thus far between *applicability* and exceptions are insufficient to respond to either the evolving nature of healthcare reform (to include public–private interactions), or to a particularly complex situation such as we see in England involving public and private delivery of healthcare. A final, recent consideration is linked to the latter point: a direction for future research is the scope for competitive delivery of SGEI, something to be addressed at EU level.[116] Consequently, examination of the English healthcare system and competition reforms may offer a distinctive perspective on this.

In terms of the resulting competition policy, therefore, what we see is an ongoing lack of clarity regarding the applicability of general competition law with regard to the delivery of NHS services, but the development of a regulatory regime to govern the NHS 'quasi-market'; thus, competition *within* the 'core' of universal access. This comprises the 'competition oversight' aspect of the Choice and Competition condition of the NHS Provider Licence, and Regulation 10 regarding anticompetitive behaviour of the 2013 Regulations.

### *3.2.2. Treatment of Purchasers and Providers*

The distinction drawn at EU level between purchasers and providers in respect of the *applicability* of competition law has arguably been complicated with regard to the English healthcare system by the apparently conflicting[117] contemporaneous judgments in *BetterCare* and *FENIN*, and the OFT's and subsequently CMA's interpretation of these.[118] Significantly, however, it has

116 W. Sauter, above n. 20, pp. 233–34.

117 Although it has also been suggested that the extent of incompatibility between the two judgments may be less than first appears in light of considerations that *BetterCare* was cited with approval by AG Maduro's Opinion, and *FENIN* has been viewed as amounting to a Pyrrhic rather than a substantive victory for shielding public healthcare provision from the application of competition law. In respect of the latter point, see J. Skilbeck, 'Just when is a public body an "undertaking"? *Fenin* and *BetterCare* compared' (2003) 12(4) *Public Procurement Law Review* 75. For further examination of the relationship between *BetterCare* and *FENIN*, see inter alia, T. Prosser, above n. 45; N. Boeger and T. Prosser, above n. 3; and T. Prosser, above n. 11.

118 Certainly the apparent attempt to conflate interpretations of *FENIN* and *BetterCare* by the former OFT has been considered unhelpful in its perceived over-emphasis on the applicability of competition law to providers, but not to purchasers unless these are also involved in provision. See T. Prosser, above n. 11.

been posited that *FENIN* should not be understood as overruling *BetterCare*.[119] This point arises in view of questions left unanswered by *FENIN*, perhaps most notably[120] the lack of consideration of competition between providers.[121]

*BetterCare* involved an abuse of dominance claim brought against an NHS Trust and other state providers of care-home care in Belfast. The OFT initially concluded that the NHS Trust in question was not subject to competition law. However, the Competition Appeals Tribunal (CAT) subsequently found that the NHS Trust was indeed an undertaking in view of its purchasing of care from independent providers, finding, inter alia, that the OFT's argument that purchase without resale was not an economic activity did not relate to the activities in question. The CAT's reasoning was based, inter alia, on the 'business dimension' of the NHS Trust's activities,[122] namely the purchasing of care from independent providers, which detracted from the 'purely social function' of providing care to elderly residents under statute, which had been the focus of the OFT's reasoning.[123] The CAT remitted the case back to the OFT, which ultimately found no infringement of the abuse of dominance provisions by the NHS Trust.[124] The OFT subsequently issued a 'Policy Note'[125] outlining its approach in view of *BetterCare* and the relevant contemporary EU case law (namely, the Commission and General Court rulings in *FENIN* and the CJEU's judgment in *AOK Bundesverband*).

The relevance of *BetterCare* – a case involving an NHS Trust in Northern Ireland – to the English NHS has been considered difficult in view of the variations in health system structure and degree of private-sector involvement in the NHS in the various countries of the UK.[126] However, as the English NHS

---

119 N. Boeger and T. Prosser, above n. 3.

120 A further point of divergence was identified in connection with the funding issue. In *FENIN*, evidence of provision of services in the Spanish system to tourists for remuneration was deemed inadmissible, and so not considered by the Court when determining whether the purchasing operations were 'economic activities'. In contrast, the CAT considered the actual percentages paid by individual residents in *BetterCare*. On this point, see B.J. Rodger, 'The Competition Act 1998 and State Entities as Undertakings: promises to be an interesting debate', CLaSF Working Paper Number 1, 2003.

121 AG Maduro proposed that further findings be made to determine whether the activities of the healthcare providers were themselves economic in nature, or based on the principle of solidarity: Case C-205/03 P, *Federación Española de Empresas de Tecnología Sanitaria (FENIN) v. Commission of the European Communities*, Opinion of Mr Advocate General Poiares Maduro delivered on 10.11.2005, ECLI:EU:C:2005:666, paragraph 70(1).

122 Thus, the CAT has been described as approaching the issue from an economic, rather than a legal, perspective. See N. Dunne, above n. 33, p. 448.

123 *BetterCare* (CAT), above n. 54, paras. 232–34.

124 OFT, Case No. CA98/09/2003, *BetterCare Group Ltd v. North & West Belfast Health & Social Services Trust* (Remitted case), 18.12.2003.

125 OFT, 'The Competition Act 1998 and Public Bodies, Policy Notel/2004', OFT443, August 2004.

126 J. Lear et al., above n. 11, p. 346.

is distinctive in the extent to which it has adopted a market-based approach, if it is possible to establish that an NHS Trust in another part of the UK is indeed subject to competition law, then this would seem likely to be the case in England as well. A further consideration is that it is difficult to follow the logic that the 'internal solidarity' demonstrated by taxpayers contributing to the support of elderly patients should not be 'exported' so as to affect the NHS Trust's transactions with external commercial providers.[127] This is because nuanced distinctions can be drawn between categories 2 and 4 in particular. It appears that private providers are certainly aware of the distinction between NHS patients and private patients as 'customers': for example, the CMA has noted that delivering services for the NHS forms part of the business model of some, but not all private providers,[128] and private providers themselves have welcomed NHS work during the economic crisis, which led to a decline in patients accessing private healthcare.[129]

A final – more convincing – view is that *BetterCare* involved the purchase of care-home places, and, by analogy with the Dutch 'cure'/'care' distinction, the characteristics of care-home markets differ from forms of healthcare provision purchased in other contexts of the English NHS, leading to the conclusion noted above that the care-home market is deemed more responsive to competition than the English hospital sector.[130] Arguments such as these therefore demonstrate that drawing parallels between *BetterCare* and category 2 in particular ought to be approached with some caution.

What remains after *FENIN* and *BetterCare* is an apparent reluctance by the OFT (and subsequently the CMA) to engage with the question of whether private providers delivering services for the NHS are subject to competition law. This can be seen in the OFT's initial interpretation which appears to conflate the two judgments by declining to pursue cases involving public-sector bodies unless purchasers were also providers, and suggesting that it would consider exceptionally cases involving bodies involved in a mix of purchasing and providing activities for non-economic purposes (such as purposes which are purely social, environmental, or national security-related).[131] However, this approach is very much influenced by the development of the *FENIN* judgments.[132]

---

127 *BetterCare* (CAT), above n. 54, para. 238.

128 CMA, *Private Healthcare Market Investigation Final Report*, CMA25, 02.04.2014, para. 2.15.

129 A number of private hospital groups recorded in their annual reports that the increased demand for private provision within the NHS and this new income from the NHS was used to compensate for falls in private patient numbers. See S. Arora, A. Charlesworth, E. Kelly and G. Stoye, 'Public payment and private provision – the changing landscape of health care in the 2000s', Institute for Fiscal Studies / Nuffield Trust Research Report, May 2013, p. 30.

130 A. Street, above n. 47.

131 OFT, above n. 125, para. 28, p. 9.

132 The OFT also references *AOK Bundesverband*. See OFT, above n. 125, p. 12.

More recent guidance[133] from 2011 – subsequently adopted by the CMA – has necessarily reflected the CJEU's approach in *FENIN*, namely:

> in determining whether a public body is acting as an undertaking in relation to [purchasing] goods or services in a market, the economic or non-economic nature of that purchasing activity depends on *the end use to which the public body puts the goods or services bought*.[134]

Thus, where an 'end use' is deemed 'economic', the purchasing activity is not dissociated from the downstream activity (provision) and may be subject to competition law. In contrast, where a public body purchases goods or services in a given market but does not directly offer or supply any goods or services in that (or a related) market, that body will not typically be acting as an undertaking for the purposes of EU and UK competition law.[135] The latter is illustrated by contrast with *Pavlov*, in which the making of pension contributions ('purchasing') by independent medical specialists was held to be subject to competition law, as their provision of medical services was considered economic.[136]

The new Clinical Commissioning Groups (CCGs), which combine purchasing and providing functions, may offer a possible test for the OFT's initial approach post-*Bettercare*/*FENIN* insofar as anticompetitive conduct by a CCG appears to involve purchasers who may also be providers. This is because the distinction between purchasing and providing functions may produce paradoxical results when these are conflated. Thus, the *applicability* of competition law to CCGs appears to risk being treated effectively as a question of whether purchasing 'trumps' providing, or vice versa. Certainly it has been suggested that if the former applies, then CCGs may not be subject to competition law (following *FENIN* and based on the logic that purchasing activities for the NHS would satisfy the solidarity principle of *Poucet and Pistre*),[137] but if the latter, then NHS commissioners are indeed undertakings for the purposes of competition law.[138]

---

133 OFT, 'Competition Law and Public Bodies, 2011', OFT1389.

134 Ibid, para. 2.14, p. 12.

135 Ibid.

136 *Pavlov*, n. 35 above. OFT, above n. 125, fn. 23, p. 12.

137 As suggested by L. Goulding, above n. 43. Joined cases C-159/91 and C-160/91 *Poucet and Pistre*, n. 41 above.

138 For a thorough elaboration of this view, see A. Sánchez Graells, 'Why are NHS Commissioners "undertakings" and, consequently, subject to competition law?' *How to crack a nut*, 02.06.2014, <http://www.howtocrackanut.com/blog/2014/06/why-are-nhs-commissioners-undertakings.html?rq=%E2%80%98Why%20are%20NHS%20Commissioners%20%E2%80%98undertakings%E2%80%99%20and%2C%20consequently%2C%20subject%20to%20competition%20law%3F%E2%80%99> accessed 24.06.2018.

The distinction between purchasing and providing functions is undoubtedly significant, for example, for clarifying the relative scope of competition law and procurement rules and understanding where gaps may exist for the purposes of tackling anticompetitive behaviour by purchasers.[139] However, whilst it is recognised that opinions diverge regarding whether anticompetitive behaviour by purchasers merits the same attention as that by providers, the separation of purchasing and providing functions by the NHS Internal Market underpinned an emphasis on *provider* competition, and there remains a significantly greater focus on competition *for* – rather than *in* – the market as regards the NHS.

Thus, the enactment of Article 122 Zvw to clarify that competition law applies to health insurers (to counteract *AOK Bundesverband*) is logical to give effect to the 'healthcare triangle' and focus on competition *in* the market in Dutch healthcare, but it does not necessarily follow that an equivalent national provision in England to counteract *FENIN* is either necessary or even desirable. This is not to deny that purchasing activity can be anticompetitive, but rather that the emphasis of the limited scope for competition *within* the English NHS (categories 1 and 2) is on providers, not purchasers: NHS patients do not choose NHS commissioners in the way that patients choose insurers in the Netherlands.[140]

### *3.2.3. National Framework Resulting from Healthcare Reforms*

The framework which emerges in English healthcare post-HSCA 2012 is shaped both by solidarity (despite the absence of formal engagement with the SGEI exception) and the distinction between purchasers and providers. Notably, section 72 HSCA 2012 builds on the uncertainty regarding the extent of applicability of competition law, by providing that NHS Improvement and the CMA share concurrent powers in applying general competition law in respect of healthcare provision. The formulation 'healthcare provision' may be interpreted broadly[141] to encompass both the NHS and private healthcare sector

---

139 O. Odudu, above n. 7, suggests that the logic behind the CJEU's judgment in *FENIN* – that instead of competition law, the purchaser is subject to public procurement rules – would make sense if procurement law could be said to address all the risks associated with monopsony power. However, as this is not the case, the 2013 Regulations appear curious for conflating competition law and procurement issues.

140 Indeed, it might be considered that the only scope for purchaser competition on the part of patients exists in connection with the private healthcare market (categories 3 and 4). However, whether the situation of a patient deciding to pay for healthcare provision themselves (as a 'self-pay' patient) rather than 'choosing' an NHS commissioner as purchaser amounts to purchaser competition is very questionable.

141 A view supported by the interpretation provisions of the HSCA 2012. The general interpretation provision, section 150 HSCA 2012, provides that 'health care' and 'health

(categories 1–4), or narrowly as limited to the NHS only (categories 1 and 2), a distinction which has particular implications for the operation of concurrent powers which is discussed in Chapter 3. In addition, 'provision' reinforces the separation between purchasing and providing activities. This may be difficult to sustain in respect of CCGs and the greater emphasis on integration in the NHS Five Year Forward View, even if it underscores the relative clarity that healthcare providers are typically subject to competition law.

In practice, however, the focus of section 72 HSCA 2012 may be narrow because it may be understood as ensuring a continuation of focus relating to categories 3 and 4, including on NHS PPUs,[142] although NHS providers, and indeed private providers delivering NHS services, could in theory be subject to competition law. Whilst the focus on provider competition of section 72 HSCA 2012 carves out a space in which general competition law can be applied, the effectiveness of this is unclear in the absence of cases brought in connection with categories 1 and 2.

This focus on 'healthcare provision' might be interpreted as indeed suggesting that an equivalent standard of application of competition law has been achieved at national level, but effectively by a (tacit) non-application of general competition law to NHS/private providers delivering services for the NHS, rather than by extending *applicability* to NHS purchasers as well as NHS/private providers. This paves the way for potential anticompetitive behaviour to be addressed not by the application of general competition law, but by a broader regulatory regime comprising the NHS Provider Licence and the 2013 Regulations, which operate in the aforementioned 'core'.

---

care service' have the meaning provided in section 64 HSCA 2012 which supplements Monitor's general duties. Section 64(3) HSCA 2012 provides: '"Health care" means all forms of health care provided for individuals, whether relating to physical or mental health, with a reference in this Part to health care services being read accordingly; and for the purposes of this Part it does not matter if a health care service is also an adult social care service'. A further permutation is made in the HSCA 2012, namely, 'health services', which are specifically linked to the NHS. 'Health services' are stipulated in sections 23 and 26 HSCA 2012 which amend the National Health Service Act 2006 in respect of functions of NHS England and CCGs respectively (Section 26 HSCA 2012 inserts the interpretation provision of section 14Z24, and section 23 HSCA 2012 inserts the interpretation provision of section 13Z4. Both define 'health services' as 'services provided as part of the health service'). This is unsurprising in view of the remits of NHS England and CCGs being limited to the NHS as distinct from the private healthcare sector, but should be treated as a separate matter from Monitor's competition functions and the meaning of 'health care services' under section 72 HSCA 2012.

142 Interestingly, the CMA has recently investigated NHS Foundation Trusts for a failure to provide private healthcare information. CMA, 'CMA demands action from hospitals on private healthcare information', Press Release, 31.08.2017, <https://www.gov.uk/government/news/cma-demands-action-from-hospitals-on-private-healthcare-information> accessed 24.06.2018.

It was suggested above that what we see in England is the development of competition *within* the 'core' of the fundamental principle of universal access. It was further suggested that, absent the clear *applicability* of competition law, the question is what a competition policy in these circumstances could look like. Would it replicate general competition law, or recognise the different scenario of the NHS quasi-market,[143] effectively enshrining the 'new style of competition law'[144] which accompanied the New Labour reforms? What has emerged in England is an attempt to apply equivalent substantive standards to NHS commissioners and providers of NHS healthcare, couched in terms which reflect the terminology of the provisions governing anticompetitive agreements but which do not explicitly distinguish between these and abuse of dominance, although hypothetical scenarios (discussed below) recognise a distinction between anticompetitive agreements and 'unilateral conduct'. Thus 'anti-competitive behaviour' is defined specifically within the context of the HSCA 2012 as meaning:

> behaviour which would (or would be likely to) prevent, restrict or distort competition and a reference to preventing anti-competitive behaviour includes a reference to eliminating or reducing the effects (or potential effects) of the behaviour.[145]

Providers delivering NHS healthcare (whether NHS Foundation Trusts or private providers) are obliged to comply with the Choice and Competition condition of the NHS Provider Licence. The 'competition oversight' element of this stipulates that:

> The Licensee shall not:
>
> (a) enter into or maintain any agreement or other arrangement which has the object or which has (or would be likely to have) the effect of preventing, restricting or distorting competition in the provision of health care services for the purposes of the NHS, or
>
> (b) engage in any other conduct which has (or would be likely to have) the effect of preventing, restricting or distorting competition in the provision of health care services for the purposes of the NHS,
>
> to the extent that it is against the interests of people who use health care services.[146]

---

143 This point was also made in connection with the NHS Internal Market reforms and associated competition policy by D. Dawson, 'Regulating competition in the NHS. The Department of Health guide on mergers and anti-competitive behaviour', *University of York Centre for Health Economics Discussion Paper* 131, March 1995.

144 I. Lianos, above n. 5.

145 Section 64(2) HSCA 2012.

146 NHS Provider Licence Annex: Standard Conditions, Condition C2, 'Competition Oversight', <https://www.gov.uk/government/uploads/system/uploads/attachment_data/file/285009/Annex_NHS_provider_licence_conditions_-_20120207.pdf> accessed 24.06.2018.

NHS commissioners – as distinct from other NHS procurement bodies[147] – are subject to the regime established by the 2013 Regulations. Regulation 10 governs anticompetitive behaviour and Regulation 10(1) notably provides:

> When commissioning health care services for the purposes of the NHS, a relevant body must not engage in anti-competitive behaviour,[148] unless to do so is in the interests of people who use health care services for the purposes of the NHS which may include –
>
> (a) by the services being provided in an integrated way (including with other health care services, health-related services, or social care services); or
> (b) by co-operation between the persons who provide the services in order to improve the quality of the services.[149]

Regulation 10(2) provides that an arrangement for providing NHS healthcare services must not include any term or condition restricting competition which is not necessary for the attainment of intended outcomes which are beneficial for NHS patients or the objective governing good procurement practice. In contrast to Regulation 10(1), this appears to reference agreements or contracts explicitly.[150]

Although these provisions indeed borrow the terminology of the general law, it is unclear whether further parallels could (or should) be drawn. Further, the different frameworks which have emerged in the Netherlands and England may also raise questions with regard to parallel application of EU competition rules.

## 3.3. PARALLEL APPLICATION OF NATIONAL AND EU COMPETITION RULES

The framework regarding the parallel application of EU and national competition rules is set out in Article 3 of Council Regulation 1/2003,[151] with

---

147 The 2013 Regulations apply only to the CCGs and NHS England (in its capacity as commissioner of specialist services). They do not apply to related bodies, such as Commissioning Support Units (CSUs), although these are expected to function in accordance with the spirit of the regulations. See Monitor, 'Substantive Guidance on the Procurement, Patient Choice and Competition Regulations', London, December 2013.

148 Defined by reference to section 64(2) HSCA 2012 above.

149 See above n. 8, Regulation 10(1).

150 While the purpose of Regulation 10(2) (above n. 8) is unclear, it might be considered to share some common features of the NZa's power to intervene in contracts under Article 45 Wmg.

151 Article 3, 'Relationship between Articles 81 and 82 of the Treaty and national competition laws'. Council Regulation (EC) No 1/2003 of 16 December 2002 on the implementation of the rules on competition laid down in Articles 81 and 82 of the Treaty. ('Council Regulation 1/2003').

differing limitations for anticompetitive agreements and abuse of dominance provisions, respectively.

Article 3(1) provides in essence that national competition authorities or national courts shall apply both national and TFEU provisions governing anticompetitive agreements and abuse of dominance.

Article 3(2) provides in essence that stricter national laws regarding the prohibition of agreements, decisions by associations or concerted practices which may affect trade between Member States may not be applied. However, an equivalent approach to *unilateral* conduct does not exist, so national laws may be stricter in prohibiting or sanctioning this.

Article 3(3) provides that Articles 3(1) and (2) do not preclude the application of provisions of national law that predominantly pursue an objective different from that pursued by Articles 101 and 102 TFEU.

### *3.3.1. The Netherlands*

As noted above, the Wmg granted the NZa two powers which have potential to interact with the application of general competition law, namely competence to conduct Significant Market Power (SMP) investigations under Article 48 Wmg, and to intervene in the drafting of contracts under Article 45 Wmg. The former has now been transferred to the ACM, but the latter remains with the NZa.

The SMP competence under Article 48 Wmg has been considered to possibly benefit from the exception in Article 3(2) Regulation 1/2003 on the grounds that the restriction on national laws being more demanding than EU competition law does not apply to unilateral conduct, which SMP clearly does.[152] In the appeal decision in *Menzis v. Van Dalen Pharmacy*,[153] the court considered the issue of compatibility between the SMP competence and Article 3(2), but established that there was no effect on trade, which has been described as arguably the easiest solution to the problem[154] as there appeared to be a lack of clarity as to whether the unilateral exception would apply.

The 'contract powers' competence of Article 45 Wmg[155] has been used most notably to date as the basis for an Electronic Networks Regulation,[156] which

---

152 W. Sauter (2014), above n. 17.

153 Which involved an expedited decision under Article 49 Wmg as well as examination under Article 48 Wmg. NZa, *Besluit als bedoeld in artikel 49 lid 1 van de Wmg 18.11.2009* (Decision under Article 49(1) Wmg of 18.11.2009) ('Article 49 Decision'). NZa, *Besluit 22.02.2011, eerste toepassing van aanmerkelijke marktmachtbevoegdheid (art. 48 Wmg)* (Decision involving the first application of SMP competence under Art. 48 Wmg of 22.02.2011) ('Article 48 Decision').

154 W. Sauter (2014), above n. 17.

155 Article 45 Wmg provides that 'The NZa may, with regard to the transparency of healthcare markets or the promotion of competition, develop rules regarding the drafting of agreements relating to healthcare or tariffs and regarding the conditions of such agreements'.

156 NZa, *Regeling CI/NR-100.099. REGELING voorwaarden voor overeenkomsten inzake elektronische netwerken met betrekking tot zorg.* (Regulation CI/NR-100.099. Regulation on

imposes mandatory access to agreements concerning the use of electronic networks to exchange patient and medication data in the Netherlands. This sets out a general prohibition whereby agreements between healthcare providers regarding setting up and maintaining healthcare-related electronic networks may not include provisions which may restrict the subsequent access of new participants to the agreement.[157] This general prohibition has been criticised as deviating from the intended purpose of Article 45 Wmg – which emphasises general obligations – and thus raising questions of compliance of the Electronic Networks Regulation with EU law in view of Article 3(2) Council Regulation 1/2003.[158] However, strictly speaking, there is no conflict with Article 3(2) Council Regulation 1/2003 since Article 45 Wmg does not comprise a prohibition, but an ex ante competence for the NZa to impose rules.[159] Furthermore, Article 45 Wmg may benefit from the exception in Article 3(3) Council Regulation 1/2003, because it serves a different purpose,[160] namely, promoting the emergence and functioning of markets in a liberalisation context (where they did not exist previously), as opposed to enforcing existing competition.

### *3.3.2. England*

In theory, questions about parallel application arise in connection with the Competition Oversight condition of the NHS Provider Licence and Regulation 10 of the 2013 Regulations. With regard to purchasers, insofar as *FENIN* can be regarded as overruling *BetterCare* and excluding the applicability of competition law to NHS commissioners (purchasers), there would seem to be no question of parallel application regarding Regulation 10. However, insofar as *BetterCare* may be considered good law, questions of parallel application may still be relevant. With regard to providers, insofar as those in category 1 are not subject to competition law,[161] then questions of parallel application may similarly not arise. With regard to category 2, private providers holding an NHS Provider Licence appear subject to competition law,[162] but recourse may be

---

Conditions for Agreements involving Electronic Networks relating to Healthcare) ('NZa Electronic Networks Regulation'). This effectively codifies previous ACM decisions which dealt with concerns about information exchange, but which failed to resolve nearly identical issues occurring elsewhere in the Netherlands. See W. Sauter, above n.17.

157 NZa Electronic Networks Regulation above n. 156, Article 2(1).

158 On this point, see M. Wiggers, *De NMa en de NZa in de curatieve zorgsector – Een toetsing aan het Europees mededingingsrecht* (The NMa and the NZa in the curative healthcare sector – an assessment against EU competition law), Kluwer, Deventer 2013, pp. 322–26.

159 See M. Wiggers, ibid, p. 150, and J. Bijkerk and W. Sauter, above n. 88.

160 See W. Sauter (2014), above n. 17.

161 See O. Odudu, above n. 7.

162 Following the logic of *BetterCare* insofar as this remains good law. See also O. Odudu, above n. 7, regarding category 1 relationships (NHS providers delivering NHS services).

had to Article 3(3) Council Regulation 1/2003 where parallel application is permitted when national competition authorities and courts apply provisions of national law that predominantly pursue an objective different from that pursued by Articles 101 and 102 TFEU. This has relevance in respect of subsections (a) and (b) of the Competition Oversight condition insofar as a distinction might be drawn between effectively delivering a universal service obligation (implicit in 'the provision of healthcare services for the purposes of the NHS') and enhancing consumer welfare – the stated (but apparently ambiguous)[163] objective of EU competition law.[164]

# 4. APPLICATION OF COMPETITION LAW IN DUTCH AND ENGLISH HEALTHCARE

The foregoing discussions of the 'undertaking' concept and the emerging EU and national frameworks in healthcare have revealed a range of complexities in applying competition law to cases of healthcare provision, ranging from varying interpretations of 'solidarity' to distinctions between provision and purchasing. However, establishing the existence of an 'undertaking', and thus the applicability of competition law, can be regarded as merely the first (albeit significant) hurdle in the actual application of the substantive provisions governing anticompetitive agreements and abuse of dominance. Further considerations include whether these provisions can reflect healthcare-specific values such as affordability and accessibility.[165]

## 4.1. APPLYING THE ANTICOMPETITIVE AGREEMENTS AND ABUSE OF DOMINANCE PROVISIONS TO THE HEALTHCARE SECTOR – GENERAL REMARKS

### 4.1.1. *Anticompetitive Agreements and Healthcare*

The anticompetitive agreements provisions – Article 101 TFEU, section 2 CA98 (the 'Chapter I' prohibition), and Article 6 Mw – constitute a prohibition on agreements between undertakings, decisions by associations of undertakings and concerted practices which have as their object or effect the prevention,

---

163 On this point, see V. Daskalova, 'Consumer Welfare in EU Competition Law: What Is It (Not) About?' (2015) 11(1) *Competition Law Review* 133. K. Cseres, 'The Controversies of the Consumer Welfare Standard' (2007) 3(2) *Competition Law Review* 121.

164 As the private healthcare sector is subject only to general competition law, concerns do not arise in this regard either.

165 For discussions of this, see J.W. van de Gronden, above n. 11.

restriction or distortion of competition within, respectively, the EU internal, UK and Dutch markets. Whilst the additional stipulation of Article 101 TFEU – that agreements may affect trade between Member States – may once have been deemed unlikely to be relevant to healthcare provision, which typically comprises markets which are regional or national in nature, this may now be changing, as even NHS healthcare provision in England can rely on input from French providers.[166] However, limited recourse has been had to Article 101 TFEU in respect of healthcare *provision*.[167]

The challenges of applying the anticompetitive agreements provisions might be described as twofold: namely, identifying those agreements which are likely to be caught by the provisions (and not protected by exceptions); and distinguishing between 'object' and 'effect' analysis.

As regards the reach of the anticompetitive agreements provisions, we have already seen the difficulties of designating 'undertakings' in healthcare. Whilst 'concerted practices' may prove as difficult to identify in healthcare as other sectors, decisions of 'associations of undertakings' have been found in some national cases regarding professional associations.[168] Regarding exceptions, it appears that Article 106(2) TFEU may offer greater protection to the healthcare sector, as Article 101(3) TFEU has been considered to be limited in connection with public services[169] (and thus healthcare). It has further been suggested[170] that exceptions based on the pursuit of legitimate objectives, and inherent restrictions[171] developed in the context of *Wouters*[172] and *Meca-Medina*,[173] may

---

166 See, for example, South Kent Coast Clinical Commissioning Group, 'French elective care contracts', News article, 08.09.2015, <http://www.southkentcoastccg.nhs.uk/news/news-articles/?blogpost=7639> accessed 24.06.2018.

167 An exception may be French pharmacists in Case T-90/11, *Ordre national des pharmaciens (ONP) and others v. European Commission*, ECLI:EU:T:2014:1049 (discussed in J.W. van de Gronden and C.S. Rusu, 'EU competition law and policy and health systems' in T.K. Hervey, C.A. Young and L.E. Bishop (eds.), *Research Handbook on EU Health Law and Policy*, Edward Elgar, Cheltenham 2017, pp. 267–90), as generally cases have dealt with issues in the pharmaceutical market. For a comprehensive discussion of these, see L. Hancher and W. Sauter, above n. 11, pp. 244–46.

168 See, for example, J. Lear et al., above n.11; O. Odudu, above n. 2.

169 T. Prosser, above n. 45, p. 27. However, connections have been drawn between the exception under Article 101(3) TFEU and a strict interpretation of Monitor's general duty to balance anticompetitive behaviour with patient interests under section 62(3) HSCA 2012. On this point, see A. Sánchez Graells, above n. 21, and A. Sánchez Graells, 'New rules for health care procurement in the UK: a critical assessment from the perspective of EU economic law' (2015) 1 *Public Procurement Law Review* 16.

170 The view that the exception afforded to collective bargaining agreements by the *Albany* case (n. 42 above) may also have limited application in healthcare is considered by J. Lear et al., above n. 11.

171 See, inter alia, J.W. van de Gronden and J. Lear et al., both above n. 11.

172 C-309/99, *J.C.J. Wouters, J.W. Savelbergh and Price Waterhouse Belastingadviseurs BV v. Algemene Raad van de Nederlandse Orde van Advocaten*, ECLI:EU:C:2002:98.

173 Case C-519/04 P, *David Meca-Medina and Igor Majcen v. Commission of the European Communities*, ECLI:EU:C:2006:492.

prove relevant to healthcare provision on the basis that healthcare providers are guided by a specific medical deontology (from the Hippocratic Oath onwards) and might apply rules that are 'inherent' in the organisation of healthcare,[174] but a distinction can be drawn between achieving *legitimate* and *public* objectives. This may suggest that this approach offers less protection to agreements in healthcare than might at first be thought.[175] Nevertheless, in applying EU competition law, the CJEU has been seen to adopt an approach capable of accommodating issues of 'general' (presumably 'public') interest.[176]

Another consideration in determining the *applicability* of the anticompetitive agreements provisions involves separating cooperation required by the state from agreements to cooperate,[177] as only the latter are subject to competition law. Indeed, the focus may be on collusive tendering, joint negotiation (collective buying or selling) and information exchange (both collection and dissemination).[178] This appears to have been borne out already insofar as guidance by the ACM clearly distinguishes colluding on a tender which could be submitted independently from 'combination agreements'[179] made because providers may be unable to tender independently, in which case a more lenient view is likely.

As regards the distinction between 'object' and 'effect' analysis, the focus of competition authorities will be on the latter in light of the difficulties of reliably predicting the welfare consequences of conduct in healthcare which may justify an 'object' approach in other sectors.[180]

The foregoing suggests that applying the general anticompetitive agreements provisions to healthcare provision is by no means a straightforward matter, so one needs to be clear about what can be achieved by applying these. Whilst some agreements may be common to any healthcare system, such as sharing patient information to ensure continuity of care or providing integrated care, further complications lie in country-specific features, such as the various structures of *zorggroepen* (care groups) which deliver integrated care. These structures mean that the anticompetitive agreements provisions apply to agreements between providers, or between providers and a 'care group' which is a legal entity forming a link between health insurers and healthcare providers (which remain

---

174 On this point, see L. Hancher and W. Sauter, above n. 11, para. 8.46, pp. 239–40.

175 Certainly the approach taken by the Commission regarding French pharmacists in *ONP* may suggest a reluctance to extend these exceptions to healthcare. See L. Hancher and W. Sauter, above n. 11, paras. 8.29–8.31, pp. 234–35.

176 Ibid, para. 8.45, p. 239. On this point, see also J.W. van de Gronden, above n. 11.

177 O. Odudu, above n. 2.

178 Ibid.

179 ACM, *Richtsnoeren voor de zorgsector* (Guidelines for the healthcare sector), March 2010, para. 267.

180 O. Odudu, above n. 2.

independent undertakings).[181] In contrast, the provisions do not apply where providers are members of a 'care group', as this involves cooperation taking place within a single undertaking. Distinctive features of English healthcare are the combination of purchasing and providing functions within CCGs and the convoluted distinctions between NHS and private providers delivering NHS services or treating private patients.

### 4.1.2. *Abuse of Dominance and Healthcare*

The abuse of dominance provisions – Article 102 TFEU, section 18 CA98 (the 'Chapter II' prohibition) and Article 24 Mw – involve a prohibition on any abuse by undertakings of a dominant position within a national market or the EU internal market. This prohibition comprises three elements: defining the market, establishing a dominant position and establishing abusive conduct. It is important to note that each element poses particular difficulties when applied to healthcare provision.

Firstly, defining markets in healthcare is complex. This is largely due to the limitations imposed on standard tests of substitutability – such as the Small but Significant and Non-transitory Increase in Price (SSNIP)/'hypothetical monopolist' test – by the 'third party pays principle' and the consequent patient insensitivity to price[182] which arises regardless of the type of healthcare system.

Secondly, the presumption of dominance may appear relatively straightforward, insofar as the definition of a 50 per cent market share, established by *AKZO*,[183] can apply to the healthcare sector. However, factors such as the existence of barriers to entry arising from law and regulation in highly regulated sectors such as healthcare can prove determinative.[184] Thus, it is necessary to distinguish barriers to entry that are natural features of the market from those created by the state, and those created by undertakings, because competition law will focus on the latter.[185] For example, a Dutch health insurance company which provides insurance to 65 per cent of inhabitants in a given region is not automatically deemed to hold a dominant position.[186] This is because its ability to act independently of its competitors is contingent upon other factors, such as whether a particular aspect of GP care is included in the statutorily-defined 'basic package' of health insurance. A further determining factor is the type of

---

181 Nederlandse Mededingingsautoriteit (NMA), Nederlandse Zorgautoriteit (NZA), *Richtsnoeren Zorggroepen* (Guidelines for Healthcare Groups), August 2010, para. 73.

182 This has led to the development of alternative econometric tests to define markets for assessing hospital mergers in the Netherlands. This is discussed further in Chapter 3 below.

183 Case C-62/86, *AKZO Chemie BV v. Commission of the European Communities*, ECLI:EU:C:1991:286.

184 See L. Hancher and W. Sauter, above n. 11, para. 8.53, p. 242.

185 O. Odudu, above n. 2.

186 ACM, above n. 179, para. 100.

insurance policy involved, as this may entail a contract between the patient and GP with the insurer providing reimbursement, but having no contract directly with the GP. In addition, distinctions can be drawn between different categories of healthcare provider. For example, entry into the hospital market is likely to be more difficult than for an individual medical practitioner to set themselves up, in view of the far lower investment needed and lighter regulatory burden involved.[187]

Finally, with regard to abusive practices, a distinction is to be drawn between exclusionary conduct (such as predatory pricing) and exploitative conduct (such as unfair trading conditions). Certainly at EU level, priority has been given to combating exclusionary rather than exploitative abuses. The reasons for this are twofold: firstly, it is very difficult to use general competition rules to combat exploitation; and secondly, fighting exploitation can be counter-productive if regulation is introduced and leads to a lack of efficiency.[188] This approach appears to be replicated in both the Netherlands and England.

A further consideration in connection with abuse of dominance concerns in healthcare is the apparent bias towards challenging monopoly power rather than monopsony power. This is perhaps unsurprising in view of the ambiguous status of purchasing activities vis-à-vis the applicability of competition law, as discussed previously. In the Netherlands, selling power was deemed a policy priority of the NZa regarding SMP,[189] and although the ACM has been asked by healthcare providers to address concerns regarding insurer buyer power, its intervention thus far has been limited. This is explained in part by its approach of not intervening unless consumer choice is threatened, but also by the statutory priority previously given to the NZa's SMP competence.[190] In England, any focus on monopoly power vis-à-vis the NHS may be attributed to the legacy of *FENIN*, in which Advocate General Maduro opined that neither does the existence of a monopsony pose a serious threat to competition (since it does not necessarily have any effect on the downstream market), nor does a monopsonist have an interest in bringing such pressure to bear on its suppliers that they become obliged to leave the upstream market.[191] However, there are examples of abuse of monopsony power – such as the restriction of patient choice as a consequence of purchasing decisions by former NHS Primary Care Trusts (now CCGs) as sole buyers,[192] or the purchase of care-home places at a discounted rate by Local

[187] L. Hancher and W. Sauter, above n. 11, para. 8.53, p. 242.
[188] Ibid, paras. 8.55–8.57.
[189] W. Sauter (2011), above n. 17.
[190] For further discussion, see W. Sauter (2014), above n. 17.
[191] AG Maduro, above n. 121, para. 66.
[192] S. Bojakowski, 'Market power: a PCT acting as a monopsony' (2012) 18(2) *British Journal of Healthcare Management* 71–76.

Authorities in England to the detriment of self-funding patients[193] – where no obvious recourse is available following *FENIN.*[194]

### *4.1.3. Competition Law and Healthcare – General Concluding Comments*

The foregoing suggests that the application of competition law in general terms in respect of healthcare provision may be difficult for various reasons. Indeed, establishing the existence of an 'undertaking' may represent merely the first (albeit significant) hurdle, before aspects such as market definition and establishing dominance are considered. A further complication emerging in both countries is the need to distinguish between different forms of cooperation in light of potential scrutiny under the anticompetitive agreements or merger control provisions.[195] It is against this background that cases and guidance from the Netherlands and England are now considered.

## 4.2. THE NETHERLANDS

### *4.2.1. Application of the Anticompetitive Agreements Provisions*

Thus far, various aspects of healthcare provision in the Netherlands have been considered in light of the anticompetitive agreements provisions. Cases have spanned both the 'cure' and the 'care' sectors.[196] In view of the focus of this chapter, decisions involving healthcare providers are considered, although it is recognised that the ACM has also issued guidance to health insurers, for example, informal opinions regarding the development of a 'preference policy' prior to the 2006 reforms.[197] Some early 'healthcare provision' cases pre-date the 2006 reforms, but appeals[198] have, to a greater or lesser extent, acknowledged

---

193 M. Hviid, above n. 48.

194 Although *BetterCare* might suggest that competition law is applicable to the latter scenario.

195 R.J.P. Jansen, '*Samenwerken of fuseren in de zorg?*' ('Collaborating or merging in healthcare?') (2013) *Markt & Mededinging*, 2, 77. A. Taylor, 'When does an alliance become a merger?', Aldwych Partners blog, 14.07.2015, <http://aldwychpartners.co.uk/when-does-an-alliance-become-a-merger/> accessed 24.06.2018. This is considered further in connection with merger control in Chapter 4.

196 Indeed, cases involving home care providers appear relatively often – ACM cases concerning market-sharing by home care organisations are considered by J.W. van de Gronden and E. Szyszczak, above n. 14; W. Sauter (2014) and (2011), both above n. 17; and E.M.H. Loozen, 'Public healthcare interests require strict competition enforcement' (2015) 119(7) *Health Policy* 882.

197 Considered further by M. Wiggers, above n. 158, pp. 229–30.

198 ACM decisions can be appealed initially to the *Rotterdam Rechtbank* (Rotterdam District Court (Rb)) and then to the *College van Beroep voor het bedrijfsleven* (Tribunal for Trade and Industry, CBb).

ongoing changes in the sector. Some early cases are considered here[199] under the headings of 'continuity of care' and 'professional associations', but the ACM's approach currently appears to involve distinguishing by specialism and sector in issuing guidance.

#### 4.2.1.1. Continuity of Care

It has been recognised that locum services are an important means to guarantee the public interest in availability of care.[200] However, ensuring continuity of care can include a range of activities and parties: two examples considered here are out-of-hours pharmacy opening and the sharing of patient data via electronic networks.

*General continuity of care – out-of-hours service provision*

Although ensuring continuity of healthcare provision is widely recognised as being in patients' interests, it risks censure under the competition rules because it is frequently implemented by agreements between parties who would typically compete with each other (such as GPs providing out-of-hours cover, or pharmacists running a 24-hour service). The conflict arises from a need to maintain services which are inherently less profitable (for example, in sparsely populated areas, or outside of general business hours) and, under a strict interpretation of the competition rules, such agreements may amount to market-sharing.

However, there is evidence to suggest that the competition authorities are willing to take a more flexible view in light of the fundamental need to ensure continuity of care. For example, ACM guidance recognises that it is unreasonable to expect a single provider to be available day and night, seven days a week, so suggests that locum schemes do not generally conflict with the anticompetitive agreements provisions.[201] However, competition concerns arise when members of a locum scheme collectively hold a position of market power which may lead to others being excluded.[202] This issue is compounded in the Netherlands in cases where GP participation in agreements may be a condition of contracts with health insurers.[203] The ACM has determined that cooperation may not exceed

199 Although M. Wiggers, above n. 158, uses groupings of different specialists/sectors in Chapter 5.

200 J.W. van de Gronden, *'Een upgrade van het zorgbeleid van de NMa: de derde versie van de Richtsnoeren voor de zorgsector'* ('Upgrade of the NMa's healthcare policy: the third edition of the Guidelines for the Healthcare Sector') (2010) Markt & Mededinging, 6, 195.

201 ACM, above n. 179, paras. 289–91.

202 Ibid, para. 291.

203 Ibid, para. 289.

what is strictly necessary for the scheme: if the cooperation includes services which can be provided independently by other providers, this aspect must be reviewed in light of the anticompetitive agreements provisions.[204] The ACM has also determined that specific conditions – for example regarding availability and accessibility – must be imposed on such agreements,[205] suggesting that the ACM distinguishes between legitimate locum schemes necessary to ensure continuity of care, and situations where continuity of care may be used as a smokescreen for anticompetitive activity. In other words, the ACM has looked at the effect, and not the object, of the agreement.

*Information-sharing and electronic networks*

Concerns about the sharing of information have arisen in the Netherlands regarding the use of electronic networks developed to store patient data. It is worth noting the importance of healthcare providers participating in electronic networks in order to maintain their position in the market because such participation is a condition of contracts with health insurers. As the existence of the networks leads to obvious benefits to patients, the concerns are more directed towards how the networks are managed and who has access. In early cases,[206] the former NMa was seen to take a relatively lenient approach (by not making full use of its ex post sanction powers, thus effectively acting as a regulator), which may reflect the transitional state of the market at the time.[207] These cases were considered to have hardly any effect on similar exclusionary practices elsewhere,[208] so the NZa adopted the aforementioned general regulation[209] on access to electronic networks in healthcare,[210] using its contract powers under Article 45 Wmg effectively to codify NMa decisions in this area.

---

204 Ibid, para. 291.

205 For example, the NMa considered the imposition of closure periods not only restricted competition between pharmacies, but also consumer choice in the absence of more extensive opening hours in Decision of the Director General of the NMa of 05.09.2003 in case 3169/37 of 05.09.2003, discussed in ACM, above n. 179.

206 For example, NMa (ACM) Decision, Case no. 3022-205, *Stichting Automatisering Gezondheidszorg Breda* (Breda Foundation for Computerising Healthcare), 15.11.2004. NMa (ACM) Decision, Case no. 2501, *Dienstapotheek Assen* (Assen Out-of-Hours Pharmacy), 21.06.2004.

207 M. Wiggers, above n. 158, pp. 322–23.

208 W. Sauter (2011), above n. 17, p. 348.

209 NZa, Regulation CI/NR-100.099, above n. 156.

210 Ibid. This provides that any agreement between healthcare providers regarding the establishment and maintenance of an electronic network may not contain any provisions which restrict new entrants to the agreement (Article 1), and that any conditions attached to membership of the network must be reasonable, objective and non-discriminatory (Articles 2 and 3).

#### 4.2.1.2. Professional Associations in the Dutch Healthcare Sector

Whilst a wide range of trade associations and professional bodies in the healthcare sector play an important role in, inter alia, disseminating clinical knowledge and sharing best practices, this must be distinguished from conduct (which may take the form of rules, regulations and recommendations) which infringes the competition rules. This can happen where a situation is created in which members engage in coordinated behaviour rather than competing.

In terms of the application of competition law, it has been considered in the Netherlands that professional associations qualify as 'associations of undertakings'.[211] This comparatively rare designation has been applied to professional groups of psychologists[212] and GPs, as opposed to their conduct merely representing an agreement between undertakings.[213]

As regards *how* professional associations could infringe the competition rules, two clear examples are: by their role in negotiating fees (or sharing information about typical fees for a service), or by imposing discriminatory rules on access to the association, where membership is necessary to practice the profession.

In the *NIP, LVE, NVP, NVVP* (Dutch Psychologists' Associations) case,[214] the ACM established that price recommendations issued by the associations infringed the anticompetitive agreements provisions on the grounds that prices were coordinated. This decision was first appealed to the *Rechtbank Rotterdam* (District Court of Rotterdam (Rb)),[215] which rejected the ACM's findings on the basis that it had not established that price recommendations were restrictive of competition. In addition, the ACM had failed to consider the role of GPs and health insurers in connection with tariffs. A further appeal to the *College van Beroep voor het bedrijfsleven* (Dutch Trade and Industry Appeals Tribunal (CBb))[216] confirmed these findings.[217]

---

211 Professional groups of anaesthetists, consultants and eye surgeons have similarly been scrutinised in the context of the UK private healthcare market. See OFT, Decision, *Anaesthetists' groups*, No. 15/04/2003. CMA, above n. 128, 'Consultant Groups', paras. 46–50.

212 ACM, *Zaak 3309, Besluit, NIP, LVE, NVP, en NVVP* (Case 3309, Decision, *NIP, LVE, NVP and NVVP* (Dutch Psychologists' Associations)), 17.03.2009.

213 M. Canoy and W. Sauter, *'De recidivist onder het mes: NMa beboet de Landelijke Huisartsenvereniging'* ('Repeat offender under the knife: the NMa fines the Dutch GPs' Association') (2012) *Markt & Mededinging* 15, 92.

214 ACM, Case no. 3309, above n. 212.

215 Dutch Psychologists' Association, first appeal, ECLI:NL:RBROT:2006:AY4928.

216 Dutch Psychologists' Association, second appeal, ECLI:NL:CBB:2008:BF8820.

217 Further discussion of this case can be found in J.W. van de Gronden and E. Szyszczak, above n. 14; E.M.H. Loozen, above n. 196; and W. Sauter (2014), above n. 17.

In the *Landelijke Huisartsen Vereiniging* (Dutch GPs' Association (LHV)) cases,[218] the ACM examined the LHV's licensing policy regarding new GPs. In 2001, the ACM found that the LHV's policy in operation at the time was in conflict with competition law and could not benefit from an exemption.[219] In 2011, the ACM investigated the LHV. It established that the LHV's practice of allowing established GPs in an area to determine whether or not to permit entry to GP groups or partnerships[220] by new GPs infringed the anticompetitive agreements provisions, and so imposed a fine and a periodic penalty. A particular concern was the need for GPs to be allowed to join GP groups, and thus locum schemes, in order to be able to enter into contracts with insurers. As the LHV had received previous warnings about its conduct, it was fined. The LHV disputed this decision on the basis, inter alia, that the fine was disproportionate, and this was subsequently reduced by the ACM, which ruled that other aspects of the appeal were unfounded.[221] The ACM considered that the LHV had made recommendations regarding the licensing of new GPs which were restrictive of competition. On appeal, the Rotterdam District Court (Rb) overturned the ACM's finding that the anticompetitive agreements provisions had been infringed.[222] This decision, whilst evidently welcomed by the LHV, appears to have prompted clarification by the ACM of the approach it will take with regard to primary care providers,[223] and criticism among competition lawyers.[224] The ACM has articulated that it is mindful of concerns among primary care providers that their collaborative work may infringe competition law and attract fines, so has suggested that its focus will be on behaviour which is contrary to patients' interests and which has prompted complaints by patients or insurers.[225] This has led to questions about whether such an approach is appropriate and whether effective lobbying within other sectors could lead to more lenient approaches being taken elsewhere too.[226] Furthermore, it has been queried whether the guidance actually has wider implications for (and intended application to) the wider healthcare sector, and not just primary care providers.[227]

---

218 ACM, Case 6888/435 (*LHV*). Decision. 30.12.2011. ACM, Case 6888_1/510 (*LHV*). Decision. 03.02.2014.

219 ACM, Case 537 (*LHV*). Decision. 11.04.2001.

220 For a discussion of the different working arrangements of Dutch GPs, see M. Canoy and W. Sauter, above n. 213.

221 Cases discussed in M. Canoy and W. Sauter, above n. 213; M. Wiggers, above n. 158, pp. 221–29; and M. Wiggers, R. Struijlaart and J. Ruigewaard, '*Landelijke Huisartsen Vereniging*' ('Dutch GPs' Association') (2014) *Markt & Mededinging*, 4, 160.

222 Dutch GPs' Association appeal case ECLI:NL:RBROT:2015:9352.

223 ACM, '*Uitgangspunten toezicht ACM op zorgaanbieders in de eerste lijn*' ('Starting points for ACM oversight of primary care providers'), 19.09.2015.

224 W. Verloren Van Themaat and M. Bosch and M. Wiggers et al., both above n. 16.

225 ACM, above n. 223.

226 M. Wiggers et al., above n. 16.

227 W. Verloren Van Themaat and M. Bosch, above n. 16.

#### 4.2.1.3. *Samenwerking* (Collaborative Working) – A Specialism-Based Approach by the ACM?

More recently, the ACM has collated guidance regarding collaborative working addressed to specific healthcare specialisms and sectors, including *eerstelijnszorg* (primary care), *specialistiche zorg* (specialist care) and *geboortezorg* (obstetrics).[228] Whilst the nature of these sectors and specialisms clearly differs, some general themes may be emerging. For example, the ACM explicitly recognises benefits of collaborative working (such as more efficient care and new treatment methods in the context of specialist care), and states that it will not intervene in collaborative working (or mergers) where the advantages to consumers outweigh the disadvantages,[229] with regard to competition, typically in the form of reduced patient choice. An example of this was seen in the positive informal Opinion the ACM gave to three hospitals in Utrecht, following a self-assessment of whether closer collaboration to deliver specialist cancer care could infringe the Mw.[230] The ACM also appears to be recognising particular forms of collaborative working in given specialisms, and linking this to competition concerns in a way which is easy to follow. For example, its guidance to practitioners in various obstetrics services suggests that forming an obstetrics *zorgketen* (care chain) could trigger merger control, that providers need to be mindful of not excluding new obstetric services providers, and that patients need to be informed which providers are involved in the obstetrics care chain.[231]

### *4.2.2. Application of the Abuse of Dominance Provisions*

Although the ACM has received complaints from healthcare providers concerning abuse of dominance by health insurers,[232] recourse to the associated provisions has been limited to the extent that some suggest there have been no notable abuse of dominance cases.[233] Whilst smaller healthcare providers

---

228 ACM, '*Samenwerken in de zorg*' ('Collaboration in healthcare'), <https://www.acm.nl/nl/onderwerpen/zorg/samenwerking-in-de-zorg/samenwerking-in-de-zorg> accessed 24.06.2018.

229 ACM, '*Informatiekaart – ACM beoordeling fuseren of samenwerken in ziekenhuiszorg*' ('Information Map – ACM assessment of mergers and collaborative working in hospital care'), <https://www.acm.nl/sites/default/files/old_publication/publicaties/12562_informatiekaart-acm-beoordeling-fuseren-of-samenwerken-in-ziekenhuiszorg.pdf> accessed 24.06.2018.

230 ACM, '*Samenwerking kankerzorg drie ziekenhuizen Utrecht goed voor patient*' ('Collaborative working in cancer care by three hospitals in the Utrecht region is good for patients'), 25.08.2016, <https://www.acm.nl/nl/publicaties/publicatie/16190/Samenwerking-kankerzorg-drie-ziekenhuizen-regio-Utrecht-goed-voor-patient> accessed 24.06.2018.

231 ACM, '*Samenwerking in de geboortezorg*' ('Collaborative working in obstetrics'), <https://www.acm.nl/nl/onderwerpen/zorg/samenwerking-in-de-zorg/samenwerking-tussen-aanbieders-van-geboortezorg> accessed 24.06.2018.

232 For an overview of these, see M. Wiggers, above n. 158.

233 W. Sauter (2011) and (2014), both above n. 17.

have complained about being effectively obliged to enter into potentially unfavourable contracts with all four major health insurers,[234] the ACM has declined so far to intervene absent threats to consumer choice or erosion of quality.[235]

The absence of abuse of dominance cases has been attributed to the NZa's competence to conduct SMP investigations and the statutory priority given to these by Article 18 Wmg.[236] ACM guidance acknowledged that certain types of behaviour – such as a dominant hospital providing orthopaedic care at predatory rates, an insurer imposing unreasonable contract terms on a healthcare provider and a GP being refused membership of an out-of-hours service[237] – fell within the remit of either the ACM or the NZa.

Some of the tensions between SMP and abuse of dominance can be illustrated by the first SMP case, *Menzis v. Van Dalen Pharmacy*.[238] This involved a complaint by health insurers (Menzis) that the Van Dalen Pharmacy refused to enter into a contract with them which involved Menzis' 'preference policy',[239] with the result that Menzis was confronted with prices which were atypical for the market,[240] and so presented problems for Menzis in complying with its 'duty of care' to its policyholders.[241] As a result, Menzis submitted complaints of abuse of dominance and SMP by Van Dalen to the NMa and NZa, respectively, and the NZa's SMP investigation took priority accordingly. The NZa issued two decisions: firstly[242] imposing an obligation on Van Dalen to enter into a contract, and secondly[243] requiring Van Dalen to comply with any reasonable requests by health insurers. Van Dalen appealed both decisions and requested that the Dutch Trade and Industry Appeals Tribunal (CBb) intervene to implement temporary remedies regarding these, and regarding a provisional

234 The insurance market having become increasingly concentrated – from 30 to 4 insurers. For further discussion, see W. Sauter (2014), above n. 17.

235 Ibid.

236 W. Sauter (2011), above n. 17.

237 This is distinguished from conduct likely to be addressed by the anticompetitive agreements provisions on the grounds that the decision to refuse membership is that of an individual healthcare provider (the service) and not a result of an agreement between competing undertakings (healthcare providers). ACM, above n. 179, p. 14.

238 See n. 153 above. A second case involving a transparency and non-discrimination obligation imposed on a collective of primary care physicians that had refused to refer patients to internet pharmacies, but which led to no further legal challenge, is mentioned by W. Sauter (2014), above n. 17.

239 Whereby an insurer determines that only one or certain products within a specific group of medicines will be included in its basic health insurance package.

240 M. Wiggers and J.J.M. Sluijs, '*Menzis – Apotheek Van Dalen*' ('Menzis v. Van Dalen Pharmacy') (2011) *Markt en Mededinging*, 4, 145.

241 Under Article 11 Zvw, insurers are obliged to ensure compensation of, and access to, healthcare for their policyholders.

242 In an expedited decision under Article 49 Wmg. NZa, Article 49 Decision, above n. 153.

243 NZa, Article 48 Decision, above n. 153.

order for penalty payment issued by the NZa when Van Dalen failed to comply with the second decision.[244] Ultimately the CBb declared the appeal of the first decision inadmissible and the second decision unfounded.[245]

Although criticised as a test case, *Menzis v. Van Dalen* nevertheless demonstrated that the fundamental distinction between NZa's ex ante and ACM's ex post intervention inherent in SMP and abuse of dominance (to allow for market development and sanction anticompetitive conduct, respectively) appeared less than clear in practice for all parties involved. As noted, the health insurers initially submitted the complaint to both the NZa and the ACM, and the NZa investigation took priority in accordance with Article 18 Wmg. This might simply be understood as a lack of clarity about the respective aims of SMP and abuse of dominance. However, perhaps a more convincing interpretation is that aggrieved parties are only likely to be motivated to bring a case[246] if they feel exploited or excluded – in other words, where there has been an *abuse* of SMP (dominance).[247] Therefore, purely preventive SMP regulation would be burdensome for the NZa in view of the difficulty of defining markets and the need for a case-by-case approach.[248] In addition, there was scope for the ACM to intervene in connection with abuse of dominance in this case, but it did not do so.[249]

The issue of which agency should deal with market power and in what way, was recently considered in the context of *maatschappen* (specialist partnerships). A 'specialist partnership' comprises a group of consultants with a particular specialism which can affect the relationships between hospitals and other providers to such an extent that concerns arise about, for example, restrictions

244 For further discussion of the permutations of this case, see the commentary: M. Wiggers and J.J.M. Sluijs, *'Menzis - Apotheek J.D. van Dalen'* ('Menzis v. Van Dalen Pharmacy') (2010) *Markt en Mededinging*, 3, 114; M. Wiggers and J.J.M. Sluijs, above n. 240; M. Wiggers and J.J.M. Sluijs, *'CBb-trilogie: Apotheek Van Dalen - NZa (en Menzis)'* ('Dutch Trade and Industry Appeals Tribunal (CBb) Trilogy: *Van Dalen Pharmacy v. NZa (and Menzis)*') (2012) *Markt en Mededinging*, 6, 213.

245 Van Dalen Pharmacy appeal case ECLI:NL:CBB:2012:BW7731. For a discussion of this decision, see M. Wiggers and J.J.M. Sluijs, above n. 244.

246 In their review of the NZa, AEF identified 25 cases in which an SMP investigation had been commenced. Of these, 1 was initiated by the NZa and 24 resulted from complaints by providers or insurers. Andersson Elffers Felix (AEF) *(in samenwerking met Radicand Economics and Tilburg Law and Economics Center (TILEC)), 'Ordening en Toezicht in de zorg: Evaluatie van de Wet marktordening gezondheidszorg (Wmg) en de Nederlandse Zorgautoriteit (NZa)'*, September 2014. (AEF in cooperation with Radicand Economics and TILEC, 'Oversight and regulation in healthcare: Assessment of the Dutch Healthcare (Market Regulation) Act 2006 (Wmg) and the Dutch Healthcare Authority (NZa)') September 2014, p. 75.

247 See M. Wiggers and J.J.M. Sluijs, above n. 244.

248 Ibid.

249 For discussion on this point, see M. Wiggers and J.J.M. Sluijs, above n. 244.

on selective contracting. Whilst the partnerships may be dealt with by means of the anticompetitive agreements provisions, or in terms of unilateral conduct,[250] it has also been suggested that the partnerships do not constitute 'undertakings' for the purposes of competition law, but may be regarded as creating a collective (as opposed to unilateral) instance of SMP.[251]

It remains to be seen how the ACM will use its new SMP competence in combination with its ability to apply the abuse of dominance provisions. However, it has been suggested that the ACM will need to focus more on abuse of dominance (rather than on anticompetitive agreements) in order to make effective use of its new competence.[252]

## 4.3. ENGLAND

The above discussion of the uncertainty surrounding the applicability of the provisions governing abuse of dominance prompts the identification, within English healthcare, of a fundamental distinction and a symbiotic relationship between the NHS quasi-market, and the private healthcare sector. Further, it would be surprising if this situation did not have implications not only for the scope of anticompetitive behaviour,[253] but also for the enforcement of competition law.

### *4.3.1. Application of the Anticompetitive Agreements Provisions*

From recent guidance by the CMA and NHS Improvement,[254] it is clear that working together and collaborative arrangements are recognised as integral parts of healthcare provision. A distinction is therefore drawn between where

---

250 M. Varkevisser et al., *'Instellingsoverstijgende maatschappen: Huidige ontwikkelingen, mogelijke gevolgen en de aanpak van eventuele mededingingsproblemen. Eindrapport'*, Maart 2013 ('Cross-institution partnerships: current developments, possible consequences and managing potential competition problems. Final Report', March 2013).

251 E. Loozen, *'Mededingingstoezicht op maatschappen van zorgaanbieders: welke rol is weggelegd voor ACM respectievelijk NZa?'* ('Competition regulation of healthcare provider partnerships: what roles do the ACM and NZa play?') (2013) *Tijdschrift voor Gezondheidsrecht*, 7(37), 622.

252 S. van der Heul, *'Wetsvoorstel voor overheveling zorgspecifieke fusietoets en het toezicht op Aanmerkelijke Marktmacht in de zorg'* ('Legislative proposal for transferring the 'healthcare-specific' merger test and SMP oversight in healthcare'), 18.04.2016, <https://www.dirkzwager.nl/kennis/artikelen/wetsvoorstel-voor-overheveling-zorgspecifieke-fusietoets-en-het-toezicht-op-aanmerkelijke-marktmacht-in-de-zorg/> accessed 24.06.2018.

253 For example, scope for price-fixing within the NHS may be limited by the existence of the National Tariff. See Monitor, 'Choice and competition: hypothetical scenarios for NHS healthcare providers', 12.09.2014, Scenario 3, 'price-fixing'.

254 See CMA, above n. 110, CMA, 'Guidance – Private medical practitioners: information about fees', 03.12.2015. Also Monitor, 'The application of the Competition Act 1998 in the healthcare sector', 12.09.2014.

competition law may be infringed, for instance, where collaborating to share commercially sensitive information (unless this meets the tests for exemptions), and where it may not, when providers share knowledge around clinical practice and make referrals based on objective reasons/clinical need.[255]

Points of divergence emerge in the guidance on particular types of behaviour emphasised by the two agencies. It might be concluded that the CMA's focus is on pricing issues[256] and the structures within which private providers work (such as Limited Liability Partnerships (LLPs)), whilst NHS Improvement's guidance seems broader in that it references a wider range of possible anticompetitive behaviours. The influence of the CMA's general competition law guidance is clear and logical. A point of similarity between both agencies' guidance, however, lies in what might perceived to be its 'educative' function; that is, making healthcare providers aware of the potential consequences of their conduct,[257] as they may generally be unfamiliar with competition law.

It is to be noted that there are relatively few cases which have involved suspected breaches of the anticompetitive agreements provisions (Chapter I prohibition) in connection with healthcare *provision* in the private healthcare sector (categories 3 and 4). In view of the above discussion of the ongoing uncertainty surrounding the applicability of competition law to the NHS (categories 1 and 2), it is perhaps unsurprising that no cases have emerged. However, NHS Improvement has produced a range of hypothetical scenarios demonstrating how competition law may be relevant to healthcare provision. The four categories are now considered in reverse numerical order in light of cases and guidance regarding anticompetitive agreements.

#### 4.3.1.1. Category 4 – Private Purchasers, Private Providers

With regard to category 4, the CMA recently investigated anticompetitive information exchange and pricing agreements in the private ophthalmology sector.[258] Consultant Eye Surgeons Partnership (CESP) Ltd, a private membership organisation, was determined to be an association of undertakings which had breached both section 2(1) CA98 (the Chapter I prohibition) and Article 101(1) TFEU. It did so by coordinating the commercial conduct of its Limited Liability Partnership (LLP) members in several ways, including acting as a conduit for the exchange of commercially-sensitive information. Having established the breach, the CMA fined CESP Ltd, but this fine was

---

255 Monitor, above n. 254.

256 CMA, above n. 254.

257 Odudu underlines the importance of 'selling' competition law in this way, with a first step being to convince [healthcare providers] '... that they inhabit a market'. O. Odudu, above n. 101.

258 CMA, Case CE/9784-13, above n. 94.

subsequently reduced, as CESP Ltd cooperated with the CMA and adopted a comprehensive competition law compliance programme. This case formed the basis for generalised CMA guidance to private providers – regarding competition law[259] and fees.[260] It is also interesting for its insights into CMA practice in defining healthcare provision markets. Although the CMA acknowledged that it was not necessary for it to define the market in this particular case,[261] it nevertheless considered the potential substitutability of NHS ophthalmology services and whether the market should be defined in general terms, or segmented according to different treatments in connection with determining the appropriate level of fine.[262] The CMA concluded that NHS ophthalmology services were not suitable substitutes in view both of the differences in cost and waiting times and of patient commitment to private medical insurance (PMI) as this would cover most costs.[263] However, it recognised that there may be limited substitutability in respect of PMI and self-funding patients.[264] As regards the scope of the market, the CMA determined that this comprised the general 'privately-funded ophthalmic services',[265] and was regional in terms of geographic definition.[266]

#### 4.3.1.2. Category 3 – Private Purchasers, Public Providers

As regards category 3, the former OFT issued warnings to NHS Foundation Trusts involved in exchanging commercially-sensitive information about their PPUs. The OFT subsequently accepted commitments by the NHS Foundation Trusts to desist from the offending activity.[267] Whilst this may amount to a 'light touch' approach, it is appropriate for a market in transition; that is, NHS providers developing their operations within the private healthcare market, which may expand since section 165 HSCA 2012 also removed the private income cap to which NHS Foundation Trusts were subject. However, whilst additional scrutiny of PPUs has been deemed necessary in the context of merger control (discussed in Chapter 4 below), it is unclear what any future approach by the CMA may be in this regard.

---

259 CMA, 'Guidance: Competition Law for Private Medical Practitioners: Cans, Can'ts, and Maybes', 03.12.2015. CMA, 'Guidance: Private Medical Practitioners: Guidance on Competition Law', 03.12.2015.
260 CMA, above n. 254.
261 CMA, Case CE/9784-13, above n. 94, para. 3.39.
262 Ibid, para. 3.41.
263 Ibid, para. 3.43.
264 Ibid, para. 3.43.
265 Ibid, para. 3.45.
266 Ibid, para. 3.48.
267 See OFT, above n. 93.

#### 4.3.1.3. Category 2 (Public Purchaser, Private Provider) and Category 1 (Public Purchaser, Public Provider)

As noted above, the scope for cases applying the anticompetitive agreements provisions of general competition law may be limited in respect of categories 1 and 2. However, NHS Improvement's guidance to NHS providers with regard to the application of the CA 98 in the healthcare sector[268] is complemented by its guidance in respect of the Competition Oversight licence condition[269] and a range of hypothetical scenarios,[270] which do not distinguish between categories 1 and 2. Whilst the general guidance inevitably draws heavily on, and directs providers to, the CMA's general guidance on competition law, the hypothetical scenarios make concessions to what might be described as 'NHS-specific' characteristics.

Thus we see that the national tariff for many procedures constrains the scope for price-fixing in connection with NHS provision, which is free to patients with the cost being paid by commissioners.[271] However, this may still occur where community service providers agree not to go below a certain price level in their negotiations with CCGs regarding non-tariff services.[272] Concerns about market-sharing are expressed in relation to areas (involving referrals to a designated clinic for an agreed postcode) and to procedures (where CEOs of NHS Trusts may agree to concentrate on different procedures).[273] Other examples of anticompetitive agreements include those denying competitors access to necessary inputs (such as adequate supplies of input or outsourced services or sufficient volumes of patient referrals),[274] those exchanging information that places competitors who do not participate in the exchange at a significant competitive disadvantage, those limiting competitors' ability to participate in tenders (such as sub-contracting agreements which might prevent the sub-contractor from bidding for future contracts with commissioners), and those with commissioners that enable them to influence strategic aspects of tenders such as service specifications, bundling of services and timing.[275]

Perhaps of most relevance to the NHS, in view of the significant focus of competition *for*, rather than *in* the market, is the elaboration of concerns

---

268 Monitor, above n. 254.
269 Monitor, 'Choice and competition licence conditions: guidance for providers of NHS-funded services', 12.09.2014.
270 Monitor, above n. 253.
271 Ibid, Scenario 3, 'price-fixing'.
272 Ibid.
273 Ibid, Scenarios 1 'market-sharing by area' and 2 'market-sharing by procedure'.
274 Ibid, Scenario 5 'agreement preventing referrals'.
275 Ibid.

about bid-rigging, which is expressed in terms of a scenario involving selective participation in tenders:

> You are the finance director of trust X. Commissioners from your region and neighbouring regions are planning to tender for various healthcare services over the next 2 years. You agree with the finance directors of trusts Y and Z in neighbouring regions B and C not to bid for tenders outside your current region: you will only bid for tenders in region A, Y will only bid for the tenders in region B, and Z for tenders in region C.[276]

As with the other scenarios listed, this is analysed in terms of effects on patients, possible benefits to the agreement, and conduct which is unlikely to raise concerns. In terms of the effects on patients, the concern is that selective participation in tenders reduces the range of providers which commissioners can choose from, so they may not be able to choose the most capable provider offering the best value for money.[277] On the provider side, the concern is that NHS trusts will have a reduced incentive to develop the most attractive offer (the best quality service for the best value for money) to maximise their chances of winning the tender.[278]

In addition to the foregoing hypothetical scenarios in respect of secondary care providers, NHS Improvement has also outlined scenarios – apparently based on real queries – for GPs working together[279] as part of its wider work on GP services.[280] The five scenarios cover a range of aspects, from bidding together for contracts, commissioners favouring GP arrangements, arrangements containing terms that prevent members from competing, excluding some providers from an arrangement, and arrangements between GPs and hospitals.[281]

As with cooperation between secondary care providers, NHS Improvement recognises that there are good reasons why GPs may wish to work together: to improve quality, to increase the scope of services provided to patients, and to enable services to be delivered more efficiently.[282] However, a further motivation for providing detailed guidance to GPs presumably stems from the introduction of the NHS Five Year Forward View setting out new models of care which involve increased cooperation between different GP practices, and between GP practices and other providers (such as hospitals).[283]

---

276 Ibid, Scenario 4 'selective participation in tenders'.
277 Ibid, para. 4.2.
278 Ibid, para. 4.2.
279 Monitor, above n. 97.
280 Monitor, 'Improving GP services: commissioners and patient choice', 01.06.2015.
281 Monitor, above n. 97.
282 Ibid, Section 1, Introduction.
283 Ibid.

NHS Improvement's guidance also sets out criteria for assessing exceptions from the anticompetitive agreements provisions. These typically comprise a need for providers (NHS trusts, consultants and community-based providers) to demonstrate possible benefits of anticompetitive agreements in terms of, for example, the nature of the benefits, whether these could have been achieved without restricting choice and competition, and the benefits being passed on to patients.[284] This is in keeping with NHS Improvement's duty under section 62(3) HSCA 2012 to balance anticompetitive conduct with patient interests. A strict interpretation of the concept of patient interests has been deemed necessary to ensure compliance with EU competition law.[285] However, it is difficult to see why this may be problematic in view of the apparently exceedingly limited scope for applying general competition law to the English NHS (categories 1 and 2).

### 4.3.2. *Application of the Abuse of Dominance Provisions*

In contrast to the guidance surrounding the anticompetitive agreements provisions, the information provided by both the CMA (regarding categories 3 and 4) and NHS Improvement (regarding categories 1 and 2) is less detailed. For example, CMA guidance merely refers providers to its generic guides,[286] which may lead to the inference that it attaches less importance to the effects of abuse of dominance within the private healthcare sector in view of its relative size compared to the NHS. In contrast, NHS Improvement sets out the factors it would consider in the analysis of the following scenario:[287]

> You are a manager at Hospital A, which is the major hospital in a local area. You agree to provide ultrasound diagnostic services (UDS) for a consortium of GP surgeries in the local area, provided that the surgeries refer at least 85% of all their patients requiring UDS to you. Hospital A is one of 5 providers of UDS in the area. It currently provides the majority of UDS in the area and benefits from an established reputation. Other local providers are relatively small and community based.

With regard to the exclusive purchasing obligation in this scenario, NHS Improvement clarifies that this limits choice of provider for patients which in turn may precipitate (other) provider exit, reduce provider incentives to introduce new services or enhance existing services, or deter (other) provider entry.[288] NHS Improvement further clarifies that the approaches it would take in respect of this scenario differ according to the Competition Oversight licence condition

---

284 Monitor, above n. 253, paras. 2.4, 3.3, 4.3 and 5.3.

285 On this point, see A. Sánchez Graells, above n. 21 and n. 169.

286 CMA, above n. 259.

287 Monitor, above n. 253, Section 6.1, Scenario 6.

288 Ibid, Section 6.2 Effects on patients.

and competition law. Thus, whereas NHS Improvement may take account of a range of benefits in connection with the licence condition, it is restricted to seeking an objective justification for the conduct for this to be permitted under competition law (for example, by Hospital A arguing that a minimum volume of referrals is needed to justify substantial investment in additional capacity or new technology to improve service quality for patients).[289]

It might be inferred from the foregoing that any focus of the abuse of dominance provisions would be on category 1 (in view of the foregoing example effectively referencing CCGs and a 'major' hospital presumably being an NHS Foundation Trust), and category 2 (on the grounds that private providers delivering services for the NHS may have a greater motivation to instigate a claim). If this analysis holds, then it remains to be seen what sort of enforcement action would follow. However, whether and how this offers insights into scenarios involving providers such as those outlined above is less clear. Elements which would benefit from further clarity include the question of who would bear any financial penalty (as passing this on to taxpayers in the form of reduced services seems difficult to justify).

The foregoing suggests that the complexities surrounding abuse of dominance are very much country- or system-specific, although some, such as problems of market definition, may be common to both England and the Netherlands.

## 5. CONCLUSIONS

This chapter has considered the applicability and application of general competition law to Dutch and English healthcare by reference to the EU competition law framework of the 'undertaking' concept and emerging national frameworks, as well as cases and guidance from both countries which give a picture of practice thus far.

The expansive definition of an 'undertaking' would appear to suggest that a wide range of healthcare provision may be subject to competition law. However, it is evident from enforcement activity in both countries that this potentially wide scope of *applicability* is not translating directly into actual *application*. There may, of course, be several reasons for this, some of which relate to the existence of the new healthcare regulators and their roles vis-à-vis the competition authorities, and these are explored further in Chapter 3 below.

The idea that the application of competition law to healthcare *provision* is likely to – and indeed should – only be appropriate in a small number of instances is uncontroversial in light of the view that there are only 'average conditions' for effective competition in hospital care and primary care, whereas

289 Ibid, Section 6.3.

'good conditions' exist for activities ancillary to healthcare provision, such as pharmacy distribution and patient transportation.[290] This is borne out by the CMA examining more (albeit still few) cases involving pharmaceutical and medical device providers than cases involving healthcare providers as such. What emerges from the foregoing analysis in this chapter, however, is that the approach of competition authorities in both countries is still developing.

Thus, for example, guidance may be informed by individual cases – such as the Dutch GPs' Association (*LHV*) case in the Netherlands and the private ophthalmology case in England – but the extent to which this can be generalised to other healthcare providers is unclear. Insofar as this may be possible with the CMA's guidance to private medical practitioners (presumably on the basis that other private providers work in similar business structures to ophthalmologists), this can perhaps be explained by the unique nature of the private healthcare market in the UK as being closer to a 'standard' market and an exception to healthcare markets elsewhere, which need to address complex interactions in order to ensure universal access. This can be demonstrated by requirements in the Netherlands for GPs to belong to specific structures in order to engage with health insurers, and thus give effect to the mandatory private health insurance scheme intended to enable universal access.

Furthermore, guidance by NHS Improvement appears to suggest that anticompetitive behaviour within the NHS quasi-market would mirror that in other, more standard markets, but in some instances may be constrained by the nature of the NHS (for example, price-fixing may be more difficult due to the existence of the National Tariff). Nevertheless, whilst it may be possible to illustrate how anticompetitive behaviour is manifest in connection with the NHS, the legal framework as determined by the 'undertaking' and SGEI concepts makes enforcement difficult. Indeed, this may be further complicated, rather than facilitated, by enforcement options emerging from the NHS Provider Licence and 2013 Regulations. The interaction between the three is examined in Chapter 3 below. However, it is noted here that, at the time of writing, no action appears to have been taken against a provider in respect of the Competition Oversight aspect of the Choice and Competition Licence Condition.[291] The absence of cases brought under Regulation 10 can be

---

290 European Commission Expert Panel on Effective Ways of Investing in Health (EXPH), 'Competition among health care providers in the European Union – Investigating Policy Options', 17.02.2015, p. 72.

291 Where licences are revoked and reasons given publicly, these refer to providers ceasing to exist as a result of acquisitions, providers ceasing to provide NHS services, providers no longer being registered with the Care Quality Commission or providers applying to have their licences revoked pursuant to section 89(a) HSCA 2012. See NHS Improvement, 'NHS Foundation Trust Directory – Related Documents', <https://improvement.nhs.uk/resources/nhs-foundation-trust-directory-and-register-licensed-healthcare-providers/> accessed 24.06.2018.

explained by NHS Improvement's sole competence to invoke the provision,[292] and its previous clarification that, where a commissioner's behaviour is in patients' interests, it will not be inconsistent with the prohibition on anti-competitive behaviour of Regulation 10.[293]

Finally, the considerations of this chapter raise questions about the underlying intention of governments in encouraging the application of competition law to healthcare sectors and whether misunderstandings may emerge. It might be possible at this stage to suggest that the application of competition law may affect particular structures within healthcare. This is demonstrated by the experience of cases involving professional associations in the Netherlands and England, so it might be inferred that competition law will shape the 'edges' of healthcare provision, rather than go directly to the heart of the doctor–patient relationship,[294] thus reinforcing the point that it is possible for the concept of 'patient choice' to operate independently of competition.[295] It is therefore interesting to note that a significant consideration in both countries is 'patients' interests', and that these may outweigh negative effects on competition. This is evident as a balancing mechanism in connection with, inter alia, the 2013 Regulations in England,[296] as well as emerging in recent ACM guidance regarding primary care providers.[297]

---

292 In contrast to the other Regulations, which may be triggered by NHS Improvement receiving complaints. See Monitor, above n. 147, p. 6.

293 Ibid, pp. 61–64. Consistency with Regulation 10 includes assessing the effect on competition (including factors such as the number of providers affected by a commissioner's conduct and the expected duration of the conduct) and assessing benefits, which may be clinical or non-clinical. These are defined respectively, inter alia, as improvements leading to better patient outcomes and improvements resulting in a better patient experience. Parallels have been drawn between these 'benefits' and the Article 101(3) TFEU exception. See A. Sánchez Graells, above n. 21.

294 Sauter has noted that the effect of competition decisions on patients as ultimate consumers has not received much attention at EU level. W. Sauter, above n. 11.

295 The EXPH is unequivocal on this point. EXPH, above n. 290, p. 4.

296 Also established in NHS Improvement's general duties under the HSCA 2012. For a critical view, see A. Sánchez Graells, above n. 169.

297 ACM, above n. 223.

# CHAPTER 3

# SECTORAL REGULATION

## The Relationship between the Competition Authority and the Healthcare Regulator in the Netherlands and England

## 1. INTRODUCTION

The development of competition in the Dutch and English healthcare systems has been accompanied by the establishment of sectoral[1] regulators for healthcare: the *Nederlandse Zorgautoriteit* (Dutch Healthcare Authority (NZa)) by the *Wet marktordening gezondheidszorg* (Dutch Healthcare (Market Regulation) Act 2006 (Wmg)) and NHS Improvement by the Health and Social Care Act 2012 (HSCA 2012), respectively. Both the Wmg and the HSCA 2012 make provision for the NZa and NHS Improvement to work with, respectively, the *Autoriteit Consument en Markt* (Authority for Consumers and Markets (ACM)) and the Competition and Markets Authority (CMA) in the context of implementing competition policy. It is to be noted that, in discussing

[1] The term 'sectoral regulator' is used in preference to 'economic regulator' in this book to underscore the ambiguity of the regulator's role vis-à-vis competition law, and because competition powers may represent merely one of the regulator's functions. In connection with the NZa, commentary has mentioned its 'competition functions' and included it in wider discussions of 'sector-specific regulation'. See, for example, W. Sauter, '*Sectorspecifiek mededingingsrecht en fusietoetsing*' ('Sector-specific competition law and merger control') (2013) *RegelMaat*, (28)2, 77, and E.M.H. Loozen, '*Inrichting van meervoudig toezicht op marktwerking*' ('Introduction of multisector regulation of competition'), (2013) *RegelMaat*, (28)2, 10. In England, Monitor's original conception as independent regulator of NHS Foundation Trusts led to it being described as closer to an economic regulator. See T. Prosser, 'Monitor, the Independent Regulator of NHS Foundation Trusts' in T. Prosser, *The Regulatory Enterprise: Government, Regulation, and Legitimacy*, Oxford University Press, Oxford 2010, pp. 136–52. However, as part of the NHS Future Forum's recommendations to refocus competition within the NHS, it proposed that Monitor's initial designation as 'economic regulator' be dropped in favour of 'sector regulator for health'. See NHS Future Forum, *Choice and Competition – Delivering Real Choice. A report from the NHS Future Forum*, London, June 2011, p. 9. No reference to 'economic regulation' is made in connection with NHS Improvement's functions. See NHS Improvement, 'Who We Are', <https://improvement.nhs.uk/about-us/who-we-are/> accessed 24.06.2018.

the evolution of this relationship in the context of the English reforms, it is necessary to be aware of the change in name from Monitor to NHS Improvement. Thus, developments in the course of the enactment of the HSCA 2012 and immediately subsequent to this will refer to Monitor and the NHS Trust Development Authority (NHS TDA) to reflect the agencies in operation during that period, whilst more general references – for example to the legal framework which is still in force – specify NHS Improvement, which has been operational since April 2016 (and incorporates the functions of both of these agencies).

The primary focus of this chapter is the particular[2] relationship between the competition authority and sectoral regulator regarding the application of competition law.[3] This relationship has been outlined by the Wmg and HSCA 2012, but how it can, or should, operate in practical terms is less obvious. Certainly it is less clear-cut than the relationship between the two agencies in respect of merger control,[4] where tensions may arise primarily from the two agencies reaching different conclusions – from different tests – about whether a merger should be approved.

Another factor which makes this relationship worthy of consideration is the benefit of national comparisons in view of the relative novelty of sectoral (economic) regulation in healthcare – the NZa being established in 2006 and Monitor's (now NHS Improvement's) designation as 'sectoral' (as opposed to 'economic')[5] regulator dating from 2012 – amid wider change within competition policy: both the ACM and CMA are relatively new agencies, having been established in 2013 and 2014, respectively. However, whilst the establishment of the ACM and CMA marks a significant change in institutional architecture relative to their predecessors,[6] this is not necessarily material in their treatment of healthcare cases. A further consideration is the distinction

---

2 The relationship between the competition authority and sectoral regulator in the context of merger control is discussed in Chapter 4 below, but is included in this chapter for comparison at various points.

3 This has also been considered with regard to other sectors. See, for example, C. Graham, 'UK: The Concurrent Enforcement by Regulators of Competition Law and Sector-Specific Regulation' (2016) 7(6) *Journal of European Competition Law & Practice* 407. M.M. Dabbah, 'The Relationship between Competition Authorities and Sector Regulators' (2011) 70(1) *Cambridge Law Journal* 113.

4 Both the Wmg and HSCA 2012 essentially allow for the competition authority to have exclusive competence in approving or blocking a merger, and an advisory function for the regulator. This is discussed in detail in Chapter 4 on merger control.

5 As noted in Chapter 1, this was one of the changes instituted by the NHS Future Forum.

6 The ACM comprises the former *Nederlandse Mededingingsautoriteit* (Dutch Competition Authority (NMa)), *Onafhankelijke Post en Telecommunicatie Autoriteit* (independent post and telecoms regulator (OPTA)) and *Consumentenautoriteit* (Consumer Authority (CA)). The CMA comprises the former Office of Fair Trading (OFT) and Competition Commission (CC).

between healthcare and other sectors, as the experience of these has shaped the development of the NZa and NHS Improvement.[7]

In the Netherlands, the NZa had powers between 2006 and approximately 2015 to conduct Significant Market Power (SMP) investigations and to intervene in the drafting of agreements/contracts (under Articles 48 and 45 Wmg, respectively). These represented 'separate' powers intended to complement the ACM's powers to apply the provisions governing abuse of dominance and anticompetitive agreements, respectively. Collectively,[8] they comprised a 'sector-specific' competition regime operating in parallel with general competition law, with all the benefits and trappings this might entail.[9] Of these two powers, recent consolidation of the ACM's armoury vis-à-vis competition in healthcare saw only the SMP competence being transferred from the NZa to the ACM. Proposals to enshrine this transfer in legislation have not proceeded beyond the Second Chamber. Furthermore, following the general election in April 2017, these proposals were deemed 'controversial',[10] meaning that their progress would be determined following the constitution of a new government. During 2018 there have been further discussions and questions raised inter alia by members of the *Socialistische Partij* (Socialist Party (SP)) and *GroenLinks-Fractie* (Green-Left Group) about the proposed refocusing of the ACM's competence

[7] With regard to the English experience, it has been considered that using utility regulation as an analytical lens offers greater value in identifying issues to be resolved rather than offering an appropriate model for healthcare regulation. See L. Stirton, 'Back to the Future? Lessons on the Pro-Competitive Regulation of Health Services' (2014) 22(2) *Medical Law Review* 180.

[8] Together with the NZa's powers within merger control, discussed in Chapter 4 below.

[9] For discussions on this point, see W. Sauter, 'Experiences from the Netherlands: The Application of Competition Rules in Health Care' in J. van de Gronden, E. Szyszczak, U. Neergaard and M. Krajewski (eds.), *Health Care and EU Law*, TMC Asser Press, The Hague 2011, pp. 337–58. W. Sauter, 'The balance between competition law and regulation in Dutch healthcare markets' (2014) *TILEC Discussion Paper*, DP 2014-041. E.M.H. Loozen, *'NMa en NZa: houd je bij je leest! Een analyse van de mededingingsbevoegdheden van beide toezichthouders aan de hand van het Samenwerkingsprotocol NMa-NZa 2010'* ('NMa and NZa, stick to what you're good at! An analysis of the competition powers of both agencies in light of the NMa–NZa Cooperation Protocol 2010') (2011) *Tijdschrift voor Toezicht*, 4, 25. E.M.H. Loozen, 'Public healthcare interests require strict competition enforcement' (2015) 119(7) *Health Policy* 882. M. Wiggers, *De NMa en de NZa in de curatieve zorgsector – Een toetsing aan het Europees mededingingsrecht* (The NMa and the NZa in the curative healthcare sector – an assessment against EU competition law) Kluwer, Deventer 2013.

[10] *Kamerstukken II, 2016–17, 34 707 Verdere behandeling van aanhangige stukken, 1 – Lijst van controversiële onderwerpen. L Volksgezondheid, Welzijn en Sport. 3. 34 445 Wijziging van de Wet marktordening gezondheidszorg en enkele andere wetten in verband met aanpassingen van de tarief- en prestatieregulering en het markttoezicht op het terrein van de gezondheidszorg.* (Second Chamber documentation, Parliamentary Session 2016–17, 34 707 Further debate of pending legislative proposals, 1 – List of controversial business. L. Ministry of Health, Wellbeing and Sport. 3. 34 445 Amendments to the Wmg and other laws to apply tariff regulation and market regulation in healthcare).

regarding healthcare.[11] A plenary debate of the legislative proposal has been scheduled in the Tweede Kamer (Second Chamber) for 3 September 2018.[12]

Whilst the transfer of the SMP competence appears to define the 'separate powers' model as a phase in the development of competition in Dutch healthcare, what appears to remain is a tension found elsewhere, namely, for the ACM to decide between ex ante and ex post intervention with regard to issues of dominance. However, the ACM is due to publish guidance on how it will use SMP when the aforementioned legislative proposal takes effect.[13]

In England, NHS Improvement and the CMA share 'concurrent' powers – also described (more accurately)[14] as 'co-competence'[15] and 'parallel jurisdiction'[16] – to apply the general provisions.[17] This is consistent with the experience of other UK sectoral regulators. As noted in Chapter 2 above, NHS Improvement also has 'separate' competition-related powers independent of the CMA's general competition law competence. These comprise the Competition Oversight condition of the NHS Provider Licence[18] and the National Health

---

11 *Kamerstukken II, 2017–18, 34 445, 12 – Wijziging van de Wet marktordening gezondheidszorg en enkele andere wetten in verband met aanpassingen van de tarief- en prestatieregulering en het markttoezicht op het terrein van de gezondheidszorg. Nr. 12 Tweede Nader Verslag. 01.08.2018* (Second Chamber documentation, Parliamentary Session 2017–18, 34 445, 12 – Amendments to the Wmg and other laws to apply tariff regulation and market regulation in healthcare, Document No. 12 Second Additional Report. 01.08.2018).

12 *Tweede Kamer der Staten-Generaal* (Second Chamber of the States-General), '*Wetsvoorstel – Aanpassingen tarief- en prestatieregulering en markttoezicht op het terrein van de gezondheidszorg*' ('Legislative Proposal – Amendments to Tariff and Market Regulation in Healthcare'), <https://www.tweedekamer.nl/kamerstukken/wetsvoorstellen/detail?cfg=wetsvoorsteldetails&qry=wetsvoorstel%3A34445#activity-2018a02393> accessed 26.08.2018.

13 *Kamerstukken II, 2017–18, 34 445, 10 – Wijziging van de Wet marktordening gezondheidszorg en enkele andere wetten in verband met aanpassingen van de tarief- en prestatieregulering en het markttoezicht op het terrein van de gezondheidszorg. Nr. 10 Nota naar aanleiding van het nader verslag. 04.05.2018* (Second Chamber documentation, Parliamentary Session 2017–18, 34 445, 10 – Amendments to the Wmg and other laws to apply tariff regulation and market regulation in healthcare, Document No. 10 Memorandum following the additional report. 04.05.2018), p. 22.

14 'Concurrent' in its ordinary meaning of 'occurring at the same time' (Oxford English Dictionary) suggests a 'separate powers' approach as outlined in this chapter.

15 As described by A. Sánchez Graells, 'Monitor and the Competition and Markets Authority', (2014) *University of Leicester School of Law Research Paper*, No. 14–32.

16 As described by N. Dunne, 'Recasting Competition Concurrency under the Enterprise and Regulatory Reform Act 2013' (2014) 77(2) *Modern Law Review* 254.

17 Section 72 HSCA 2012. Similar provision is made by section 73 HSCA 2012 for NHS Improvement and the CMA to share concurrent powers in respect of market investigations, although these are governed by Part 4, Enterprise Act 2002 (EA02), not the Competition Act 1998 (CA98). Concurrent powers in respect of market investigations are largely beyond the scope of this chapter as these cannot be compared for the purposes of the present discussion in a meaningful way with market assessments in the Netherlands.

18 Section 96 HSCA 2012 sets limits on NHS Improvement's (formerly Monitor's) functions to set or modify licence conditions. Under section 96(2)(b) HSCA 2012, NHS Improvement (formerly Monitor) may exercise its duty to determine the standard licence conditions to be included in each licence, exercise its powers to include or modify a special condition in

Service (Procurement, Patient Choice and Competition) (No. 2) Regulations 2013[19] ('the 2013 Regulations'). At first glance, these might be considered complementary insofar as, as noted in Chapter 2, they borrow the terminology of general competition law and operate in a space where the extent of its applicability remains unclear.

It is notable that the impact (actual in the Netherlands and potential in England) of these statutory relationships between the competition authority and regulator regarding the application of competition law and pursuit of cases has already been highlighted as a matter of concern.[20]

A solution proposed in both countries[21] has been to transfer the regulator's competition powers to the competition authority. This appears to reflect in part Littlechild's conception of UK economic regulation as merely 'holding the fort' pending the arrival of competition,[22] although the experience of other regulated sectors in the UK suggests that regulation has taken on a more permanent character. Interestingly, this solution also finds expression in the Netherlands in connection with the design of the NZa in comments by Edith Schippers before becoming Minister for Health, Wellbeing and Sport: 'we can well imagine that the NZa will ultimately become a Healthcare team within the NMa, but we are not at that stage yet', as well as the *Raad van State* (Dutch Council of State) taking the view that competition regulation belonged with the ACM.[23] Indeed, this solution has taken effect in practical terms in the Netherlands with the transfer of SMP investigations[24] to the ACM,

---

a licence or exercise the power to modify the standard conditions applicable to all licences 'for the purpose of preventing anti-competitive behaviour in the provision of health care services for those purposes which is against the interests of people who use such services.' This has been described as 'expressly confirm[ing] the power to impose obligations on healthcare service providers to comply with competition law obligations' by O. Odudu, 'Competition law and the welfare state' in J. Galloway (ed.), *Intersections of Antitrust: Policy and Regulations*, Oxford University Press, Oxford (forthcoming), at fn. 48, <https://papers.ssrn.com/sol3/papers.cfm?abstract_id=3160784> accessed 10.05.2018.

19 National Health Service (Procurement, Patient Choice and Competition) (No. 2) Regulations 2013, SI 2013/500.

20 On this point with regard to the Netherlands, see in particular E.M.H. Loozen and M. Wiggers, both above n. 9. With regard to England, see A. Sánchez Graells above n. 15, and A. Sánchez Graells, 'New rules for health care procurement in the UK: a critical assessment from the perspective of EU economic law' (2015) 1 *Public Procurement Law Review* 16.

21 Championed in the Netherlands, inter alia, by M. Wiggers, above n. 9; and in England by A. Sánchez Graells, above n. 15.

22 S. Littlechild, *Regulation of British Telecommunications' Profitability*, Department of Trade and Industry, London 1984, para. 4.11.

23 As discussed by S. van der Heul and F. Cornelissen, *'Markttoezicht in de gezondheidszorg na wijziging Wmg'* ('Market regulation in healthcare after Wmg amendments') (2016) *Markt & Mededinging*, 5, 175.

24 The NZa's 'healthcare-specific' merger assessment powers have also been transferred, but this is discussed in Chapter 4 below.

prompted by formal reviews in 2014 of the NZa's role.[25] It has been suggested that the formal transfer will take place in 2018.[26]

Nevertheless, this apparently common solution – of transferring the regulator's competition powers to the competition authority – is unexpected in view of the obvious differences between both countries, not only regarding consensus about the extent of the *applicability* of competition law and the distinctions between the insurance-based and taxation-funded healthcare system models, which affect the feasibility of competition in healthcare, but also regarding the different implications of 'separate' and 'concurrent' powers models.

It is against the backdrop of such issues that this chapter unfolds. Section 2 sets out the relationship between the ACM and NZa in the Netherlands in operation between 2006 and 2015 and elucidates this in terms of a 'separate powers' model. Section 3 sets out the relationship between the CMA and NHS Improvement in England since 2014 in terms of a 'concurrent powers' model, which operates alongside a variant 'separate powers' model comprising the 'NHS-specific' competition regime of the NHS Provider Licence and the 2013 Regulations. Section 4 considers two factors which influence the relationship between the competition authority and sectoral regulator in both countries, namely the regulators' focus on patients and the evolving role of government oversight.[27] Section 5 draws conclusions concerning the predominance in practice of the 'separate powers' model.

## 2. DEFINING THE RELATIONSHIP BETWEEN THE COMPETITION AUTHORITY AND SECTORAL REGULATOR IN DUTCH HEALTHCARE – A SEPARATE POWERS MODEL

The Dutch separate powers model in operation between 2006 and 2015 was established by the Wmg and further elaborated through a series of *Samenwerkingsprotocollen* (Cooperation Protocols) between the ACM and

[25] E. Schippers, *'Kwaliteit loont'* ('Quality Pays'), Letter from the Minister for Health, Wellbeing and Sport to the Chairman of the Second Chamber, 06.02.2015.

[26] As discussed by law firms, for example, Maverick Law, *'Druk NZa en ACM bij Zorg en Farma neemt toe'* ('Increasing pressure on the NZa and ACM in healthcare and pharma'), 05.03.2018, <https://www.maverick-law.com/nl/blogs/druk-nza-en-acm-bij-zorg-en-farma-neemt-toe.html> accessed 24.06.2018.

[27] These are also explored in M. Guy, 'Competition and sectoral regulation in Dutch and English healthcare: factors shaping the competition focus of the new healthcare regulators and their relationship with the competition authorities' (2017) 2 *Ius Publicum* ISSN 2039 2540, <http://www.ius-publicum.com/pagina.php?lang=en&pag=fascicolo> accessed 24.06.2018.

the NZa in 2006, 2010 and 2015.[28] The Cooperation Protocols deal with the relationship between the ACM's general competition law powers and the NZa's SMP and contract powers under Articles 48 and 45 Wmg, respectively.

It is recognised that the NZa's powers, although ex ante in nature, may intersect with the ACM's ex post powers regarding anticompetitive agreements[29] and abuse of dominance[30] under the Dutch Competition Act (Mw).[31] This has been described as *samenloop* (overlap)[32] and is defined in Article 18(2) Wmg as referring specifically to the overlap between SMP and abuse of dominance.[33] Where overlap occurs, parties should address concerns to the NZa first.[34] Furthermore, in instances of such overlap, the NZa's SMP competence was intended to take precedence over the ACM's abuse of dominance power, unless the two agencies agreed that the ACM was better placed to act, or that the two agencies should act together.[35] Consistency was intended to be ensured by the NZa applying the same definitions as the ACM with regard to competition law.[36] Thus SMP is defined by reference to 'dominance',[37] namely the ability of one or more healthcare providers or health insurers to behave independently of its competitors or consumers, whether individually or collectively, and thereby to restrict the development of competition on the Dutch market or a part thereof.

In order to understand the effects these separate powers and overlap might have and why this approach has been criticised,[38] it is first useful to consider the NZa's competition powers under Articles 48 and 45 Wmg.

---

28 These are based primarily on Article 17 Wmg, which requires the NZa to develop protocols with different bodies to ensure effective and efficient decision-making with regard to matters of mutual interest and the collection of information. The 2015 Protocol has extended this legal basis to include Article 5.1.(2)(c) *Wet handhaving consumentenbescherming* (Dutch Consumer Protection (Enforcement) Act (Whc)), which requires the ACM to develop protocols with different bodies and reflects the ACM's extended remit compared to that of the former Dutch competition authority (NMa).

29 Article 6 *Mededingingswet* (Dutch Competition Act (Mw)) (also known as the 'cartel prohibition' in Dutch literature).

30 Article 24 Mw.

31 There is further scope for intersection with the ACM's powers regarding commitment decisions under Article 49 Mw.

32 For clarification of why '*samenloop*' has been translated as 'overlap' in this book, see the Preface.

33 The concept of overlap is defined in different ways in connection with Dutch criminal and administrative law. For a consideration of these by reference to the Wmg definition, see E.M.H. Loozen (2011), above n. 9.

34 Article 18(1) Wmg.

35 Articles 18(3) and (5) Wmg respectively.

36 Article 18(4) Wmg.

37 Article 47 Wmg.

38 See in particular E.M.H. Loozen (2011) and (2015), both above n. 9.

## 2.1. THE NZA'S COMPETITION POWERS, 2006–15

### *2.1.1. SMP Powers (Article 48 Wmg)*

Article 48 Wmg empowered the NZa to impose obligations (ranging from separating types of service provision to equal treatment of service users)[39] where it assessed that one or more healthcare providers or health insurers holds SMP. SMP is a concept borrowed from the telecommunications sector,[40] but has been considered 'loosely based' on this[41] and may operate differently in healthcare.[42]

The NZa clarified that its SMP competence may interact not only with its other rule-making powers, but also with its general tariff-setting powers. For example, where healthcare providers hold market power and there is insufficient countervailing buyer power, then general tariff-setting should address this (by means of price limits and yardstick competition), rather than widespread use of the SMP tool.[43]

The original design of the SMP power set out in the Wmg and clarified by the NZa appears to have been intended to distinguish clearly between this and the ACM's abuse of dominance powers. For example, whilst both provisions assessed conduct, SMP was intended to do so from a preventive (ex ante) approach, and abuse of dominance from a repressive (ex post) approach.[44] In addition, differences in approach are evident in the NZa's ability to impose obligations in contrast to the ACM's ability to impose fines.[45]

The previous distinction between the ex ante SMP powers of the NZa and the ACM's ex post abuse of dominance powers can be summarised thus:[46]

| Power | Role of ACM | Role of NZa |
|---|---|---|
| **Abuse of dominance/ significant market power (SMP)** | Enforcement of prohibition on abuse of a dominant position (Article 24 Mw). Repressive (*ex post*) assessment of conduct. Possibility of imposing sanctions. | May impose obligations on parties with significant market power (Article 48 Wmg). Preventive (*ex ante*) test of conduct. |

**Figure 4. Overview of the NZa's SMP powers and the ACM's abuse of dominance powers**

39 Article 18(1) (a)–(l) Wmg.

40 For a discussion of the relationship between abuse of dominance and SMP in connection with telecommunications, see M. Harker, 'EU competition law as a tool for dealing with regulatory failure: the broadband margin squeeze cases' [2013] *Journal of Business Law* 817.

41 W. Sauter (2014), above n. 9.

42 Ibid. An example being that the Dutch courts have observed that a different standard for SMP has been applied in healthcare than in the electronic communications sector.

43 NZa, *'Toelichting op de beleidsregel Aanmerkelijke Marktmacht in de Zorg'* ('Explanatory Notes to the Policy Rule Significant Market Power in Healthcare'), September 2010, p. 9.

44 Ibid, p. 11.

45 Ibid, p. 10.

46 Based on table clarifying the different functions of the ACM and NZa more generally. ACM, *Richtsnoeren voor de zorgsector* (Guidelines for the healthcare sector) March 2010, para. 35.

As discussed in Chapter 2 above, the *Menzis v. Van Dalen* case suggested that the distinction between SMP and abuse of dominance was less clear in practice.

The NZa was considered to make little use of its SMP competence, with it being described as a 'remedy of last resort'.[47] Although the NZa received a range of complaints of SMP, it appeared to address these by other means,[48] apparently in contravention of its own policy.[49] Potential SMP cases rejected by the NZa involved issues of buyer power,[50] consistent with the NZa's previous focus on seller power.

Prior to the transfer of the SMP competence to the ACM, the NZa recognised areas for improvement in connection with the econometric tools used to establish SMP and the need for a clearer formulation of obligations regarding vertical relationships, duty to contract and excessive prices.[51]

### *2.1.2. Power to Intervene in the Drafting of Contracts (Article 45 Wmg)*

In essence, under 45 Wmg, the NZa may develop rules regarding the drafting of agreements relating to healthcare or tariffs (or conditions of these agreements). Whilst the potential scope for NZa intervention under Article 45 Wmg is broad, the main use of these powers thus far has been effectively to codify ACM decisions in an Electronic Networks Regulation,[52] which imposes mandatory access to agreements concerning the use of electronic networks to exchange patient and medication data, as discussed in Chapter 2 above. This would appear to suggest a useful distinction between the ACM ex post powers regarding anticompetitive agreements and this ex ante NZa power. However, the NZa has

---

47 W. Sauter (2014), above n. 9.

48 In its 2014 review of the NZa, AEF observed that between 2009 and 2014, 'hundreds' of possible SMP cases were identified via signals, opinions or requests. Many of these were addressed informally, or in the context of other matters. Andersson Elffers Felix *in samenwerking met Radicand Economics and Tilburg Law and Economics Center (TILEC), 'Ordening en Toezicht in de zorg: Evaluatie van de Wet marktordening gezondheidszorg (Wmg) en de Nederlandse Zorgautoriteit (NZa)'* (AEF in cooperation with Radicand Economics and TILEC, 'Oversight and regulation in healthcare: Assessment of the Dutch Healthcare (Market Regulation) Act 2006 (Wmg) and the Dutch Healthcare Authority (NZa)') September 2014, p. 75.

49 See C.C. Meijer, *'Beleidsregel AMM in de zorg – een groeimodel'* ('Policy Rule SMP in Healthcare – a Growth Model') (2007) *Markt en Mededinging*, 8, 219.

50 AEF, above n. 48, p. 79.

51 NZa, Position paper: *'Werking van het zorgstelsel'* ('Operation of the Healthcare System'), April 2015.

52 NZa, *Regeling CI/NR-100.099. REGELING voorwaarden voor overeenkomsten inzake elektronische netwerken met betrekking tot zorg* (Regulation CI/NR-100.099. Regulation on Conditions for Agreements involving Electronic Networks relating to Healthcare). ('NZa Electronic Networks Regulation').

clarified that its power to intervene under Article 45 Wmg is not restricted to general unreasonable contract terms, but is linked with general competition law by a focus on contract terms which restrict or limit competition.[53] Consequently, the Article 45 Wmg powers have been considered a competition power – as well as a regulatory power – for the NZa,[54] and halfway between a competition rule and a regulatory power.[55] Furthermore, Article 45 Wmg may be considered to strengthen both the NZa's ex ante and ACM's ex post roles, with the implication that the threshold for NZa intervention is not lower, but different: it does not target a single restriction to set an example, but seeks to address several less serious restrictions at the same time to resolve the underlying problem in a structural manner.[56] In the current transfer of NZa competition powers to the ACM, it is important to note that the Article 45 Wmg competence remains with the NZa, thus underlining the apparently truly discrete nature of this power.

### *2.1.3. Possible Overlap between NZa and ACM Powers, 2006–15*

The 2006 Cooperation Protocol clarified that overlap may occur with regard to the NMa and NZa producing reports, (informal) opinions, decisions, guidelines/policy rules, consultation and vision documents and regulatory frameworks.[57] This explanation has remained intact in the subsequent Protocols. The 2006, 2010 and 2015 Protocols have also been consistent in following Article 18(3) Wmg with regard to managing overlap, namely, that the NZa may first apply its Wmg powers before the ACM applies its Mw powers.

The substantive scope of overlap was defined in Article 18(2) Wmg specifically by reference to the possible complementarity of the NZa's SMP competence and the ACM's abuse of dominance powers, and was briefly reconceptualised by the 2010 Cooperation Protocol[58] as follows:

---

53 Ibid.

54 J. Bijkerk and W. Sauter, *'Een nieuwe mededingingsbevoegdheid voor de NZa? Artikel 45 Wmg over ingrijpen in de voorwaarden en de wijze van totstandkomen van overeenkomsten met betrekking tot zorg of tarieven'* ('A new competition power for the NZa? Article 45 Wmg and intervention in the conditions and formulation of agreements relating to healthcare or tariffs') (2010) *Markt en Mededinging*, 4, 145.

55 W. Sauter (2014), above n. 9.

56 J. Bijkerk and W. Sauter, above n. 54.

57 Nederlandse Mededingingsautoriteit (NMa), *Protocol tussen de Nederlandse Mededingingsautoriteit en de Nederlandse Zorgautoriteit over de wijze van samenwerking bij aangelegenheden van wederzijds belang* (Protocol signed by the Dutch Competition Authority and the Dutch Healthcare Authority regarding cooperation in matters of mutual interest), October 2006 ('2006 Cooperation Protocol'), Article 6.

58 Nederlandse Mededingingsautoriteit en Nederlandse Zorgautoriteit (NMa/NZa), *Samenwerkingsprotocol NMa–NZa* (NMa–NZa Cooperation Protocol), December 2010, ('2010 Cooperation Protocol').

| NZa power | ACM power | Source |
|---|---|---|
| Article 48 Wmg (SMP) | Article 24 Mw (Abuse of dominance) | Article 18(2) Wmg; Article 7, 2006 Cooperation Protocol, Article 11, 2010 Cooperation Protocol and Article 18, 2015 Cooperation Protocol |
| Article 45 Wmg (contract powers) | Article 6 Mw (Anticompetitive agreements) | Article 13, 2010 Cooperation Protocol |
| Article 48 Wmg (SMP) | Article 6 Mw (Anticompetitive agreements) | Article 12, 2010 Cooperation Protocol |

**Figure 5. Overview of the varying scope of 'overlap', 2006–15**

There are two particularly contentious areas of this wider definition of overlap purporting to link the ACM's competence to apply the anticompetitive agreements provision, not only with the NZa's competence to intervene in contracts (agreements), but also with its SMP competence.[59] Whilst the first pairing appears relatively coherent,[60] although not formally recognised as equivalent,[61] the latter appears to require substantial clarification, which is not forthcoming in the 2010 Cooperation Protocol. However, it has been considered that both provisions may offer protection against market power, and thus satisfy the requirement of wider Dutch administrative law that 'overlapping' powers share a focus, but not the requirement that both powers target the same behaviour.[62]

However, both of these additional purported areas of overlap have been removed from the 2014 Protocol, which reverts to the earlier focus on overlap between SMP and abuse of dominance.[63] Furthermore, the NZa's Article 45 Wmg powers appear to continue to be considered rule-making powers regarding problems that resemble cartels, without actually forming a direct equivalent to anti-cartel powers.[64]

---

59 E.M.H. Loozen (2011), above n. 9, criticises both pairings, using a wider framework of 'overlap' drawn from Dutch criminal and administrative law. Against this framework, two requirements must be fulfilled in order to be able to speak of 'overlap', namely that provisions must target the same conduct or have the same effect.

60 The connection between the anticompetitive agreements provision of Article 6 Mw and NZa contract powers of Article 45 Wmg is considered by J. Bijkerk and W. Sauter, above n. 54.

61 For example, in describing the division of effort between the then NMa and NZa, it was considered that the NZa had no competence regarding the enforcement of the anticompetitive agreements provision. See ACM (2010), above n. 46, p. 13.

62 E.M.H. Loozen (2011), above n. 9.

63 ACM/NZa, *Samenwerkingsprotocol Autoriteit Consument en Markt en Nederlandse Zorgautoriteit* (ACM and NZa Cooperation Protocol), December 2014 ('2014 Cooperation Protocol'), Articles 18 and 19.

64 W. Sauter (2014), above n. 9.

## 2.2. THE SEPARATE POWERS MODEL 2015–18 AND FUTURE DIRECTION

At the time of writing, the separate powers model of regulation and overlap in Dutch healthcare had been undergoing a substantial overhaul with the transfer of the NZa's SMP powers (and role within the healthcare-specific merger test) to the ACM. The transfer is intended to focus the application of competition powers with regard to the healthcare sector.[65] Furthermore, the Minister for Health, Wellbeing and Sport will retain powers to issue policy rules as the 'responsible Minister' (it being noted that the ACM is overseen ultimately by the Minister for Economic Affairs),[66] apparently in keeping with shared regulation in other sectors. However, the proposal that the Minister retains competence to set policy rules in connection with, for example, SMP, has been criticised on the basis that such provision is not made in postal or telecommunications regulatory legislation and that the ACM already has experience of this tool.[67] As noted above, however, whilst the transfer was to be enshrined in legislation, the progress of the legislative proposal has stalled pending decisions about its future progression by the new Coalition Government following the general elections in April 2017, with updates anticipated in the first part of 2018. At the time of writing, it appears that a plenary debate in the *Tweede Kamer* (Second Chamber) and a technical briefing by the Ministry of Health, Wellbeing and Sport were scheduled for 18 and 20 June 2018, respectively.[68]

From the legislative proposal drafted to implement this transfer,[69] it appears that, where possible, NZa powers will still take priority over ACM competition

65 E. Schippers, *Kabinetsreactie rapport commissie Borstlap en evaluatie Wmg en NZa* (Cabinet response to the Borstlap and AEF reports, Letter from the Minister for Health, Wellbeing and Sport to the Chairman of the First Chamber), 02.04.2015.

66 E. Schippers, above n. 25.

67 *Kamerstukken II, 2015–16, 34 445, 4 – Wijziging van de Wet marktordening gezondheidszorg en enkele andere wetten in verband met aanpassingen van de tarief- en prestatieregulering en het markttoezicht op het terrein van de gezondheidszorg. Nr. 4 Advies Afdeling Raad Van State en nader rapport* (Second Chamber documentation, Parliamentary Session 2015–16, 34 445, 4 – Amendments to the Wmg and other laws to apply tariff regulation and market regulation in healthcare, Document No.4, Opinion of the Dutch Council of State (*Raad van State*)), p. 7.

68 *Tweede Kamer der Staten-Generaal* (Second Chamber of the States-General), above n. 12.

69 *Kamerstukken II, 2015–16, 34 445, 2 – Wijziging van de Wet marktordening gezondheidszorg en enkele andere wetten in verband met aanpassingen van de tarief- en prestatieregulering en het markttoezicht op het terrein van de gezondheidszorg. Nr. 2 Voorstel van Wet* (Second Chamber documentation, Parliamentary Session 2015–16, 34 445, 2 – Amendments to the Wmg and other laws to apply tariff regulation and market regulation in healthcare, Document No.2, Legislative Proposal).

law powers.[70] Furthermore, 'overlap' as defined under Article 18 Wmg is redefined to refer to NZa powers under the Wmg relating to implementation of the *Zorgverzekeringswet* (Dutch Health Insurance Act 2006 (Zvw)) or the *Wet langdurige zorg* (Dutch Long-Term Care Act 2015 (Wlz)).[71]

Although the amendments to Article 48 Wmg largely involve substitution of 'ACM' for 'NZa'[72] as might be anticipated, the Explanatory Memorandum elaborates some significant refinements. For example, SMP will be established not by recourse to the market definition principles of general competition law, but by other methods designed for the healthcare sector,[73] such as the Logit Competition Index (LOCI) and Option Demand Method (ODM), tools developed by the NZa and used in its assessment of mergers.

In addition, there are three new obligations which may be imposed under Article 48.[74] First, the ACM may impose a duty to supply on a healthcare provider, whereas currently there is merely a requirement for healthcare providers to enter into contracts with insurers.[75] Second, is a duty on healthcare providers to allow patients to choose another provider. Thus, a GP who refers patients to a specific pharmacy will be obliged to offer patients a choice of pharmacies.[76] Thirdly, the ACM may impose maximum prices, minimum prices or fixed prices on either healthcare providers or health insurers.[77]

Overall, the proposed transfer of the NZa's SMP competence to the ACM appears to signal the end of the separate powers model. However, such a transfer is not as radical as may first appear, having been called for at various intervals in the past. This may suggest that the idea of separate powers vis-à-vis SMP in Dutch healthcare has merely been refocused, as the tension between ex ante SMP intervention and ex post abuse of dominance sanction remains, albeit in the hands of a single agency, the ACM. In the meantime, concerns about the transfer have emerged among practitioners. For example, the

70 Ibid, p. 6, proposed amendments to Article 18(3) Wmg.
71 Ibid, p. 6, proposed amendments to Article 18(2) Wmg.
72 Ibid, p. 8, proposed amendments to Article 48 Wmg.
73 *Kamerstukken II, 2015–16, 34 445, 3 – Wijziging van de Wet marktordening gezondheidszorg en enkele andere wetten in verband met aanpassingen van de tarief- en prestatieregulering en het markttoezicht op het terrein van de gezondheidszorg. Nr. 3 Memorie van Toelichting* (Second Chamber documentation, Parliamentary Session 2015–16, 34 445, 3 – Amendments to the Wmg and other laws to apply tariff regulation and market regulation in healthcare, Document No. 3, Explanatory Memorandum), para. 4.3.1, p. 19. Apparently in response to feasibility and enforceability tests conducted by the ACM. See Letter of 22.05.2015 to the Minister for Health, Wellbeing and Sport from Chris Fonteijn, Chairman of the Board of the ACM, <https://www.eerstekamer.nl/overig/20161107/uitvoerbaarheids_en/meta> accessed 24.06.2018.
74 The first two are clarified in the Explanatory Memorandum, above n. 73, at p. 20.
75 Intended to be a new subsection (f). See Legislative Proposal, above n. 69, at p. 8.
76 Intended to be a new subsection (n). See Legislative Proposal, above n. 69, at p. 9.
77 Intended to be a new subsection (j). See Legislative Proposal, above n. 69, at p. 8.

apparent focusing of the new SMP obligations on healthcare providers appears a questionable step in the face of growing concerns about the consolidation and buyer power of health insurers.[78] In addition, the supplementing of ACM capacity with a Healthcare Task Force comprising 20 full-time staff – effectively to implement the transfer of competence – has also been criticised as being insufficient in light of the view that the Dutch healthcare sector has a turnover of approximately €95 billion, so requires the ACM's full attention.[79] A further concern was that it may be possible to distinguish between the ACM, on the one hand, and the Healthcare Task Force on the other, vis-à-vis management of SMP cases.[80] This would suggest that the ACM's experience of SMP in the post and telecommunications sectors will not serve to shape the further development of SMP in healthcare.[81] Furthermore, the connection between SMP and abuse of dominance may be less helpful than intended, as abuse of dominance has been considered the 'Achilles' heel' of the ACM, which has focused on pursuing anticompetitive agreements cases.[82] Although the Healthcare Task Force has subsequently gained the status of a *Directie* (Directorate) within the ACM,[83] more time may yet be needed to see if these criticisms remain valid – particularly regarding the distinction between SMP and abuse of dominance powers.

## 3. DEFINING THE RELATIONSHIP BETWEEN THE COMPETITION AUTHORITY AND SECTORAL REGULATOR IN ENGLISH HEALTHCARE – CONCURRENT POWERS AND SEPARATE POWERS MODELS?

In contrast to the Netherlands, there appear to be two models of relationship in evidence between the competition authority and sectoral regulator in English healthcare. On the one hand, NHS Improvement was granted concurrent powers with the CMA with regard to applying competition law and conducting market investigations, under sections 72 and 73 HSCA 2012,

---

78 D.W.L.A. Schrijvershof and J.C. Plettenburg, *'Toetsing van zorgfusies en toezicht in de zorg door ACM: hoe nu verder?'* ('Healthcare merger assessment and regulation of healthcare by the ACM: where now?') (2016) *Tijdschrift Mededingingsrecht in de praktijk*, 3, 21. S. van der Heul and F. Cornelissen (2016), above n. 23.

79 D.W.L.A. Schrijvershof and J.C. Plettenburg, ibid.

80 S. van der Heul and F. Cornelissen, above n. 23.

81 Ibid.

82 Ibid.

83 ACM, 'Organogram', <https://www.acm.nl/nl/organisatie/organisatie/organogram> accessed 24.06.2018.

respectively. On the other hand, a separate powers model is in evidence as regards merger control, as only the CMA is competent to approve or block a merger. A separate powers model may also be used to describe the relationship between the two agencies in respect of regulatory rules, since only NHS Improvement is competent to administer the NHS Provider Licence or apply the 2013 Regulations.

In order to understand the concurrent powers shared by NHS Improvement and the CMA in respect of applying competition law, this section considers three aspects which may impact how section 72 HSCA 2012 *may* operate in practice, since these powers have yet to be used,[84] and may indeed never be used.

Firstly, it is useful to recall the position of the competition authority vis-à-vis healthcare prior to the HSCA 2012 and what the legislation purported to change by instituting a concurrent powers model.

Secondly, it is important to consider briefly the reforms of the Enterprise and Regulatory Reform Act 2013 (ERRA 13) and the Competition Act 1998 (Concurrency) Regulations 2014[85] ('the 2014 Concurrency Regulations'), which – as regards NHS Improvement (Monitor) – were also influenced by the experience of enacting the HSCA 2012.

Finally, it is useful to examine NHS Improvement's competition-related powers – primarily its licensing authorisation regime (specifically the Choice and Competition condition of the NHS Provider Licence), but also Regulation 10, governing anticompetitive behaviour, of the 2013 Regulations – in order to assess whether these may impact NHS Improvement's ability to exercise its concurrent powers under section 72 HSCA 2012. In contrast to the relatively clear ex ante/ex post distinction drawn between SMP and abuse of dominance in the Netherlands, this range of interventions available to NHS Improvement suggests that a different classification is needed. Certainly, whilst, in the preamble to its early cases,[86] NHS Improvement (Monitor) explicitly recognised that it may have recourse to any of the 2013 Regulations, licence authorisation or concurrent powers in addressing a complaint, its practice thus far has made use of the 2013 Regulations and not its concurrent powers. It would therefore appear that any conflict between whether NHS Improvement should employ the 2013 Regulations or its concurrent powers would be

---

84 As confirmed by the CMA's Concurrency Reports of 2014, 2015, 2016, 2017 and 2018. CMA, '"Baseline" annual report on concurrency – 2014', 01.04.2014, CMA24. CMA, 'Annual Report on Concurrency 2015', 01.04.2015, CMA43. CMA, 'Annual Report on Concurrency 2016', 28.04.2016, CMA54. CMA, 'Annual Report on Concurrency 2017', 28.04.2017, CMA63. CMA, 'Annual Report on Concurrency 2018', 30.04.2018, CMA79.

85 SI 2014/536.

86 See, inter alia, Monitor, Case CCD 04/13, *Commissioning Cancer Surgery Services in Greater Manchester and Cheshire*; and Monitor, Case CCD 01/13, *Commissioning of radiosurgery services*.

determined – appropriately – by the offending behaviour in question and the *applicability* of competition law in a given case, rather than a specific policy direction.

## 3.1. THE POSITION OF THE COMPETITION AUTHORITY VIS-À-VIS THE HEALTHCARE SECTOR IN ENGLAND PRE-HSCA 2012 AND THE DEVELOPMENT OF CONCURRENT POWERS

Prior to enactment of HSCA 2012, the competition authority's focus was effectively reserved to the private healthcare sector, in an apparent understanding that conduct of NHS entities was exempt by fiat from oversight by the then Office of Fair Trading (OFT).[87] It is uncontroversial to suggest that this fiat encompassed the NHS (categories 1 and 2). This was underscored by the creation of the NHS Co-operation and Competition Panel (NHS CCP) and the NHS-specific competition regime discussed in Chapter 1 above. The situation of category 3 (private purchaser and public provider) appeared less clear. In 2011, the then OFT took limited enforcement action by requiring NHS Foundation Trusts to desist from sharing information about their Private Patient Units (PPUs).[88] This might be construed as the OFT's first intervention with regard to the NHS. However, such an interpretation fails to distinguish between the NHS (categories 1 and 2) on the one hand, and the private healthcare sector (categories 3 and 4) on the other. This particular case clearly concerned the private healthcare sector (category 3),[89] as the NHS Foundation Trusts operate PPUs as private providers, so is entirely consistent with the OFT's focus on the private healthcare sector and practice at that time. It seems obvious to suggest that the lack of competition authority intervention prior to the HSCA 2012 can be attributed to questions of the *applicability* of competition law to the English NHS. Thus, possible intervention in the NHS was circumscribed by the *FENIN* judgment, which prompted the OFT to close its investigations into public-sector activity for several years prior to re-engaging with the theme of opening up public-sector markets.[90]

---

87 As explained by M. Gaynor and R.J. Town, 'Competition in Health Care Markets' in M. Pauly et al. (eds.), *Handbook of Health Economics, Part 2*, Elsevier, North-Holland Elsevier 2012, p. 559.

88 OFT, 'OFT welcomes action by NHS Trusts to ensure compliance with competition law' Press Release, 71/12, 16.08.2012.

89 The OFT clearly included category 3 in its delineation of the private healthcare market. See Office of Fair Trading (OFT), *Private Healthcare Market Study*, OFT1396, p. 13.

90 For a comprehensive discussion of this change in policy, see O. Odudu, 'Why it matters – Selling competition law in the new frontier', *Competition Law Insight*, 10.12.2013.

The question therefore arises of whether (and how) section 72 HSCA 2012 changed this arrangement. Certainly the White Paper[91] preceding the HSCA 2012 was explicit in its intention that the then OFT (now CMA) should have oversight of the NHS by means of concurrent powers shared with Monitor (now NHS Improvement).

Concurrent powers are a feature of the wider UK economic regulation landscape and have recently been subject to revision by ERRA 2013.[92] Importing this style of regulatory relationship into healthcare involves various implications, including the suggestion that this model of regulation is misguided for competition in English healthcare,[93] and is fundamentally problematic in view of the very questionable assumption that a single, unified healthcare sector exists in England. What makes this assumption questionable is primarily the relative lack of clarity regarding the extent of *applicability* of competition law to the NHS and private healthcare sector, respectively, and the ongoing distinction between the two drawn by the CMA despite acknowledging increasing 'linkages'.

This fundamental problem – of the absence of a single healthcare sector, but existence of closely interlinked NHS and private healthcare markets – is compounded by what concurrent powers in healthcare are intended to achieve. The White Paper preceding the HSCA 2012 made a single reference to concurrent powers as explicitly linked to Monitor's duty to promote competition.[94] However, as part of its wider recommendations to remove this duty, the NHS Future Forum reconceptualised concurrent powers as a safeguard against competition being applied disproportionately,[95] and a mechanism to ensure sector-specific expertise[96] – a benefit of this model recognised in connection with other

---

91 Department of Health, *Equity and Excellence: Liberating the NHS*, Cm 7881, July 2010, p. 38.

92 For a comprehensive overview of the reforms, see N. Dunne (2014), above n. 16.

93 Indeed, N. Dunne (2014), above n. 16, has queried the logic of granting powers to Monitor (now NHS Improvement) and the CMA in light of the uncertainty surrounding the applicability of competition law to the English NHS.

94 One of Monitor's roles was defined thus: 'Promoting competition, to ensure that competition works effectively in the interests of patients and taxpayers. Like other sectoral regulators, such as OFCOM and OFGEM, Monitor will have concurrent powers with the Office of Fair Trading to apply competition law to prevent anti-competitive behaviour', Department of Health, above n. 91, p. 38.

95 'We therefore think that the Bill should be clear that Monitor is the sector-specific regulator and takes concurrent powers to the Office of Fair Trading as a safeguard against competition being applied disproportionately': NHS Future Forum, above n. 1, p. 30.

96 Hence its recommendation to 'maintain the provisions to give Monitor concurrent powers with the Office of Fair Trading. Under current rules, any challenge under competition law would be for the OFT to deal with. However, we think that this job would be best done by a dedicated regulator with a greater knowledge of the unique nature of healthcare, including the importance of cooperation through clinical networks and the benefits of integrating services to improve quality': NHS Future Forum, above n. 1, p. 11.

sectors.[97] Interestingly, this distinction reflects, from a healthcare perspective, wider concerns about concurrent powers in general, namely, the extent to which regulatory bodies are well-suited to investigating competition-related issues and the desirability of having specialist competition authorities in particular sectors.[98] Certainly, Monitor's suitability for investigating competition issues and applying competition law was queried.[99]

This refocusing of concurrent powers by the NHS Future Forum to comprise elements of ensuring sector-specific expertise and especially to avoid disproportionate use of competition (effectively a counterpoint to the Coalition Government's original ambition for Monitor as 'economic regulator' to 'promote competition') was reinforced in the HSCA 2012 by the articulation of Monitor's (now NHS Improvement's) general duty to include an obligation to prevent 'anti-competitive behaviour',[100] defined by reference to the terminology of the anticompetitive agreements provisions.[101] Whilst this set Monitor aside from other sectoral regulators in the ERRA 13 reforms, since the latter have a duty to promote competition, the articulation of Monitor's duty in these terms arguably links it more within a 'social solidarity' rationale for regulation,[102] as distinct from one based on economic principles. Certainly, discussions of other regulator roles help explain why a model inspired by the experience of other sectors is problematic for English healthcare, as a significant tension may arise between social tasks and a primarily economic focus.[103] The reframing of Monitor's role by the NHS Future Forum suggests that a social role remains following the removal of any economic focus – including the term 'economic regulator'.[104]

As the wording of section 72 HSCA 2012 remained unchanged during the passage of the Health and Social Care Bill,[105] this potentially significant

---

97 T. Prosser, 'Competition, Regulators and Public Service' in B. Rodger and A. MacCulloch (eds.), *The UK Competition Act – A New Era for UK Competition Law*, Hart Publishing, Oxford 2000.

98 Ibid.

99 A. Sánchez Graells (2014) and (2015), above n. 15 and n. 20, respectively.

100 Section 62(3) HSCA 2012.

101 Section 64(2) HSCA 2012.

102 T. Prosser, 'Regulation and Social Solidarity' (2006) 33(3) *Journal of Law and Society* 364.

103 See further on this point, T. Prosser, 'Theorising Utility Regulation' (1999) 62(2) *Modern Law Review* 196.

104 The NHS Future Forum recommended that Monitor's designation as an 'economic regulator' be removed and substituted by 'sectoral regulator'. 'We suggest that other safeguards should include the removal of the provision in the Bill for Monitor to "promote competition" and to clarify Monitor is a sector regulator for health not an "economic regulator"' (p. 9). 'We also feel that the language of "economic regulator" is misleading, suggesting an organisation like a utilities regulator – a model that is unhelpful and inaccurate' (p. 28), NHS Future Forum, above n. 1.

105 Health and Social Care Bill (HC Bill 132) Session 2010–11, as introduced 19.01.2011, Clause 60; Health and Social Care Bill (HC Bill 177) Session 2010–11, 02.04.2011, Clause 64; Health and Social Care Bill (HC Bill 221) Session 2010–12, 18.07.2011, Clause 67; Health and

distinction – between concurrent powers as a mechanism to ensure sector-specific expertise and a safeguard against disproportionate application of competition – is lost in the legislation.[106] However, it is questionable whether concurrent powers – essentially an institutional arrangement – can achieve such ambitious aims, either of promoting competition or avoiding disproportionate use of competition law, which may only be limited in its applicability.

The scope of concurrent powers is further defined by reference to the 2014 Concurrency Regulations on the one hand, and the ring-fencing of NHS Improvement's sectoral powers under section 74 HSCA 2012 (with regard to general duties under section 62 HSCA 2012) and section 67 HSCA 2012 (regarding the interaction between licensing and competition powers) on the other. These aspects are now considered.

## 3.2. DEFINING THE SCOPE OF CONCURRENT POWERS BY REFERENCE TO SECTION 72 HSCA 2012, ERRA 2013 AND THE 2014 CONCURRENCY REGULATIONS

How concurrent powers operate in English healthcare can be understood in substantive terms by reference to section 72 HSCA 2012, and in institutional terms with regard to ERRA 2013 and the 2014 Concurrency Regulations as follows.

### *3.2.1. Section 72 HSCA 2012 – The Legal Basis for Concurrent Powers in English Healthcare*

Section 72 HSCA provides that NHS Improvement and the CMA have concurrent functions in respect of applying the UK and EU competition provisions regarding anticompetitive agreements and abuse of dominance. Of particular note is that these concurrent functions 'concern the *provision* of *health care services* in England' (emphasis added). The discussion of this substantive scope in Chapter 2 concluded that the substantive focus of section 72 HSCA 2012 may actually be very narrow in practice, and possibly even limited to anticompetitive behaviour by PPUs in view of the focus on *provision*. Further support for this interpretation emerged from the difficulty of separating purchasing and providing functions in the NHS and the lack of clarity about the extent of *applicability* of competition law post-*FENIN*.

Social Care Bill (HL Bill 92) Session 2010–12, 12.09.2011, Clause 68; Health and Social Care Bill (HL Bill 119) Session 2010–12, 22.12.2011, Clause 70; Health and Social Care Bill (HL Bill 132) Session 2010–12, 14.03.2012, Clause 72.

106 The Explanatory Notes to the HSCA 2012 merely outline that Monitor has concurrent powers and what these empower Monitor to do in respect of enforcement action, paragraph 711, <http://www.legislation.gov.uk/ukpga/2012/7/notes/division/5/3/2/1> accessed 24.06.2018.

Of greater relevance to the present discussion of concurrent powers is the focus of section 72 HSCA 2012 on *'healthcare services'*. The issue of whether these are interpreted widely, as encompassing the NHS and private healthcare sectors (categories 1–4), or narrowly, as limited to the NHS (categories 1 and 2), despite the expansive wording, provides insights into the problems of concurrent powers operating in English healthcare. These can be illustrated as follows:

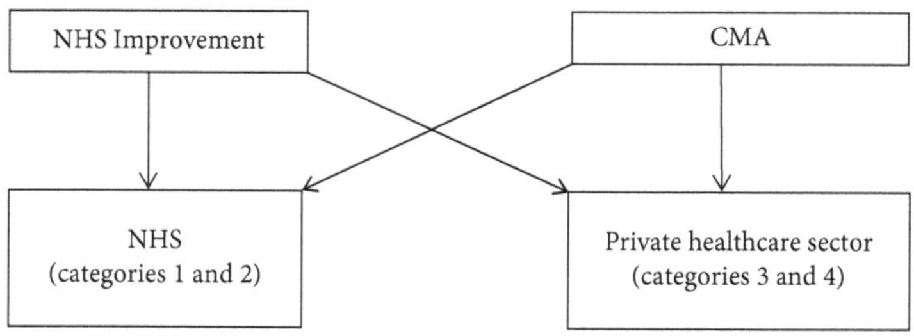


**Figure 6. 'Concurrent powers' under s. 72 HSCA 2012 in light of a broad interpretation of 'healthcare services' (as encompassing categories 1–4)**

On a broad reading, by which 'healthcare services' encompasses categories 1–4, concurrent powers can be understood as meaning that either the CMA or NHS Improvement may apply competition law regardless of whether the case involves the private healthcare sector or the NHS. Thus, the CMA would be granted oversight of the NHS and NHS Improvement oversight of the private healthcare sector.

Alternatively, on a narrow reading, with 'healthcare services' equating to the NHS only, again either the CMA or NHS Improvement may apply competition law under section 72 HSCA 2012 as follows:

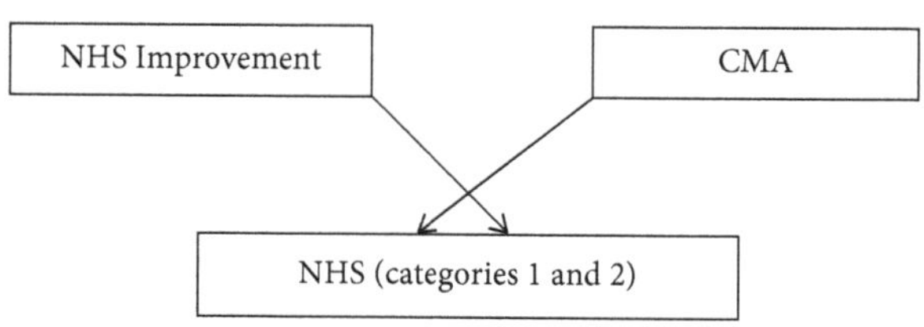


**Figure 7. 'Concurrent powers' under s. 72 HSCA 2012 in light of a narrow interpretation of 'healthcare services' (as encompassing categories 1 and 2 only)**

In a departure from the pre-HSCA 2012 situation, either scenario serves to grant the CMA explicit oversight of the NHS – which can be inferred as the overarching intention of section 72 HSCA 2012 from the White Paper onwards. Certainly there appears to be nothing in practice to suggest that the intention behind section 72 HSCA 2012 was to grant NHS Improvement oversight of the private healthcare sector.

Further clarification as to the scope of concurrent powers under section 72 HSCA 2012 is provided by the ERRA 2013 reforms and the 2014 Concurrency Regulations, and these are now considered.

### *3.2.2. ERRA 2013 and the 2014 Concurrency Regulations*[107] *– Refocusing the Scope of Concurrent Powers in English Healthcare*

In addition to merging the OFT and CC to create the CMA, ERRA 2013 made provision to overhaul the UK concurrency regime.[108] While Monitor (now NHS Improvement) was included in some of the ERRA 2013 developments vis-à-vis concurrency, it was explicitly excluded from others. For instance, Monitor was not subject to the new power for the Secretary of State to remove concurrent powers from regulators.[109] In addition, Monitor was not made a full member of the UK Competition Network (UKCN), but attends with observer status.[110] This was attributed to Monitor's statutory duty to prevent anticompetitive behaviour,[111] in contrast to the duty imposed on other regulators to promote competition. Some of the exceptions granted to Monitor appear to be provisional. For example, the duty on sectoral regulators to

---

107 The Competition Act 1998 (Concurrency) Regulations 2014, SI 2014/536. It is to be noted that the 2014 Concurrency Regulations relate exclusively to the concurrent powers shared by the CMA and NHS Improvement in respect of applying competition law. Thus, it might be surmised that the broad interpretations regarding 'healthcare provision' pertain with regard to market investigations under section 73 HSCA 2012. In other words, in theory either the CMA or NHS Improvement may make a market investigation reference in respect of either the NHS or the private healthcare sector. However, again, it is to be noted that, despite the broad terminology of section 73 HSCA 2012, there appears to be little intention for NHS Improvement to have oversight of the private healthcare sector. However, the CMA's management of its private healthcare market investigation can be linked to the market study being contemporaneous with the enactment of the HSCA 2012. Nevertheless, the CMA noted overlaps between its private healthcare remit and Monitor's focus on private healthcare-related aspects, such as the provider licensing regime and supervision and interpretation of the private patient income cap rules. (See Competition and Markets Authority (CMA), *Private Healthcare Market Investigation Final Report*, CMA25, 02.04.2014, para. 2.69). However, Monitor appeared to rule itself out of overseeing the Private Patient Unit (PPU) remedy in the CMA private healthcare market investigation by virtue of its focus extending to the NHS in England, as opposed to the UK-wide private healthcare market. See CMA25, above, para. 11.294.

108 For an excellent discussion, see N. Dunne, above n. 16.

109 Section 52 ERRA 2013 lists OFCOM, OFGEM, OFWAT, the ORR, the Northern Ireland Authority for Utility Regulation and the CAA as the 'sectoral regulators' whose concurrent powers may be removed. It is worth noting, however, that Monitor's concurrent powers with regard to market regulations under section 73 HSCA 2012 may be removed by the Secretary of State by virtue of section 52(2)(b) ERRA 2013 if this is ultimately extended to Monitor as well as other sectoral regulators.

110 CMA, 'Network launched to help drive competition in regulated sectors', Press Release, 03.12.2013.

111 Under section 62(3) HSCA 2012.

consider whether it would be more appropriate to use their competition law powers before using their direct regulatory powers to enforce licence conditions did not initially apply to Monitor, but the Secretary of State may extend this duty at a future date.[112] (This is a separate matter from Monitor (NHS Improvement) deciding which of its concurrent powers, its licensing powers or its 2013 Regulations competence is best suited to a given case – which has been acknowledged in cases thus far ultimately assessed under the 2013 Regulations.)[113] Indeed the mere suggestion that the Secretary of State would extend this consideration requirement in the future was deemed sufficient[114] in the Lords' debates preceding ERRA 2013 to justify the otherwise apparent anomaly of including Monitor as one of the sectoral regulators in the CMA's new annual concurrency reports.[115] Indeed, during the Lords' Debates of the Enterprise Bill, it was recommended that Monitor be removed from the list of sectoral regulators on the grounds that the interaction between Monitor and the CMA would be entirely different from the latter's interaction with other sectoral regulators.[116] Furthermore, the experience of enacting the

---

112 CMA (2014), above n. 107, para. 5, and fn. 8, p. 5.

113 See, for example, Monitor, Case CCD 04/13 (above n. 86), 'Notice of Initiation of Investigation', where Monitor considered its scope to use the 2013 Regulations, the competition condition of the NHS Provider Licence and, the NHS Principles and Rules of Competition and Cooperation in respect of behaviour prior to April 2013 (when the 2013 Regulations came into force).

114 See comments by Viscount Younger of Leckie: 'The Government have been clear in response to the consultation on competition reform that Monitor's explicit new duty to consider Competition Act enforcement before taking enforcement action through the provider licence provided under Schedule 14 to the Enterprise Bill will not be commenced until a future date, reflecting the unique characteristics of the health sector. Subject to this, Monitor will become part of the same concurrency regime as the other sectoral regulators. So it is right that the concurrency arrangements between the CMA and Monitor and the use of concurrent powers in the health sector should be covered by the concurrency report. This will provide greater transparency and assurance that concurrent competition powers are being used effectively and in the interests of users of healthcare services.' Enterprise and Regulatory Reform Bill, HL Deb, 12.12.2012, col GC363.

115 Section 16(7) ERRA 2013. Section 16 ERRA 2013 provides that the CMA must consult sectoral regulators in preparing concurrency reports, which must include details of the CMA and/or the regulator exercising its powers under CA98 or EA02, and where a regulator has elected not to use its concurrent powers, information about the powers it has used.

116 See Lord Whitty's proposed Amendment 24BFA to remove Monitor from the list of regulators to be included in the CMA concurrency reports and comments: 'I advise the Government, gently, not to reopen this matter – health service reform was difficult enough for them. People are settling down now to make it work but the idea that another authority [presumably a reference to the CMA] might come in under this Bill and overrule a health service body trying to square off competition and co-operation would reopen huge anxieties among health service professionals, patient groups and the new commissioning body [presumably a reference to NHS England]. The Government would be wise to take it out [i.e. remove Monitor from the list of sectoral regulators included in the concurrency reports]. They can do it at this point without too much attention but if what they are proposing gets out there, they will be in serious trouble.' Enterprise and Regulatory Reform Bill, HL Deb, 12.12.2012, Col GC362.

HSCA 2012 seemed to inform this cautious approach, as drawing attention to possible CMA oversight of the NHS would likely prove controversial.

It is to be noted that these aforementioned amendments in respect of Monitor appear not to have changed in the interim, so may be deemed to relate equally to NHS Improvement. For example, NHS Improvement is now included within the CMA's annual concurrency reports.[117]

Of particular relevance to the present discussion are important exceptions which were made for Monitor in respect of cases which are '*principally concerned with the provision of healthcare services for the purposes of the NHS in England* under Regulations 5 and 8 of the 2014 Concurrency Regulations, (emphasis added). Thus Monitor was empowered to lead on such cases[118] and the CMA may not take these over.[119] However, it may be the case that Monitor would agree to let the CMA act in a case.[120] This would appear to suggest that there may be other instances not affected by Regulations 5 and 8 of the 2014 Concurrency Regulations – for example, in cases where healthcare provision for the purposes of the NHS in England is incidental, rather than the 'principal concern' – but no further elaboration was provided.

It is to be noted that the CMA and Monitor's successor, NHS Improvement, clarified the basis of case allocation, which respects the limitations outlined here, in their Memorandum of Understanding.[121]

The situation regarding concurrent powers under section 72 HSCA 2012 and (now) NHS Improvement's and the CMA's respective competences following Regulations 5 and 8 of the 2014 Concurrency Regulations can be illustrated as follows:

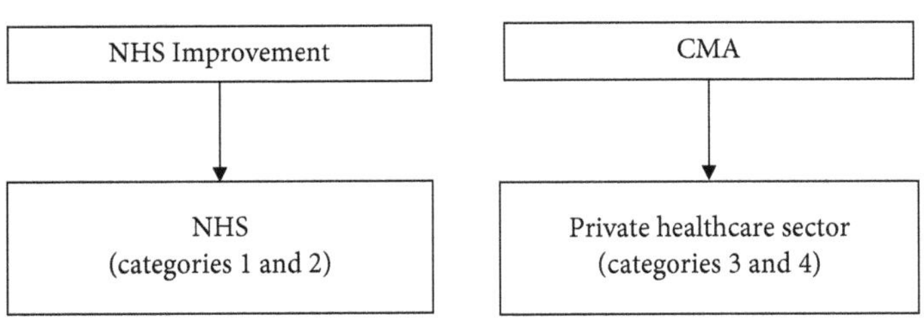


**Figure 8. How concurrent powers under s. 72 HSCA 2012 operate following amendments by Regulations 5 and 8 of the 2014 Concurrency Regulations**

117 See CMA (2017) and (2018), above n. 84.

118 Regulation 5(5), 2014 Regulations, above n. 85.

119 Regulation 8(1)(b), 2014 Regulations, above n. 85.

120 By virtue of Regulation 4(2), 2014 Regulations. See CMA, *Guidance on concurrent application of competition law to regulated industries*, CMA 10, 29.03.2014, at fn. 44.

121 Part A – Cooperation in relation to the competition prohibitions (Competition Act 1998 and Articles 101 and 102 of the Treaty on the Functioning of the European Union), para. 36, p. 11. CMA and NHS Improvement, *Memorandum of Understanding between the Competition and Markets Authority and NHS Improvement*, 01.04.2016.

The amendments to concurrency powers under section 72 HSCA 2012 by the 2014 Concurrency Regulations are important for at least two reasons.

Firstly, they significantly refine the scope for CMA intervention, and in so doing effectively re-establish the situation which existed prior to the HSCA 2012. Thus, the CMA may intervene in cases which involve the private healthcare sector, but not the NHS, in an arrangement which appears to enshrine the pre-HSCA 2012 situation in secondary legislation.

Secondly, they do nothing to clarify explicitly NHS Improvement's position vis-à-vis the private healthcare sector, which might be implicit from concurrent powers under a broad reading of 'healthcare provision' of section 72 HSCA 2012 as noted above. Rather, the amendments of the 2014 Concurrency Regulations support the view advanced during the Lords' Debates preceding ERRA 2013,[122] namely that concurrent powers function differently in healthcare. This is because allocation of cases is determined by factors (notably the *applicability* of competition law) other than which agency is best placed to act. Furthermore, insofar as concurrent powers have been used in other sectors, distinctions are not drawn between the markets comprising a sector. So, for example in the energy sector, it is not the case that the wholesale market is reserved to the competition authority and the retail market to the regulator.

Indeed, the practical implementation of concurrent powers under section 72 HSCA 2012 appears closer to the ordinary dictionary definition of 'concurrency' in the sense of occurring at the same time, in that the NHS and private healthcare sector both co-exist and operate separately, than to 'concurrency' as typically understood ('co-competence'[123]) in UK economic regulation.

In light of this convoluted institutional arrangement and the lack of clarity regarding the extent of applicability of competition law, it is unsurprising that NHS Improvement (and formerly Monitor) has not yet made use of its concurrent powers.[124]

As noted above, the focus for section 72 HSCA 2012 may be restricted to activities of PPUs in practical terms in view of the *applicability* of competition law to the English NHS (discussed in Chapter 2 above). If this is borne out and more cases emerge, which is a possibility in light of the removal of the private patient income cap under section 165 HSCA 2012,[125] then the foregoing analysis

---

122 See Lord Whitty's comments to this effect, above n. 116.

123 A. Sánchez Graells, above n. 15.

124 Certainly the five reports available at the time of writing demonstrate this, with an overview of cases addressed under the 2013 Regulations being given. See CMA (2014) pp. 90–93, (2015) pp. 64–68, (2016) pp. 71–74, (2017), pp. 100–101, and (2018), pp. 108–09, all n. 84 above.

125 The possibility that section 165 HSCA 2012 may precipitate an expansion in PPUs has been recognised by the CMA in its development of a separate test to assess PPUs as these do not meet the thresholds of general merger control. See, inter alia, CMA, *Private Healthcare Market Investigation Final Order*, 01.10.2014, Part 2, 'PPU arrangements'.

leads to the conclusion that oversight of such cases would be by the CMA, consistent with the 2011 case overseen by the OFT. This is because PPUs provide healthcare for the UK-wide private healthcare market, so would presumably not be caught by the limitation of providing healthcare services for purposes of the NHS in England under the 2014 Concurrency Regulations (which would trigger oversight by NHS Improvement).

Nevertheless, Monitor – and latterly NHS Improvement – has featured consistently in the CMA's annual concurrency reports, and these reveal an interesting insight into a sector in transition – partly in view of the NHS Five Year Forward View, which was launched in October 2014. For example, the reports offer an overview of the regulatory cases and advocacy activities of Monitor/NHS Improvement in the absence of competition law cases and market studies. It has consistently been noted that Monitor/NHS Improvement has no duty to promote competition, but rather a duty to prevent anticompetitive behaviour.[126] Furthermore, the amount of attention given to Monitor/NHS Improvement within the concurrency reports has declined from an elaboration of competition in the English NHS in the 'baseline' 2014 report (12 pages), via discussions of cases brought under the 2013 Regulations in the 2015 and 2016 reports (eight pages and six pages, respectively), to an overview of the sense of transition emerging from the NHS Five Year Forward View and the Sustainability and Transformation Partnerships, with no mention of competition (outside acknowledging the statutory framework), in the 2017 and 2018 reports (two pages each).[127]

## 3.3. NHS IMPROVEMENT'S 'COMPETITION-RELATED' POWERS – A VARIATION ON THE SEPARATE POWERS MODEL?

A final consideration in connection with NHS Improvement's exercise of concurrent powers under section 72 HSCA 2012 arises out of its use of its regulatory tools: the Competition Oversight condition of the NHS Provider Licence and the 2013 Regulations. In a sense, these comprise an NHS-specific competition regime operating in parallel with general competition law, so may suggest a further separate powers model.

### *3.3.1. The Competition Oversight Condition of the NHS Provider Licence*

The NHS Provider Licence includes nine General Conditions which cover areas such as the provision and publication of information, 'fit and proper person'

126 See CMA (2015), para. 187, p. 62, and CMA (2016), para. 234, p. 71, both above n. 84.

127 See CMA, above n. 124.

requirements and a requirement for providers to be registered with the Care Quality Commission (CQC).[128] The Competition Oversight condition is part of a wider Choice and Competition licence condition,[129] one of several further specific conditions.[130] It applies to all licence-holders, whether private sector, voluntary sector or NHS Foundation Trust providers. As noted in Chapter 2 above, the Competition Oversight condition imposes a two-fold prohibition on providers, with terminology clearly influenced by the anticompetitive agreements and abuse of dominance provisions of the Competition Act 1998 (CA98) and the Treaty on the Functioning of the European Union (TFEU). Furthermore, the condition has been interpreted as ensuring that the competition rules are applied equally across the NHS, and raising the possibility of two different competition regimes being applied.[131]

The existence of the Competition Oversight condition offers an alternative to applying competition law insofar as anticompetitive conduct may be addressed (in a theoretical example) by removing a provider's licence, thus effectively causing them to exit the NHS market. This may obviate any need to apply competition law, and all the cost and complexity that the latter would entail. However, it is important to note that the condition is intended to extend the spirit of competition law to *all* licencees, even those which may not be regarded as carrying out an 'economic activity', and thus are not 'undertakings' which trigger the application of competition law. It is notable that the introduction of a Competition Oversight licence condition has been deemed to fill the potential enforcement gap under CA98,[132] apparently by extending the application of competition rules to *all* providers delivering services for the purposes of the English NHS. This appears a curious distinction to make in view of the relative clarity that competition law may apply to NHS *provision*[133] (as distinct from purchasing, insofar as the two may be separated). However, as noted in Chapter 2, at the time of writing, no action has been taken in respect of the Competition Oversight licence condition.[134]

---

128 Monitor, 'The New NHS Provider Licence – Monitor's response to the statutory consultation on the new NHS provider licence', 14.02.2013.

129 The patient choice element is intended to protect patients' rights to choose between providers by obliging these to make information available and act in a fair way. 'Choice' in this context refers to a choice of provider under the NHS Constitution or a choice conferred locally by CCGs. See Monitor, above n. 128, Condition 6 – Choice and Competition Conditions.

130 Others relate to pricing, integrated care, continuity of services and Foundation Trusts.

131 C. Graham, above n. 3.

132 See Monitor, above n. 128, '6.1 Purpose of the Choice and Competition licence conditions'.

133 For a discussion of this, see O. Odudu, 'Are State-owned healthcare providers undertakings subject to competition law?' (2011) 32(5) *European Competition Law Review* 231.

134 However, NHS Improvement issued enforcement undertakings in June 2016 in respect of financial governance breaches by Nottingham CityCare Partnership CIC. See NHS Improvement, 'Regulatory Action: licensed independent healthcare providers', 16.06.2017,

### 3.3.2. The 2013 Regulations

The 2013 Regulations cover a wide range of potential behaviour by NHS commissioners, although the focus, unsurprisingly, relates to procurement activity. However, Regulation 10, which places a prohibition on anticompetitive behaviour by NHS commissioners, may have relevance to NHS Improvement's relationship with the CMA. As discussed in Chapter 2 above, Regulation 10 appears to extend the spirit of competition law to NHS commissioners, which could serve to address the inconsistency in approach between purchasers and providers with regard to applying competition law as evidenced by cases such as *FENIN*.[135] Regulation 10 therefore appears to operate in a space where competition law may not apply, thus reducing potential conflict between this and NHS Improvement's concurrent powers in respect of general competition law. It has been queried whether Regulation 10(1)'s focus on patients' interests as a counterbalance to anticompetitive behaviour[136] may inhibit future enforcement activity by the CMA similar to that previously taken by the OFT regarding PPUs.[137] However, this view demonstrates the limitations of trying to discuss a single, unified healthcare sector in England, as it conflates not only the NHS (categories 1 and 2) and the private healthcare sector (PPUs being an example of category 3 activity) in terms of the varying applicability of competition law, but also the respective competences of NHS Improvement and the CMA in terms of concurrent powers as developed by the 2014 Concurrency Regulations. Nevertheless, it also raises interesting questions about how competition in the English NHS (and indeed private healthcare sector) may develop in future and

<https://improvement.nhs.uk/about-us/corporate-publications/publications/regulatory-action-licensed-independent-healthcare-providers/> accessed 24.06.2018. More generally, where licences are revoked and reasons given publicly, these refer to providers ceasing to exist as a result of acquisitions, providers ceasing to provide NHS services, providers no longer being registered with the Care Quality Commission or providers applying to have their licences revoked pursuant to section 89(a) HSCA 2012. See NHS Improvement, 'NHS Foundation Trust Directory – Related Documents', <https://improvement.nhs.uk/resources/nhs-foundation-trust-directory-and-register-licensed-healthcare-providers/> accessed 05.05.2018.

135 However, there is a lack of clarity about what behaviour is at issue: 'anti-competitive behaviour' in Regulation 10 is defined by reference to section 64(2) HSCA 2012, which provides that '"Anti-competitive behaviour" means behaviour which would (or would be likely to) prevent, restrict or distort competition and a reference to preventing anti-competitive behaviour includes a reference to eliminating or reducing the effects (or potential effects) of the behaviour.'

136 And also, Monitor's general duty under section 62(3) HSCA 2012.

137 See A. Sánchez Graells, above n. 20, pp. 4–5. 'One can wonder whether this type of enforcement activity will still be possible when NHS commissioners argue that the anti-competitive behaviour of healthcare providers is justified on the basis of reg. 10(1) of the NHS Procurement, Patient Choice and Competition Regulations 2013, since it was carried out in the 'patients' interest', measured in qualitative terms.'

the potential influence of linkages between the two on enforcement activity under the discrete NHS-specific and general competition regimes.

### *3.3.3. Relationship between NHS Improvement's Competition-Related Powers and its Concurrent Powers*

NHS Improvement (Monitor) has previously considered that it has three tools at its disposal to address competition concerns, namely, its licence authorisation powers, the 2013 Regulations and its concurrent powers. At the time of writing, only the 2013 Regulations have been used.

However, it is useful to elaborate which concerns may influence NHS Improvement (Monitor)'s decision to use one set of powers rather than another. This can be summarised as follows:

| Possible combination of powers | Governed by | Description in NHS Improvement (Monitor) terminology |
|---|---|---|
| Competition oversight licensing condition + concurrent powers | Applicability of competition law and section 67(3) HSCA 2012 | 'Functional conflict' |
| Competition oversight licensing condition + Regulation 10 | Section 67(3) HSCA 2012 | 'Functional conflict' |
| Concurrent powers + Regulation 10 | Applicability of competition law and NHS Improvement guidance | 'Competing regulatory functions' |

**Figure 9. NHS Improvement's choice of powers**

A limited guidance framework is offered by the HSCA 2012. Section 67(3) HSCA 2012 stipulates that NHS Improvement must ignore its functions in respect of imposing and removing licence conditions[138] when exercising its competition or pricing functions. 'Competition functions' relate to functions under Chapter 2 (competition), so in theory relate to NHS Improvement's concurrent powers or its Regulation 10 powers by virtue of section 75 HSCA 2012. Such tension between competition and licensing functions amounts to a 'functional conflict'.[139] This would appear to describe a situation in which NHS Improvement decides between using its power under the Competition Oversight licence condition on the one hand, and either its concurrent powers or Regulation 10 powers on the other. However, the question of the *applicability* of competition law to a given situation should not be overlooked.

[138] Sections 111 and 113 HSCA 2012.

[139] See further on this point, Monitor, *Functional conflicts and balancing competing regulatory interests policy*, 02.07.2015, <https://www.gov.uk/government/publications/functional-conflicts-and-balancing-competing-regulatory-interests-policy> accessed 11.05.2018.

In contrast to this 'functional conflict', there appears to be less guidance regarding the choice between using concurrent powers and Regulation 10. As this constitutes a choice between two 'competition functions', it is questionable whether this amounts to a need to balance 'competing regulatory functions', a designation used by NHS Improvement to describe any situation which is not a 'functional conflict'.[140] Insofar as a choice between deploying the 2013 Regulations and concurrent powers is possible, this appears determined primarily by the *applicability* of competition law.

In contrast to the Dutch separate powers model, it is difficult to see how either the Competition Oversight licence condition or Regulation 10 may have a detrimental impact on NHS Improvement's concurrent powers. This is because these two powers operate in a space where the scope to actually apply competition law to the English NHS remains in question. Certainly, there appears to be less scope for overlap between the 2013 Regulations and general competition law, and no formal framework for the former to take precedence over the latter. For example, a complaint brought under the 2013 Regulations may deal with issues of competitive neutrality and patient choice – such as whether NHS patients have been made aware of their entitlement to a choice of NHS or private healthcare provider – which are not obviously addressed by general competition law. This is in contrast to the high degree of complementarity evident in the NZa's (former) SMP competence and the ACM's abuse of dominance powers.

The relative breadth of NHS Improvement's competition-related powers suggests that it would not be surprising if these are deployed in preference to general competition law, perhaps reflecting the experience of other sectors. This is interesting in view of the suggestion that the Secretary of State may seek to extend the requirement to NHS Improvement in the future to use its general competition law powers rather than its regulatory tools, as noted above in connection with the ERRA 2013 reforms. However, it is difficult to see how this can operate in practice in view of questions concerning the *application*, if not the *applicability* of competition law. Certainly there is no evidence (either in the Concurrency Reports or elsewhere) to suggest that NHS Improvement is

140 While NHS Improvement recognises 'balancing competing regulatory interests' as a source of potential conflict, the examples it gives are wide-ranging and involve cross-over between different functions, such as 'enforcement action in relation to foundation trusts' and 'duties in respect of the accounts of foundation trusts'. See MONITOR, above n. 139, para. 5. In any event, NHS Improvement appears to perceive these less as a conflict of interest and more an overlap of functions to be addressed by 'legitimately and reasonably balancing potentially competing interests' (para. 7). This is quite different from whether, for example, there can be a conflict between the 2013 Regulations and NHS Improvement's concurrent powers under section 72 HSCA 2012. Both of these are instances of NHS Improvement's 'competition functions' and presumably complementary rather than antagonistic.

choosing to make use of its direct regulatory powers instead of its competition prohibition powers where the latter could have been exercised.[141]

# 4. FACTORS INFLUENCING THE RELATIONSHIP BETWEEN REGULATOR AND COMPETITION AUTHORITY

Having outlined the separate powers and concurrent powers models in operation in the Netherlands and England, two further factors may influence the relationship between regulator and competition authority with regard to applying competition law.

Firstly, the focus of both the NZa and NHS Improvement on patients may suggest a different approach to the ACM and CMA's objective of enhancing consumer welfare, which is commonly understood as the purpose of competition law.[142]

Secondly, a common concern regarding the relationship between the regulator and government is that the former is insufficiently independent of the latter. This may present concerns insofar as there may be scope for the Minister for Health to influence the approach of the competition authority as well. This is perhaps more evident in the Netherlands in view of the Minister for Health, Wellbeing and Sport setting policy direction, which may affect how the ACM uses its new competition powers in healthcare cases. However, provision is also made for NHS England (in lieu of the Department of Health), NHS Improvement and the CMA to work together.

## 4.1. THE REGULATOR'S FOCUS ON PATIENTS

### *4.1.1. The Netherlands: The NZa's Separate Powers and the General Consumer Interest*

The NZa's explicit focus on patients as motivation for its activities finds expression in its obligation to prioritise the general consumer interest under Article 3(4) Wmg. Although it has been queried whether the general consumer interest constitutes a source of legitimacy for regulatory intervention,[143] this section

141 See the CMA Concurrency reports of 2015, 2016, 2017 and 2018, all n. 84 above.

142 However, it has been suggested that competition law has a role to play in providing an 'incentive to improve' (O. Odudu, above n. 18), which may be seen as a different focus/purpose.

143 W. Sauter, 'Is the general consumer interest a source of legitimacy for healthcare regulation? An analysis of the Dutch experience' (2009) 2–3 *European Journal of Consumer Law* 419.

asks whether the NZa's focus on patients may impact the separate powers model that underpinned the relationship between the NZa and ACM between 2006 and 2015, and what happens following the transfer of competence to the ACM.

#### 4.1.1.1. Overview of the General Consumer Interest under Article 3(4) Wmg

The general consumer interest in Dutch healthcare relates to a general body of consumers and long-term interests, and thus operates as a means to ensure that the market mechanism works effectively.[144] It comprises the healthcare values of accessibility, affordability and quality, which are defined in specific terms[145] – 'affordability' encompassing both micro and macro dimensions; 'accessibility' distinguishing physical and financial aspects; and 'quality' relating to the proper functioning of markets – and which are further underpinned by freedom of choice and transparent information.

There is potential for tension in at least two ways with regard to the overarching values and NZa regulation.[146] Firstly, it may be necessary to clarify where trade-offs between affordability, accessibility and quality are necessary, or acceptable. For example, it was suggested at the time of the 2006 reforms that quality should be given the highest priority.[147] Secondly, tension may arise from potential divergence of interests within the 'dual identity' of patients on the one hand, and insured parties on the other. For example, proposals to amend Article 13 Zvw[148] – which operates to mitigate the limited choice of providers available to patients with cheaper 'benefits in kind' policies – could have produced lower premiums, but were voted down amid concerns about the effects of impacting health outcomes.

#### 4.1.1.2. The NZa's Separate Powers (2006–15) and the General Consumer Interest Framework

The public interests of quality, affordability and accessibility have constituted a framework which the NZa used in its assessment process, particularly with regard to proportionality.[149] For example, in connection with its SMP competence, the NZa has clarified that it will only intervene when the consumer interest will be promoted as a result, suggesting a lesser focus on exclusionary rather

144 Thus has been related to the market failure rationale for regulation. See W. Sauter, ibid.
145 NZA, *'Visiedocument: (In) het belang van de consument'* ('Vision Document: (In) the general consumer interest') (November 2007), Section 2.1.
146 W. Sauter, above n. 143.
147 R.D. Friele, *Evaluatie Wet marktordening gezondheidszorg* (Assessment of the Wmg), ZonMw, Den Haag 2009.
148 Discussed in Chapter 1 above.
149 For example, in connection with expedited SMP investigations under Article 49 Wmg. See NZa (2010), above n. 43, Section 3.7.

than on exploitative conduct.[150] However, the ultimate effects for public interests of both types of conduct are thought to often be similar, illustrated as follows:[151]

| | |
|---|---|
| Accessibility | Access for individual consumers may be seriously restricted or, in the most serious cases, completely debarred. |
| Affordability | Excluding competitors and/or exploiting consumers may result in prices higher than those which would have emerged in a (sufficiently) competitive market. Consequences regarding affordability may affect either the individual consumer (for example, regarding individual payments, excesses or non-insured care) or society as a whole. If the latter, these may be consequences for the premia consumers pay for health insurance. |
| Quality | Parties which exclude competitors and/or have so much seller power that the market is not sufficiently competitive are no longer responsive to competitive pressures to maintain or increase quality. |

**Figure 10. Overview of the 'general consumer interest' in light of exclusionary and exploitative behaviour**

Furthermore, in imposing SMP obligations, the NZa is required to describe the extent to which the actual or potential conduct is expected to lead to consequences for market relations and (consequently) public interests.[152] In connection with the *Menzis v. Van Dalen Pharmacy* case, the public interests of accessibility, affordability and quality played a part in satisfying requirements for an expedited investigation,[153] and 'advantages within the meaning of public interests' were deemed a criterion for judging the reasonableness of a contract.[154] Furthermore, affordability formed a particular focus in justifying the use of preference policies[155] and the imposition of the SMP obligation.[156]

150 Ibid, p. 28.

151 Ibid, p. 29.

152 Ibid.

153 See the expedited decision under Article 49 Wmg. NZa, *Besluit als bedoeld in artikel 49 lid 1 van de Wmg 18.11.2009* (Decision under Article 49(1) Wmg of 18.11.2009), paragraph 39. This is in accordance with the requirements set out in the policy guidance in respect of Article 49 Wmg, NZa, above n. 43, Section 3.7.

154 NZa, *Besluit 22.02.2011, eerste toepassing van aanmerkelijke marktmachtbevoegdheid (art. 48 Wmg)* (Decision involving the first application of SMP competence under Art. 48 Wmg of 22.02.2011), (NZa Article 48 Wmg Decision), paragraph 180.

155 For example, in the recognition that preference policies, as a type of selective purchasing, may be beneficial for consumers and have a positive effect on affordability of healthcare. However, these positive effects can only be realised by health insurers if a pharmacist agrees to cooperate with the preference policy. See NZa Article 49 Decision, above n. 153, paras. 75 and 76.

156 On the basis that not imposing the obligation would mean that positive effects on affordability would not be obtained. See NZa Article 49 Decision, above n. 153, para., 98, and NZa Article 48 Decision, above n. 154, paras. 234–237.

As regards the NZa's Article 45 Wmg contract powers, here too the general consumer interest has been recognised as paramount.[157] Furthermore, the NZa's Regulation on Agreements concerning healthcare-related electronic networks states that it serves the public interests of quality, accessibility and affordability[158] under Article 3(4) Wmg in two ways. Firstly, by promoting competition, which benefits consumers by increasing freedom of choice (such as being able to choose new providers, and creating more options with existing providers), and thereby also in the sense of affordability. Secondly, by the advantages of electronic networks in healthcare for quality by offering greater access for healthcare providers, and thus for consumers who direct their healthcare requests/demands to them.

The Electronic Networks Regulation also makes clear that healthcare providers having access to patient data (such as diagnoses and X-ray results) and medication data can be important for patient safety, and that managing prescriptions and appointments online by reference to data connected to waiting times is directly in patients' interests (in terms of accessibility), and particularly important for their healthcare.[159] An implication of this is that there can be benefits to patients which may go beyond NZa compliance with Article 3(4) Wmg. Such wide-ranging benefits may suggest – at least in connection with healthcare providers' access to electronic networks and online services for patients – that the consistent approach envisaged by the Regulation may address the tension outlined above and produce benefits for patients on the one hand, and insured parties on the other.

#### 4.1.1.3. Effect of the General Consumer Interest on the Separate Powers Model

The effect of the general consumer interest on the separate powers model varies according to the scope for the respective powers of the NZa and ACM to be considered separate.

Thus, in connection with the NZa's SMP competence, in view of its relationship with the ACM's abuse of dominance powers, the general consumer interest may add little to a standard competition assessment based on the effects of exclusionary and exploitative conduct for public interests, as outlined above. However, insofar as a general competition assessment may achieve different outcomes, the general consumer interest appears to offer a mechanism to draw on non-competition matters and use these to balance the NZa's approach to, for instance, sanctions in the healthcare sector, as suggested by the examples above.

---

157 See NZa, *'Toelichting Toepassing artikel 45 Wmg'* ('Explanatory Notes regarding the application of Art. 45 Wmg'), December 2009, Section 3.5, p. 13.

158 NZa Electronic Networks Regulation, above n. 52, p. 3.

159 Ibid, p. 11.

In contrast, the relationship between the NZa's contracts power and the ACM's anticompetitive agreements power is markedly less clear. We have seen that the NZa's power can offer a useful consolidation of ACM decision-making practice, as evidenced by the Electronic Networks Regulation. However, the justification of benefits in the general consumer interest does not extend beyond what the ACM could offer.

Ultimately, it may be the case that the effect of the general consumer interest on the separate powers model can only be viewed in light of the transfer of the SMP competence to the ACM, and how the latter takes account of the public interests of affordability, accessibility and quality in its assessments. Certainly, the Explanatory Memorandum to the legislative proposal enshrining this transfer of competence suggests that the ACM will similarly be bound by considerations of the general consumer interest.[160]

#### 4.1.2. *England: The Concurrent Powers and Separate Powers Models, NHS Improvement's Focus on Patients and the Effect of NHS Improvement's Duty on the Separate Powers and Concurrent Powers Models*

NHS Improvement's focus on patients is set out in section 62 HSCA 2012 and is important for reinforcing the inconsistency elsewhere in the HSCA in referencing 'healthcare' (potentially categories 1–4) and separately 'the NHS' (categories 1 and 2). However, this nevertheless reflects the complexity of the English system, which permits patients to switch between the NHS and private healthcare sector.

Section 62(1) HSCA 2012 places a main general duty on NHS Improvement to protect and promote the interests of people who use healthcare services by promoting provision of healthcare services which (a) is economic, efficient and effective, and (b) maintains or improves the quality of the services. This is elaborated further, with 'protect' meaning that NHS Improvement will act to ensure that the interests of people who use health services are not diminished, whilst 'promote' is intended to mean furthering their interests.[161] As the reference to 'healthcare services' appears to extend beyond the NHS,[162] this suggests that NHS Improvement's duty under section 62(1) HSCA 2012 is owed to *all* patients in England, whether accessing NHS or private healthcare services. Indeed, this is logical in view of the possibility for a single patient to move between the two sectors, subject to Department of Health and NHS

---

160 34 445 Explanatory Memorandum, above n. 73, p. 40.

161 Explanatory Notes to the HSCA 2012, above n. 106, para. 666.

162 Since these are defined under section 64(3) HSCA 2012 as 'all forms of health care provided for individuals, whether relating to physical or mental health …; and … it does not matter if a health care service is also an adult social care service'.

England rules[163] intended to avoid NHS resources being used to subsidise private healthcare. Against this background of complex interactions between the private healthcare sector and the English NHS, it is perhaps unsurprising that NHS Improvement's general duty should be couched in the broad, even unwieldy, terms of 'people who use healthcare services'. However, it should be noted that NHS Improvement's duty under section 62(1) HSCA 2012 is qualified by section 62(3) HSCA 2012, which centres its focus clearly on NHS patients, and preventing anticompetitive behaviour which is not in their interests.

The distinction between NHS patients on the one hand, and private patients on the other, reveals different interests which may come into play in conducting competition assessments. Thus, NHS patients may be considered to have a dual identity as patients and taxpayers, whilst private patients may be more generally considered similar to 'consumers' in view of the supplementary nature of the private healthcare market. The 'dual identity' of patients and taxpayers is evident in other contexts – notably in the exhortation by NHS England's CEO Simon Stevens to 'think like a patient, act like a taxpayer'.[164] In view of Monitor's (latterly NHS Improvement's) and the UK government's commitment to the NHS as a taxation-funded service free at the point of delivery[165] and its close partnership with NHS England, the failure to couch its general duty in terms of 'patients and taxpayers' in the HSCA 2012 appears as something overlooked, even remiss. The lack of explicit reference to taxpayers may be explained by the resulting focus of the HSCA 2012 on competition on quality (not price) – as this is something patients may be responsive to[166] – and by the suggestion that taxpayers' and patients' interests align to such a degree that the distinction becomes superfluous: the preferences of a state's citizens in their role as taxpayers are unlikely to be very different from their preference in

163 Department of Health, 'Guidance on NHS patients who wish to pay for additional private care', 23.03.2009. NHS Commissioning Board (now NHS England), 'Commissioning Policy: Defining the boundaries between NHS and Private Healthcare', April 2013. Ref: NHSCB/CP/12.

164 NHS England, New – Full text of Simon Stevens' Speech, 01.04.2014, https://www.england.nhs.uk/2014/04/simon-stevens-speech/> accessed 24.06.2018. This emphasis has been reiterated more recently in the context of curbing prescriptions for 'over-the-counter' medicines. NHS England, 'NHS England frees up millions of pounds which could be used for frontline services', *News*, 29.03.2018, <https://www.england.nhs.uk/2018/03/nhs-england-frees-up-millions-of-pounds-which-could-be-used-for-frontline-services/> accessed 24.06.2018.

165 Monitor, 'Monitor's Strategy 2014-2017 – Helping to redesign healthcare provision in England', 10.04.2014. The UK government (Department of Health) remains committed to the guiding principles of the NHS: 'that access to healthcare is based on need and not the ability to pay, and that services are comprehensive and available to all'. Department of Health, 'The Government's Revised Mandate to NHS England for 2017–18' March 2018, paragraph 1.1, p. 7.

166 Whereas taxpayers may favour competition on price insofar as this achieves value for money in keeping with the emphasis on competition for the market in the context of the English NHS.

their role as users.[167] However, the precedent in Ofcom's dual duty to consumers and citizens[168] could have justified NHS Improvement in adopting a similar dual duty approach. Indeed, similar to Ofcom, NHS Improvement too can be described as having a broad remit of functions.[169]

Against this background, it becomes necessary to draw a clearer distinction between competition as a mechanism to improve NHS care (which is in the interests of both taxpayers and patients, given that the former seem likely to benefit from the NHS at some stage in their lives, if not within a single treatment episode), and competition between the NHS and the private healthcare sectors (which might serve the interests of patients where they can move between the two). NHS Improvement's focus might be understood as making market mechanisms work with regard to the former (both in terms of competition *for* and *in* the market) – as suggested by its duty to prevent anticompetitive behaviour that is not in the interests of NHS patients. However, the explicit focus on 'people who use healthcare services' – as distinct from taxpayers – suggests a concern for the latter.

This dual identity of patient/taxpayer is ultimately helpful – and appears thus far to have been largely overlooked – in understanding how competition works within the NHS and consequently NHS Improvement's focus with regard to this. So, to borrow NHS England terminology, whilst 'acting like a patient' may appear to equate patients with consumers as a demand-driven impetus as per the Dutch system, 'thinking like a taxpayer' suggests a form of constraint, most obviously in the form of accountability for securing value for money as associated with public procurement rules. The latter is essential in view of the apparent ongoing commitment to keeping the NHS as a taxation-funded service which has nevertheless sought to incorporate elements of competition.

The link between NHS Improvement's duty under sections 62(1) and 62(3) HSCA 2012 and its separate powers in connection with the NHS Provider Licence and the 2013 Regulations appears consistent and coherent, as all are directed towards managing anticompetitive behaviour in connection with the NHS (categories 1 and 2).

The link between NHS Improvement's duty and its concurrent powers also appears relatively clear. Insofar as Regulations 5 and 8 of the 2014 Regulations operate to reserve any potential claims under general competition law regarding the NHS to NHS Improvement rather than the CMA, possible scope for conflict

---

167 J. Le Grand, *The Other Invisible Hand – Delivering Public Services through Choice and Competition*, Princeton University Press, Princeton NJ 2007.

168 T. Prosser, above n. 102.

169 Enumerated under section 62 HSCA 2012.

is avoided. A further safeguard is nominally provided by section 74 HSCA 2012. This provides that NHS Improvement's general duties under section 62 do not apply in relation to anything done by NHS Improvement in the carrying out of its functions by virtue of section 72, but that where NHS Improvement exercises its concurrent powers, it may nevertheless have regard to any of the matters in respect of which section 62 imposes a duty if it is a matter to which the CMA is entitled to have regard. This appears to prompt two questions: firstly, whether there are different areas of interest for NHS Improvement and the CMA; and secondly, whether NHS Improvement's duty to prevent anticompetitive behaviour which is not in patients' interests under section 62(3) is consistent with exceptions to general competition law.

The first is answered, to a limited extent, by the Explanatory Notes to the HSCA 2012, which provide that whilst both agencies may have regard to patients' interests regarding the provision of healthcare services for the purposes of the NHS, the CMA will not always have regard to considerations relating to promoting research into matters relevant to the NHS.[170]

The second question has been considered in terms of a comparison and contrast of NHS Improvement's approach to the prohibition on anticompetitive behaviour in the 2013 Regulations[171] with approaches to applying Article 101(3) TFEU.[172] That analysis concludes that NHS Improvement must ensure that it takes a strict approach in determining 'patients' interests', but that there is no fundamental inconsistency between the 2013 Regulations and EU economic law.

Overall, NHS Improvement's duty under section 62(1), as elaborated further by section 62(3), HSCA 2012 has little impact on the concurrent powers model insofar as it does not affect the CMA's application of competition law, particularly in view of the safeguard afforded by section 74 HSCA 2012, which should ensure a consistent approach. However, the elaboration of NHS Improvement's duty serves to reinforce the development of concurrent powers as entailing the continuing distinction between the NHS and the private healthcare sectors, which in turn raises questions about the purpose of section 74 HSCA 2012. The ongoing uncertainty about the extent of the *applicability* of competition law to the English NHS and the healthcare-specific style of concurrency seen to develop from the 2014 Concurrency Regulations, suggest that the purpose of section 74 HSCA 2012 as a safeguard to ensure consistent application of competition law by the CMA and NHS Improvement becomes highly questionable, if not actually redundant.

---

170 Explanatory Notes to the HSCA 2012, above n. 106, para. 721.

171 Similarly defined by reference to section 64(2) HSCA 2012.

172 See A. Sánchez Graells (2014) and (2015), above n. 15 and n. 20, respectively.

## 4.2. CHANGING MINISTERIAL OVERSIGHT AND THE RELATIONSHIP BETWEEN THE REGULATOR AND COMPETITION AUTHORITY

The development of competition in Dutch and English healthcare also involves evolution in ministerial oversight, and this too can affect the relationship between the regulator and competition authority.

In view of the relative facility for developing competition and relative clarity about the applicability of competition law regarding Dutch healthcare, a lesser degree of ministerial oversight might be anticipated as the ACM and NZa become more embedded regarding healthcare regulation. Conversely, the limited scope for competition within the English NHS and relative lack of clarity about the extent of applicability of competition law would suggest that more ministerial oversight could be expected. However, the developments in both countries appear counterintuitive.

### *4.2.1. The Netherlands*

The NZa and ACM are both *zelfsbestuurorganen* (Autonomous Administrative Agencies (ZBOs)), an administrative form shared by other sectoral regulators in the Netherlands.[173] In general terms, this status confers a relationship with government which sees the relevant Minister issue general policy direction whilst the regulator is responsible for day-to-day implementation of the policy. Thus the ACM is subject to oversight by the Minister for Economic Affairs, but the Minister may only intervene in ACM practice in limited circumstances.[174] The NZa is overseen by the Minister for Health, Wellbeing and Sport, and since 2006 links between the two have existed which affect the development of competition, perhaps most notably the requirement for the two to cooperate with regard to setting tariffs, with the NZa making recommendations to the Minister regarding which hospital service prices can be liberalised. Furthermore, the Explanatory Memorandum to the Wmg clarifies that the Dutch government is, and remains, responsible for oversight of

[173] However, there has been a reduction in the creation of ZBOs as the preferred legal and administrative form for new regulators. This has been explained by the ZBO model being criticised as not offering a satisfactory answer to the inherent conflict between the necessary 'independence' (*of* the regulator) and 'Ministerial responsibility' (*for* the regulator). For further discussion, see M. Aelen, '*Beginselen van goed toezicht: het onafhankelijkheidsbeginsel*' ('Principles of good regulation: the principle of independence') (2015) *Tijdschrift voor Toezicht*, 2, 15.

[174] An example being to overturn an ACM decision to block a merger under Article 47(1) Mw, a power not used thus far in a healthcare context. For further general discussion, see A. Ottow, *Market & Competition Authorities – Good Agency Principles*, Oxford University Press, Oxford 2015, pp. 114–17.

public interests in healthcare.[175] Between 2006 and 2015, there appears to have been no explicit framework for the Minister for Health, Wellbeing and Sport to influence the ACM's practice in healthcare. However, the Minister has been critical of the ACM's widespread approval of hospital mergers, and tackling this has been identified as a priority in the consolidation of the ACM's armoury regarding competition in healthcare.[176] Whilst the current transfer of powers to the ACM entails additional functions and responsibilities, it appears not to rectify the limited substantive scope of competition law, and this has been recognised as potentially problematic.[177] How the new arrangements evolve in practice obviously remains to be seen. However, it is notable that senior figures in the ACM have already expressed reservations about what the new SMP powers can achieve, namely that the transfer of powers would not necessarily lead to *more* intervention on the basis of sector-specific regulation.[178] This is because the ACM has consistently (and correctly) taken the view that it can only intervene where it establishes a breach of the competition rules. This leads to the inference that there may be quite a substantial disconnect between what the Minister for Health, Wellbeing and Sport wishes to achieve in terms of developing competition in Dutch healthcare, and what the ACM (and competition law) may realistically deliver. Certainly this view appears supported by a discrepancy noted between the Minister being quite active in terms of refocusing competition following the Borstlap and AEF reports in 2014 (discussed in Chapter 1 above), and the ACM's relative lack of explicit engagement with the healthcare sector as a whole, as evidenced by the ACM apparently not updating its comprehensive 'Guidelines for the Healthcare Sector' from 2010.[179] Nevertheless, the ACM has been more active in calling on the Minister for Health, Wellbeing and Sport to introduce clear and concrete criteria for assessing mergers in healthcare[180] – although the legislative proposal allows scope for this via Ministerial Decrees, the Explanatory Memorandum suggests that this is not yet necessary.[181]

---

175 *Kamerstukken II, 2004–05, 30 186, 3 – Regels inzake marktordening, doelmatigheid en beheerste kostenontwikkeling op het gebied van de gezondheidszorg (Wet marktordening gezondheidszorg), Nr. 3 Memorie van Toelichting* (Second Chamber documentation, Parliamentary Session 2004–05, 30 186, 3 (Explanatory Memorandum) – Rules governing market organisation, efficiency and managed cost development in healthcare (Dutch Healthcare (Market Regulation) Act 2006 (Wmg)), p. 2.

176 E. Schippers, above n. 25.

177 D.W.L.A. Schrijvershof and J.C. Plettenburg, above n. 78; and S. van der Heul and F. Cornelissen, above n. 23.

178 ACM, *'Spreekpunten Henk Don bij rondetafelgesprek "kwaliteit loont" in de Tweede Kamer op 17.04.2015'* ('Points for discussion by Henk Don at the "Quality Pays" round table discussion in the Second Chamber 17.04.2015').

179 D.W.L.A. Schriversho and J.C. Plettenburg, above n. 78.

180 Ibid.

181 34445 Explanatory Memorandum, above n. 73, p. 31.

#### 4.2.2. *England*

In addition to the development of the competition framework, including concurrent powers of the CMA and NHS Improvement, the HSCA 2012 also instituted significant changes to the oversight landscape. This was most notable in the creation of NHS England,[182] and the amendment of section 1H(2) NHS Act 2006 to provide that NHS England, concurrently with the Secretary of State, is under a duty[183] – subject to limited exceptions[184] – to continue the promotion in England of a comprehensive health service. The Explanatory Notes to the HSCA 2012 clarify that NHS England's duty would not apply to those services falling within the public health functions of the Secretary of State or Local Authorities.[185] Certainly NHS England appears to interpret its remit in expansive terms as leading the NHS in England and setting priorities and direction,[186] whilst the Department of Health provides strategic leadership for public health, the NHS and social care in England.[187] Nevertheless, it is NHS England which has devised a 'strategic vision' for the NHS in the form of the NHS Five Year Forward View,[188] in partnership with other bodies (including what is now NHS Improvement), whilst acknowledging the need for consensus and input from government.

Limited oversight by the Secretary of State might be inferred by annual publication of 'The Mandate', which sets out the ambitions which the government wants NHS England to achieve,[189] and reaffirms the government's commitment to an NHS built on the guiding principles that access to healthcare is based on need, and not the ability, to pay, and that services are comprehensive and available to all.[190] The Mandate had previously limited reference to competition as an example of how NHS England will need to balance different ways of ensuring local and national delivery, and as

---

182 Section 9 HSCA 2012 amends the National Health Service Act 2006 to incorporate the functions of the NHS Commissioning Board (now renamed NHS England).

183 Section 1(1) National Health Service Act 2006.

184 Namely, 'the part of the health service that is provided in pursuance of the public health functions of the Secretary of State or local authorities', which is beyond the scope of the present discussion.

185 Explanatory Notes to the Health and Social Care Act 2012, above n. 106, para. 97.

186 NHS England, 'About NHS England', <https://www.england.nhs.uk/about/about-nhs-england/> accessed 24.06.2018.

187 NHS England, 'Understanding the New NHS – A guide for everyone working and training within the NHS', p. 8, 'Structure of the NHS in England'.

188 NHS England website, above n. 186.

189 Department of Health, 'The Mandate – A Mandate from the Government to the NHS Commissioning Board: April 2013 – March 2015', November 2013.

190 Department of Health, above n. 165, para. 1.1.

a means to achieving better quality,[191] but this has been removed in the current version.[192]

The relationship between NHS Improvement and the Secretary of State for Health, in contrast to the situation in the Netherlands, has received comparatively little attention and appears less straightforward. This is because the HSCA 2012 makes provision for the CMA to take over some functions of the Department of Health, separate from its competition oversight function. These are the new mechanisms for modifying licence conditions and determining the National Tariff.

The CMA can now serve as a review body in cases where NHS Improvement proposes to include or modify a special condition[193] in the NHS Provider Licence and this is rejected by the applicant or licence-holder.[194] The CMA's review is intended to examine whether any matters relating to the (proposed) provision of a healthcare service for the purposes of the NHS (may) operate against the public interest.[195] The CMA must focus on the public interest, so could not consider references in terms of the impact on competition as an end in itself.[196] Furthermore, the CMA must have regard to the matters in respect of which NHS Improvement has general duties under section 62 HSCA 2012.[197] Whilst this might be construed as meaning that the CMA must have regard to NHS Improvement's duty to balance anticompetitive behaviour with patient interests under section 62(3) HSCA 2012, there has yet been no recourse to this mechanism at the time of writing.

The HSCA 2012 also introduced a new system for determining the National Tariff. This is important because the NHS tariff has been instrumental in facilitating conditions for competition with regard to the NHS, such as 'payment by results' to incentivise NHS providers and as a benchmark for private and voluntary sector providers to adhere to, thus effectively creating a market for 'NHS provision'. Pre-HSCA 2012, the National Tariff was determined by the Department of Health, but now NHS Improvement must publish a

---

191 See paragraphs 6.4 of both Department of Health, 2013–2015 Mandate, above n. 189, and 'The Mandate – A Mandate from the Government to the NHS England: April 2015–March 2016', December 2015. 'The objectives in this mandate can only be realised through local empowerment. The Board's role in the new system will require it to consider how best to balance different ways of enabling local and national delivery. These may include ... the transformative effect of information and transparency, enabling patients to make fully informed decisions, and encouraging competition between peers for better quality'.

192 Department of Health, above n. 165.

193 Provided for by section 96 HSCA 2012.

194 Section 101 HSCA 2012.

195 Section 101(2) HSCA 2012.

196 Explanatory Notes to the HSCA 2012, above n. 106, para. 798.

197 Section 101(6) HSCA 2012.

'national tariff' document specifying, inter alia, certain healthcare services which are or may be provided for the purposes of the NHS and the method used for determining the national prices of those services.[198] Prior to publication of this, NHS Improvement must consult on its proposals by sending a notice outlining the proposed healthcare services and method(s) used to determine prices to each CCG and relevant provider and such other persons as it considers appropriate.[199] This notice must include, inter alia, the healthcare services to be included and the method(s) used to determine prices, both of which are subject to agreement between NHS Improvement and NHS England.[200] If the consultation reveals objections which exceed certain thresholds determined separately for CCGs and providers,[201] then NHS Improvement may not publish the tariff and must refer it for CMA[202] review of whether the method proposed is appropriate.[203] This review function of the CMA is not one of its general purposes under CA98, but is governed by the HSCA 2012.[204] Thus far, objections to the 2015–16 tariff were raised, but apparently resolved by NHS England and Monitor (now NHS Improvement) offering providers a choice between an 'enhanced tariff option' and a 'default tariff rollover';[205] thus no recourse to CMA review was deemed necessary. In 2016, the objection threshold was not reached[206] and a two-year tariff document – spanning 2017–19 – was published.[207]

What emerges from the foregoing is a complicated picture in which the relationship between NHS Improvement and the CMA is not only dependent

198 Section 116 HSCA 2012.

199 Section 118 HSCA 2012.

200 Section 118(7) and (8) HSCA 2012.

201 Expressed as the 'objection percentage' in section 120(2) HSCA 2012. Section 120(3)(a) defines this for CCGs as the proportion of CCGs or relevant providers who objected to the proposed method. Section 120(3)(b) defines this as the 'share of supply percentage' of relevant providers who objected to the proposed method, weighted according to their share of supply in England of such services as may be prescribed.

202 Sections 120(1)(b) and 120(4) HSCA 2012 specify the Competition Commission.

203 Further guidance is provided by Competition Commission, *National Tariff Methodology Reference Rules under the Health and Social Care Act 2012*: Guide, February 2014, CC22.

204 Section 120(5) HSCA 2012. Schedule 12 HSCA 2012 sets out the procedure on a reference under section 120 HSCA 2012.

205 See, inter alia, Monitor and NHS England, NHS National Tariff Payment System 2015–2016 Engagement Documents, <https://www.gov.uk/government/consultations/nhs-national-tariff-payment-system-201516-engagement-documents>, accessed 24.06.2018. S. Stevens and D. Bennett, Letter to Chief Executives of providers of NHS-funded care, 18.02.2015, <https://www.england.nhs.uk/wp-content/uploads/2015/02/tariff-arrangmnts-2015-16nhs-activity.pdf> accessed 24.06.2018.

206 NHS Improvement, 'National Tariff Payment System 2017/18 and 2018/19: a consultation notice', 22.12.2016, <https://improvement.nhs.uk/resources/national-tariff-1719-consultation/> accessed 24.06.2018.

207 NHS Improvement, 'National Tariff Payment System 2017/18 and 2018/19', 23.02.2018, <https://improvement.nhs.uk/resources/national-tariff-1719/> accessed 24.06.2018.

upon it sharing concurrent powers under section 72 HSCA 2012, although a distinction is drawn between these and the separate roles considered above.[208]

## 5. CONCLUSIONS

This chapter has reviewed the relationship between the new healthcare regulator and the competition authority in the Netherlands and England to attempt to clarify how intervention by the former may affect the application of general competition law by the latter in each country. This is necessary as the underlying institutional relationship may offer some measure of explanation for the absence of competition cases in both countries and, more widely, the potential success of the competition reforms to both the Dutch and English healthcare systems.

This chapter also examined the extent of the separate powers and concurrent powers models. This enabled an understanding of the potential limitations of each model – for example, that the separate powers model may represent in essence the tension between ex ante and ex post intervention, but not offer a resolution of this, despite the removal of separate powers with the transfer of SMP competence to the ACM.

Perhaps most significantly, the chapter demonstrated that the concurrent powers granted to NHS Improvement and the CMA under section 72 HSCA 2012 operate in a very different way to those in other sectors in view of the distinction between the NHS and private healthcare sectors and the consequent *applicability* of competition law. Indeed, the actual relationship between the CMA and NHS Improvement which has developed from the HSCA 2012, the ERRA 2013 reforms and the 2014 Concurrency Regulations represents 'concurrency' as a concept closer to the literal dictionary definition of concurrent [powers] existing at the same time, rather than the 'co-competence' intended as per other sectors. The recent establishment of NHS Improvement and development of a Memorandum of Understanding with the CMA in theory offered an opportunity to revisit and clarify this institutional framework. However, the reluctance to have recourse to primary legislation following the experience of enacting the HSCA 2012 appears to suggest that the current framework is increasingly entrenched. The connection between the concurrent powers under section 72 HSCA 2012 and 'healthcare provision' underscores again the fact that it remains difficult, even impractical, to speak of 'healthcare' as a single sector in England. Whilst other sectors may comprise various markets, the distinction between the NHS and the private healthcare sector

[208] Namely 'the functions of the CMA in its separate role of considering references related to proposed action by NHS Improvement under healthcare sector legislation, for example in relation to setting the national tariff for healthcare services.' CMA and NHS Improvement, above n. 121.

is so pronounced that it is difficult to speak of concurrent powers, since NHS Improvement's expertise is effectively reserved to the NHS (a position reinforced as much by the ERRA 2013 and the 2014 Concurrency Regulations as by the HSCA 2012), and the CMA's to the private healthcare sector. This appears to undermine the argument typically advanced in favour of concurrent powers of the benefits of sector-specific expertise both in assessing competition cases and also in terms of reputation which may facilitate the development of competition policy in a sector. Both – and particularly the latter – appear to have obvious relevance to healthcare. However, the extent to which knowledge of the NHS can be imputed from the CMA's experience of the private healthcare sector is questionable. These are two very distinctive markets for different reasons: the NHS due to its commitment to universal coverage, and the private healthcare sector due to its supplementary nature bringing it closer to 'standard' markets, which is unusual for healthcare (at least in Europe).

The chapter also examined two factors which may prove influential in shaping the relationship between the regulator and competition authority in England and the Netherlands, namely, the focus of the regulator on patients and the evolving role of government in connection with this relationship.

Examination of the regulators' focus on patients was intended to indicate whether any significant discrepancy existed between this and the competition authority's motivation to enhance consumer welfare by applying competition law, as this may have implications for whether and how competition law is applied. With regard to the Netherlands, the chapter examined the NZa's focus as encapsulated in its duty to promote the general consumer interest, understood in terms of the values of accessibility, affordability and quality commonly associated with healthcare provision. This provided a framework for grounding the NZa's decisions using its separate powers, and the chapter found that as this is not automatically replicated in the ACM's assessment criteria, there may be a need to include these by other means, such as policy directions. In England, NHS Improvement's general duty to protect and promote the interests of people who use healthcare services under section 62(1) HSCA 2012 was examined and found to reinforce still further the potential scope for distinction between NHS and private patients. This – together with the qualification of section 62(3) – appears to support further the view advanced in this chapter that 'concurrency' in connection with regulating English healthcare takes on a different meaning in the absence of a single, unified sector. This chapter examined the implications of this new style of concurrency for potential competition cases and found that the situation which existed prior to the enactment of the HSCA 2012 – namely, that the CMA would take enforcement action only in connection with the private healthcare sector – may well continue.

In Section 4, the chapter considered the evolving role of the government and how this may impact the relationship between the competition authority and regulator with regard to applying competition law. Here too we see counterintuitive developments. In the Netherlands, where the *applicability* of competition law is considerably less in question, it may be the case that the Minister intervenes to try to direct how the ACM responds. In England, the creation of NHS England marked a significant turning-point and raised questions about the operation of NHS Improvement despite being at least nominally independent of the Department of Health. In light of the perhaps limited applicability of competition law, it seems reasonable to query the role of the CMA. This chapter has established that, even where the CMA has limited scope to apply competition law, it has other functions in connection with competition in the NHS, namely, effectively as an arbitrator in resolving disputes regarding the setting of the National Tariff by NHS England and NHS Improvement. This creation of semi-independent bodies, coupled with a reduced role for the Secretary of State for Health, clearly offers a potentially rich area for future research.

Finally, the original motivation for the research question of this chapter came from criticisms made in both England and the Netherlands, that the power to apply general competition law should be the exclusive preserve of the competition authority. Indeed, this is taking place in the Netherlands with the current transfer of SMP competence to the ACM, although it remains to be seen whether further policy directions may serve to complicate the picture of a competition authority applying general competition law. Certainly the idea that general competition law is applied by a single agency has the merit of simplicity. In England, the concerns surrounding the enactment of the HSCA 2012 suggest that sole oversight of the NHS by the CMA is problematic, over and above questions of the applicability of competition law to the NHS. This may suffice to explain the effective obviation of CMA oversight of the NHS by the 2014 Concurrency Regulations. Consequently, the common 'solution' of transferring the regulator's competition powers to the competition authority should be treated with caution.

It was suggested in the Introduction to this chapter that proposals to transfer the regulator's competition powers to the competition authorities may have been influenced in part by Littlechild's conception of economic regulation as merely 'holding the fort' pending the arrival of competition; an image developed further by the description that the regulators would 'wither away'.[209] On the one hand, this might be considered to describe what has happened with the Dutch legislative proposal to transfer the majority of the NZa's competition powers to the ACM. On the other hand, even if the NZa is 'withering away' from a competition perspective, it does not necessarily follow that competition has fully arrived in Dutch healthcare, as the ACM has merely assumed the NZa's

209 T. Prosser, above n. 97.

competence. Indeed, the arrival of fully-functioning markets in healthcare is proving to be a mythical end point as complications surrounding ministerial understanding of what competition can achieve, and what a democratically-elected government can do, prove to be determining factors. In England, it is interesting to note that NHS Improvement's role vis-à-vis competition has not so much 'withered away' as been refocused. This is particularly true in the context of merger control and is discussed in Chapter 4 below.

# CHAPTER 4

# MERGER CONTROL

## Hospital Mergers, General Merger Control and the Development of 'Healthcare-Specific' Merger Control in the Netherlands and England

## 1. INTRODUCTION

In contrast to the Dutch and English experiences of applying competition law to healthcare, the applicability of general merger control to hospital mergers is notably less contentious in either country. The relationship between the competition authority and sectoral regulator is also notably clearer: the former has exclusive competence to approve or block a merger, whilst the latter's input is limited to an advisory function. A further contrast is seen in hospital mergers representing a comparatively active area in terms of the number of cases. In the Netherlands, the trend has been towards a steady number of hospital mergers: 15 between 2012 and 2014,[1] 9 in 2014, and 8 in 2015 and 2016.[2] Within the wider Dutch 'healthcare sector', the number of mergers is increasing, from 73 in 2015 and 81 in 2016[3] to 90 in 2017.[4] In England, there were six hospital mergers (involving NHS Foundation Trusts) between 2012 and 2016[5] subsequent to the

---

1 This marks an increase on the 9 hospital mergers assessed between 2004 and 2011. R. Kemp, M-L. Leijh-Smit and K. Schep, *'Concentratietoezicht ACM in de ziekenhuissector – Inzicht in en reflectie op de praktijk'* ('ACM merger control in the hospital sector – insights into, and reflections on practice') (2015) *Markt en Mededinging*, 3, 103.

2 Boer & Croon, *'Fusies en overnames in de gezondheidszorg: onderzoek 2017'*. Executive summary – maart 2017, Amsterdam ('Mergers and takeovers in healthcare: 2017 Investigation'. March 2017), <https://bccf.nl/wp-content/uploads/2017/04/BCCF-Healthcare-Onderzoek-maart-2017.pdf> accessed 24.06.2018.

3 Ibid.

4 Boer & Croon, *'Fusies en overnames in de gezondheidszorg: onderzoek 2018'*. Executive summary – maart 8 Amsterdam ('Mergers and takeovers in healthcare: 2018 Investigation'. March 2018), <https://bccf.nl/wp-content/uploads/2018/03/Fusies-en-overnames-in-de-gezondheidszorg_onderzoek-2018-1.pdf> accessed 24.06.2018.

5 For an overview, see A. Taylor, 'Competing over health – What's next for the National Health Service in England?', *Competition Law Insight*, 16.02.2016.

Health and Social Care Act 2012 (HSCA 2012) reforms. The period of 2016–17 saw a 'marked increase'[6] in NHS mergers, some of which are reviewable under general merger control, and the number of mergers is expected to rise.

Indeed, merger activity has been considered a logical response to the opening up of Dutch hospital markets[7] as previously unregulated markets strived for efficiency. Dutch hospitals have cited the bargaining power of health insurers, stricter quality requirements and increased competition between hospitals as reasons for merging.[8] However, motivation for merging in Dutch healthcare more generally appears to vary across different types of treatment. For example, mergers in the home care sector appear driven primarily by insolvencies, whereas scale plays a notable role in maternity care mergers and healthcare chains, often supported by private equity partners driving mergers in the oral care sector.[9]

In England, it might be considered that a similar logic for merging would apply to the NHS quasi-market as well, as it increasingly operates within a financially straitened environment: certainly motivation for mergers has included concerns about workforce size and the delivery of good outcomes across all services when a smaller provider is involved.[10] However, 'political drivers' may also play a part alongside economic and clinical drivers for hospital mergers[11] in connection with the English NHS. This has been clearly evidenced by episodes of 'merger mania' accompanying previous NHS reform – notably successive policy (between approximately 2004 and 2014) under the New Labour and Coalition Governments to 'upgrade' NHS Trusts to NHS Foundation Trust status[12] in a process latterly termed the 'NHS Foundation Trust pipeline'. Prior (and immediately subsequent) to the HSCA 2012 reforms, these mergers

---

6 A. Taylor, 'Making NHS mergers more successful', *Aldwych Partners* blog, 22.09.2017, <http://aldwychpartners.co.uk/making-more-nhs-mergers-more-successful/> accessed 24.06.2018.

7 M. Canoy and W. Sauter, 'Out of control? Hospital mergers in the Netherlands and the public interest' (2010) 31(9) *European Competition Law Review* 377.

8 ACM, *'Prijs- en volume-effecten van ziekenhuisfusies – Onderzoek naar effecten van ziekenhuisfusies 2007–2014'* ('Price and volume effects of hospital mergers – investigation into the effects of hospital mergers 2007–2014'), *Zaaknummer* (Reference) ACM/17/009041, 05.12.2017, pp. 2 and 6.

9 Boer & Croon, above n. 2.

10 NHS Improvement, *Advice to the Competition and Markets Authority – Proposed merger of Burton Hospitals NHS Foundation Trust and Derby Teaching Hospitals NHS Foundation Trust*, February 2018, pp. 4–5.

11 Economic/financial drivers have been defined as encompassing economic gains, reduced management costs through economies of scale and scope, and reduced operating costs arising from rationalisation of service provision. Client care/clinical quality drivers typically refer to improvements in clinical quality, whether by means of increased effectiveness of higher volume activity of specialised units, higher quality medical training or the capacity to retain and recruit staff more effectively. See M. Cereste, N. Doherty and C. Travers, 'An investigation into the level and impact of merger activity amongst hospitals in the UK's National Health Service' (2003) 17(1) *Journal of Health Organization and Management* 6.

12 As noted in Chapter 1 at fn. 117.

were assessed not under the general merger control regime but a parallel, two-stage NHS-specific merger test.[13]

Nevertheless, applying a two-stage general merger-control regime to hospital mergers[14] in both the Netherlands and England has proved difficult, even contentious, in light of tensions between mergers and promoting competition[15] and, more generally, the ability of a general competition test to accommodate healthcare-specific concerns, or public interest criteria such as accessibility.

The transitional nature of the healthcare markets in the Netherlands and the quasi-market of the English NHS complicates the picture further. In the Netherlands, the gradual liberalisation of hospital service prices and encouragement of selective contracting by health insurers proved instrumental in the *Autoriteit Consument en Markt* (Authority for Consumers and Markets (ACM))'s Phase II approval in 2012 of the *Tilburg Hospitals* merger,[16] a decision which has attracted criticism. Furthermore, widespread merger approval proved a particular concern in the Netherlands prior to the blocking of the *Albert Schweitzer Hospital–Rivas Care Group* merger[17] in July 2015. This led to criticism that the ACM did not apply Dutch general merger control correctly.[18] The ACM has consistently rebuffed such criticism on the grounds that it can only block a merger if it poses competition problems,[19] and has subsequently suggested that competition law may not be capable of delivering what the Minister for Health, Wellbeing and Sport wants to achieve with competition in Dutch healthcare.[20]

In England, the distinctive nature of the NHS quasi-market raised questions about the use of general merger control and varying perceptions of merger benefits within the NHS and by the Competition and Markets Authority (CMA)

---

13 NHS Co-Operation and Competition Panel (NHS CCP), *Merger Guidelines*, 25.10.2010.

14 As distinct from mergers involving, for example, health insurers or pharmaceutical companies, which typically appear to attract less political sensitivity.

15 On this point, see M. Canoy and W. Sauter, above n. 7.

16 ACM, Case 7295/402 *TweeSteden Ziekenhuis–St Elisabeth Ziekenhuis* (TweeSteden Hospital–St Elisabeth Hospital) ('*Tilburg Hospitals* merger'), 16.11.2012 (Phase II decision).

17 ACM, Case 14.0982.24 *Stichting Albert Schweitzer Ziekenhuis–Stichting Rivas Zorggroep* (*Albert Schweitzer Hospital–Rivas Care Group* merger), 22.07.2015 (Phase II decision).

18 See, for example, E.M.H. Loozen, 'Public healthcare interests require strict competition enforcement' (2015) 119(7) *Health Policy* 882. See further on the tension between healthcare-specific merger control and the correct application of general merger control, E.M.H. Loozen, '*ACM en ziekenhuisfusies: hoeder van het publiek belang?*' ('Hospital mergers and the ACM: guardian of the public interest?') (2015) *Markt en Mededinging*, 5, 178.

19 See R. Kemp et al., above n. 1.

20 ACM, '*Spreekpunten Henk Don bij rondetafelgesprek "kwaliteit loont" in de Tweede Kamer op 17.04.2015*' ('Points for discussion by Henk Don at the "Quality Pays" round table discussion in the Second Chamber 17.04.2015').

when the latter's predecessor blocked[21] the *Dorset Hospitals* merger;[22] the first to be assessed under the HSCA 2012 reforms and to include consideration of 'relevant customer benefits'[23] identified by Monitor (now NHS Improvement), at Phase II. Although subsequent NHS Foundation Trust mergers have been approved both at Phase I[24] and Phase II,[25] questions may arise about how general merger control is to be used in future in view of the current wider policy changes implementing new care models under the NHS Five Year Forward View and Accountable Care Organisations within the context of Sustainability and Transformation Partnerships. The 2017 *Manchester Hospitals* merger[26] was the first NHS Foundation Trust merger to be decided – and approved – against this backdrop (and under an expedited Phase II assessment), and the CMA used this decision as a platform to articulate its view that competition currently plays a limited role in the NHS, and is not the basic organising principle for the provision of NHS services.[27] Subsequently, it has continued to maintain this and placed significant weight on NHS Improvement's opinion and identification of 'relevant patient benefits'[28] in order to clear mergers at Phase I, notably the 2017 *Birmingham Hospitals*[29] merger.[30] So there may now be a trend towards

---

21 See, for example, F. Barnes, 'Competition law and patient choice in the NHS: help or hindrance?' *Oxera Agenda*, January 2014, <https://www.oxera.com/Latest-Thinking/Agenda/2014/Competition-law-and-patient-choice-in-the-NHS-help.aspx> accessed 24.06.2018.

22 Competition Commission, *Royal Bournemouth and Christchurch Hospitals NHS Foundation Trust/Poole Hospital NHS Foundation Trust Merger Inquiry* (CC), 17.10.2013 (Phase II decision).

23 Under section 30(1)(a) Enterprise Act 2002 (EA02). See Sections 2 and 5 below for consideration of how this exception mechanism functions within general merger control.

24 For example, CMA, Case Reference ME/6432-14, *Anticipated acquisition of Heatherwood and Wexham Park Hospitals NHS Foundation Trust by Frimley Park Hospital NHS Foundation Trust*, 03.06.2014. CMA, Case Reference ME/6481-14, *Anticipated acquisition by Chelsea and Westminster NHS Foundation Trust of West Middlesex University NHS Trust*, 19.01.2015.

25 CMA, *A report on the anticipated merger of Ashford and St Peter's Hospitals NHS Foundation Trust and Royal Surrey County Hospital NHS Foundation Trust*, 16.09.2015 (Phase II decision).

26 CMA, *Central Manchester University Hospitals/University Hospital of South Manchester Merger Inquiry, Final Report*, 01.08.2017.

27 Ibid, paragraph 7, p. 5.

28 A term used in preference to 'relevant customer benefits', but with the same meaning. See, for example, NHS Improvement, *Advice to the Competition and Markets Authority: Proposed merger of Central Manchester University Hospitals NHS Foundation Trust and University Hospitals of South Manchester NHS Foundation Trust*, June 2017, p. 6.

29 CMA, Case ME/6666-17, *Anticipated merger between University Hospitals Birmingham NHS Foundation Trust and Heart of England NHS Foundation Trust*, 14.09.2017.

30 For example, 'In its recent merger investigations between NHS hospitals in Manchester and Birmingham, the CMA found that NHS providers were facing significant growth in demand for services, while working under tight budgetary, capacity and regulatory constraints. The CMA also found that, although competition between NHS service providers was possible, it may be more limited than had previously been the case. The CMA has taken account of these findings in its investigation of the merger'. CMA, Case reference ME/5726-17, *Anticipated merger between Derby Teaching Hospitals NHS Foundation Trust and Burton Hospitals NHS Foundation Trust*, 05.04.2018, paragraph 4. Near identical comments had been made in Case ME/6666-17, above n. 29, at paragraph 7.

the CMA clearing a significant majority of NHS Foundation Trust mergers at Phase I, effectively directed by NHS Improvement's view and identification of relevant patient benefits arising from a merger[31] – this would suggest a healthcare-specific approach to assessment under general merger control insofar as it marks a divergence from the CMA's approach to mergers in other sectors.

In view of such concerns and ambivalence about general merger control, it is not surprising that a range of modifications have been introduced in both countries. These can be described collectively as 'healthcare-specific' merger control. This can be understood further as comprising both 'jurisdictional' and 'substantive assessment' aspects which have been introduced both prior and subsequent to the application of general merger control in relation to the 2006 reforms in the Netherlands and HSCA 2012 reforms in England. These modifications form the focus of the discussions in this chapter, but, in overview, comprise the following:

| | Jurisdictional aspects | Substantive assessment aspects |
|---|---|---|
| **The Netherlands** | - Temporary lower turnover thresholds;<br>- *Zorgspecifieke fusietoets* (healthcare-specific merger test). | - Temporary additional assessment criteria;<br>- *Nederlandse Zorgautoriteit* (Dutch Healthcare Authority, hereinafter NZa) Opinions. |
| **England** | - Section 79 HSCA 2012 – NHS Foundation Trusts;<br>- NHS-specific merger test ('NHS Foundation Trust pipeline');<br>- NHS Improvement Authorisation ('Transactions oversight');<br>- New test for Private Patient Units (PPUs). | - NHS Improvement advisory function under section 79(5) HSCA 2012 to identify 'relevant patient benefits' to assist CMA assessment under Enterprise Act 2002 (EA02). |

**Figure 11. Overview of 'healthcare-specific' merger control**

These modifications are affected by the ongoing wider developments regarding competition in healthcare in both countries. Thus the refocusing of the ACM's powers in connection with healthcare includes the transfer of the healthcare-specific merger test to the ACM from the NZa, and a refocusing of how public interests are to be incorporated in the merger assessment process. In England, the development of a new test for PPUs arises from concerns about an expansion in these as a result of section 165 HSCA 2012 removing the private patient income cap.[32] The recent *Manchester Hospitals* and *Birmingham Hospitals* mergers

31 Provided by section 79(5) HSCA 2012.

32 CMA, *Private Healthcare Market Investigation Final Report*, CMA25, 02.04.2014, paragraph 11.249, pp. 11–58. CMA, *Private Healthcare Market Investigation Final Order*, 01.10.2014, Part 2, pp. 5–6.

both saw significant reliance on NHS Improvement's advice on relevant patient benefits, which arguably suggests a refocusing of the use of general merger control, rather than the design of a new substantive or jurisdictional test. Recourse to the CMA's 'fast-track' procedure in the *Manchester Hospitals* merger similarly does not constitute a new substantive assessment or jurisdictional approach, yet may prove notable if it marks a change in procedure which is adopted in other hospital merger cases.

This chapter therefore provides an assessment of what healthcare-specific merger control can achieve by reference to the development of the aforementioned modifications. These might be considered a response to general concerns about hospital mergers[33] – typically relating to increased costs – as well as to specific concerns about apparent preference for merger over other forms of cooperation. These arise in view of the relative clarity of navigating merger assessment (as evidenced by widespread merger approval) when contrasted with perceived uncertainty regarding the anticompetitive agreements provisions.[34]

The chapter is structured as follows:

Section 2 considers in overview the general merger-control regimes in operation in the Netherlands and England and how these have been applied in hospital merger cases. From a Dutch perspective, the cases considered comprise the *Zeeland Hospitals*, *Tilburg Hospitals*, *Albert Schweitzer Hospital–Rivas Care Group* and recent *Amsterdam Universities Hospitals*[35] mergers. From an English perspective, attention is paid to the *Dorset Hospitals*, *Surrey Hospitals*, *Manchester Hospitals* and *Birmingham Hospitals* NHS Foundation

---

33 It has been established in both countries that merged entities can exceed the optimal hospital size. M. Canoy and W. Sauter, above n. 7, refer to OECD data to conclude that the size of Dutch hospitals is above the EU average. This has also been a concern in England, see A. Charlesworth, 'Size may not be everything: reviewing hospital mergers', *Nuffield Trust Blog Post*, 24.02.2012, <https://www.nuffieldtrust.org.uk/news-item/size-may-not-be-everything-reviewing-hospital-mergers> accessed 24.06.2018. In addition, government-mandated mergers in England have been deemed to produce no more benefit than those arising between private hospitals: M. Gaynor, M. Laudicella and C. Propper, 'Can governments do it better? Merger mania and hospital outcomes in the English NHS' (2012) 31(1) *Journal of Health Economics* 528.

34 On this point, see R.J.P. Jansen, *'Samenwerken of fuseren in de zorg?'* ('Collaborating or merging in healthcare?') (2013) *Markt en Mededinging*, 2, 77. E. Loozen, M. Varkevisser and E. Schut, *'Beoordeling ziekenhuisfusies door ACM: staat de consument wel echt centraal?'* ('Are consumers really at the centre of the ACM's hospital merger decisions?') (2014) *Markt en Mededinging*, 1, 5. A. Taylor, 'When does an alliance become a merger?', *Aldwych Partners blog*, 14.07.2015, <http://aldwychpartners.co.uk/when-does-an-alliance-become-a-merger/> accessed 24.06.2018.

35 This developed between 2016 and 2017, following an informal opinion by the ACM in 2015 that a proposed reconfiguration would qualify as a merger. ACM, Case no. 13.1466.22, *Informal Opinion regarding the merger of AMC–VUmc*, 13.05.2015, <https://www.acm.nl/sites/default/files/old_publication/publicaties/14244_amc-vumc-informele-zienswijze-2015-05-13.pdf> accessed 24.06.2018.

Trust mergers.[36] These are compared and contrasted with the recent *Cygnet Healthcare Ltd and Cambian Adult Services* merger,[37] since this falls outside the scope of the healthcare-specific merger-control regime established by the HSCA 2012, yet nevertheless affects the NHS.

Section 3 considers in detail the jurisdictional and substantive aspects of healthcare-specific merger tests in both countries set out in Figure 1.

Section 4 examines the intentions behind healthcare-specific merger tests and lessons emerging from their design and application in the Netherlands and England.

Section 5 provides concluding remarks about the treatment of hospital merger assessment in the Netherlands and England in light of the complex framework established by the interaction between general merger control and the development of healthcare-specific merger control.

## 2. OVERVIEW OF GENERAL MERGER CONTROL AS APPLIED IN DUTCH AND ENGLISH HEALTHCARE

### 2.1. MARKET DEFINITION AND HOSPITAL MERGERS IN THE NETHERLANDS AND ENGLAND

A factor common to substantive merger assessment in both countries is market definition, and this can prove outcome-determinative in hospital merger cases.[38] However, this factor is characterised by different approaches in the

36 With regard to the 'four categories of English healthcare' outlined in Chapter 1 above, these mergers, and indeed the HSCA 2012 regime, may be considered to relate to categories 1 and 2 (that is, NHS and private / voluntary sector providers delivering NHS services).

37 CMA, *A report on the completed acquisition by Cygnet Health Care Ltd and Universal Health Services, Inc. of the Cambian Adult Services Division of Cambian Group plc*, 16.10.2017. This might be considered to relate specifically to category 2 (private sector delivery of NHS services) of the 'four categories of English healthcare' outlined in Chapter 1 above. A case combining private and NHS providers which could similarly be considered to fall within the scope of category 2 (but within the HSCA 2012 merger regime) is CMA, Case reference ME/6252-13, *Anticipated Pathology Services Joint Venture between Basildon and Thurrock University Hospitals NHS Foundation Trust, Southend University Hospitals NHS Foundation Trust and Integrated Pathology Partnerships Ltd.*, 10.09.2014. Although NHS Improvement (at the time Monitor) did not identify any relevant patient benefits arising from the proposed joint venture, the CMA did not establish any substantial lessening of competition either, and granted approval at Phase I.

38 As seen in a range of US hospital merger decisions, and also the *Hilversum-Gooi Noord* merger, where a wider market based on patient willingness to travel was established at Phase II, thus leading the ACM to grant a licence and permit the merger to proceed. For discussion of this case, see J.W. van de Gronden and E. Szyszczak, 'Introducing Competition Principles into Health Care through EU Law and Policy: A Case Study of the Netherlands' (2014) 22(2) *Medical Law Review* 238.

two systems. For example, the 'hypothetical monopolist' test appears largely rejected in the Netherlands, but has been used by the CMA as a guide in defining both product and geographic markets in NHS mergers.[39] Furthermore, the approaches to geographic market definition differ, with the development of modern econometric methods applicable to Dutch hospital markets relying on patient willingness to travel, or time-elasticities as a proxy for price substitution.[40] In England, the CMA distinguishes between the NHS and private healthcare sector and has clarified that the relevant geographic market may be based on the location of providers and will be informed by an assessment of the willingness of patients to travel for consultation or treatment (the 'catchment area').[41]

Finally, there are different approaches to defining product markets which reflect the two systems. In the Netherlands, the ACM typically distinguishes 'inpatient' and 'outpatient' general hospital care[42] from separate markets for highly specialist care which may be offered only by providers with a licence under the *Wet op bijzondere medische verrichtingen* (Special Medical Procedures Act 1997 (WBMV)) or by university hospitals.[43] However, the ACM may focus on specialties where these would result in different consequences for a merger than an assessment based on markets for general hospital care. In England, the CMA's approach to product market definition now encompasses both the NHS and private healthcare sector and is based on specialties,[44] then disaggregated further within each specialty to 'inpatient and outpatient activities', 'elective and non-elective services', and also 'community and hospital-based care'. Whilst distinctions can be drawn within these (sub-)markets, matters may not always be that straightforward. For example, maternity services are classified as 'non-elective' services, yet because they constitute planned services, they are included with 'elective services' within CMA assessments.[45]

---

39 See, for example, the *Surrey Hospitals* merger, above n. 25, para. 5.51.

40 See M. Varkevisser, C. Capps and F. Schut, 'Defining Hospital Markets for Antitrust Enforcement: New Approaches and their Applicability to the Netherlands' (2008) 3(1) *Health Economics, Policy and Law* 7. Also, M. Varkevisser and F. Schut, 'The Impact of Geographic Market Definition on the Stringency of Hospital Merger Control in Germany and the Netherlands' (2012) 7 *Health Economics, Policy and Law* 363.

41 Competition and Markets Authority, *CMA guidance on the review of NHS mergers*, 31.07.2014, CMA29, para. 6.40. This follows the OFT's use of catchment areas in the *Dorset Hospitals* merger case. OFT, ME/5351/12, *Anticipated Merger between The Royal Bournemouth and Christchurch Hospitals NHS Foundation Trust and Poole Hospital NHS Foundation Trust*, 07.02.2013, (Phase I Decision), para. 47.

42 A similar approach to that taken in the United States. For discussions of how the Dutch approach to defining product markets has developed, see M. Varkevisser et al., and M. Varkevisser and F. Schut, both above n. 40.

43 For further discussion, see R. Kemp et al., above n. 1.

44 Based on CMA, above n. 41, paras. 6.37–6.39. See also subsequent cases.

45 See, for example, CMA, Case reference ME/6653/16, *Anticipated Merger between Central Manchester University Hospitals NHS Foundation Trust and University Hospital of South Manchester NHS Foundation Trust*, 09.03.2017, (Phase I Decision), paragraph 53.

A further stage in determining the product market definition in earlier cases saw the CMA considering at Phase I the effect of the merger on competition *in* the market and competition *for* the market.[46] With regard to competition *in* the market, the CMA analyses competition for the provision of NHS elective inpatient and outpatient services and private services,[47] and so makes an assessment based on the perceived effects of a merger on the choice of hospital available to (individual) NHS patients. With regard to competition *for* the market, the CMA analyses competition for winning contracts for commissioned NHS elective and non-elective inpatient services and outpatient services, including specialised services,[48] and so makes an assessment based on the perceived effects of a merger on the choice available to NHS commissioners (whether Clinical Commissioning Groups or NHS England in respect of specialist services). More recently, the distinction between competition *in* the market and competition *for* the market has been used as a basis for identifying theories of harm[49] to underpin competition concerns.

Although these aspects do not always feature in discussions of other elements of healthcare-specific merger control,[50] how measurement tools are interpreted in the context of general merger control can be pertinent in itself,[51] as well as for the development of healthcare-specific merger control. For example, in England, the interpretation of GP referral data was considered significant to the outcome of the *Surrey Hospitals* merger, but the premise that the NHS Foundation Trusts/NHS Trusts with the most referrals represent the main competitors was considered misleading, and the CMA's focus on random variation of patient choices problematic.[52] In the Netherlands, the potential for

46 See, for example, *Heatherwood and Frimley* (2014), above n. 24, para. 5.

47 *Heatherwood and Frimley* (2014), para. 5, and *Chelsea and Westminster-West Middlesex* (2015), para. 5, both above n. 24.

48 Ibid.

49 CMA, above n. 45, para. 50.

50 See, for example, W. Sauter, '*Sectorspecifiek mededingingsrecht en fusietoetsing*' ('Sector-specific competition law and merger control') (2013) *RegelMaat*, (28)2, 77. E.M.H. Loozen, '*Inrichting van meervoudig toezicht op marktwerking*' ('Introduction of multisector regulation of competition') (2013) *RegelMaat*, (28) 2, 105.

51 Although it is recognised that the CMA has previously not deemed it necessary to conclude on the precise scope of the product or geographic markets in Phase I decisions. See, for example, *Heatherwood and Frimley* (2014), paras. 5 and 6, and *Chelsea & Westminster-West Middlesex* (2015), paras. 5 and 6, both above n. 24. See also *Birmingham Hospitals* merger, paras. 57 and 61, above n. 29. In the *Cygnet Health Care-Cambian Adult Services* merger, the CMA took the view that direct analysis of competition on a local specific basis was more appropriate than attempting to generalise findings in the relevant product or geographic markets. CMA, above n. 37, paragraphs 5.4 and 5.60.

52 For discussions of this, see A. Taylor, 'Is clearance for hospital mergers about to get easier?' *Nuffield Trust Blog*, 10.09.2015, <https://www.nuffieldtrust.org.uk/news-item/is-clearance-for-hospital-mergers-about-to-get-easier> accessed 24.06.2018. Also A. Taylor, 'Using patient referrals to analyse hospital competition', *Aldwych Partners blog*, 26.11.2015,

relatively small relevant geographic markets in specific aspects of healthcare (such as long-term care or social care) has raised concerns about the potential for notable market power even where providers have a relatively low turnover, and so has motivated the Dutch government's decision to extend the timeframe of operation for lower turnover thresholds for healthcare provider mergers.[53] These concerns are discussed further in Section 3 below under 'jurisdictional aspects' of healthcare-specific merger control.

## 2.2. DUTCH GENERAL MERGER CONTROL AND HOSPITAL MERGER CASES

In the Netherlands, the general merger-control regime is set out in the *Mededingingswet* (Dutch Competition Act (Mw))[54] and is heavily influenced by the EU Merger Regulation (EUMR).[55] Jurisdiction is established by a requirement for 'undertakings'[56] and satisfaction of threshold tests for turnover and degree of transfer of control to distinguish notifiable mergers[57] from collaborations subject to a self-assessment regime.[58]

Dutch general merger control comprises a two-phase assessment. Phase I is a mandatory 'notification' phase[59] intended to establish whether a merger will

<http://aldwychpartners.co.uk/using-patient-referrals-to-analyse-hospital-competition/> accessed 24.06.2018.

53 Staatsblad 2017, 503, *Besluit van 13.12.2017, houdende wijziging van het Besluit van 06.12.2007, houdende tijdelijke verruiming van het toepassingsbereik van het concentratietoezicht op ondernemingen die zorg verlenen (Stb. 2007, 518) in verband met een verlenging van het besluit en de reikwijdte van het concentratietoezicht op aanbieders van maatschappelijke ondersteuning* (Bulletin of Acts and Decrees 2017 503, Decree of 13.12.2017 extending the Decree of 06.12.2007 instituting temporary measures regarding the applicability of merger control to undertakings providing care (Bulletin of Acts and Decrees (Stb) 2007, 518) in connection with extending the time period of operation of the Decree and the scope of merger control regarding providers of social care).

54 Chapter 5 Mw (Articles 26–49 Mw).

55 Council Regulation (EC) No. 139/2004 of 20.01.2004 on the control of concentrations between undertakings (the EC Merger Regulation).

56 Defined as 'economic activities' by reference to competition law – Case C-41/90, *Klaus Höfner and Fritz Elser v. Macrotron GmbH*, ECLI:EU:C:1991:161 – and elaborated as 'offering goods or services on a market' in Case C-35/96, *Commission of the European Communities v. Italy*, ECLI:EU:C:1998:303.

57 Dutch general merger control distinguishes between three types of notifiable 'concentration': merger, takeover and joint venture. See ACM, *Richtsnoeren voor de zorgsector* (Guidelines for the healthcare sector), March 2010, para. 5.1.

58 See ACM, 'Assessing mergers and collaborations in hospital care', 27.09.2013, <https://www.acm.nl/en/publications/publication/12304/Assessing-mergers-and-collaborations-in-hospital-care> accessed 24.06.2018.

59 It is prohibited for undertakings to operate as a merged undertaking prior to approval by the ACM. This is referred to as 'gun-jumping' and comprises premature implementation of a notifiable merger or breach of the anticompetitive agreements provision (Article 6 Mw) for mergers regardless of whether they are notifiable. See ACM, above n. 57, section 5.2.3.

lead to a significant impediment to effective competition (SIEC) on the Dutch market or part of it by creating or strengthening an economically dominant position. Where the ACM determines that there is no SIEC, the merger can be approved. However, where the ACM finds an SIEC, a licence is required for the merger and a Phase II assessment is undertaken, unless the merger parties propose 'remedies' to offset the SIEC.[60] Phase II is a 'licence authorisation' phase involving an in-depth investigation of the SIEC, which results either in the merger being blocked or the granting of a licence to enable the merger to proceed.

This section examines three merger cases approved at Phase II (the *Zeeland Hospitals, Tilburg Hospitals* and *Amsterdam Universities Hospitals* mergers), as well as the first hospital merger to be blocked – involving the Albert Schweitzer Hospital and Rivas Care Group.

### *2.2.1.* Zeeland Hospitals *Merger*

The *Zeeland Hospitals* case[61] involved a merger between the sole direct competitors in a remote and westerly province in the Netherlands which resulted in a market share of over 80 per cent and was finally[62] approved in 2009. This approval followed a Phase II assessment subject to remedies to implement an efficiency defence advanced by the merging parties. After a SIEC was established at Phase I, the hospitals claimed that the merger was necessary to ensure an adequate level of quality regarding the provision of even basic care. This argument was endorsed by the quality regulator, the *Inspectie voor de Gezondheidszorg en Jeugd* (Dutch Health and Youth Care Inspectorate (IGJ)),[63] whereas the NZa was more sceptical.[64] The ACM initially took the view that the conditions for a successful efficiency defence had not been satisfied because the claimed benefits were not

---

60 This option of avoiding a Phase II assessment has proved successful in some merger cases involving home care organisations. For example, ACM, Case No. 5206 *Stichting Pantein–Stichting Thuiszorg Brabant Noord-Oost*, cited in ACM, above n. 57, section 5.3.1, paragraph 137.

61 Discussed further by W. Sauter, 'Experiences from the Netherlands: The Application of Competition Rules in Health Care' in J.W. van de Gronden, E. Szyszczak, U. Neergaard and M. Krajewski (eds.), *Health Care and EU Law*, TMC Asser Press, The Hague 2011; and J. W. van de Gronden and E. Szyszczak, above n. 38.

62 The merger was officially notified in 2005 (under Case no. 5196 *Ziekenhuis Walcheren–Stichting Oosterscheldeziekenhuizen*, (*Zeeland Hospitals* merger) 18.11.2005) but was withdrawn after a Phase II assessment was deemed necessary. The merger was notified a second time in 2008 under Case no. 6424/427 *Ziekenhuis Walcheren–Oosterscheldeziekenhuizen*, (*Zeeland Hospitals* merger) 25.03.2009.

63 Formerly known as the Inspectie voor gezondheidszorg (Dutch Healthcare Inspectorate (IGZ), which merged with the Inspectie voor jeugdzorg (IJZ) in 2018.

64 This prompted the question of the relative predominance of the three agencies. See Y. Maasdam and J-K. Sluijs, *'Wie van de drie is de echte marktmeester in de zorg: de IGZ, de NMa of toch de NZa?'* ('Who is the real market umpire in healthcare? The IGZ, the NMa or actually the NZa?') (2009) *Actualiteiten Mededingingsrecht*, 5, 103.

verifiable, nor was it clear that these would be passed on to patients. However, on the authority of the IGJ, the ACM accepted that the benefits were merger-specific. This proved critical, as the ACM then proposed a range of behavioural remedies to implement the efficiency defence, namely, a price cap, commitments regarding the claimed quality improvements, and the opening-up of the collective agreement between the hospitals and their consultants so that the latter could compete with the merged entity. This approach by the ACM is notable not only for being the first of its kind, but has been described as 'unique' by both lawyers and health economists[65] and 'creative'[66] in its use of the efficiency defence.

### *2.2.2.* Tilburg Hospitals *Merger*

The 2012 *Tilburg Hospitals* case[67] involved a merger of two hospitals in the city of Tilburg in the south of the Netherlands with a predicted combined market share of 70–80 per cent and price increases of 25–33 per cent. The ACM ultimately cleared this merger at Phase II subject to a voluntary price cap on the grounds that wider changes in the sector – namely that the government subsidy supporting insurer and hospital purchasing decisions was due to be withdrawn from January 2015 – would be sufficient to correct any SIEC. The price cap was therefore intended to provide some protection against the anticipated price increase in the transition period from 2015–16. It is surprising to note that the ACM itself[68] contended that the price cap constituted neither a 'remedy' in the sense of the Remedies Guidelines 2007,[69] nor a condition or restriction in accordance with Article 41(4) Mw, which provides that a licence may be issued subject to restrictions, or with conditions attached to it. In addition, the ACM acknowledged in a press release that it was powerless to enforce this behavioural remedy.[70] This approach was strongly criticised as an inappropriate

---

65 Specifically M. Wiggers, *De NMa en de NZa in de curatieve zorgsector – Een toetsing aan het Europees mededingingsrecht* (The NMa and the NZa in the curative healthcare sector – an assessment against EU competition law) Kluwer, Deventer 2013; and M. Varkevisser et al., above n. 40.

66 By, inter alia, M. Canoy and W. Sauter, above n. 7, and J.W. van de Gronden and E. Szyszczak, above n. 38.

67 Discussed by E.M.H. Loozen, M. Varkevisser and F. Schut, 'Dutch Authority for Consumers and Markets fails to meet the standard of proof in recent hospital merger decisions' (2014) 35(1) *European Competition Law Review* 16.

68 ACM, above n. 16, *Bijlage 3, Prijsplafond* (Appendix 3, Price Cap).

69 ACM, *Richtsnoeren Remedies 2007* (Remedies Guidelines 2007) 21.09.2007.

70 Autoriteit Consument en Markt (ACM), *'Regierol zorgverzekeraar cruciaal bij toestaan ziekenhuisfusies'* ('Leading role of health insurers critical in approving hospital mergers'), 07.12.2012, <https://www.acm.nl/nl/publicaties/publicatie/10934/NMa-regierol-zorgverzekeraar-cruciaal-bij-toestaan-ziekenhuisfusies> accessed 24.06.2018.

use of remedies, which, together with inconclusive market definitions, made it difficult to see why the merger was cleared.[71]

### 2.2.3. Albert Schweitzer Hospital–Rivas Care Group *Merger*

The 2015 proposed *Albert Schweitzer Hospital–Rivas Care Group* merger is notable for being the first hospital merger to be blocked by the ACM. The Albert Schweitzer Hospital in Dordrecht operates in the field of inpatient and outpatient general hospital care and specialist hospital care. Rivas Care Group comprises a hospital, an outpatient clinic and several care facilities including residential care and nursing homes, home care services, and maternal and child health centres near Rotterdam. At Phase I the ACM established that the merging parties were each other's main competitor; thus competitive pressure would be removed by the merger, and this could not be offset by the health insurers' buyer power.[72] This finding was supported by arguments advanced by health insurers and patient organisations that the hospitals had not demonstrated the benefits of the merger. The ACM considered that the Phase II investigation should examine three aspects: the extent of the relevant geographic market; the competitive pressure exerted by the surrounding hospitals; and the possible benefits of the proposed merger.[73] The ACM established that the geographic market had been correctly determined at Phase I,[74] and the merged entity would hold market shares of 70–80 per cent on the markets for inpatient and outpatient general hospital care. Ultimately the ACM concluded that the merger would result in the removal of a considerable amount of competitive pressure and that scope to discipline the merged entity by patients 'voting with their feet' and choosing other hospitals, or by health insurers negotiating more favourable prices and quality, was limited.[75] As a result, the ACM declined to issue a merger licence in July 2015, having considered that the remedy proposed by the parties was insufficient to offset the significant impediment to effective competition. This decision was challenged by the parties on the basis that the ACM had not included an adequate analysis of the counterfactual, had overstated the competitive pressure between the parties, had understated the scope for health insurers and patients to discipline the merged entity, and had not demonstrated

71 E.M.H. Loozen et al., above n. 67.

72 ACM, 'Further investigation needed into merger between hospitals', Press Release, 18.03.2014, <https://www.acm.nl/en/publications/publication/12845/Further-investigation-needed-into-merger-between-hospitals> accessed 24.06.2018.

73 ACM, above n. 17, para. 2.

74 Ibid, paras. 59–60.

75 ACM, 'ACM prohibits proposed merger between two Dutch hospital groups', Press Release, 15.07.2015, <https://www.acm.nl/en/publications/publication/14503/ACM-prohibits-proposed-merger-between-two-Dutch-hospital-groups> accessed 24.06.2018.

that its theory of harm – that the merger would result in increased prices and lower quality – was plausible. However, the *Rechtbank Rotterdam* (Rotterdam District Court (Rb Rotterdam)) supported the ACM's analysis on appeal and upheld the prohibition on the merger in October 2016.[76] The parties decided not to pursue a further appeal[77] to the *College van Beroep voor het bedrijfsleven* (Dutch Trade and Industry Appeals Tribunal (CBb)).

### *2.2.4.* Amsterdam Universities' Hospitals *Merger*

In September 2017, a merger between two university hospitals in Amsterdam – the Academic Medical Centre (AMC) of the University of Amsterdam and the Vrije Universiteit Medical Centre (VUmc) in Amsterdam – was finally cleared with a licence by the ACM. This case is notable for being the first university hospitals merger to be assessed by the ACM, which required consideration of factors beyond patient care and product market definition based on specialty. In its Phase I assessment of whether a licence would be required, the ACM defined its focus in terms of the applicability of general merger control.[78] Thus undergraduate- and postgraduate-level medical education, specialist medical continuing professional development, and certain aspects of medical research were exempted as these were not deemed to be 'economic activities', largely due to the levels of government funding these receive. In contrast, the ACM deemed teacher training and aspects of medical research subsidised by bodies such as the *Koninklijke Nederlandse Akademie van Wetenschappen* (Royal Netherlands Academy of Arts and Sciences (KNAW)) to be subject to general merger control under Chapter 5 Mw. The ACM's assessment comprised judgements on medical and paramedic education and training, medical scientific research and patient care.

The ACM established that there were no competition concerns arising in connection with medical and paramedic education and training and medical scientific research. With regard to patient care, the ACM conducted an extensive analysis which took account of the public function of university medical centres in providing experimental and innovative treatment and their function effectively as providers of last resort for patients requiring highly specialist care

---

76 Albert Schweitzer Hospital–Rivas Care Group appeal, ECLI:NL:RBROT:2016:7373.

77 Albert Schweitzer Ziekenhuis, *'Albert Schweitzer Ziekenhuis en Rivas Zorggroep zien af van fusie, geen hoger beroep'* ('Albert Schweitzer Hospital and Rivas Care Group will not merge – no further appeal'), Press Release, 10.11.2016, <https://www.asz.nl/nieuws/nieuwsberichten/2016/11/21396/> accessed 24.06.2018.

78 ACM, Case reference 16.0685.22, *Vergunningseis voor de concentratie tussen het Academisch Medisch Centrum en Stichting VUmc* (Licence request for merger between the AMC and VUmc), 14.12.2016 (Phase I Decision). Section 5, *Toepasselijkheid van het concentratietoezicht* (Applicability of merger control).

where no further referral is possible (referred to as the 'academic healthcare provision' by the NZa).[79] These public functions mean that university medical centres receive a government contribution and are classified as delivering services of general economic interest (SGEI), so their function in this regard would fall outside the scope of general merger control.[80] Having considered the extensive range of providers involved in delivering care via university medical centres, the ACM outlined two product markets – broadly, 'basic healthcare' (*basiszorg*) and 'highly specialist healthcare' (*topzorg*),[81] the latter being only provided in specific hospitals, typically university hospitals – with relevant geographic markets relating to the municipality of Amsterdam and the wider North Holland province. Ultimately, concerns about a reduction in patient choice regarding 'highly specialist healthcare' contributed to the ACM's ultimate finding that a licence – and thus a Phase II investigation – was required for the proposed *Amsterdam Universities Hospitals* merger.

In its Phase II decision, the ACM focused on competition concerns in the market for highly specialist healthcare. However, it concluded that the AMC and VUmc held a combined market share of 30–40 per cent, and so did not pose any competition concerns in this market. Although the ACM approved the *Amsterdam Universities Hospitals* merger, the NZa had advised that the merger should be blocked due to negative effects on the public interests of affordability and quality; inter alia, on the grounds that the resulting hospital would be 'too big to fail', that there would not be sufficient choice of providers for health insurers purchasing general care, and that the price of care would increase and/or the quality of care would decrease.[82]

Overall, the foregoing illustrates how the ACM's assessment includes factors such as the position of affected undertakings on the relevant market, the position of other operators on the market, the independence of suppliers from the proposed merged entity and the possibilities for new entry.[83] However, critiques of ACM decisions focus specifically on how the ACM interprets elements of

---

79 ACM, ibid, section 8.1 *Rol van UMC's* (Function of University Medical Centres), paragraphs 74–75.

80 Provision is made within Dutch general merger control for SGEI. Article 41(3) Mw provides that where at least one party to a merger is entrusted with a service of general economic interest, a licence may only be refused if the refusal does not hinder the performance of the SGEI activity.

81 The ACM explains '*topzorg*' as such complex healthcare that patients mostly cannot attend a basic hospital. '*Topzorg*' is generally only provided in university medical centres and Cooperative Specialist Care and Teaching Hospitals (*Samenwerkende Topklinische opleidingsZiekenhuizen* (STZ)). ACM, Case reference 17.0166.24. *Besluit Verlening vergunning voor concentratie tussen het Academisch Medisch Centrum en Stichting VUmc*, 05.09.2017, (*Amsterdam Universities Hospitals* merger), (Phase II decision), section 1, paragraph 3.

82 Ibid, section 7.4.

83 ACM, above n. 57, section 5.3.1, para. 134.

general merger control. For instance, it has been suggested that if the merging hospitals together hold a market share of 50 per cent, this is sufficient proof of an SIEC[84] (in line with the EU presumption of dominance). However, this has been criticised on the basis that market share may not of itself indicate dominance, or equate to a SIEC, but nevertheless may provide a starting-point for the ACM's assessment.[85] This kind of critique is interesting because it sets a framework for discussion separate from the healthcare-specific merger control by suggesting that the real problem lies with how general merger control is interpreted and applied by the ACM, as distinct from any perceived problem with the general test as such.[86] A further critique suggests that a different legislative framework to the Mw may be beneficial. This would be based on the premise that the ACM starts from a 'yes, unless …' approach to approving hospital mergers in line with other sectors of the economy, whereas a 'no, unless …' starting-point would require further legislative development, perhaps following the example instituted for media mergers.[87]

## 2.3. UK GENERAL MERGER CONTROL AND HOSPITAL MERGER CASES IN ENGLAND

In England, the UK general merger control regime of the Enterprise Act 2002 (EA02) comprises a system of voluntary notification[88] and a two-stage assessment conducted by the CMA.

Its jurisdiction is determined by the identification of two or more 'enterprises' satisfying either the turnover test[89] or 'share of supply' test,[90] ceasing to be distinct and creating a 'relevant merger situation'. Cases involving NHS Foundation Trusts post-HSCA 2012 have satisfied the turnover threshold test.[91]

---

84 E.M.H. Loozen et al., above n. 34.

85 R. Kemp et al., above n. 1.

86 For an overview of this perspective, see E.M.H. Loozen, above n. 18.

87 D.W.L.A. Schrijvershof and J.C. Plettenburg, *'Toetsing van zorgfusies en toezicht in de zorg door ACM: hoe nu verder?'* ('Assessment of healthcare mergers and regulation in healthcare by the ACM: where do we go from here?') (2016) *Tijdschrift Mededingingsrecht in de Praktijk*, 3, 21.

88 Although the CMA can also investigate a merger on its own initiative. CMA, *Mergers: Guidance on the CMA's jurisdiction and procedure*, January 2014, CMA2, paragraphs 6.5–6.19.

89 Section 23(1)(b) EA02 provides that the value of the turnover in the UK of the enterprise being taken over must exceed £70 million.

90 The CMA's approach involves a flexible definition: 'The share of supply can relate to any reasonable description of goods and services': CMA, above n. 41, para. 5.17.

91 The *Dorset Hospitals, Heatherwood-Frimley Park, Chelsea & Westminster-West Middlesex, Surrey Hospitals, Manchester Hospitals* and *Birmingham Hospitals* mergers. The turnover of a business contributing to a proposed joint venture similarly satisfied the turnover threshold test in OFT, ME/6094/13, *Anticipated pathology joint venture between University College London Hospitals NHS Foundation Trust, Royal Free London NHS Foundation Trust and the Doctors Laboratory Limited*, 22.11.2013.

Phase I assessment determines whether the relevant merger situation may lead, or has led to a Substantial Lessening of Competition (SLC). A merger must pass from Phase I to Phase II assessment unless no SLC is established at Phase I, or an exception applies.[92] The most relevant exception for hospital mergers is the identification of 'relevant customer benefits', under section 30(1)(a) EA02, which pertain to reductions in price or improvements in quality. A regime for mergers involving NHS Foundation Trusts was established under section 79 HSCA 2012, which includes an advisory role for NHS Improvement under section 79(5) HSCA 2012 to identify what have become known as 'relevant patient benefits', which share the aforementioned definition of 'relevant customer benefits'.[93] How these benefits have operated in the context of the *Dorset*, *Surrey* and *Manchester Hospitals* mergers is considered in Section 3 below. However, it is important to note that the exception may not always be invoked in cases which fall outside the HSCA 2012 framework, or only within the context of assessing efficiencies.[94]

Phase II involves an in-depth investigation of whether the SLC can be mitigated, for example by the CMA determining relevant customer benefits. Following HSCA 2012, two NHS Foundation Trust mergers have proceeded to Phase II assessment, with one being blocked (the *Dorset Hospitals* merger) and one approved (the *Surrey Hospitals* merger). The *Manchester Hospitals* merger is also discussed here as it represents the first case to be determined within the context of Sustainability and Transformation Partnerships and marks a change in approach, namely engaging with general merger control by being assessed under the CMA's fast-track procedure rather than proceeding to Phase II in the standard way.

### *2.3.1.* Dorset Hospitals *Merger*

The *Dorset Hospitals* merger involved a two-to-one merger to monopoly of two 'closest geographical competitors' in Dorset in the south-west of England.[95] The parties articulated the view that the merger would achieve economies of scale, improved consultant cover, realised synergies and greater financial resilience for both NHS Foundation Trusts. Ultimately the Competition Commission (CC) established that the proposed merger would lead to an SLC in 19 elective inpatient services, 33 outpatient services, maternity services and private cardiology services. The CC concluded that the parties had identified no 'relevant customer

---

92 Section 22 EA02. The CMA has acknowledged the possibility that the 'de minimis' exception may be relevant. CMA, above n. 41, para. 7.29.

93 See above n. 28.

94 See CMA Cambian, *Merger Assessment Guidelines*, CC2 (Revised) OFT1254, sections 5.7.3–5.7.4 cited in CMA, above n. 37, fn. 482, p. 189.

95 Discussed, inter alia, by R. Curran and S. Albert, 'It seemed like a good idea at the time: the application of competition law to the health sector in England' (2014) 35(9) *European Competition Law Review* 419.

benefits' which could offset the SLC, and not only blocked the merger but also took the further step of requiring the parties not to merge for 10 years.[96] The case has been considered a difficult test case, but one offering useful lessons regarding, inter alia, the difficulty of advancing failing firm arguments in the NHS context where providers do not exit the market in any conventional sense, but rather change organisational form to ensure continuity of service.[97]

### *2.3.2.* Surrey Hospitals *Merger*

The *Surrey Hospitals* case involved a proposed merger of hospitals in Surrey, near London. The merger was considered by the parties to be the most effective way of ensuring that they could continue to deliver high-quality services to patients amid financial and capacity-related challenges. At Phase I the CMA established that the merger could result in reduced quality and less scope for patient choice in several elective specialty services, and so referred it for an in-depth investigation. At Phase II the CMA inquiry group approved the merger, having established that there would be sufficient competition and choice for patients in the area due to the presence of a number of nearby hospitals as credible alternatives.

### *2.3.3.* Manchester Hospitals *Merger*

The *Manchester Hospitals* case involved a proposed merger of two NHS Foundation Trusts comprising nine hospitals in the Greater Manchester area in the north-west of England. In view of the obvious significant lessening of competition that such a merger would entail, the parties requested that the CMA conduct a fast-track assessment[98] which effectively bypasses the Phase I assessment stage. The CMA has the option of conducting such expedited Phase II investigations where, typically, parties agree to waive certain procedural rights and the SLC affects a substantial element of the proposed merger.[99] The CMA approved the merger in light of the substantial 'patient benefits' which would flow from the merger, and would offset the loss of competition between the NHS Foundation Trusts.

### *2.3.4.* Cygnet Healthcare Ltd–Cambian Adult Services *Merger*

The *Cygnet Healthcare Ltd and Cambian Adult Services* case represents an example of merger activity which has implications for the NHS and NHS

---

96 Ibid.

97 Ibid.

98 CMA, News Story, 'Manchester hospitals trust request fast track merger reference', 09.02.2017, <https://www.gov.uk/government/news/manchester-hospital-trusts-request-fast-track-merger-reference> accessed 24.06.2018.

99 CMA, above n. 94, sections 6.61–6.65.

patients, yet is not subject to the section 79 HSCA 2012 merger assessment regime because it does not involve NHS Foundation Trusts. This case involved the acquisition by Universal Health Services, Inc. (via its subsidiary Cygnet Healthcare) of Cambian Adult Services, which created a relevant merger situation giving rise to a Substantial Lessening of Competition in the supply of hospital-based inpatient mental health rehabilitation services to local authorities and NHS clinical commissioning groups (CCGs) in the East Midlands.[100] The type of healthcare provision at issue in this case arguably justified a particular approach being taken – for example, a clearer distinction being drawn between NHS and independent (private) sector providers in defining the product market;[101] and also the 'customer' (for rehabilitation services) being taken to be CCGs, NHS Trusts and Local Authorities, rather than NHS patients. The latter assumption was made in view, perhaps, of the limited capacity for the latter to exercise choice in respect of mental healthcare service provision,[102] a factor which was acknowledged in the clearance of the merger subject to divestment of a hospital.[103] However, mental health services provision is an area of NHS healthcare delivery which is subject to ongoing policy changes, notably reducing out-of-area placements. This inevitably affects plurality of providers in different regions, and highlights the potentially controversial distinction between private and NHS provision.[104] Even so, the extent to which such policy changes can be incorporated into CMA assessments in the absence of the dedicated section 79(5) HSCA 2012 'relevant patient benefits' mechanism is unclear.

---

100 CMA, above n. 37, sections 5.49–5.58.

101 Ibid, section 5.67.

102 'Mental health services' and detention under the Mental Health Act 1983 are included within specific exceptions to the duty on CCGs and NHS England under Regulation 13 of the National Health Service (Procurement, Patient Choice and Competition) (No. 2) Regulations 2013, SI 2013/500, to offer patients requiring an elective referral a choice of provider in respect of their first outpatient appointment by reference to Standing Rule 39 of the National Health Service Commissioning Board and Clinical Commissioning Groups (Responsibilities and Standing Rules) Regulations 2012 (SI 2012 No. 2996). See, in particular, Standing Rules 40(1) and 41 of the aforementioned 2012 Regulations. For an insightful consideration of how patient choice operates regarding mental health services and how this may impact anticipated NHS mental health trust mergers (thus subject to the section 79 HSCA 2012 merger regime), see A. Taylor, 'Has patient choice made it harder for mental health trusts to merge?', *NHS Competition Regulation*, 15.05.2015.

103 CMA, 'CMA requires sale of East Midlands adult mental health hospital', Press Release, 16.10.2017, <https://www.gov.uk/government/news/cma-requires-sale-of-east-midlands-adult-mental-health-hospital> accessed 24.06.2018.

104 A. Taylor, 'Unintended effects of limiting out-of-area placements?', *Aldwych Partners blog*, 13.11.2017, <http://aldwychpartners.co.uk/unintended-effects-of-limiting-out-of-area-placements/> accessed 24.06.2018.

# 3. JURISDICTIONAL AND SUBSTANTIVE ASPECTS OF HEALTHCARE-SPECIFIC MERGER CONTROL

This section examines the development of modifications to Dutch and UK general merger control which collectively constitute healthcare-specific merger control in order to understand how the two regimes are related and may complement each other. Healthcare-specific merger control can be understood in terms of modifications relating to 'jurisdictional aspects', that is, clarification of which arrangements are subject to general merger control, and 'substantive assessment aspects', or attempts to incorporate wider, typically non-economic, concerns which may not otherwise receive much attention in general merger control.

The healthcare-specific modifications in the Netherlands include lower turnover thresholds and a healthcare-specific merger test (now transferred from the NZa to the ACM) with a 'merger effects' report, which might be linked to questions of determining jurisdiction for assessing a merger. Further elements are additional criteria for the ACM to consider in its assessment and the NZa Opinions, which might be related to the substantive assessment process. In England, the modifications include a role for NHS Improvement to identify relevant customer benefits under section 79(5) HSCA 2012 as part of the CMA's assessment of mergers involving NHS Foundation Trusts; thus a substantive assessment aspect. However, perhaps more prominent modifications are evident in terms of jurisdictional aspects in the form of different tests being developed for NHS Trusts and Private Patient Units (PPUs), alongside the application of general merger control to NHS Foundation Trusts by section 79 HSCA 2012.

## 3.1. JURISDICTIONAL ASPECTS

### *3.1.1. The Netherlands*

The jurisdictional aspects of Dutch healthcare-specific merger control comprise two elements – lower turnover thresholds and a healthcare-specific merger test.

#### 3.1.1.1. Lower Turnover Thresholds

Mergers involving at least two parties involved in the provision of healthcare[105] (thus including hospitals) and where each party has an individual turnover

105 'Healthcare' is interpreted by reference to the definitions of the *Zorgverzekeringswet* (Dutch Health Insurance Act 2006 (Zvw)) and the *Wet maatschappelijke ondersteuning* (Dutch Social Support Act 2015 (Wmo)). See Article 2, STAATSBLAD 2007, 518, *Besluit van 06.12.2007,*

of at least €5,500,000 are subject to lower turnover thresholds than those of Dutch general merger control. These lower turnover thresholds were introduced initially between 2008 and 2013,[106] but were extended until 2018 and recently have been retained until 2023.[107]

The relationship between the general merger-control thresholds of Article 29(1) Mw[108] and these lower thresholds[109] can be illustrated broadly as follows:

| | ***General merger control*** | ***Healthcare merger control*** |
|---|---|---|
| ***Combined global turnover of all undertakings in the previous calendar year*** | Must exceed €113,450,000 | Must exceed €55,000,000 |
| ***Individual turnover in the Netherlands of at least two of the undertakings concerned in the previous calendar year*** | Must exceed €30,000,000 | Must exceed €10,000,000 |

**Figure 12. Lower turnover thresholds applicable to Dutch healthcare mergers 2008–2023**

The response to these different turnover thresholds has been varied. The care turnover threshold of €5,500,000 has been considered effective in avoiding notification of mergers not intended to be covered by the lower thresholds.[110] A review in 2012 established that the ACM had examined twice as many mergers, and that a considerable number of mergers which (potentially) raised competition concerns were caught by the notification obligation.[111] A subsequent review established that the ACM had scrutinised 35 additional mergers between 1 January 2012 and 1 January 2017, of which 32 were approved because they

*houdende tijdelijke verruiming van het toepassingsbereik van het concentratietoezicht op ondernemingen die zorg verlenen.* (Bulletin of Acts and Decrees (Stb) 2007, 518, Decree of 06.12.2007 instituting temporary measures regarding the applicability of merger control to healthcare providers).

106 The Decree of 06.12.2007 instituted temporary measures extending the applicability of merger control to healthcare providers. These measures took the form of lower turnover thresholds for mergers between undertakings in the healthcare sector between 2008 and 2013. See Staatsblad 2007, ibid.

107 Staatsblad 2017, above n. 53, following an interim extension between 2013 and 2018 by the Decree of 19.10.2012 extending the 2007 Decree. Staatsblad 2012, 515, *Besluit van 19.10.2012, houdende wijziging van het Besluit tijdelijke verruiming van het toepassingsbereik van het concentratietoezicht op ondernemingen die zorg verlenen in verband met een verlenging van het besluit* (Bulletin of Acts and Decrees 2012, 515, Decree of 19.10.2012 extending the Decree instituting temporary measures regarding the applicability of merger control to undertakings providing care).

108 Article 29(1) Mw provides that the combined global turnover threshold is €150,000,000.

109 Article 29(3) Mw provides that turnover thresholds may be reduced for particular categories of undertaking for a specified period of time.

110 Explanatory Note in the Staatsblad 2012, above n. 107.

111 Ibid.

did not restrict competition and three did not require adjudication by the ACM (for example, because the parties decided not to proceed with the merger).[112]

The logic behind the introduction, and subsequent extension, in 2012 of the lower turnover thresholds has been that the Dutch healthcare sector remains in transition following the 2006 reforms. The development of a demand-driven system underpinned by mandatory private health insurance has been subject to review,[113] and changes identified, such as the further development of the risk equalisation scheme, and an increased willingness of health insurers to bear risks. Such developments have significant effects for parties involved in healthcare, their roles and their incentives.[114] The development of a demand-driven system in Dutch healthcare means that it is important for both patients and health insurers (as purchasers of healthcare) to be able to exercise choice. Consequently, effective merger control is needed to prevent mergers which restrict competition and choice, and thereby to ensure healthcare provision which is affordable, accessible and of high quality. The number of healthcare mergers has increased over time in the Netherlands, with 2016 seeing the highest number yet[115] (and 2017 expected to exceed this). The Dutch government was therefore concerned about the need to maintain effective merger control and decided to extend the period of operation of the lower turnover thresholds from 2018 until 2023 as a way of addressing potential risks to the interests of patients and health insurers in a timely manner.[116] The Dutch government further justified its decision to extend the period of operation of the lower turnover thresholds by underscoring specific characteristics of the healthcare sector, such as the 'information lead' of healthcare providers vis-à-vis healthcare insurers (purchasers) and patients, the potential for small relevant geographic markets in certain sectors (discussed above), and the risk such characteristics pose for facilitating positions of market power.[117] In reviewing whether or not to extend the lower turnover thresholds, the Dutch government held a consultation and received responses from law firms, the *Nederlandse Vereniging van Participatiemaatschappijen* (Dutch Venture Capital Association (NVP)) and the *Federatie Medisch Specialisten* (Dutch Federation of Medical Specialists). Although it was suggested that extending the period of operation of these lower turnover thresholds is likely,[118] various issues emerged from this consultation,

---

112 Explanatory Note in the STAATSBLAD 2017, above n. 53.

113 See KPMG PLEXUS, *'Evaluatie Zorgverzekeringswet – Eindrapportage'* ('Zvw assessment – Final Report') September 2014, cited in Explanatory Note in STAATSBLAD 2017, above n. 53. This follows a previous review in 2009.

114 Explanatory Note in STAATSBLAD 2017, above n. 53.

115 Ibid.

116 Ibid.

117 Ibid.

118 D.W.L.A. SCHRIJVERSHOF, *'Kostbare zorgfusietoetsing en lage ACM-drempels'* ('Expensive healthcare merger assessment and low ACM thresholds'), *Zorgvisie*, 19.07.2017, <https://www.zorgvisie.nl/zorgfusietoetsing-en-de-acm-drempels/> accessed 24.06.2018.

with several respondents being opposed to an extension[119] and others suggesting new developments, such as an expedited notification procedure and lower filing fee.[120] Concerns about the lower turnover thresholds included, for example, whether or not the original motivation for the lower turnover thresholds regarding markets in transition was still valid.[121] In addition, concerns arose about which parties are affected negatively by falling below the lower turnover thresholds, including developing 'healthcare networks' which comprise smaller providers[122] and venture capital companies which may invest in smaller providers.[123] Respondents also used the consultation as an opportunity to elaborate possible changes to the healthcare-specific merger test, and even suggest that a 'voluntary notification' system be implemented along the lines of the UK system, with the *Manchester Hospitals* and *Surrey Hospitals* mergers being cited as examples of potentially problematic mergers which had been scrutinised following voluntary notification.[124]

#### 3.1.1.2. The Healthcare-Specific Merger Test and Merger Effects Report

The core element of this test, introduced in January 2014, was a prohibition[125] on consummating any merger involving healthcare providers without prior approval by the NZa. This effectively meant an additional stage prior to, and distinct from, the competition test conducted by the ACM. The prohibition did not apply to healthcare providers comprising fewer than 50 people,[126] and an exemption could be applied in exceptional circumstances (such as the imminent insolvency of a provider which would otherwise be saved by a merger).[127]

---

119 M. ALINPOUR, Loyens & Loeff response to consultation 21.08.2017, <https://www.internetconsultatie.nl/zorgconcentraties/reactie/d41ac314-818a-4e1c-8b39-c89a6787038d> accessed 24.06.2018.

120 F.S.A. ZWART, *Nedelandse Vereniging van Participatiemaatschappijen* (NVP) response to consultation, 18.08.2017, <https://www.internetconsultatie.nl/zorgconcentraties/reactie/219f2288-46f8-4a10-a556-c05f6972f994> accessed 24.06.2018. The 2017 Decree also makes provision for a one-off fee of €17,450 to notify a merger, and a one-off fee of €34,900 if a licence is required. See Explanatory Note in STAATSBLAD 2017, above n. 53, Section 5, '*Regeldruk*' ('Regulatory Burden').

121 C.J. DE BOER, Van Doorne Advocaten, Notarissen, Fiscalisten, response to consultation, 10.08.2017, <https://www.internetconsultatie.nl/zorgconcentraties/reactie/79ec6634-6385-464a-941b-f6425f4ed80f> accessed 24.06.2018.

122 I.H.E. SENGERS, *Federatie Medisch Specialisten* response to consultation, 20.08.2017, <https://www.internetconsultatie.nl/zorgconcentraties/reactie/c8bfdf1f-dfbe-4f16-818a-8d83512f5542> accessed 24.06.2018.

123 F.S.A. ZWART, above n. 120.

124 D.W.L.A. SCHRIJVERSHOF, Maverick Advocaten response to consultation, 08.08.2017, paragraphs 7–9, <https://www.internetconsultatie.nl/zorgconcentraties/reactie/f30a08d1-3a15-418e-ae17-553246839253> accessed 24.06.2018.

125 Article 49a(1) Wmg.

126 Article 49a(3)Wmg.

127 Explanatory Notes cited in C.T. DEKKER and J.G. SIJMONS, '*Continuïteit van zorg en zorgspecifieke fusietoetsing*' ('Continuity of healthcare and healthcare-specific merger assessment') (2013) *Tijdschrift voor Gezondheidsrecht*, (37)2, 136.

In order to avoid the prohibition, healthcare providers wishing to enter into a merger were obliged to apply to the NZa for approval and submit a 'merger effects' report. This was intended to demonstrate that the merger parties had considered the following aspects as a minimum:[128]

a. The aims of the merger.
b. The reasons for merging.
c. The structure of the envisaged merged entity of healthcare provider(s).
d. The financial consequences of the merger for the healthcare provider(s).
e. The consequences of the merger for healthcare provision to clients.
f. The risks which the merger may entail for quality and accessibility of care and the ways in which these risks can be managed.
g. The ways in which stakeholders have been consulted about the proposed merger and how their contribution has been dealt with.
h. The ways and timeframe in which the merger will be implemented.

The NZa was able to withhold approval under the healthcare-specific merger test in four circumstances: firstly, if 'stakeholders' (such as patients and staff) had not been adequately consulted;[129] secondly, if the views and recommendations of such stakeholders had not been convincingly considered in the decision to merge;[130] thirdly, if continuity of critical care (as defined by statute) was endangered by the proposed merger;[131] and finally, if the merger effects report did not provide sufficient insight into anticipated effects of the merger.[132]

Following the 2015 reforms, this healthcare-specific merger test will now be implemented by the ACM and will apply to mergers which involve undertakings directly or indirectly involved in the provision of care, meeting specific turnover thresholds in the preceding calendar year.[133] Significantly, it is now intended that the healthcare-specific merger test should coincide with the initial notification phase of general merger assessment.[134] The merger effects

---

128 Article 49b(2) Wmg.

129 Article 49c(2)(a) Wmg.

130 Article 49c(2)(b) Wmg.

131 Article 49c(2)(c) Wmg.

132 Article 49c(2)(d) Wmg.

133 Proposed amendments – Article 49a(1)(a) and (b) Wmg – provide that one of the merger parties must have a turnover of at least €7,000,000 and the other(s) a turnover of at least €500,000 in the Netherlands. See *Kamerstukken II, 2015–16, 34 445, 2 – Wijziging van de Wet marktordening gezondheidszorg en enkele andere wetten in verband met aanpassingen van de tarief- en prestatieregulering en het markttoezicht op het terrein van de gezondheidszorg. Nr. 2 Voorstel van Wet.* (Second Chamber documentation, Parliamentary Session 2015–16, 34 445, 2 – Amendments to the Wmg and other laws to apply tariff regulation and market regulation in healthcare, Document No. 2, Legislative Proposal), p. 9.

134 *Kamerstukken II, 2015–16, 34 445, 3 – Wijziging van de Wet marktordening gezondheidszorg en enkele andere wetten in verband met aanpassingen van de tarief- en prestatieregulering*

report is amended to emphasise that parties must demonstrate that they have considered other forms of collaboration and state why a merger has been chosen in preference to these.[135] The ACM may – similarly to the NZa – withhold its approval if critical care is endangered by the proposed merger or if clients and stakeholders have not been appropriately consulted and their views given due consideration.[136]

### *3.1.2. England*

The modifications which comprise the 'jurisdictional aspects' within healthcare-specific merger control in England are separate scrutiny for NHS Trusts (initially via the NHS Foundation Trust and transactions 'pipelines' and latterly by transactions oversight processes) and Private Patient Units (PPUs).

As noted in the Introduction to this chapter, the applicability of general merger control has not been subject to the same level of questioning as general competition law. However, two separate questions have been posed, namely, whether NHS mergers should benefit from the Secretary of State's public interest exception category,[137] and also how general merger control and CMA oversight can apply to NHS mergers following the rejection of the *Dorset Hospitals* merger.[138]

An underlying intention of section 79 HSCA 2012 was to create 'a single regime for merger control, which avoids duplication of the roles of [NHS Improvement] and the [CMA] and eliminates risk of double-jeopardy'.[139] Thus section 79 HSCA 2012 clarifies that general merger control applies to NHS Foundation Trusts, and there is no longer a grey area in which mergers involving NHS Foundation Trusts may in theory be subject both to the EA02 test and the NHS-specific merger test conducted by the NHS CCP[140] prior to the HSCA 2012. Whether this desire to create a single merger-control regime was merely a reflection of the policy in operation at the time (now discontinued) for NHS Trusts to achieve NHS Foundation Trust status is unclear. Certainly, as it has now been recognised that not all NHS Trusts

*en het markttoezicht op het terrein van de gezondheidszorg. Nr. 3 Memorie van Toelichting* (Second Chamber documentation, Parliamentary Session 2015–16, 34 445, 3 – Amendments to the Wmg and other laws to apply tariff regulation and market regulation in healthcare, Document No. 3, Explanatory Memorandum), para. 4.3.2, p. 22.

135 *Kamerstukken II 2015–16*, above n. 133. Proposed amendments – Article 49b Wmg.

136 Ibid. Proposed amendments – Article 49d Wmg.

137 K. Desai, 'Public hospital mergers: a case for broader considerations than competition law?' (2013) 34(12) *European Competition Law Review* 646.

138 P. Corrigan and A. Taylor, 'The CMA can improve the NHS merger regime: here's how', *Health Service Journal*, 26.03.2014.

139 Health and Social Care Act 2012 Explanatory Notes, Section 79 – Mergers involving NHS foundation trusts, para. 740.

140 NHS CCP, above n. 13.

will achieve NHS Foundation Trust status via the 'NHS Foundation Trust pipeline', the evolution of 'transactions' oversight (initially by Monitor and the NHS Trust Development Authority (NHS TDA), and subsequently by NHS Improvement) suggests that alternative organisational forms are being pursued in connection with the new care models of the NHS Five Year Forward View and Sustainability and Transformation Partnerships.

It is important to note that, perhaps surprisingly, the (primary) jurisdictional requirement for an 'enterprise'[141] has not proved decisive in separate scrutiny of NHS Trusts and PPUs. Thus NHS Foundation Trusts,[142] NHS Trusts (despite their less autonomous status)[143] and PPUs are all deemed 'enterprises' and no discussion of any implications of providing services 'free for the patient at the point of delivery' has emerged in connection with merger control[144] comparable with that found in connection with the *applicability* of competition law.[145]

---

[141] Section 79(6) HSCA 2012 provides that the definitions of Part 3 EA02 apply. Section 129 EA02 defines an 'enterprise' as the activities, or part of the activities, of a business. A 'business' is defined as including a professional practice and any other undertaking which is carried on for gain or reward or which is an undertaking in the course of which goods or services are supplied otherwise than free of charge.

[142] Although section 79 HSCA 2012 was advanced as authority for NHS Foundation Trusts being 'enterprises' in all four cases discussed in this chapter, this was clarified further in the *Dorset Hospitals* merger. Thus an NHS Foundation Trust is an 'enterprise' on the grounds that it provides clinical services for gain or reward, has a substantial amount of financial and corporate autonomy to manage its finances, and can retain and benefit from surplus generated from income received from commissioning for the provision of clinical services. This appears uncontroversial, as does the further determining factor that regulation of Foundation Trusts did not prevent providers from maintaining sufficient scope for autonomy to make organisational, financial and other operational decisions with a substantial impact on the sector. See OFT, above n. 41, paragraphs 4.1–4.3.

[143] The logic for considering NHS Foundation Trusts to be 'enterprises' as articulated in the *Dorset Hospitals* merger decision (OFT, above n. 41) appears to have informed CMA guidance that NHS Trusts are similarly considered to be 'enterprises'. See CMA, above n. 41, para. 5.19, fn. 36. However, it might be considered that the CMA regards all NHS Trusts as – in effect – a single 'enterprise' for jurisdictional purposes, but not for the purposes of its economic analysis, since this appears to treat NHS Trusts as individual entities.

[144] This is because, since commissioning organisations procure and pay a consideration for the provision of such services depending on the number of patients that are treated, NHS Foundation Trusts have the incentive to re-invest such income to attract patients. See OFT, above n. 41, para. 4.1. Indeed, CMA guidance clarifies that 'enterprises' in healthcare can comprise entire organisations, such as NHS Foundation Trusts or NHS Trusts controlling hospitals, ambulance services, mental health services, community services and individual services or specialties. The CMA emphasises a case-by-case approach, but distinguishes NHS mergers by considering what is necessary to operate the relevant service or clinical specialty. See CMA, above n. 41, paras. 5.3 and 5.4. So, for example, it is not always necessary for the transaction to include the transfer of an NHS contract (governing the supply of goods and services to the NHS), if the acquiring provider is already able to supply the services without requiring the NHS contract to be transferred and acquires staff and assets.

[145] However, it might be considered that the Coalition Government's intention was that the EA02 general merger-control regime would be extended to mergers involving NHS Foundation Trusts, but not NHS Trusts. Clause 65 of Bill 132, 2010–11, as introduced on 19.01.2011

Rather, it is the related jurisdictional threshold of a requirement for a 'relevant merger situation' which appears to prompt the need for separate scrutiny of NHS Trusts and PPUs. This is discussed below, but in overview, the reach of the EA02 test (as amended by section 79 HSCA 2012) can be summarised as follows:

| **Merger Parties** | **Test used** | **Approval granted by** | **Advisory input** |
|---|---|---|---|
| 'Enterprise' (e.g. private healthcare provider) + 'Enterprise' (e.g. private healthcare provider) | EA02 | CMA | N/A |
| 'Enterprise' (e.g. private healthcare provider) + NHS Foundation Trust | EA02 (section 79 HSCA 2012) | CMA | NHS Improvement |
| 'Enterprise' (e.g. private healthcare provider) + NHS Foundation Trust | One-stage 'PPU arrangement' test | CMA | N/A |
| NHS Foundation Trust + NHS Foundation Trust | EA02 (section 79 HSCA 2012) | CMA | NHS Improvement |
| NHS Foundation Trust + NHS Trust | EA02 (section 79 HSCA 2012) | CMA | NHS Improvement |
| NHS Trust + NHS Trust | Oversight in the context of NHS Foundation Trust authorisation or Transactions oversight | NHS Improvement | N/A |

**Figure 13. Overview of the applicability of the EA02 to NHS mergers**

### 3.1.2.1. The Requirement for a 'Relevant Merger Situation' – NHS Trusts and NHS Foundation Trusts

The requirement for a 'relevant merger situation', namely the change in control necessary for two or more enterprises to cease to be distinct, serves to draw a distinction between how NHS Trusts and NHS Foundation Trusts are viewed vis-à-vis general merger control.

---

(which eventually became section 79 HSCA 2012), was explained thus: 'This clause provides that the merger control regime in Part 3 of the Enterprise Act 2002 would apply to foundation trusts which are not enterprises for the purposes of that regime in relation to mergers between foundation trusts or between NHS foundation trusts and other organisations. This means that the OFT and the Competition Commission would be responsible for reviewing mergers involving all foundation trusts whether or not they are enterprises.' Explanatory Notes to the Health and Social Care Bill – Bill 132 EN, paragraph 575, <https://publications.parliament.uk/pa/cm201011/cmbills/132/en/11132en.htm> accessed 24.06.2018. This explanation goes on to clarify the reference to 'businesses' (see also n. 141 above for the EA02 definition) as 'other organisations' – which is vague enough to encompass both private providers and NHS Trusts. However, in contrast, as noted above, the CMA has stated that it considers NHS Trusts to be 'enterprises'.

As regards NHS Foundation Trusts, section 79(1) HSCA 2012 provides that there are two instances where two or more enterprises cease to be distinct. Firstly, this occurs where the activities of two or more NHS Foundation Trusts cease to be distinct activities.[146] This appears straightforward and has been illustrated by mergers between NHS Foundation Trusts such as *Heatherwood–Frimley Park* and *Chelsea & Westminster–West Middlesex* decided at Phase I, and the *Surrey Hospitals* and the *Manchester Hospitals* mergers determined at Phase II. Secondly, it occurs where the activities of one or more NHS Foundation Trusts and the activities of one or more businesses cease to be distinct activities.[147] This would appear to apply to mergers between NHS Foundation Trusts and NHS Trusts[148] (in view of the CMA's approach as noted above) or between NHS Foundation Trusts and private healthcare providers under arrangements for private healthcare providers to deliver NHS services.[149]

In contrast, a merger involving two or more NHS Trusts has been deemed by the CMA not to constitute the requisite change in control since the resulting entity would remain overseen ultimately by the Secretary of State for Health.[150] A distinction was thus drawn between NHS Trusts which were able to achieve NHS Foundation Trust status and those which were not, and so faced alternative organisational arrangements involving private providers. This distinction was reflected in two different kinds of assessment, named the 'NHS Foundation Trust pipeline' and 'Transactions pipeline', respectively. This distinction now appears superseded, primarily[151] by NHS Improvement's 'Transactions Guidance' which sets out a range of authorisation procedures, including the need to comply with CMA competition assessment where necessary. These three mechanisms are now considered.

*The NHS Foundation Trust pipeline*

This was the more established of the two pipelines and developed to give effect to successive New Labour and Coalition Government policies for all NHS Trusts

146 Section 79(2) HSCA 2012.

147 Section 79(3) HSCA 2012. Section 79(4) HSCA 2012 clarifies that the references to 'activities' include a reference to part of an NHS Foundation Trust's or a business's activities.

148 These, prior to HSCA 2012, appear to have been scrutinised under the NHS-specific merger test only, regardless of the potential to be subject to EA02. See, for example, NHS CCP, *Merger of Bexley Care Trust with Oxleas NHS Foundation Trust and South London Healthcare Trust*, February 2010.

149 Thus category 2 (private sector delivery of NHS services) of the 'four categories of English healthcare' outlined in Chapter 1 above. Such arrangements were within the scope of the NHS CCP, above n. 13, at para. 4.10.

150 CMA, above n. 41, para. 5.7.

151 Although other assessment procedures are now involved, for example to achieve specific Care Quality Commission (CQC) ratings. See further, NHS Improvement, 'Single Oversight Framework for NHS Providers', 30.09.2016, <https://improvement.nhs.uk/resources/single-oversight-framework/> accessed 24.06.2018.

to achieve NHS Foundation Trust status. Indeed, that the motivation for NHS Trust mergers stemmed directly from this policy was explicitly acknowledged in individual cases, for example: 'The merger was arranged within the broader policy context that requires the majority of NHS trusts to become NHS foundation trusts by April 2014.'[152]

Between 2009 and 2013 the NHS Co-operation and Competition Panel (NHS CCP) reviewed mergers between NHS Trusts and NHS Foundation Trusts and produced recommendations regarding approval by the Secretary of State for Health or Monitor (now NHS Improvement), who respectively had exclusive competence to approve mergers involving NHS Trusts and NHS Foundation Trusts.

The NHS CCP's Merger Guidelines were based on Principle 10 of the NHS Principles and Rules for Cooperation and Competition (NHS PRCC) which provided that:

> Mergers, including vertical integration, between providers are permissible where there remains sufficient choice and competition or where they are otherwise in patients' and taxpayers' interests, for example because they will deliver significant improvements in the quality of care.

The NHS CCP adopted a wide definition of 'merger', but explicitly excluded mergers between commissioners.[153]

The procedural approach of the NHS CCP's assessment broadly reflected general merger control with a two-phase test, but the substantive content differed markedly, as its focus was to establish whether a proposed merger was consistent with the provisions about patient choice and competition of the NHS PRCC. The test comprised a 'cost–benefit analysis' in which potential benefits such as improved clinical outcomes, better services or greater efficiency were weighed against any possible adverse effects on patients and/or taxpayers (including both financial and non-financial impacts) arising from a loss of patient choice or competition.[154]

However, there are at least two further points of note[155] regarding overlap and divergence between the NHS CCP and EA02 regimes. Firstly, although

---

152 NHS CCP, *Proposed merger of Royal Free London Foundation Trust with Barnet and Chase Farm Hospitals NHS Trust, Final Report*, 13.08.2013, para. 29.

153 NHS CCP, above n. 13, para. 4.9.

154 Ibid, para. 6.3.

155 A third point of note being the NHS CCP's rejection of a 'share of supply' test to establish jurisdiction, on the grounds that existing turnovers were easier and simpler to apply. NHS Cooperation and Competition Panel, 'Response to Consultation Document', 04.10.2010, para. 48.

the NHS CCP regime was nominally a voluntary regime, in practice all NHS mergers were examined prior to consummation.[156] Secondly, the NHS CCP's jurisdictional thresholds operated in a different manner, focusing on the revenue of the combined entity in the last financial year, with different thresholds for different sectors:[157]

- £70 million in the case of acute and mental health trusts;
- £35 million in the case of community service providers; or
- £15 million in the case of primary care providers.

Concurrently with the implementation of the HSCA 2012, ultimate decision-making powers were transferred from the Secretary of State for Health to the then newly-established NHS TDA[158] (now incorporated into NHS Improvement), although Secretary of State oversight appeared to be ongoing in 2014.[159] Prior to the NHS TDA's involvement, it had been envisaged that Monitor (now NHS Improvement) would adopt a similar approach to the NHS CCP's under the NHS PRCC.[160]

The subsequent move away from the NHS Foundation Trust pipeline was heralded by a recognition that Care Quality Commission (CQC) ratings represent a better indicator of quality than Foundation Trust status,[161] and a growing acceptance that not all NHS Trusts are able to achieve NHS Foundation Trust status.[162] It is recognised that, from a general competition perspective,

---

156 K. Desai, above n. 137.

157 NHS CCP, above n. 13, para. 4.20.

158 Under Direction 4(g)(iii)(bb) of the NHS Trust Development Authority (NHS TDA), National Health Service Trust Development Authority Directions, <https://www.gov.uk/government/uploads/system/uploads/attachment_data/file/175350/NTDA_Directions_2013.pdf> accessed 24.06.2018.

159 See, for example, NHS Trust Development Authority (NHS TDA), 'The acquisition of Barnet and Chase Farm Hospitals NHS Trust by the Royal Free London NHS Foundation Trust', July 2014.

160 Monitor, Briefing Note: 'The respective roles of Monitor, the Office of Fair Trading and the Competition Commission in relation to mergers involving NHS trusts and NHS foundation trusts', 17.10.2013.

161 The Former Secretary of State for Health, Jeremy Hunt, has expressed the view that CQC ratings are a better indicator of success for NHS providers. See C. Dowler, 'Exclusive Hunt Interview: CQC ratings have replaced Foundation Trust status as a definition of success', *Health Service Journal*, 09.09.2015. David Bennett (former CEO of Monitor) and Simon Stevens (CEO NHS England) have both recently called for the 'Foundation Trust pipeline' (of NHS Trusts seeking to achieve Foundation Trust status, typically via merger) to be discontinued. See C. Dowler, 'Bennett calls for freeze of Foundation Trust pipeline', *Health Service Journal*, 05.11.2015. C. Ham, 'Simon Stevens' vision for the NHS: welcome but challenging to deliver', *The King's Fund blog*, 14.10.2015, <https://www.kingsfund.org.uk/blog/2015/10/simon-stevens-vision-nhs-welcome-challenging-deliver> accessed 24.06.2018.

162 As acknowledged by Simon Stevens, CEO of NHS England, in comments to Health Select Committee on 21.07.2015 in response to Question 36. 'Increasingly, for many providers the foundation trust/NHS trust distinction is a distinction without a difference, and, frankly,

there may be a tension between a policy for NHS Trusts to achieve NHS Foundation Trust status and resisting consolidation in light of the limitations on benefits considered to flow from hospital mergers.[163] However, the extent to which this apparent conflict holds in connection with the distinctive nature of the NHS 'quasi-market' is questionable in view of the reluctance to engage with the concept of provider exit[164] and the need to ensure universal access. Certainly a more logical interpretation of the discontinuation of the NHS Foundation Trust pipeline arises from the explanation of ensuring universal acccess rather than a desire to resist consolidation.[165] That is, in the interests of ensuring universal service and continuity of care, it is recognised that 'one size does not fit all', and that the NHS Foundation Trust model may be unsuitable, so there is little, if any, need for a policy of mergers to create new NHS Foundation Trusts.

*The Transactions pipeline*

Between 2013 and 2016, oversight of NHS Trusts included assessment by the NHS TDA (now NHS Improvement) against annual accountability frameworks.[166] These allowed for two broad options for ensuring NHS Trust

---

lying behind that, exactly as you say, is that the kinds of tests that were being set by Monitor for becoming a Foundation Trust are unlikely to be met by some of those institutions despite the fact that we are going to continue to need them to provide valued and important local services. One of the tasks for the newly paired Monitor and TDA will be to answer the exam question you have just set, which is, "Let's not kid ourselves that, for some of these institutions, they are on a path to Foundation Trust status, because they're not, but we need them, so what is the right way of recognising their governance and ensuring that in concert with other parts of the health service locally they have a future that works?" We have to stop pretending that everybody is going to meet the current set of Foundation Trust tests, and instead just get real about the circumstances facing different parts of the country', <http://data.parliament.uk/writtenevidence/committeeevidence.svc/evidencedocument/health-and-social-care-committee/nhs-current-issues/oral/18809.html> accessed 24.06.2018.

163 Certainly it has been considered that government-mandated mergers produce no more benefit than other mergers. See M. Gaynor et al., above n. 33.

164 Indeed, a further tension might be inferred from Monitor's development of a failure regime as acknowledged by the former OFT, and the development of a 'success regime' to ensure provider sustainability in the context of the NHS Five Year Forward View. See, respectively, OFT, 'Orderly Exit – Designing continuity regimes in public markets', OFT1468, December 2012, and NHS England, 'Five Year Forward View – The Success Regime: A whole systems intervention', 03.06.2015.

165 See comments by Simon Stevens, above n.162.

166 NHS TDA, 'Delivering High Quality Care for Patients – The Accountability Framework for NHS Trust Boards', April 2013. NHS TDA, 'Delivering for Patients – The 2014/15 Accountability Framework for NHS Trust Boards', 31.03.2014. NHS TDA, 'Delivering for Patients – The 2015/16 Accountability Framework for NHS Trust Boards', 02.04.2015.

sustainability: application for NHS Foundation Trust status, or one of a range of transactions.

With regard to ensuring the sustainability of NHS Trusts, the NHS TDA recognised six types of transaction as follows:[167]

| Type of transaction | Description |
|---|---|
| Trust – Trust mergers | These are 'statutory mergers' and take place when two NHS Trusts come together to form a new, merged entity. |
| Foundation Trust acquisition | When an NHS Foundation Trust 'takes over' the running of assets previously owned by an NHS Trust. |
| Trust acquisition | A much larger NHS Trust could 'take over' a much smaller NHS Trust, retaining the identity of the larger NHS Trust. |
| Operating franchises (also described as Operating Competition) | A long-term contract or franchise could be awarded to the private sector to run services previously delivered by an NHS Trust. |
| Management contracts | A short-term contract could be awarded to another NHS organisation or to the private sector to run an NHS facility. |
| Divestments | An NHS Trust could decide to sell assets it owns to another organisation, yet remain viable as an NHS Trust. |
| Demergers | An NHS Trust could decide to split its assets into two or more parts, with each part representing a viable solution. |

**Figure 14. Types of 'Transaction' available to ensure NHS Trust sustainability**

The NHS TDA had oversight of the majority of these, with the exception of 'Foundation Trust acquisition', which was overseen by the CMA and Monitor (now NHS Improvement) under the EA02 test. Monitor similarly recognised various forms of 'transactions',[168] and further clarified that the regulatory framework governing transactions involving NHS Foundation Trusts comprised its own risk assessment of transactions, as well as CMA competition review of mergers.[169]

167 Adapted from NHS TDA Accountability Frameworks 2013 (p. 85), 2014–15 (pp. 1–2) and 2015–2016 (pp. 35–36), all above n. 166.

168 Including those which should be reported under the threshold set out in Monitor's 'Risk assessment framework' (including most mergers or acquisitions as well as larger capital investment projects), statutory transactions (mergers or acquisitions involving one or more NHS Foundation Trusts, and separations and dissolutions of NHS Foundation Trusts as defined by sections 56–57A NHS Act 2006 as amended by HSCA 2012) and transactions which could be reviewed by the CMA under EA02. Monitor, 'Supporting NHS Providers: Guidance on Transactions for NHS Foundation Trusts – Updated March 2015', p. 7.

169 Ibid, p. 8.

### *The NHS Five Year Forward View, NHS Improvement Transactions Guidance and the CMA's competition test: the need for a 'business case' or a 'patient benefits' case*[170]

The development of the transactions pipeline coincided to a certain extent with the start of implementing new care models as part of the NHS Five Year Forward View. It appears that NHS Improvement has played a role in approving at least some of these new care models, apparently by reference to its Foundation Trust authorisation process – an example being the emergence of an integrated care organisation, Torbay and South Devon Foundation Trust, from the acquisition of community provider Torbay and Southern Devon Health and Care Trust by South Devon Healthcare Foundation Trust.[171] It is unclear why such a restructuring was not examined under the EA02 regime, since the creation of a NHS Foundation Trust would presumably include the requisite change in control. However, this can perhaps be explained[172] by the vertical nature of some of the integration relationships involved, which may be considered to raise fewer competition concerns than would a horizontal merger. An example of the latter would be the *Manchester Hospitals* merger, which was indeed examined under general merger control.

What is perhaps surprising is the distinction maintained between NHS Trusts and NHS Foundation Trusts in NHS Improvement's Transactions Guidance published in November 2017. This clarifies to some extent when a transaction may constitute a merger subject to scrutiny by the CMA: either because it is notified by the parties involved, or because the CMA decides to conduct its own investigation into a completed merger[173] (it being recalled that the notification system under the EA02 is a voluntary regime). The Transactions Guidance is clear that the CMA will not review a merger which involves only NHS Trusts[174] – despite it being recognised in earlier CMA guidance that NHS Trusts may also be subject to general merger control. What the Transactions Guidance does is to emphasise the importance of early engagement by the parties with NHS Improvement in the first instance, and the CMA where appropriate, in order to secure a successful review of a transaction or merger. This is a welcome development since it offers some clarity for parties wishing to enter into a new organisational arrangement.

170 For a good overview of the distinction between the two, see A. Taylor, above n. 6.

171 Monitor, 'Patients in South Devon set to get integrated care after hospital acquisition', Press Release, 01.10.2015, <https://www.gov.uk/government/news/patients-in-south-devon-set-to-get-integrated-care-after-hospital-acquisition> accessed 24.06.2018.

172 It may also be explained by the existence of the voluntary notification regime underpinning EA02.

173 NHS Improvement, *Transactions Guidance – for Trusts undertaking transactions, including mergers and acquisitions*, November 2017, section 2.1, 'The CMA's competition review of transactions'.

174 Ibid.

NHS Improvement's Transactions Guidance makes clear that a transaction/merger is only reviewable by the CMA where it raises competition concerns, for example, where merging providers are located close to each other and provide similar services.[175] However, questions start to emerge in view of the CMA's acknowledgement of the limited role for competition currently within the English NHS. In particular, a concern arises if, by virtue of the thresholds for general merger control, and section 79 HSCA 2012 explicitly including NHS Foundation Trusts within this, NHS providers are compelled to engage with the merger review process only because they satisfy the threshold tests, and not because the merger entails competition concerns, since patient benefits outweigh these. In other words, submitting to the merger control process risks becoming a 'rubber-stamping' exercise for parties on both sides: for the CMA because a merger has been notified to it,[176] and for the merging parties who may fear reprisals if they do not engage with this process because no clear categories of exemption appear to be available.[177] Certainly, this scenario appears plausible in light of the CMA's comments in the *Manchester Hospitals* merger decision[178] (and effectively reiterated in subsequent cases)[179] about the limited role for competition within the English NHS at present. If it is the case that mergers involving NHS bodies are increasingly approved because they deliver 'relevant patient benefits', then the question arises of the proper role of general merger control within a system which is acknowledged – by the competition authority itself! – not to rely on competition.

#### 3.1.2.2. The Requirement for a 'Relevant Merger Situation' – PPUs

The new test for PPUs proposed by the CMA is mentioned here because it appears to be motivated by the prospect of an expansion in these units following the removal of the private patient income cap by section 165 HSCA 2012.[180] Furthermore, the new test marks a first modification of the EA02 regime for the private healthcare sector, as it appears intended primarily to target the scope for individual private healthcare providers to consolidate their market share by operating PPUs.[181] It is to be noted that, typically, both private

175 Ibid. p. 11.

176 In the apparent absence thus far of the CMA acting on its own initiative to investigate a merger involving NHS bodies.

177 As noted previously, the option of the Secretary of State creating a further public interest category for public healthcare appeared not even to be considered, let alone actively rejected, in the design of the HSCA 2012. For further discussion of this exemption category, see K. Desai, above n. 137.

178 See CMA, above n. 26.

179 See CMA, above n. 30.

180 CMA, *Final Report*, above n. 32, para. 11.249.

181 The CMA found that an adverse effect on competition could arise in connection with PPUs on the private healthcare market because private healthcare providers can benefit from NHS

and NHS providers operate PPUs,[182] and so both appear to be included in the definition of a PPU as:

> a facility within a national health service [site] providing inpatient, day-case patient or outpatient privately-funded healthcare services to private patients; such units may be separate units dedicated to private patients or be facilities within a main national health service site which are made available to private patients either on a dedicated or non-dedicated basis.[183]

In jurisdictional terms, a new test is necessary because previous PPU arrangements – such as commercial leasing, the use of (but not title to) equipment and the secondment of support staff (as opposed to transfer of employees),[184] and use of an NHS Foundation Trust name on the branding and promotion of PPU facilities[185] – had not previously constituted a 'relevant merger situation', so could not be reviewed under general merger control. The new test therefore comprises a jurisdictional threshold of 'PPU arrangement' and assessment involving 'relevant customer benefits' based on market investigation criteria.[186] At the time of writing, the test has not been used. Insofar as private healthcare providers consolidating their market share can be seen as organic growth (of the private healthcare market), the development of a 'merger-control-like' test to monitor this appears unusual, although it may be understood in light of the complex symbiotic relationship between the NHS and private healthcare sector, which cannot be explained simply in terms of competition.

### *3.1.3. Relationship between the Jurisdictional Aspects and General Merger Control*

How the jurisdictional aspects of healthcare-specific merger control complement general merger control appears to both extend and narrow the oversight by the ACM and CMA, and accordingly the range of mergers assessed.

In the Netherlands, the lower turnover thresholds and separate 'care turnover' threshold have the function of *extending* the ACM's oversight in terms

---

infrastructure and the possibility of partnership with an NHS Trust to manage a PPU offers a low-risk means of market entry for private hospital operators. Ibid, paras. 11.249–11.252.

182 The CMA established that of the 83 dedicated PPUs in the UK, 74 are managed in-house by the NHS and 9 are managed by private hospital groups. Ibid, para. 2.28.

183 CMA, *Final Order*, above n. 32.

184 All established in OFT, ME/2524/06 *Award of management contract to provide private in-patient bone marrow transplants and sarcoma cancer treatments at UCLH NHS Foundation Trust to HCA International Limited*, 12.10.2006.

185 As considered in OFT, ME/5641/12 *Anticipated lease by HCA International Limited of premises from Guy's and St Thomas' NHS Foundation Trust*, 07.11.2012, para. 17.

186 Defined under section 134(8) EA02. See CMA, 'Private Healthcare Market Investigation – Explanatory Note to accompany the Private Healthcare Market Investigation Order 2014', 01.10.2014, paragraph 24.

of the number of hospital mergers examined. This is an important consideration in view of healthcare as a sector in transition, but, albeit with the benefit of hindsight, may have contributed to the problem of widespread hospital merger approval by increasing the number of mergers available for approval. It is interesting to note that in the consultation regarding whether or not the turnover thresholds be maintained, one law firm proposed that a voluntary notification regime be adopted for Dutch hospital mergers based on the experience of the *Surrey Hospitals* and *Manchester Hospitals* mergers.[187] This is an interesting suggestion since it is unclear whether all NHS Foundation Trust mergers are being notified in practice (as appeared to be the experience with mergers scrutinised under the NHS-specific merger test)[188] despite the EA02 merger-control regime being based on voluntary notification. If this is the case, then perhaps the regime established by section 79 HSCA 2012 – in conjunction with NHS Improvement engagement – is effectively operating as a substitute mandatory notification regime.

In England, the clarification by section 79 HSCA 2012 that general merger control covers mergers involving NHS Foundation Trusts, together with the new PPU test, may extend the scope of CMA oversight, if not the range of mergers examined.

The new PPU test clearly extends the scope for CMA oversight by introducing a new threshold of 'PPU arrangement', which is not dependent upon a change in control. This appears to enable the CMA to scrutinise any new NHS Foundation Trust PPUs which arise as a result of removing the private patient income cap, thus extending oversight to NHS Foundation Trusts acting as private providers on the private healthcare market. However, the CMA's overarching concern in its private healthcare Market Investigation was to avoid further consolidation of, and distortions of competition by, private healthcare providers acquiring PPUs. This would appear to suggest that the intended scope behind the new test is narrower than first appears. However, the permutations of PPUs operated by NHS Foundation Trusts and those operated by private healthcare providers may be less clear-cut in practice, so merits further research if these develop as anticipated.

Section 79 HSCA 2012 extends the scope for CMA oversight by making explicit the applicability of general merger control to the NHS. As noted previously, this is because a merger between an NHS Trust and an NHS Foundation Trust seems likely to be caught on the grounds that the requirement for 'enterprises' is satisfied and there will presumably be sufficient change in control for a 'relevant merger situation' insofar as the resulting entity is likely to be an NHS Foundation Trust, thus no longer subject to Secretary of State control.

---

187 D.W.L.A. Schrijvershof, above n. 124.

188 K. Desai, above n. 137.

However, section 79 HSCA 2012 may limit the scope for CMA oversight by explicitly referencing mergers involving NHS Foundation Trusts, thereby avoiding oversight of emerging arrangements in connection with the 'transactions oversight' or the new care models. These arrangements clearly involve 'enterprises' in the form of private companies and NHS Trusts. However, whether they entail the requisite change in control necessary for a 'relevant merger situation' remains unclear, unless the resulting body remains subject to Secretary of State control, so avoidance of CMA oversight is then not associated with section 79 HSCA 2012.

It is interesting to note that the CMA appears increasingly ready to acknowledge the limited scope for competition within the NHS – as evidenced in comments in relation to both the *Manchester Hospitals* and *Birmingham Hospitals* mergers. However, whilst different approaches may be taken as to how subsequent NHS Foundation Trust mergers are assessed – namely, whether this would amount to a full, two-phase investigation; an expedited investigation at the request of the parties (as per the *Manchester Hospitals* merger); or significant weighting being given to NHS Improvement assessment of relevant customer benefits enabling approval at Phase I (as per the *Birmingham Hospitals* merger) – this may represent a change in *procedure* by the CMA, and not a material change to the *jurisdictional* aspects of merger assessment.

In the Netherlands, the original version of the healthcare-specific merger test, with its requirement for submission of a 'merger effects' report and the option for the NZa to prohibit a proposed merger which endangered the provision of critical care, would appear to operate potentially to *reduce* the ACM's oversight of hospital mergers. In other words, the healthcare-specific merger test would appear to serve as a filter for Dutch general merger control – a notable feature in view of the system of mandatory notification.[189] It is interesting to note that the refocusing of the healthcare-specific merger test with the 2015 reforms saw the merger effects report being retained, and a new requirement for parties to apparently justify a merger over other forms of collaboration. This may serve to refocus the jurisdiction of general merger control by a filter which not only may reduce the number of notified mergers, but distinguishes other forms of collaboration. An example of this can be seen in recent questions regarding

---

[189] This would presumably serve to increase the number of mergers examined by the ACM, and in which the main 'filter' available to the ACM appears to be the establishment of an SIEC leading to a dominant position. In view of the complexities surrounding market definition for hospitals and establishing 'dominance' in a healthcare context, this is a significant hurdle. The ACM has recently reiterated that it can only take action where there are instances of market power from a competition perspective, which only emerges in a limited number of cases. See Autoriteit Consument en Markt (ACM), *'Position Paper Autoriteit Consument en Markt Rondetafelgesprek "Kwaliteit loont"'* ('ACM Position Paper on the "Quality Pays" roundtable discussion'), 17.04.2015.

the applicability of general merger control to *Maatschappen* (Specialist Partnerships) – partnerships of medical specialists across different hospitals and regions – and how best to manage any resulting competition concerns.[190] As regards merger control, the question arose of whether the Specialist Partnership was a separate entity from a hospital. The ACM clarified that it regards partnerships and hospitals as forming a single undertaking, subject to as yet unclarified exceptions.[191] Consequently, if the Specialist Partnership of one hospital merges with another partnership from another hospital, the ACM does not consider this as a merger between two independent undertakings, but as cooperation between the two hospitals regarding the same specialty. The formation of Specialist Partnerships at city or region level are therefore considered by the ACM to be agreements between hospitals, which must be examined under the anticompetitive agreements provisions (Article 6 Mw).[192]

## 3.2. SUBSTANTIVE ASSESSMENT ASPECTS

### 3.2.1. *The Netherlands*

The 'substantive assessment aspects' of healthcare-specific merger control comprise additional assessment criteria for the ACM and NZa Opinions.

#### 3.2.1.1. Additional Assessment Criteria for the ACM

In 2013, new Policy Rules were introduced regarding mergers between healthcare providers and between health insurers.[193] These clarified healthcare-specific

---

190 See, for example, M. Varkevisser et al., *'Instellingsoverstijgende maatschappen: Huidige ontwikkelingen, mogelijke gevolgen en de aanpak van eventuele mededingingsproblemen. Eindrapport'* ('Cross-institution partnerships: current developments, possible consequences and managing potential competition problems. Final Report'). IMBG, Erasmus Universiteit Rotterdam. Maart 2013. E.M.H. Loozen, *'Mededingingstoezicht op maatschappen van zorgaanbieders: welke rol is weggelegd voor ACM respectievelijk NZa?'* ('Competition regulation of healthcare provider partnerships: what roles do the ACM and NZa play?') (2013) *Tijdschrift voor Gezondheidsrecht*, 7(37), 622.

191 ACM, *'ACM-lijn maatschappen en ziekenhuizen'* ('ACM guidance on healthcare provider partnerships and hospitals'), 06.06.2013.

192 Ibid.

193 *Beleidsregel van de Minister van Economische Zaken van 05.07.2013, nr. WJZ/13118300, houdende bijzondere regels betreffende concentraties van zorgaanbieders en zorgverzekeraars* (Policy Rule by the Minister for Economic Affairs of 05.07.2013, No. WJZ/13118300, setting out special rules governing mergers of healthcare providers and mergers of health insurers). Article 3 of these rules is concerned with mergers between health insurers, but this is beyond the scope of this discussion. A legislative proposal (*Kamerstukken II 2011–12, 33 362, nr. 2. Wijziging van de Wet marktordening gezondheidszorg en enkele andere wetten, teneinde te voorkomen dat zorgverzekeraars zelf zorg verlenen of zorg laten aanbieden door zorgaanbieders*

criteria for the ACM to consider in assessments of mergers between healthcare providers where the combined market share exceeds 35 per cent. These Policy Rules are now in force until 1 January 2023,[194] and in essence, the ACM must consider four factors:[195] the transparency of care quality; clients' travel behaviour or willingness to travel; possibilities for entry by other healthcare providers; and the ways in which healthcare purchasers[196] can influence client choice. These criteria may influence the definition of relevant markets, as well as reflect the consequences of a merger for competition.[197] In addition, the ACM must request an Opinion from the 'client councils' of the healthcare provider most affected by the merger regarding the relevant market(s).[198] In connection with the cases discussed in this chapter, the additional healthcare-specific assessment criteria have all been considered at Phase I.[199]

#### 3.2.1.2. NZa Opinions

The requirements for the ACM to consult the NZa during the merger assessment process, and for the NZa to provide a non-binding Opinion at either or both stages of the merger-review process, were set out in soft law documentation such as the ACM's Guidelines for the Healthcare Sector[200] and the NZa–ACM

---

*waarin zij zelf zeggenschap hebben* (Amendment of the Wmg and other Acts to prohibit the provision of healthcare by health insurers, or by healthcare providers over which they have control)) was put forward which comprised a prohibition (with exemptions) on vertical integration of health insurers and healthcare providers. This approach had been criticised by economists and on grounds of incompatibility with EU law. See further, W. Sauter, above n. 50.

194 Article 4 of the 2013 Policy Rules stipulates that the timeframe of their operation is linked with the 2007 Decree (see above n. 105), so has recently been extended to 2023. The 2013 Policy Rules consolidate the 2009 Policy Rules which were repealed on 16.07.2013 and were addressed specifically to healthcare providers but remain broadly unchanged in substantive terms. *Beleidsregel van de Minister van Economische Zaken van 01.09.2009, nr. WJZ/9145416, houdende bijzondere regels betreffende concentraties van zorgaanbieders* (Policy Rule by the Minister for Economic Affairs of 01.09.2009, No. WJZ/9145416, setting out special rules governing mergers of healthcare providers).

195 Article 2(1) 2009 Policy Rules, above n. 194.

196 The broad definition of 'healthcare purchasers' in Article 1(h) 2009 Policy Rules, above n. 194, as referring to health insurers in the 'cure' sector, and regional 'care agencies' in the 'care' sector or municipalities appears retained by Article 1(i) of the 2013 Policy Rules, above n. 193.

197 Explanatory Notes to the 2013 Policy Rules, above n. 193.

198 Article 2(2) 2009 Policy Rules, above n. 194.

199 ACM, Case reference 16.0685.22, above n. 78, section 9, p. 42. With regard to the *Albert Schweitzer-Rivas Care Group* merger, see ACM, Case reference 13.1464.22. *Besluit van de Autoriteit Consument en Markt als bedoeld in artikel 37, eerste lid, van de Mededingingswet* (ACM decision as defined by Article 37(1) Mw), 18.03.2014, (Phase I decision), section 6, p.17. With regard to the *Tilburg Hospitals* merger, see ACM, Case reference 7295/101, *Besluit van de Raad van Bestuur van de Nederlandse Mededingingsautoriteit als bedoeld in artikel 37, eerste lid, van de Mededingingswet* (Decision of the NMa Board as defined by Article 37(1) Mw), 20.12.2011, (Phase I decision).

200 ACM, above n. 57.

Cooperation Protocols.[201] The NZa's duty to prioritise the 'general consumer interest',[202] defined in terms of affordability, accessibility and quality, formed the basis for its Opinions, although it was obliged to follow the advice of the quality regulator (IGJ) in its assessments of quality.[203] In addition, the NZa developed two econometric methods – the Option Demand Method (ODM) and the Logit Competition Index method (LOCI) – with the ACM to assess possible post-merger price increases.[204] These two models are used to assess whether a merger may result in price increases in the markets for inpatient and outpatient care, and informed the 'affordability' aspect of the NZa Opinions. Furthermore, changes in the sector have led to the inclusion of other factors in NZa Opinions, such as selective contracting. Whilst the healthcare-specific merger test introduced in January 2014 was referenced in some NZa Opinions, it appears that the test was intended to replace the NZa's Opinions.[205] However, the NZa provided an Opinion in the 2015 *Albert Schweitzer Hospital–Rivas Care Group* merger, although it is unclear how its assessment of possible price increases influenced the ACM's decision to block this merger, as the latter considered that these did not necessarily reflect the extent of underlying competitive tension between the parties.[206] With the proposed refocusing of the ACM's competence vis-à-vis healthcare mergers, it appeared that the NZa would no longer be required to submit an Opinion, and that any emphasis given to the public interest factors of affordability, accessibility and quality would be the exception, rather than the rule, in ACM assessments. Furthermore, as noted previously, the NZa provided an Opinion in the *Amsterdam Universities Hospitals* merger case,[207] highlighting concerns on public interest grounds and proposing that the merger be blocked.

---

201 NMA, *'Protocol tussen de Nederlandse Mededingingsautoriteit en de Nederlandse Zorgautoriteit over de wijze van samenwerking bij aangelegenheden van wederzijds belang'* ('Protocol signed by the Dutch Competition Authority and the Dutch Healthcare Authority regarding cooperation in matters of mutual interest'), October 2006. NMA/NZA, *'Samenwerkingsprotocol NMa-NZa'* ('NMa–NZa Cooperation Protocol'), December 2010. ACM/NZA, *'Samenwerkingsprotocol Autoriteit Consument en Markt en Nederlandse Zorgautoriteit'* ('ACM and NZa Cooperation Protocol'), December 2014.

202 Article 3(4) Wmg. See also ACM, above n. 57, section 5.3.3.

203 Article 19 Wmg.

204 The ODM is related to the insurance aspects of hospital care by translating patient willingness to pay (WTP) into the inclusion of a hospital in the contracted care offer of health insurers. LOCI is an index which characterises the competitiveness of a hospital between 0 (monopoly) and 1 (perfect competition) as determined by the overlap of products/services provided by health insurers in different segments. As described in, for example, the NZa Opinion in the *Tilburg Hospitals* case. NZA, *Zienswijze vergunningsaanvraag Stichting TweeSteden ziekenhuis en Stichting St. Elisabeth ziekenhuis, Juli 2012* (NZa, Opinion on the licence request in the *Tilburg Hospitals* merger, July 2012).

205 W. Sauter, above n. 50.

206 See ACM, above n. 17, paras. 79–82.

207 NZA, Case Reference 255248/372686, *Opinion in the Amsterdam Universities Hospitals merger case* (correspondence between M.J. Kaljouw and C. Fonteijn 24.08.2017).

Among the 2015 reforms of the healthcare-specific merger test, it was intended that the ACM may examine a proposed merger in the light of criteria to be determined by Ministerial Decrees regarding the protection of public interests in healthcare.[208] However, it was intended that these would apply where, as a result of a merger, there were insufficient alternatives for specific types of care or a health insurer was unable to fulfil its duty of care obligations.[209] The proposals allowed for the possibility, and not the obligation, to set further criteria, as this recourse would only be employed if general merger control failed to safeguard public interests.[210]

### *3.2.2. England – NHS Improvement's Advisory Function under Section 79(5) HSCA 2012*

NHS Improvement's advisory function under section 79(5) HSCA 2012 to identify 'relevant patient benefits' appears, at least prima facie, to be capable of complementing CMA assessments, since this mechanism exists in the wider context of the EA02 test. Indeed, the terminology of 'relevant customer benefits' (as stated in section 79(5) HSCA 2012) and 'relevant patient benefits' (which appears increasingly to be used in discussions of NHS mergers) appears interchangeable.[211] Furthermore, NHS Improvement and the CMA have adopted a broad definition of 'customer' in relation to the healthcare sector as meaning 'a current or future user of healthcare services (often but not always referred to as a 'patient') or a commissioner.'[212] However, NHS Improvement has acknowledged that it relies on the definition in section 30(1)(a) EA02 of 'relevant benefits', that is, lower prices, higher quality or greater choice of goods or services in any market in the United Kingdom.

NHS Improvement's examination of relevant patient benefits involves assessing whether the benefits put forward by the merger parties qualify as such by examining three questions: whether the proposal is likely to represent a real improvement in quality, choice or innovation of services for patients, or in value for money for commissioners; whether the proposal is likely to be realised within a reasonable period as a result of the merger; and whether the proposal is unlikely to accrue without the merger or similar lessening of competition.[213] Examples of relevant patient benefits in NHS Improvement

---

208 *Kamerstukken 2015–16*, above n. 133, para. 5.3.2, p. 23.

209 Ibid.

210 Ibid.

211 While section 79(5) HSCA 2012 makes explicit reference to 'relevant customer benefits' under section 30(1)(a) EA02, subsequent references have been to 'patient benefits'. See, for example, Monitor, above n. 160 and latterly NHS Improvement, above n. 28, fn. 6, p. 6.

212 NHS Improvement, above n. 173, fn. 8, p. 13, and CMA, above n. 41, para. 7.3. This is based in part on the definition of a 'customer' under section 30(4) EA02.

213 NHS Improvement above n. 173, section 4.1 'The framework for assessing the proposals'.

guidance – consistent with *CMA guidance on the review of NHS mergers*[214] – include higher quality services arising through implementing a particular model of care, service reconfiguration, increased consultant or staff cover, or access to equipment; or greater innovation through research and development; or financial savings.[215]

Whilst NHS Improvement's assessment of 'relevant patient benefits' is typically reserved to input at Phase I,[216] it appears, with the *Manchester* and *Birmingham Hospitals* mergers, to be gaining significance in terms of being outcome-determinative, although this was arguably less true with earlier cases.

In the *Dorset Hospitals* merger, although Monitor (NHS Improvement) emphasised the relevant customer benefit associated with reconfiguring maternity services at Phase I, this was not submitted by the parties to the Phase II assessment. Ultimately the then Competition Commission (CC) concluded that the merger would result in an SLC in 55 services and found no relevant customer benefits. The CC also rejected the parties' proposed behavioural remedy of assessing quality that might be affected by the SLCs by using the metric of the Friends and Family Test (FFT).[217] Having considered that partial divestiture would not provide a feasible structural remedy, as the services affected by the SLCs were not easily divisible, the CC concluded that prohibition was the only proportionate remedy that would address the SLCs and adverse effects that they established. However, it would be unfair to consider NHS Improvement's input into this merger as indicative of its approach. It is acknowledged that this merger provided a difficult test case, not least as a two-to-one merger to monopoly would always encounter tough scrutiny from the competition authorities.[218] Furthermore, this was compounded by the wider changes in the sector at the time,[219]

---

214 CMA, above n. 41, para. 7.13, pp. 44–46.

215 Monitor, Supporting NHS Providers: Guidance on merger benefits, 26.08.2015, pp. 13–20.

216 The only exception to this so far is the advice provided in the context of the *Manchester Hospitals* merger, which involved a fast track Phase II investigation at the request of the merging parties. See NHS Improvement, above n. 173, section 1.3, p. 6. However, it is acknowledged that where merger parties only submit relevant patient benefits during a Phase II inquiry, the CMA will seek NHS Improvement's views in Phase II. See CMA, above n. 41, para. 8.6.

217 The FFT was implemented in April 2013 and asks patients to rate the likelihood of their recommending a ward/service etc. to friends and family if they needed similar treatment, <http://www.nhs.uk/NHSEngland/AboutNHSservices/Pages/nhs-friends-and-family-test.aspx>, accessed 24.06.2018.

218 R. Curran and S. Albert, above n. 95.

219 For a comprehensive analysis of this based on interviews with groups involved in the merger, see E. Spencelayh and J. Dixon, 'Mergers in the NHS – Lessons from the decision to block the proposed merger of hospitals in Bournemouth and Poole', *The Health Foundation Policy Analysis*, December 2014.

namely enactment of the HSCA 2012 with all the changes this entailed, such as the change between the NHS CCP and NHS Improvement and refocused substantive tests.

In the *Surrey Hospitals* merger, NHS Improvement identified potential relevant patient benefits in respect of increased access to consultants (via the introduction of weekend ward rounds and out-of-hours consultant rota) across gastroenterology, stroke and interventional radiology.[220] However, the CMA did not consider that these were sufficient to offset the SLC it identified at Phase I, and thus did not obviate the need for a Phase II assessment.[221] Nevertheless, these relevant customer benefits serve to highlight the role that government policy may continue to play in NHS merger decisions. At Phase II the CMA considered NHS Improvement's advice in connection with 'the requirement for seven-day services', following the establishment of the NHS Services Seven Days a Week Forum in February 2013 to consider how NHS services could be improved to provide a more responsive and patient-centred service across the seven-day week.[222] This would appear to suggest that government policy to provide a 'seven-day NHS' found reflection in CMA assessment. However, in its Phase II decision, the CMA also paid attention to NHS Improvement's assessment of the merging parties in its capacity as NHS Foundation Trust regulator.

In the *Manchester Hospitals* merger, NHS Improvement considered that 11 of the 15 proposals by the parties would be likely to result in improvements for patients by providing more timely and effective care in three ways.[223] Firstly, in relation to acute coronary syndrome, heart rhythm abnormalities, acute aortic surgery and stroke proposals, through combining workforces to increase the availability of sub-specialist consultants and access to services on the weekends. Secondly, in relation to urgent gynaecology, kidney stones treatment and elective orthopaedics, through sharing capacity and resources to provide dedicated surgical lists for urgent patients, increase treatment options available and ring-fence elective care. Thirdly, in relation to vascular, head and neck cancer, general surgery, and urology cancer, through creating higher volume hubs which have been shown to produce better patient outcomes and survivorship. NHS Improvement further considered that more work was necessary to ensure that the proposals were likely to be delivered within a reasonable timeframe.[224] In considering the counterfactual, NHS Improvement

---

220 Monitor, 'Monitor's advice to the Competition and Markets Authority on the merger benefits of the proposed merger of Ashford and St Peter's Hospitals NHS Foundation Trust and Royal Surrey County Hospital NHS Foundation Trust', March 2015.

221 CMA, ME/6511/14 *Anticipated Merger of Ashford and St Peter's Hospitals NHS Foundation Trust and Royal Surrey County Hospital NHS Foundation Trust*, 12.03.15, (Phase I decision), paragraphs 24–33.

222 CMA, above n. 25, paragraphs 4.18–4.23.

223 NHS Improvement, above n. 173, section 4.3.1, p. 19.

224 Ibid, section 4.3.2, pp. 20–21.

assessed that a merger appeared to be the most effective way to achieve the improvements at scale across Manchester, since the merger would mean that the parties were more likely to work together to ensure delivery of the improvements.[225] From the CMA's assessment, it is clear that relevant patient benefits beyond those proposed by the parties were taken into consideration. For example, attention was paid to the parties' specific plans in 75 distinct clinical service areas, and NHS Improvement's experience of finding that mergers between NHS providers can generate improvements in clinical service delivery and financial savings.[226]

### *3.2.3. Relationship between the 'Substantive Assessment Aspects' and General Merger Control*

How the substantive assessment aspects complement general merger control is largely related to the (limited) scope for the latter to accommodate non-competition concerns. This is evidenced primarily by the inclusion of NZa Opinions in the Netherlands and NHS Improvement's advisory role regarding 'relevant customer benefits' under section 79(5) HSCA 2012.

With regard to the inclusion of NZa Opinions, whilst the ACM has acknowledged these and the NZa's econometric assessments, this arises out of a period of tension following the *Zeeland Hospitals* merger discussed above, although how public interests will be incorporated into merger assessment following the current reforms is unclear. However, it appears that these may be incorporated less routinely and less explicitly in view of the anticipation that general merger control will accommodate public interests as a rule, as noted above. Whether this will result in a 'creative' – as opposed to a 'strict' – interpretation of Dutch general merger control remains to be seen. However, this underscoring of the potential flexibility of Dutch general merger control suggests a willingness to engage with the criticism that what is at fault is not the underlying substantive test, but the interpretation and implementation of this.[227]

NHS Improvement's advisory function under section 79(5) HSCA 2012 may also have been construed initially as an attempt to incorporate public interests, albeit within the confines of 'relevant customer benefits'.[228] However, the

---

225 Ibid, section 4.3.3, pp. 21–22.

226 CMA, above n. 26, pp. 136–50.

227 See E.M.H. Loozen, above n. 18.

228 M. Guy, 'Monitor's Advice to the OFT and the New Healthcare Regulation', *Competition Policy Blog*, 20.03.2013, <https://competitionpolicy.wordpress.com/2013/02/20/monitors-advice-to-the-oft-and-the-new-healthcare-regulation/> accessed 24.06.2018. M. Guy, 'The Meaning of "Relevant Customer Benefits" in the Context of Health Care: Monitor's Advice and the Competition Commission's Response', *Competition Policy Blog*, 28.10.2013, <https://competitionpolicy.wordpress.com/2013/10/28/the-meaning-of-relevant-customer-benefits-in-the-context-of-health-care-monitors-advice-and-the-competition-commissions-response/> accessed 24.06.2018.

references to the development of a seven-day NHS within the context of the *Surrey Hospitals* merger case, and the significance attached to patient benefits in the *Manchester Hospitals* merger suggests that relevant customer benefits may equally serve as a means of advancing policy, so these will be interpreted in a more flexible way. A further – presumably unintended – consequence of NHS Improvement's advisory function has been the potential for change in working practices between NHS Improvement and the CMA which can be traced across the *Dorset*, *Surrey* and *Manchester Hospital* mergers. It might be considered that the blocking of the *Dorset Hospitals* merger led the CMA to delay its assessment of the *Surrey Hospitals* merger pending delivery of Monitor's (NHS Improvement's) advice. This delay coincided with the outlining and promotion of Sustainability and Transformation Partnerships, which prompted the NHS Foundation Trusts not to pursue a merger.[229] In light of the complications of the CMA conducting its general merger assessment subsequent to NHS Improvement's advisory function, the choice of the expedited Phase II assessment in the *Manchester Hospitals* merger takes on a different dimension, as this procedure would enable the CMA's and NHS Improvement's respective assessments to occur concurrently.[230]

## 4. INTENTIONS BEHIND HEALTHCARE-SPECIFIC MERGER TESTS AND LESSONS EMERGING FROM THEIR DESIGN AND APPLICATION

Having examined in overview the constituent elements of healthcare-specific merger control, it is useful to consider what purposes these serve, or what they are intended to achieve. To this end, various conceptions are possible, but at least four issues can be identified in connection with the application of general merger control to hospital mergers. These range from the introduction of competition reforms as a way of counteracting the limitations of a competition-based test, to considering the role of merger control in a sector heavily dependent upon different types of agreement and cooperative relationships.

### 4.1. 'SELLING' COMPETITION REFORMS AND ENGAGING WITH THE HEALTHCARE SECTOR

In moving away from healthcare provision as a public service overseen by government to a market-based system overseen by a competition authority,

---

229 Royal Surrey County Hospital NHS Foundation Trust, 'Update on proposed hospital merger', <http://www.royalsurrey.nhs.uk/update-on-proposed-hospital-merger/> accessed 24.06.2018.

230 I am grateful to Andrew Taylor (Aldwych Partners) for highlighting this sequence of events.

it has been acknowledged that the success of such reforms will depend largely on public perception,[231] which in turn relies on perception of the reforms by the parties which comprise the healthcare sector. Thus there is a need for broader efforts to 'sell' competition[232] and engage with healthcare providers involved in the implementation of the reforms. In terms of healthcare-specific merger control, the role of the regulators in both countries and the Dutch healthcare-specific merger test seem particularly relevant.

Underpinning the competition reforms in both the Netherlands and England has been the incorporation of the NZa's and NHS Improvement's advisory functions into merger assessment. As approving or blocking a merger is the exclusive preserve of the ACM or CMA, it is necessary to have a clearly-defined role for the NZa and NHS Improvement.

The relationship between the ACM, NZa and quality regulator (IGJ) can be illustrated as follows, with white arrows denoting the lack of statutory consultation requirement:

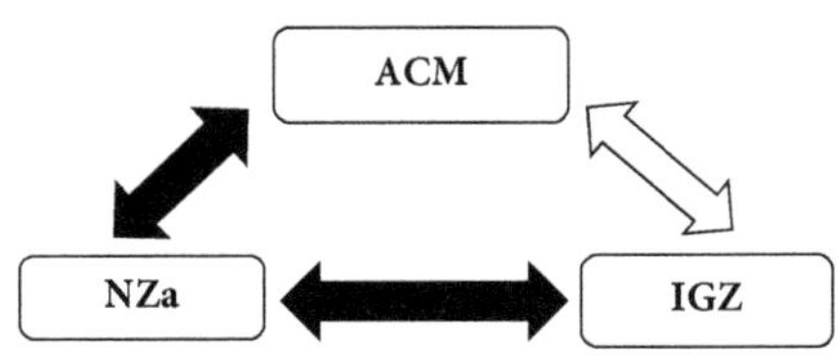


**Figure 15. The institutional relationship between the ACM, NZa and IGJ in healthcare merger assessment, 2006–15**

Whilst this framework appeared to afford the NZa a defined role within merger assessment, this was challenged in the context of the *Zeeland Hospitals* merger, as the ACM appeared to give greater weight to the IGJ's advice, effectively sidelining the NZa's Opinion. This led to the purpose of the NZa being questioned.[233]

In England, it is interesting to note that NHS Improvement's function within NHS Foundation Trust merger assessment was only incorporated in the final debates prior to enactment of the HSCA 2012,[234] in stark contrast to modifications of its other roles which are largely attributable to the NHS Future Forum's recommendations in refocusing competition. Nevertheless, inclusion of

231 W. Sauter, above n. 61.

232 On this point in connection with wider public service reform in England, see O. Odudu, 'Why it matters: Selling competition law in the new frontier', *Competition Law Insight*, 10.12.2013.

233 Y. Maasdam and J-K. Sluijs, above n. 64.

234 No mention appears to be made of any interaction between the then OFT and Monitor regarding NHS Foundation Trust mergers prior to the inclusion of Clauses 79(4) and (5) to the Health and Social Care Bill (HL Bill 132) Session 2010–12 (as amended on report), 14.03.2012. The HSCA 2012 received Royal Assent on 27.03.2012.

a function for NHS Improvement within merger control may be considered to be motivated by the same intention to facilitate the transfer between an NHS-specific and general merger control regime. The fact that NHS Improvement was assigned a pre-existing function within general merger control (identifying 'relevant customer benefits' exceptions), rather than a new role related to, but independent of, the EA02 test would seem to support this.

It seems uncontroversial to suggest that the 'merger effects' report of the Dutch healthcare-specific merger test serves an important function in engaging with healthcare providers, as well as facilitating communication between these and the competition authority. The NZa's ability to prohibit a merger on the basis that stakeholders have not been adequately consulted appears to reinforce this. Although not a feature of healthcare-specific merger control in England, emphasis on considering merger effects can be inferred from the significant efforts made by the CMA, NHS Improvement and competition lawyers to bridge any communication gap between the CMA and the NHS, particularly following the *Dorset Hospitals* merger. This is evident in the range of publications by the agencies and in the trade press outlining the merger control process and assessment criteria,[235] and has been significantly consolidated recently by more formal research and guidance.[236]

## 4.2. ENSURING APPROPRIATE OVERSIGHT OF MERGERS IN A SECTOR IN TRANSITION

Dutch experience of uncertainty regarding the potential for hospitals to raise competition concerns in the period 1998–2004, coupled with an ongoing move towards the 2006 reforms, suggests that the timing of the application of general merger control is critical. Indeed, it has been suggested that the lack of application of general merger control amounted to a 'regulatory holiday' creating market distortions, with the implication that these were subsequently aggravated by ongoing merger approval.[237]

---

235 See, for example, D. Bennett, 'Monitor's plan for a better merger regime', *Health Service Journal*, 23.01.2014. G. Hanratty, 'Heatherwood-Frimley Park shows the way through merger process', *Health Service Journal*, 26.06.2014. T. Akinrinade, J. Christoforou and E. Clark, 'How to navigate a competition review to get trust merger approval', *Health Service Journal*, 14.10.2014.

236 Demonstrated, inter alia, by Aldwych Partners, 'Benefits from mergers: lessons from recent NHS transactions'. NHS Improvement, 'Making Mergers Work: Improvements NHS providers have achieved through merger', May 2016. Cass Business School City University London and NHS Improvement, 'Mergers in the NHS: lessons learnt and recommendations – Summary', May 2016. Cass Business School City University London and NHS Improvement, 'Mergers in the NHS: Lessons Learnt and Recommendations – Update 2017'. All available via <https://improvement.nhs.uk/resources/how-make-nhs-mergers-work-better-patients/> accessed 24.06.2018.

237 M. Canoy and W. Sauter, above n. 7.

This would appear to suggest that there is a need for healthcare-specific amendments which are both prospective as well as reactive to the application of general merger control. Many of the elements of healthcare-specific merger control are reactive, such as the introduction of lower turnover thresholds in the Netherlands. However, the development of the NHS-specific test in England might be deemed prospective, at least with the benefit of hindsight,[238] as the application of general merger control seems a logical step for NHS Trusts which have attained NHS Foundation Trust status and are consequently independent of government oversight. Whether the PPU test can be deemed prospective is questionable. While it appears to anticipate an expansion of PPUs, it also can be construed as a *reaction* to PPUs being found not to qualify for Phase I assessment thus far.[239]

## 4.3. COUNTERACTING THE LIMITATIONS OF A COMPETITION-BASED TEST

This offers a healthcare perspective on the wider issue of the flexibility of general competition law to accommodate public interest concerns.[240] More specifically, the issue is the importance of making healthcare values of affordability, accessibility and quality 'sufficiently operational' for competition authorities to handle.[241] In other words, how effectively to apply a standard test to the healthcare sector, characterised by atypical consumers and (at least in England) a move away from competition on price.

This 'operationalisation' is demonstrated in part by the additional criteria for the ACM, but mainly by the incorporation of regulator advice into the merger-assessment process, as exemplified by NHS Improvement's input into merger control under section 79(5) HSCA 2012 and NZa Opinions in the Netherlands. In a sense, an intention of the additional assessment criteria is to

238 Whether competition in the NHS would have developed along the same lines as the HSCA 2012 reforms in the absence of the Coalition Government is a moot point. While the HSCA 2012 reforms build on previous New Labour reforms, they have also been criticised for taking earlier reforms in a wrong direction. See comments by the former Secretary of State for Health Alan Milburn in T. Gash and T. Roos, 'Choice and competition in public services: learning from history', *Institute for Government*, August 2012.

239 See OFT, above n. 184, and OFT, above n. 185.

240 On this wider point in connection with mergers, see D. Reader, 'Accommodating Public Interest Considerations in Domestic Merger Control: Empirical Insights', CCP Working Paper 16-3; and more generally in connection with the Dutch context, J.W. van de Gronden, *'Een upgrade van het zorgbeleid van de NMa: de derde versie van de Richtsnoeren voor de zorgsector'* ('Upgrade of the NMa's healthcare policy: the third edition of the Guidelines for the Healthcare Sector') (2010) *Markt en Mededinging*, 6, 195.

241 M. Canoy and W. Sauter, above n. 7. This 'operationalisation' has been identified as a lesson in the context of it being crucial to employ merger control.

understand aspects of patient behaviour – such as willingness to travel further for specialist rather than basic care, and responding to greater availability of information about quality[242] – which may not otherwise be reflected in the competition test of Dutch general merger control. In essence, the 2013 Policy Rules can be seen very much as a reflection of a sector in transition. There is an acknowledged need for the ACM's decision-making process to be as transparent as possible, as developments such as the change in classification of hospital services may influence elements such as market definition which are fundamental to the merger control process.[243]

As regards the regulator's role, in England, NHS Improvement's duty to advise on 'relevant customer benefits' is an example of regulator input found in other sectors,[244] but is now developing in a healthcare context as a significant assessment mechanism in its own right, as evidenced by the weight given by the CMA to elaborating relevant patient benefits in the *Manchester Hospitals* merger. An extra dimension to this is afforded by considerations of the limited role for competition in the English NHS.

In the Netherlands, the focus of the NZa's Opinions in merger cases was on the general consumer interest,[245] which refers to long-term interests,[246] and so can be distinguished from the interests of individual consumers or healthcare providers. The NZa interpreted this in terms of the wider public interests of affordability, accessibility and quality. These have been further defined in connection with healthcare. For example, 'accessibility' can be understood in terms of physical and financial accessibility. The former acknowledges access to the right care within a reasonable distance and time period, based on norms regarding waiting time for elective care. The latter provides that ability to pay is no barrier to receiving medical care. 'Affordability' can be considered both at a micro level (relating to affordable basic insurance) and macro level (relating to lack of reduction of purchasing power or a dramatic increase in public spending).[247] The 'quality' dimension of the NZa's Opinions was previously focused on the transparency of quality and whether markets worked well – presumably to complement IGJ assessments regarding the medical quality of

---

242 Explanatory Notes to the 2013 Policy Rules, above n. 193.

243 Ibid.

244 For example, Ofwat considers relevant customer benefits in the context of comparative competition and mergers in the water sector. See OFWAT, 'Ofwat's approach to mergers and statement of methods', October 2015, p. 2. A similarly formal process is in place for Ofcom to produce a report at Phase I regarding media mergers. However, other sectoral regulators may also be consulted in merger assessment accordingly.

245 Article 3(4) Wmg.

246 W. SAUTER, 'Is the general consumer interest a source of legitimacy for healthcare regulation? An analysis of the Dutch experience' (2009) 2–3 *European Journal of Consumer Law* 419.

247 NZA, '*Visiedocument: (In) het belang van de consument*' ('Vision Document: (In) the general consumer interest') (November 2007), section 2.1.

healthcare – whereas more recent NZa Opinions included a section on 'quality' devoted to the IGJ's advice.[248]

The 2015 reforms include a potentially significant refocusing of how public interests may be incorporated, with the suggestion that recourse to Ministerial Decrees may be had only where general merger control proves insufficient. Whilst the ACM has acknowledged that affordability and accessibility of healthcare comprise part of its competition assessment, an in-depth analysis of the effects of a merger on the *quality* of the healthcare provided does not.[249]

## 4.4. ELABORATING THE APPROPRIATE PLACE OF MERGER CONTROL IN A SECTOR HEAVILY DEPENDENT UPON COOPERATIVE RELATIONSHIPS

The creation of the NHS-specific test, the 'Transactions' oversight and PPU test in England underscore the existence of different forms of cooperation within the hospital sector. Recognising that such arrangements may not fall within the scope of general merger control may raise the question of whether the anticompetitive agreements provisions were triggered instead. However, this is perhaps more likely in the Netherlands, where both merger control and the anticompetitive agreements provision (Article 6 Mw) are addressed to 'undertakings' by the Dutch Competition Act (Mw). In England, although NHS Foundation Trusts and NHS Trusts are indeed 'enterprises' for the purposes of EA02, their respective status as 'undertakings' for the purposes of the Chapter I prohibition of the Competition Act 1998 is less clear if an NHS Foundation Trust and NHS Trust are to enter into a potentially anticompetitive agreement.[250] It has been suggested – albeit in view of the widespread merger approval by the ACM – that navigating merger control is a more attractive proposition to healthcare providers than confronting the relative uncertainty of the anticompetitive agreements provisions.[251] As mergers represent a more definitive form of 'consolidation' than other types of cooperation,[252] this appears

---

248 See, for example, NZA, above n. 204.

249 ACM, *'Position paper Autoriteit Consument en Markt. Rondetafelgesprek fusietoets zorginstellingen'* ('ACM Position Paper on the roundtable discussion of the healthcare institution merger test'), 29.06.2015.

250 See O. Odudu, 'Competition Law and the National Health Service', *Competition Bulletin: Competition Law Views from Blackstone Chambers*, 08.10.12, <https://competitionbulletin.com/2012/10/08/competition-law-and-the-national-health-service/> accessed 24.06.2018.

251 R.J.P Jansen and A. Taylor, both above n. 34.

252 In England, the 'Dalton Review' of organisational reforms which accompanied the NHS Five Year Forward View and the development of the 'transactions' pipeline identified three levels of organisational form: Collaborative (comprising Federations and Joint Ventures), Contractual (comprising service level chains and management contracts) and

not only counterintuitive, but also counterproductive if such perceptions were to lead to mergers in lieu of less involved forms of cooperation.

## 5. CONCLUSIONS

This chapter has examined the question of what healthcare-specific merger control *can*, and *is intended to*, achieve in Dutch and English healthcare by reference to the elements which it comprises, and how it complements general merger control as applied to hospital mergers in both countries.

The deliberately broad definition of healthcare-specific merger control has demonstrated that there are elements which enable general merger control to accommodate aspects which it may not typically consider.

Consideration of what healthcare-specific merger control is *intended* to achieve offers a framework against which what it *can* achieve might be evaluated. Thus the intended goal for the ACM to examine a greater number of hospital mergers has been achieved by the introduction of lower turnover thresholds and the 'care turnover' threshold. Similarly, aims to improve engagement with hospitals have been achieved as a result of the 'merger effects report', particularly in view of the criticism that the healthcare-specific merger test is merely procedural, not substantive in nature.[253] Equally, the inclusion of NHS Improvement and the NZa in the general merger assessment processes appears to have fulfilled the intention of facilitating the move away from government to competition authority oversight. This seems to be the case particularly in the Netherlands in view of the 2015 reforms.

Perhaps the most important – and unifying – example of what healthcare-specific merger control is both *intended* to and can *actually achieve* is the recognition that general merger control may be unsuitable as a mechanism for evaluating all organisational forms or cooperative relationships. This is illustrated by the distinction the ACM draws between 'mergers' and 'collaborations' in respect of, for example, Specialist Partnerships in the Netherlands, as noted above. This distinction is strengthened by the requirement for parties to justify the choice of a merger under the 2015 reforms. However, defining of the limits of general merger control is evidenced most strongly by the creation of NHS-specific and PPU tests in England, as these serve to reinforce the threshold filter of a 'relevant merger situation' based on degree of change in control rather than proof of 'enterprises'.

Consolidation (comprising integrated care organisations, multi-site trusts and multi-service chains or Foundation-Groups). D. Dalton, *Examining new options and opportunities for providers of NHS care*, December 2014, p. 18.

253 See W. Sauter and E.M.H. Loozen, both above n. 50.

Of course, what healthcare-specific merger control *can* achieve can also produce distinctions from what may have been *intended*. For example, although some of the healthcare-specific amendments may have been intended to counter widespread merger approval, it is difficult to claim that the blocking of the *Albert Schweitzer Hospital–Rivas Care Group* merger in 2015 was solely attributable to these amendments as distinct from the finding of a SIEC under Dutch general merger control, which could not be offset by countervailing buyer power and market conditions. However, this is not to suggest that healthcare-specific merger control is somehow distinct from general merger control – in an assessment of the ACM's practice, the healthcare-specific elements are also included.[254]

In a similar vein, if government policy is continuing to influence NHS mergers, as evidenced by the focus on a seven-day NHS in connection with the *Surrey Hospitals* merger, then it is questionable whether NHS Improvement's advice regarding 'relevant customer benefits' under section 79(5) HSCA 2012 adds anything to the CMA assessment at Phase II, which appears to examine the wider policy context anyway. However, although NHS Improvement's input may contribute little in substantive terms, its presence is significant in terms of perception of how NHS mergers are treated by the CMA.

A further example of what healthcare-specific merger control can achieve lies in raising awareness of differences in healthcare and consequently of potential limitations in developing competition in the sector.

The 2015 reforms in the Netherlands may prove instructive in this regard. It will be recalled that the NZa's role vis-à-vis Opinions and the healthcare-specific merger test is being removed. This has the effect of streamlining general merger-control assessment as prospective merging parties will only deal with one agency – the ACM – thus saving time and money, as well as avoiding confusion about the NZa's role.[255] It appears that consideration of healthcare values of affordability, accessibility and quality will be incorporated by other means, questioning the NZa's role in merger assessment in the first place, over and above 'selling' competition reforms. Furthermore, the healthcare-specific

254 R. Kemp et al., above n. 1.

255 The latter being criticised by the Borstlap and AEF reports discussed in Chapter 1 above. Andersson Elffers Felix *(in samenwerking met Radicand Economics and Tilburg Law and Economics Center (TILEC)), 'Ordening en Toezicht in de zorg: Evaluatie van de Wet marktordening gezondheidszorg (Wmg) en de Nederlandse Zorgautoriteit (NZa)'*, September 2014 (AEF in cooperation with Radicand Economics and TILEC, 'Oversight and regulation in healthcare: Assessment of the Dutch Healthcare (Market Regulation) Act 2006 (Wmg) and the Dutch Healthcare Authority (NZa)') September 2014. H. Borstlap, P.F.M. van der Meer Mohr and L.J.E. Smits, *'Het rapport van de onderzoekscommissie intern functioneren NZa'*, 02.09.2014 ('Report of the investigation committee on the internal operation of the NZa'), 02.09.2014.

merger test is to be refocused in terms of whom it is addressed to, and with regard to some of the considerations for the 'merger effects' report. This suggests that the experience of the NZa's inclusion in merger assessments has produced lessons which have been heeded.

It may appear, in the round, that one effect of these reforms is to refocus, as much as simplify, the general merger control procedure. However, this appears to suggest that elements of healthcare-specific merger control in the Netherlands have proved needlessly complicated. Whilst healthcare-specific merger control may not have counteracted the problem of widespread merger approval, it has nevertheless served a useful function with regard to how competition in Dutch healthcare may be perceived. It has therefore provided a basis on which the 2015 reforms can build.

With regard to healthcare-specific merger control in England, a less complicated picture emerges in which general merger control appears comparatively unencumbered by regulator intervention: the 'relevant customer benefits' exception, although perhaps not widely used in other sectors, is already incorporated into the test of EA02, and appears merely 'refocused' to involve NHS Improvement.

Overall, the foregoing suggests that there are indeed limits to what healthcare-specific merger control can achieve. However this, in turn, highlights limitations of applying general merger control to a sector in transition, and therefore at least marks an important developmental stage.

# CONCLUSION

In general terms, this book has examined the applicability and application of competition law to Dutch and English healthcare, the relationship between the new healthcare regulators and competition authorities, and the modifications made to general merger control regarding hospital mergers. It has also outlined what competition policy in healthcare can look like by reference to the Dutch and English experiences, which encompass the broad typologies of the insurance-based healthcare system and the taxation-funded model. In particular, it has sought to contribute to understanding where competition law may be applied and where exemptions and modifications may be deemed necessary if a competition policy in healthcare is to be workable for benefits to materialise from competition reforms.

Over the course of writing this book and discussing initial research findings with academic and non-academic audiences (primarily) in the UK and the Netherlands, it has become apparent that competition in healthcare is a theme of interest beyond a niche issue within the confines of either competition law or health law. Thus, it is impossible to divorce competition in healthcare entirely from either general competition policy or understandings of healthcare system organisation: it draws heavily from both, so a competition policy for healthcare cannot exist in isolation.

However, the wide-ranging events which have occurred in the past six years have affected the concept of a competition policy for healthcare to varying degrees. For example, the creation of the *Autoriteit Consument en Markt* (Authority for Consumers and Markets (ACM)) and the Competition and Markets Authority (CMA) can be perceived as having had little impact on the development of competition in healthcare beyond this potentially being treated as less of a priority for larger agencies.[1] Further, although proposals to repeal the Health and Social Care Act 2012 (HSCA 2012) by the Labour, Green and Liberal Democrat parties ahead of the UK General Election in 2015[2]

1 Although it is recognised that the ACM incorporates the former Dutch Consumer Authority, and its advice also includes healthcare-related issues.

2 M. Guy, 'What could repeal of the Health and Social Care Act 2012 mean for the application of competition law and the English NHS?', *Competition Policy Blog*, 05.05.2015, <https://competitionpolicy.wordpress.com/2015/05/05/what-could-repeal-of-the-health-and-social-care-act-2012-mean-for-the-application-of-competition-law-and-the-english-nhs/> accessed 24.06.2018.

(and subsequently) failed to materialise, the main impact this could have had would have been to simplify competition policy vis-à-vis the National Health Service (NHS) by leaving intact the (UK and EU) general competition regime. Thus, there may have been greater licence to explore questions of categorising the NHS in terms of a Services of General Interest (SGI) exemption or Services of General Economic Interest (SGEI) exception. Conversely, the vote in the 2016 UK referendum to leave the EU could seem, in theory, to have the opposite effect: that of removing the EU competition law framework and leaving intact the HSCA 2012. While the option of exploring exemptions and exceptions still remains, the absence of a pre-existing framework makes this more difficult. Certainly, the lack of enthusiasm of subsequent Conservative governments to engage with further reform has unsurprisingly led to the criticism of the HSCA 2012 reforms that 'we are left with some pretty unworkable ideas in primary legislation',[3] and more recently, that the NHS has 'a statutory framework which is not entirely future-facing for what we are seeking to achieve'[4] regarding the current development of Sustainability and Transformation Partnerships.

Over the past six years there have also been ongoing and increasing calls to review and refocus competition reforms in both countries by diverse actors – for example, the '*het roer moet om*' ('we must change course') campaign[5] in the Netherlands by healthcare providers, inter alia, to challenge the power of health insurers, and recommendations by committees in both the House of Lords[6] (in 2017) and the House of Commons[7] (in 2018) to review the HSCA 2012 market reforms in England. But perhaps what is most notable is the emerging delineation of a competition policy in healthcare by the competition authorities themselves. This can be seen in the ACM's reiteration of the limits to its powers of intervention,[8] and the recent clarification by the CMA that competition is not the 'organising principle' of NHS healthcare provision.[9] There is clearly a need, then, at this point in time, for this extended examination of competition policy in healthcare.

---

3 K. Walshe, 'Queen's Speech: We can't avoid legislation for ever', *Health Service Journal*, 28.05.2015.

4 NHS England CEO Simon Stevens in response to Question 326. House of Commons Health and Social Care Committee, Oral evidence: Integrated care: organisations, partnerships and systems, HC 650, 20.03.2018.

5 <http://www.hetroermoetom.nu/> accessed 24.06.2018.

6 House of Lords Select Committee on the Long-Term Sustainability of the NHS. Report of Session 2016–17, *The Long-term Sustainability of the NHS and Adult Social Care*, 05.04.2017. Recommendation 4 (paragraph 101).

7 House of Commons Health and Social Care Committee, *Integrated care: organizations, partnerships and systems*. Seventh Report of Session 2017–19, 11.06.2018, paragraphs 32–44.

8 See, for example, ACM, *'Spreekpunten Henk Don bij rondetafelgesprek "kwaliteit loont" in de Tweede Kamer op 17.04.2015'* ('Points for discussion by Henk Don at the "Quality Pays" round table discussion in the Second Chamber 17.04.2015').

9 Competition and Markets Authority (CMA), *Central Manchester University Hospitals/ University Hospital of South Manchester merger inquiry. Final Report*, 01.08.2017.

The Introduction to this book set out a 'healthcare structure' of macro, meso and micro levels – to reflect state intervention, healthcare purchasers and healthcare providers – as well as acknowledging two 'narratives' – that healthcare does not merit special treatment, so can be treated in the same way as other liberalised sectors (such as telecommunications); and that competition could function as a means to an end, for example, to deal with rising costs and demand, rather than an end in itself, that is, to initiate a fundamental system change – which accompanied the competition reforms in Dutch and English healthcare. The discussions of this book suggest two main findings with regard to these conceptions.

Firstly, there is a need to consider competition in healthcare by reference to the three main actors of the 'healthcare structure', and thus a 'systemic', rather than an 'individual' (consumer-level) focus is needed. A systemic focus certainly undermines overblown comparisons between the functioning of healthcare and other sectors (which appear based on an individual/consumer focus), although more modest comparisons may remain valid. Furthermore, it is only by reference to the macro, meso and micro levels that we can understand the limits to competition reforms, in other words, that competition can – and should – only be a means to an end, and not an end in itself. This necessitates further thinking about how we understand markets and what we want them to achieve.[10] However, what that 'end' to which competition is the means is, can vary. For example, it has recently been suggested that using a competitive private health insurance market to achieve the 'end' of achieving universal access is institutionally complex and requires broad political and societal support.[11] With regard to England, one interpretation of the HSCA 2012 competition reforms belongs with narratives of increasing the efficiency of NHS providers in the wider context of achieving competitive neutrality with private providers delivering NHS services. Perhaps a more compelling use of competition vis-à-vis the NHS would be to help manage the interactions between NHS and private providers, by emphasising a focus on the latter should this be required – in other words, reconceptualising 'the NHS' (that is, NHS patients and NHS commissioners) as the 'consumer' in need of protection against anticompetitive behaviour, consistent with the approach taken by the CMA in

---

10 T. Zuiderant-Jerak, K. Grit and T. van der Grinten, 'Markets and Public Values in Healthcare', *iBMG Working Paper* W2010.01.

11 R.A.A. Vonk and F.T. Schut, 'Can universal access be achieved in a voluntary private health insurance market? Dutch private insurers caught between competing logics', *Health Economics, Policy and Law* 1, 07.05.2018, <https://www.cambridge.org/core/journals/health-economics-policy-and-law/article/can-universal-access-be-achieved-in-a-voluntary-private-health-insurance-market-dutch-private-insurers-caught-between-competing-logics/0CBA1AFA497BCD5D2FF8F06D2896E1E2> accessed 24.06.2018.

pharmaceutical cases.[12] While both of these interpretations suggest an 'end' of modernisation in order to maintain the NHS, the former courts controversy by hinting at system change, whilst the latter remains underexplored in the healthcare provision context.

Secondly, whilst all three levels of the 'healthcare structure' may be considered to be engaged within competition policy – including, for example, the relative non-applicability of general competition law to healthcare purchasing bodies, and the design of 'healthcare-specific' merger control which is targeted primarily at healthcare providers, typically hospitals – the most significant impact may be seen at the macro level of state intervention. This is because, put simply, the decision to introduce competition reforms – and the form and extent of these – is primarily a political one, especially within healthcare systems which remain committed to the principle of solidarity, or universal access to healthcare. Whilst concerns are acknowledged that the scope for governments to 'experiment' with competition reforms and public/private interactions is constrained by the application of EU competition law,[13] it remains the case that the influence of national governments is pervasive in other aspects of developing competition policy in healthcare. This has become evident most notably in calls by the ACM for further clarity – even new legislation – regarding the Dutch government's ambitions for implementing competition reforms.[14] It is also demonstrated by the controversy surrounding the enactment of the HSCA 2012 and the resulting refocusing of competition to constrain CMA oversight of the NHS,[15] at least with regard to applying competition law.

The remainder of this Conclusion rounds off the discussions of this book as follows.

Section 1 provides a summary of the findings of the substantive chapters regarding the development of competition policy (Chapter 1), the applicability and application of competition law (Chapter 2), the interaction between the sectoral regulator and competition authority (Chapter 3), and general and 'healthcare-specific' merger control in the context of hospital mergers (Chapter 4).

---

12 See, for example, CMA, Case CE/9742-13, *Decision of the Competition and Markets Authority – Unfair pricing in respect of the supply of phenytoin sodium capsules in the UK*, 07.12.2016, p. 12. Whilst the Competition Appeals Tribunal (CAT) set aside part of its decision and remitted the case to the CMA, it nevertheless acknowledged the importance of the case for the public interest ([2018] CAT 11, paragraph 465, p. 146). The CMA is currently considering whether to appeal, in view of the implications for similar cases. CMA, 'CMA considers appeal in phenytoin case' News Story, 07.06.2018, <https://www.gov.uk/government/news/cma-considers-appeal-in-phenytoin-case> accessed 26.08.2018.

13 See further on this point, W. Sauter, 'Services of general economic interest and universal service obligations as an EU law framework for curative health care' (2007) *TILEC Discussion Paper* 29, <https://www.tilburguniversity.edu/upload/23c6e429-7ff9-44cd-9844-407c0bf3dfaf_SGEI-USO.pdf> accessed 24.06.2018.

14 ACM, above n. 8.

15 By the Competition Act 1998 (Concurrency) Regulations 2014, SI 2014 No. 536.

Section 2 elaborates two broad themes to emerge from these discussions to offer a starting-point for future research and policy: the need to recognise the distinctive features of the healthcare sector and the relationship between the EU competition law framework and the emergent national competition policies in healthcare.

## 1. OVERVIEW OF FINDINGS BY CHAPTER

### 1.1. COMPETITION REFORMS IN DUTCH AND ENGLISH HEALTHCARE AND THE DEVELOPMENT OF COMPETITION POLICY

Chapter 1 charted the development of competition policy in Dutch and English healthcare by reference to relevant legislation and policy documentation and set out two conceptualisations of how competition works – the Dutch 'healthcare triangle' and the 'four categories of English healthcare'.

The Dutch 'healthcare triangle' elaborated the relationship between patients (consumers), health insurers and healthcare providers, in connection with the system of mandatory private health insurance introduced in 2006, as follows:[16]

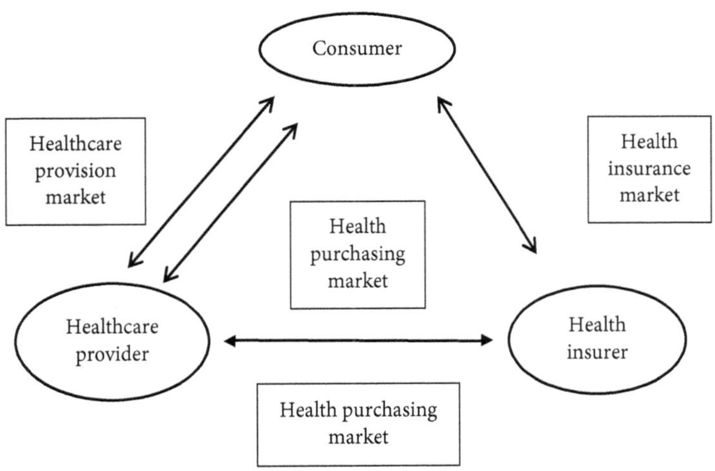


**Figure 2. The Dutch 'healthcare triangle'**

Although the triangle may suggest that patients (consumers) form the driving force behind the relationship, successive developments discussed in this book

16 Figure 2 in Chapter 1, page 21. See also W. Sauter, 'Is the general consumer interest a source of legitimacy for healthcare regulation? An analysis of the Dutch experience' (2009) 2–3 *European Journal of Consumer Law* 419.

suggest this can be challenged: both insurers and providers can be considered to provide the impetus for the interaction. For example, insurers were considered to be the 'motor' for the system,[17] but concerns about the power of large insurance firms has grown. Indeed, whilst the additional assessment criteria were discussed in Chapter 4 in the context of healthcare provider mergers, these also relate to health insurers.[18] As noted above, healthcare providers have also proved instrumental in calling for change. In 2018, the current emphasis on solidarity and integration can, however, perhaps be read as re-instating patients as the focus of the relationship/triangle.

Chapter 1 also considered the legislation underpinning the 'healthcare triangle' – notably the *Zorgverzekeringswet* (Dutch Health Insurance Act 2006, (Zvw)) and the *Wet marktordening gezondheidszorg* (Dutch Healthcare (Market Regulation) Act 2006, (Wmg)). However, the current focus is on how the proposed transfer of NZa competence to the ACM[19] may develop beyond the 'Healthcare Taskforce' being given a more permanent status as a *Directie* (Directorate) within the ACM, separate from 'competition' and alongside Directorates for energy, consumers, telecommunications, transport and post.[20] Chapter 1 also examined the elaboration of the relevant legislation by policy documentation, specifically the 2002, 2007 and 2010 *Richtsnoeren voor de zorgsector* (Guidelines for the healthcare sector) issued by the ACM and the former *Nederlandse Mededingingsautoriteit* (Dutch Competition Authority, NMa), and the 2006, 2010 and 2014 *Samenwerkingsprotocollen* (Cooperation Protocols) governing the interactions between the ACM/NMa and the *Nederlandse Zorgautoriteit* (Dutch Healthcare Authority (NZa)). The subsequent discussions of Chapter 3 suggested that further 'cooperation protocols' may need to be elaborated in light of the transfer of competence, particularly with regard to merger control, where the NZa provided an Opinion in the *Amsterdam Universities Hospitals* merger, so continues to provide useful input.

---

17 For discussion of how this analogy works and is constrained in practice, see R. Halbersma, J. van Manen and W. Sauter, *'De verzekeraars als motor van het zorgstelsel'* ('Health insurers as motor of the healthcare system') (2012) *Zorg en Financiering*, 11(10), 10.

18 Article 3, *Beleidsregel van de Minister van Economische Zaken van 5 juli 2013, nr. WJZ/13118300, houdende bijzondere regels betreffende concentraties van zorgaanbieders en zorgverzekeraars* (Policy Rule by the Minister for Economic Affairs of 5 July 2013, No. WJZ/13118300, setting out special rules governing mergers of healthcare providers and mergers of health insurers).

19 Intended to be given legal effect by *Kamerstukken II, 2015–16, 34 445, 2 – Wijziging van de Wet marktordening gezondheidszorg en enkele andere wetten in verband met aanpassingen van de tarief- en prestatieregulering en het markttoezicht op het terrein van de gezondheidszorg. Nr. 2 Voorstel van Wet* (Second Chamber documentation, Parliamentary Session 2015–16, 34 445, 2 – Amendments to the Wmg and other laws to apply tariff regulation and market regulation in healthcare, Document No. 2, Legislative Proposal).

20 ACM, 'Organogram', <https://www.acm.nl/nl/organisatie/organisatie/organogram> accessed 24.06.2018.

In England, competition can be conceptualised by reference to the complex relationship between the NHS and private healthcare sector and the separation of purchasing and providing functions in operation between the late 1980s and approximately 2014 – otherwise named in this book the 'four categories of English healthcare'.[21]

| 1. Public Purchaser and Public Provider | 2. Public Purchaser and Private Provider | 3. Private Purchaser and Public Provider | 4. Private Purchaser and Private Provider |
|---|---|---|---|

**Figure 3. The 'four categories of English healthcare'**

The introduction of the NHS Five Year Forward View in October 2014 and the subsequent emphasis on integrated care models may yet come to be regarded as marking a second, post-purchaser/provider separation phase in NHS reform where a competition framework exists but there is acknowledged to be limited scope for competition, following the CMA's comments to this effect in the 2017 *Manchester Hospitals* merger. However, what persists is the complex interaction between the NHS and private healthcare sector, and a need for this to be acknowledged and managed in a coherent manner. The substantive discussions of this book reveal further nuance to the 'four categories'. For example, the current focus on Accountable Care Organisations (ACOs) and Sustainability and Transformation Partnerships (STPs), coupled with the expansion in private sector delivery of NHS services, suggests that category 2 in particular is undergoing expansion. Whilst the expansion of Private Patient Units (PPUs) in category 3, anticipated by section 165 HSCA 2012, may not be materialising in practical terms, it remains the case that the CMA is taking decisive action to develop the private healthcare sector following its 2014 Market Investigation, for example, by requiring NHS Foundation Trusts to share information for private patients.[22] In addition, the discussions of merger control in Chapter 4 reveal that further nuance may be needed within category 1 to distinguish NHS Trusts and NHS Foundation Trusts. Insofar as the 'four categories' are intended

21 Figure 3 in Chapter 1, page 40. Adapted from the relationships as set out in Office of Fair Trading (OFT), *Private Healthcare Market Study*, OFT1396, p. 13; and O. Odudu, 'Competition Law and the National Health Service', *Competition Bulletin: Competition Law Views from Blackstone Chambers*, 08.10.12, <https://competitionbulletin.com/2012/10/08/competition-law-and-the-national-health-service/> accessed 24.06.2018.

22 CMA, Press Release 'CMA demands action from hospitals on private healthcare information', 31.08.2017, <https://www.gov.uk/government/news/cma-demands-action-from-hospitals-on-private-healthcare-information> accessed 24.06.2018.

to provide a snapshot in time and an accessible insight into English healthcare, these remain 'fit for purpose'. However, it is recognised that further development may be needed to reflect current and future reforms.

With regard to competition policy in English healthcare, Chapter 1 charted the development of differing approaches in three chronologically consecutive phases: the NHS 'internal market' under the Conservative governments of the 1980s and 1990s, the 'choice and competition' reforms of the NHS 'quasi-market' under New Labour, and the 'Opening Up Public Services' reforms of the Liberal Democrat and Conservative Coalition Government which coincided with the HSCA 2012 reforms. Chapter 1 also detailed the enactment of the HSCA 2012 reforms to demonstrate that the competition policy which has materialised was not that originally envisaged by Andrew Lansley, and which can also help explain why implementation has been difficult. Indeed, what has emerged is arguably the worst of all worlds: a policy which is both found wanting by those actively in favour of competition as a principle in itself, and which does little to allay the worst suspicions of those of us more sceptical of competition reforms in healthcare. In the absence of governmental appetite to review the HSCA 2012 reforms, we appear to be witnessing a period in which future development is in the hands of the CMA and NHS Improvement. This may equate to more or less active 'non-enforcement', rather than an explicit engagement with exception mechanisms.

## 1.2. COMPETITION LAW: ITS APPLICABILITY AND APPLICATION IN DUTCH AND ENGLISH HEALTHCARE

The discussions of Chapter 2 underscore an important distinction regarding competition law and Dutch and English healthcare – namely, between *applicability* (which may be a largely theoretical question) and actual *application* (which suggests a requirement for 'active enforcement' in practical terms) – and reveal that problems may attach to both.

With regard to applicability of competition law, Chapter 2 underscored the fundamental relevance of solidarity in defining the scope for this. What emerges is that applicability of competition law may be a dynamic concept in light of questions arising in the Netherlands regarding the ongoing applicability of Dutch competition law to the private health insurers if these are required to fulfil solidarity-inspired obligations regarding profit distribution.[23] Chapter 2 also

[23] See L. Glas, A. Looijestijn and J.W. van de Gronden, *'Advies 2: Beoordeling van verschillende voorgenomen zorgmaatregelen in het licht van het EU-recht en het EVRM. Avies in opdracht van VGZ en Zilveren Kruis'* ('Opinion 2: Assessment of different proposals for healthcare

reflected upon the recent change in approach at EU level in view of deeming competition law applicable to healthcare purchasers within an insurance-based healthcare system, away from *AOK Bundesverband*[24] to discussions of profit-making in connection with Slovak state-owned health insurers in *DZP/UZP*.[25] Despite the wide-ranging criticism of the *FENIN*[26] decision, which has given rise to uncertainty about the extent of the applicability of competition law regarding NHS commissioners, Chapter 2 established the significance of this case as an analytical framework for examining the interaction between the NHS and private healthcare sector in England by underscoring the distinction which arises from providers operating within the NHS and/or the private healthcare sector.

The concept of solidarity, or universal access to healthcare, was also identified as providing a 'core' for determining the development of competition reforms more generally. Thus the Dutch experience suggests that it is possible to develop competition *around* the core by this being protected by the risk equalisation scheme as an SGEI. In contrast, the English experience suggests that attempts have been made to develop competition *within* the core, that is, the NHS-specific competition regime. This is curious since it can be accepted on balance that general competition law would apply to providers of NHS services, and since the NHS can be seen as serving a 'provider of last resort' function relative to the private healthcare sector, which would effectively suggest an informal SGEI function.

With regard to actual *application* of competition law, Chapter 2 identified difficulties of implementation beyond the parallel application of EU and national competition rules.[27] This is particularly evident in the NHS-specific competition regime of prohibitions imposed on NHS commissioners (under Regulation 10 of the National Health Service (Procurement, Patient Choice and Competition) (No. 2) Regulations 2013[28] (the 2013 Regulations)) and on providers delivering services for the NHS (under the 'competition oversight' element of the Choice and

measures in light of EU law and the European Convention on Human Rights. Opinion commissioned by VGZ and Zilveren Kruis').

24 Joined cases C-264/01, C-306/01, C-354/01 and C-355/01, *AOK Bundesverband, Bundesverband der Betriebskrankenkassen (BKK) et al. v. Ichthyol-Gesellschaft Cordes et al.*, ECLI:EU:C:2004:150.

25 Case T-216/15, *Dôvera zdravotná poisťovňa, a.s. v. European Commission*, ECLI:EU:T:2018:64.

26 Case C-205/03 P, *Federación Española de Empresas de Tecnología Sanitaria (FENIN) v. Commission of the European Communities*, ECLI:EU:C:2006:453.

27 This is a separate issue to the potential divergent application of EU competition law by national competition authorities conceptualised as 'Euro-national competition rules for healthcare' by J.W. van de Gronden and E. Szyszczak, 'Introducing Competition Principles into Health Care through EU Law and Policy: A Case Study of the Netherlands' (2014) 22(2) *Medical Law Review* 238.

28 National Health Service (Procurement, Patient Choice and Competition) (No. 2) Regulations 2013, SI 2013/500.

Competition condition of the NHS Provider Licence), to avoid 'anticompetitive behaviour' (as defined by section 64(2) HSCA 2012) – a concept itself couched in the terminology of the EU (and UK) provisions governing anticompetitive agreements. The difficulties arising from this regime include the commitment to holding purchasers and providers to the same standard, which fails to recognise the differing role each plays, and the conflation of purchasing and providing functions (for example, within Clinical Commissioning Groups).

A further consideration is that 'healthcare provider' may be too wide a category. This is evidenced by the 'one-size-does-not-fit-all' approach apparently adopted by the ACM in issuing specific guidance according to the differing working practices of diverse healthcare providers (from primary care to obstetrics) in the Netherlands. In England, the interactions between the NHS and private healthcare sector complicate matters and mean that it is always necessary to ask whether a provider (NHS or private) is operating in the NHS or private healthcare sector. However, the relative clarity found in connection with the private healthcare sector (categories 3 and 4) would suggest that the CMA may continue to focus its efforts here, perhaps in connection with Private Patient Units.

## 1.3. SECTORAL REGULATION: THE RELATIONSHIP BETWEEN THE COMPETITION AUTHORITY AND SECTORAL REGULATOR IN DUTCH AND ENGLISH HEALTHCARE

Chapter 3 identified two possible models to describe the relationship between the competition authority and sectoral regulator in applying competition law – 'separate powers' and 'concurrent powers'.

'Separate powers' described primarily the situation in the Netherlands, to reflect the interaction between the ACM and NZa in applying the provisions governing anticompetitive agreements and abuse of dominance, and the competence to intervene in contract terms and to correct Significant Market Power (SMP), respectively. However, it was acknowledged that this term could also be used in relation to the situation which has emerged in England following the HSCA 2012 reforms and the Competition Act 1998 (Concurrency) Regulations 2014, which effectively enshrines the pre-HSCA 2012 situation. In other words, the CMA has oversight of the private healthcare sector only (categories 3 and 4) with regard to applying competition law, whilst NHS Improvement can apply competition law in cases concerning anticompetitive behaviour in respect of NHS provision (categories 1 and 2). In addition, 'separate powers' can be used in connection with the distinction between general competition law and the regulatory regime emerging out of the 2013 Regulations and the NHS Provider Licence.

In contrast, 'concurrent powers' refers to a relationship characteristic of wider UK economic regulation,[29] which involves a competence for *either* the competition authority *or* the sectoral regulator to apply certain rules. This situation still exists in connection with section 73 HSCA 2012,[30] whereby either the CMA or NHS Improvement may conduct a market investigation of the NHS. This appears curious in view of the controversy which resulted in the refocusing of competition following the NHS Future Forum's report and the subsequent curtailment of CMA oversight of competition law cases noted above, as it suggests that the CMA may have a potentially wide-ranging competence to influence re-structuring of the NHS if a critical market investigation were to emerge. However, controversy surrounding the HSCA 2012 reforms is not the only reason why the model of concurrent powers does not work for English healthcare in the way it functions in other sectors: the findings of Chapter 3 also demonstrate that the reference to 'healthcare provision' in section 72 HSCA 2012 is also problematic for not distinguishing between the private healthcare sector and NHS quasi-market, in view of the relative extent of applicability of competition law to each. Indeed, it can be considered that unequivocal applicability is a prerequisite for concurrent powers to apply competition law, so this may be better suited to the Dutch system. Furthermore, the decision to adopt and, following the NHS Future Forum report,[31] to retain, concurrent powers appears to be based on two related, but discrete, logics: incorporating the benefit of regulator sectoral expertise and underscoring proportionality in applying competition law. This nuance is significant, but appears lost in the simple wording of 'concurrent powers'.

By examining the NZa and NHS Improvement and their respective interactions with the ACM and CMA (as opposed to a healthcare regulator and another sectoral regulator), Chapter 3 offers an initial in-depth assessment of aspects prominent in, if not unique to, healthcare, namely the focus on patients (and their dual identity as insurance policyholders and taxpayers in the Netherlands and England, respectively) and the evolving Ministerial intervention in light of the establishment of the healthcare regulators and growing role for competition authorities. The dual identity is significant as it may affect the focus and effective implementation of the reforms, both by raising questions about who the competition policy is intended to protect, and by

29 As discussed in Chapter 1, this appeared to underpin the HSCA 2012 reforms, consistent with the narrative of healthcare resembling other sectors.

30 Discussed further in M. Guy, 'Competition and sectoral regulation in Dutch and English healthcare: factors shaping the competition focus of the new healthcare regulators and their relationship with the competition authorities' (2017) 2 *Ius Publicum Network Review*, ISSN 2039 2540, <http://www.ius-publicum.com/pagina.php?lang=en&pag=fascicolo> accessed 24.06.2018.

31 NHS Future Forum, *Choice and Competition – Delivering Real Choice*. A report from the NHS Future Forum, June 2011.

suggesting that whilst NHS patients and taxpayers may have differing interests, the distinction between Dutch patients and insurance policyholders can be more clearly linked with two separate provision and insurance markets.

Chapter 3 also identified some counterintuitive developments in view of the ongoing intervention by the Minister for Health, Wellbeing and Sport within the Dutch system, which might be considered to allow greater scope for competition, and thus amenability to greater, if not exclusive, competition authority oversight. In contrast, with regard to the NHS quasi-market, where scope for competition is limited, direct Secretary of State for Health oversight has been curtailed significantly by the establishment of NHS England and its interaction with NHS Improvement, as well as by the CMA's lesser-noted review functions under the HSCA 2012 in respect of the National Tariff and the NHS Provider Licence.

## 1.4. MERGER CONTROL: GENERAL MERGER CONTROL, HOSPITAL MERGERS AND THE DEVELOPMENT OF HEALTHCARE-SPECIFIC MERGER TESTS IN THE NETHERLANDS AND ENGLAND

Chapter 4 distinguished the use of general merger control and healthcare-specific merger tests based on two aspects: 'jurisdictional' and 'substantive assessment'.

'Jurisdictional aspects' outline in essence *which* healthcare (typically hospital) mergers a competition authority should examine. In the Netherlands, these aspects include lower turnover thresholds and the healthcare-specific merger test insofar as the latter enables a hospital merger to be blocked prior to general merger assessment if, for example, critical care is endangered. In England, 'jurisdictional aspects' reflect the different types of hospital provision across the NHS and private healthcare sector. Thus section 79 HSCA 2012 delineates a specific focus for the CMA in assessing mergers involving NHS Foundation Trusts against the general merger control regime of the Enterprise Act 2002, while NHS Improvement's 'transactions oversight' can involve NHS Trusts specifically, and does not involve general merger control. In contrast, the CMA's new test for Private Patient Units, whilst prima facie concerned with units operated either by NHS Foundation Trusts or private providers across the UK,[32] actually appears intended to be a narrow solution to the specific problem of over-consolidation of the private healthcare market in London.

'Substantive assessment aspects' provide further detail regarding *what* a competition authority should consider in assessing a hospital merger. In the

[32] The private healthcare market being UK-wide in its focus, in contrast to the reach of the NHS being defined in terms of the individual countries of the UK.

Netherlands, these aspects include the incorporation of additional assessment criteria and NZa Opinions into the ACM's decisions. In England, the predominant 'substantive assessment' aspect is the reformulation of the 'relevant customer benefits' exception (under section 30(1)(a) Enterprise Act 2002, which can form part of general merger assessment) as 'relevant patient benefits' which are developed by NHS Improvement in conjunction with the merging parties under section 79(5) HSCA 2012.

Chapter 4 further considered the motivations for healthcare-specific merger tests, as ranging from 'selling' competition reforms and engaging with the healthcare sector, to ensuring appropriate oversight of mergers in a sector in transition and counteracting the limitations of a competition-based test, to elaborating the appropriate place of merger control in a sector heavily dependent upon cooperative relationships. It also considered briefly the *Cambian* merger[33] to demonstrate how mergers which may have significant implications for the NHS are not subject to the 'patient benefits' scrutiny of section 79(5) HSCA 2012.

In particular, Chapter 4 underscored concerns that the ease of navigating merger control relative to questions about the applicability and enforcement of the prohibition on anticompetitive agreements may lead healthcare providers to merge rather than explore less involved forms of cooperation. With reference to the English experience, Chapter 4 suggested that subjecting NHS Foundation Trust mergers to merger control may amount to little more than a 'rubber-stamping' exercise in view of the increasing significance of 'relevant patient benefits' in prompting CMA approval of these. This view is particularly pertinent in view of the CMA's explanation of the limited role for competition within the English NHS at present, following the shift in focus towards integrated care with Sustainability and Transformation Partnerships.

## 2. CONCLUSIONS BY REFERENCE TO BROAD THEMES: FUTURE RESEARCH AND POLICY DIRECTIONS

### 2.1. THE NEED TO RECOGNISE THE DISTINCTIVE FEATURES OF THE HEALTHCARE SECTOR

There is a clear need for competition policy in healthcare to address, or at a minimum reflect, the distinctive features of the healthcare sector. These can be defined in various ways, but may be common to many healthcare systems and how they are addressed may vary at national and EU levels. The research underpinning this book has engaged with at least three aspects of the distinctive

33 CMA, *A report on the completed acquisition by Cygnet Health Care Ltd and Universal Health Services, Inc. of the Cambian Adult Services Division of Cambian Group plc*, 16.10.2017.

features of the healthcare sector, both in England and the Netherlands, though this section ultimately focuses on England to indicate how an approach to competition policy in healthcare based on distinctive features can raise useful questions for future research.

The first and perhaps foremost distinctive feature which needs to be recognised is the importance of solidarity (universal access) as an organising principle of healthcare provision. Chapter 2 demonstrated how solidarity forms a 'core' *around*, or *within* which competition and competition policy may be developed with regard to the experiences of the Netherlands and England, respectively. Whilst this can be reflected within competition policy by the use (or not) of exceptions, such as SGEI, there may also be implications for oversight as well – as demonstrated in particular in England by the reluctance to grant the CMA explicit oversight of competition law cases involving the NHS. In both countries, ongoing government support for solidarity as an organising principle for healthcare may form part of the retreat from competition reforms. This has been evidenced by the 2017 Dutch Government Agreement.[34] In England this might be inferred from the former Secretary of State for Health and Social Care's recent comments that the Prime Minister remains 'unbelievably committed' to the NHS,[35] and the current Secretary of State for Health and Social Care outlining his vision of one NHS and social care system, working together to improve patient safety and outcomes, 'In a spirit of collaboration, not competition …'.[36]

The inherent tension between competition and solidarity means that a range of considerations – both substantive and institutional – arise in shaping a competition policy, and appear to hold regardless of whether a healthcare system comprises an insurance-based model or is funded by general taxation. Thus the Dutch 2006 reforms have been considered to demonstrate that achieving universal access in a competitive private health insurance market is institutionally complex and requires broad political and social support.[37] Whilst the HSCA 2012 competition reforms may be considered less ambitious in light of the wider commitment to maintaining the NHS as a taxation-funded system, the relative absence of broad political and social support may similarly be considered to have been a factor in the variable development of the reforms and the difficulty in their implementation.

---

34 VVD, CDA, D66 en ChristenUnie, *Regeerakkoord 2017–2021 'Vertrouwen in de toekomst'* ('Trust in the Future'), 10.10.2017, p. 14.

35 D. Campbell, 'May to give NHS "significant" cash boost, Jeremy Hunt reveals', *The Guardian*, 06.06.2018.

36 Department of Health and Social Care, 'Matt Hancock: my priorities for the health and social care system', 20.07.2018, <https://www.gov.uk/government/speeches/matt-hancock-my-priorities-for-the-health-and-social-care-system> accessed 26.08.2018.

37 R.A.A. Vonk and F.T. Schut, above n. 11.

From a substantive perspective, solidarity may be considered to be reflected in competition policy in terms of whether and how values associated with healthcare – namely, accessibility, affordability and quality – can be incorporated in competition assessments. Solidarity is also connected, particularly within the English context, with the concept of the 'dual identity' of patients and taxpayers. The importance of this concept as emphasised in this book, lies in the potential for the two groups to have differing perspectives and needs, and the implications these have for the focus of competition policy.

'Distinctive features' can also include the nature of relationships in healthcare provision and the different characteristics of the various actors involved. These may equally be common to all healthcare systems, but may need to be addressed more at national (rather than EU) level in light of characteristics within different competition regimes as well as healthcare systems. For example, the emphasis on collaboration and cooperation between healthcare providers in both countries suggests that there is a need for the competition authorities and regulators to continue to develop guidance about how they will interpret the prohibition on anticompetitive agreements and the interaction between this and merger control.[38] This could build on pre-existing work such as the requirement for merging parties in the Netherlands to justify why a merger is chosen over other forms of collaboration, and the clarification of 'business cases' and 'patient benefit' cases by NHS Improvement in England. The need for this additional guidance – primarily in England – appears to stem from decisions not to explore exceptions to national merger control and competition law regimes, as well as concerns that mergers may be chosen in preference to other, less involved, forms of collaboration simply because the legal framework appears easier to navigate.

As regards the different characteristics of the actors, the ACM has already started to differentiate its guidance according to different types of healthcare provider, and recent research in the Netherlands calls for merger assessment to be reviewed to recognise that increases in price resulting from hospital mergers are managed better by smaller, rather than larger health insurers,[39] perhaps suggesting a differentiation which has not received much attention thus far. In England, whilst relative size of provider and purchaser can be relevant, the underlying interaction and distinction between the NHS and private healthcare sector would appear to be as pertinent as considering different categories of healthcare provider; thus the CMA has issued guidance specifically addressed to

---

38 R.J.P. Jansen, 'Samenwerken of fuseren in de zorg?' ('Collaborating or merging in healthcare?') (2013) *Markt & Mededinging*, 2, 77. A. Taylor, 'When does an alliance become a merger?', *Aldwych Partners blog*, 14.07.2015, <http://aldwychpartners.co.uk/when-does-an-alliance-become-a-merger/> accessed 24.06.2018.

39 See the doctoral research of Anne-Fleur Roos. See also B. Kiers, '*Kleine zorgverzekeraar ontloopt prijsstijging bij ziekenhuisfusie*' ('Small health insurers avoid price increases in hospital mergers'), Zorgvisie, 08.06.2018, <https://www.zorgvisie.nl/kleine-verzekeraar-ontloopt-prijsstijging-bij-ziekenhuisfusie/> accessed 24.06.2018.

private healthcare providers operating in the private healthcare sector, but not to those operating in the NHS.

Overall, the need to recognise and pay attention to the distinctive features of the healthcare sector is well-illustrated by the discussions of the English system in this book, and the conclusion that there is no single, unified 'healthcare' sector which may be amenable to competition reforms and the application of competition law. Rather, there are two increasingly interlinked markets of the NHS and private healthcare sector which behave in fundamentally different ways. The NHS is still – correctly – referred to as a 'quasi-market' which serves to justify the existence of separate regimes such as the 2013 Regulations. The private healthcare sector resembles a standard market, yet its supplementary nature represents an anomaly among European healthcare systems insofar as it does not engage with questions of universal coverage or solidarity.

Despite this, the word 'healthcare' is used in various ways in the context of the HSCA 2012 reforms, notably as a distinction from other liberalised sectors (such as energy and telecommunications). However, what is curious about the use of the word 'healthcare' in the HSCA 2012 is that it offers scope for interpretation that acknowledges the coexistence of the NHS and private healthcare sectors; for example, section 72 HSCA 2012 could prima facie relate to either, but ultimately fails to address the distinctions between these. As the underlying intention of the HSCA 2012 appears to have been NHS reform, it is notable that the term 'healthcare' should be used at all – as opposed to 'NHS' being used consistently throughout.

What emerge from the discussions in this book are different conceptions of competition in connection with the English NHS. Thus, the merger assessment system under section 79 HSCA 2012 appears to build on previous policy reforms – namely, for NHS Trusts to achieve Foundation Trust status in order to operate alongside, or even merge with, private providers delivering services for the NHS. In contrast, mergers between private providers which deliver services for the NHS (such as the aforementioned *Cambian* case) are subject to the 'lesser' degree of scrutiny by the CMA under the general merger-control regime of the Enterprise Act 2002, with no obvious involvement of NHS Improvement. The latter suggests a scenario which could benefit from the alternative interpretation of competition, whereby the NHS is conceptualised as the 'consumer' in need of protection against anticompetitive practices, as per the CMA's approach in pharmaceutical cases. However, whilst the reluctance to review the HSCA 2012 or propose new legislation pertains, it is recommended that clarification of the distinction between, and coexistence of, the NHS and private healthcare sectors be implemented by other means – for example, by further comment by the CMA and NHS Improvement.

While the juxtaposition of the NHS and private healthcare sectors within the English system as outlined in this book may represent a similarity with types of public/private interaction found within other healthcare systems, it nevertheless serves to highlight the need to consider the distinctive features of healthcare systems in designing and developing competition policies for healthcare elsewhere.

## 2.2. THE RELATIONSHIP BETWEEN THE EU COMPETITION LAW FRAMEWORK AND THE EMERGENT NATIONAL COMPETITION POLICIES IN HEALTHCARE

The research in this book contributes to three separate areas of discussion of the relationship between the EU competition law framework and the emergent national competition policies in healthcare. The first two discussions draw on the 'exemption' and 'exception' perspectives outlined in Chapter 2: namely the *applicability* of competition law to the healthcare sector; and understanding how the SGEI framework can operate. The third discussion reflects on Brexit.

Questions of the extent of applicability of EU competition law within social sectors and healthcare have received a renewed impetus in the past couple of years with cases such as *CEPPB*[40] regarding education and *DZP/UZP* regarding Slovak health insurers,[41] which in turn has reignited academic discussion.[42] The latter case in particular would seem to mark a change in approach by the EU courts from the framework previously established by *AOK Bundesverband*, which could raise questions about the implementation of national provisions, for example Article 122 *Zorgverzekeringswet* (Dutch Health Insurance Act 2006 (Zvw)) which extended the applicability of Dutch (but not EU) competition law to Dutch private health insurers. Whilst further clarity and discussion at EU level is most welcome, these cases appear to be coinciding with a retreat from a focus on competition within Dutch and English healthcare. Nevertheless, insofar as wider EU fiscal policy is producing Country-Specific Recommendations to develop greater efficiency in healthcare provision (which may involve introducing or developing competition) within the European Semester,[43] EU-level elaboration of competition law is helpful, particularly in addressing the anomaly which had arisen from the disparate approaches taken to purchasers and providers.

The extent to which this new case law is helpful with regard to a taxation-funded system remains less clear, so further clarification may be welcome,

---

40 Case C-74/16, *Congregación de Escuelas Pías Provincia Betania v. Ayuntamiento de Getafe*, ECLI:EU:C:2017:496.

41 *Dôvera zdravotná poisťovňa, a.s. v. European Commission*, above n. 25.

42 J.W. van de Gronden, 'Services of General Interest and the Concept of Undertaking: Does EU Competition Law Apply?' (2018) 41(2) *World Competition* 197.

43 Which may suggest at least a theoretical conflict with Article 168(7) TFEU, which specifies that healthcare system organisation is a Member State competence. This has been interpreted in a competition context as meaning that Member States have a certain degree of freedom in opting to develop competition.

as *FENIN* continues to represent the EU courts' approach in this connection. Insofar as the reasoning in *DZP/UZP* recognises competition on quality, this would appear to have application within, for example, the English system as well. These case law developments already suggest that it may be time for the CMA to update its guidance regarding public services and competition law to reflect these changes, and certainly to revisit the simplistic[44] interpretation of *FENIN* it adopted from the Office of Fair Trading. Elaboration by the CMA of the general competition law framework regarding public services in the UK may, in turn, enable further clarification of the function of the prohibition on anticompetitive behaviour by NHS commissioners within Regulation 10 of the 2013 Regulations. However, as a minimum, it is recommended that the CMA re-evaluate its interpretation of *FENIN* and clarify its understanding of the relationship between the NHS and private healthcare sector in light of its more recent and specific guidance to private practitioners, applying only to their private healthcare sector work (category 4) and not their NHS work (category 2). This is necessary because this approach by the CMA appears to be explained more by alternative interpretations of *FENIN*[45] based on the ultimate end purpose of the purchase (that is, to provide healthcare services for the NHS, which can equate to providing healthcare services based on clinical need, not the ability to pay).

Ostensibly, this may leave a jurisdictional gap with regard to potential anticompetitive behaviour by private providers delivering NHS services (category 2), so further clarification by the CMA is to be welcomed. It is recognised that the CMA's capacity to take action with the concurrent powers of section 72 HSCA 2012 in individual cases regarding NHS provision is now constrained by Regulations 5 and 8 of the Concurrency Regulations 2014. However, this is a different matter to the CMA producing more general guidance about its interpretation of *FENIN*, or joint guidance with NHS Improvement regarding private providers and/or the constraints on potential anticompetitive behaviour resulting from structures such as the National Tariff (limiting scope for price-fixing) or the NHS Provider Licence. This could complement general CMA guidance, for example, regarding bid-rigging in the public sector which has been linked with the NHS.[46]

---

44 Further on this point see T. Prosser, 'EU competition law and public services' in E. Mossialos, G. Permanand, R. Baeten and T.K. Hervey (eds.), *Health Systems Governance in Europe: The Role of European Union Law and Policy*, Cambridge University Press, Cambridge 2010; and N. Boeger and T. Prosser, 'United Kingdom' in M. Krajewski, U. Neergaard and J.W. van de Gronden (eds.), *The Changing Legal Framework for Services of General Interest in Europe – Between Competition and Solidarity*, TMC Asser Press, The Hague 2009; as well as the General Court judgment in *FENIN*.

45 See further, N. Dunne, 'Knowing when to see it: state activities, economic activities, and the concept of undertaking' (2010) 16(3) *Columbia Journal of European Law* 427.

46 S. Calkin, 'CMA warning over public sector bid rigging', *Health Service Journal*, 21.06.2016.

As regards the SGEI exception, the research in this book offers conclusions regarding the English perspective. It has identified two ways in which the English NHS can be regarded as sharing common characteristics with SGEI, in essence by ensuring universal access to healthcare through the NHS being a system based on clinical need, not the ability to pay, and by serving a 'provider of last resort' function relative to the private healthcare sector. In this regard, private providers and NHS providers competing to deliver services for the NHS may provide an example of 'competitive provision of universal service obligations',[47] whilst the HSCA 2012 competition framework may continue to be regarded as a 'new style of competition law'.[48] However, in view of the recent comments by the CMA regarding the lack of competition in the NHS, it may prove more productive to explore further the protection which may be afforded by the SGEI exception and to develop a public service obligation as necessary in order to give effect to the apparent ongoing commitment to keeping the NHS as a taxation-funded service free at the point of delivery, evident in the Government's Mandate to NHS England.[49]

Overall, this book has offered an insight into how two Member States – the Netherlands and England (UK) – have engaged with the EU competition law framework to develop national competition policies for healthcare.

As a UK academic writing in 2018, it would be remiss not to conclude by offering a tentative consideration of the effect Brexit may have for competition policy and the English NHS. Insofar as it is recommended that new freedoms created by Brexit should be constrained and immediate changes to current competition policy avoided,[50] this would appear to suggest a 'business as usual' approach regarding the NHS, which would leave unchanged current uncertainty about the extent of applicability of (EU and national) competition law. As emphasised in this book, this uncertainty arises in particular with regard to category 2 delivery of NHS services by private providers. Further clarity by the CMA regarding such activity, or even by the EU courts (insofar as post-Brexit approaches to competition law enforcement may seek to align as far as possible) would therefore be most welcome.

---

47 Sauter has identified this as a discernible preference at EU level regarding public services by reference to the priority assigned to competitive conditions where feasible in the 2002 Universal Service Directive. W. Sauter, *Public Services in EU Law*, Cambridge University Press, Cambridge 2015, pp. 233–34.

48 I. Lianos, 'Toward a Bureaucracy-Centred Theory of the Interaction between Competition Law and State Activities' in T.K. Cheng, I. Lianos, and D.D. Sokol (eds.), *Competition and the State*, Stanford University Press, Stanford CA 2014.

49 Department of Health, 'The Government's Revised Mandate to NHS England for 2017–18' March 2018, paragraph 1.1, p. 7.

50 B. Lyons, D. Reader and A. Stephan, 'UK competition policy post-Brexit: taking back control while resisting siren calls' (2017) 5 *Journal of Antitrust Enforcement* 347.

Whilst not directly affected by the EU framework, the research in this book has identified two aspects of competition policy which should not be overlooked in future, namely the option for the CMA or NHS Improvement to conduct a market investigation of the English NHS under section 73 HSCA 2012, and the possibility of mergers not involving NHS Foundation Trusts (that is, involving private healthcare providers) not to be subject to the additional scrutiny of 'relevant patient benefits' by NHS Improvement under section 79 HSCA 2012. It is not difficult to see that both of these may have implications in an environment where international private healthcare providers may seek to deliver services for the English NHS.

# BIBLIOGRAPHY


AELEN, M., 'Beginselen van goed toezicht: het onafhankelijkheidsbeginsel' ('Principles of good regulation: the principle of independence') (2015) *Tijdschrift voor Toezicht*, 2, 15.

AKINRINADE, T., CHRISTOFOROU, J. and CLARK, E., 'How to navigate a competition review to get trust merger approval', *Health Service Journal*, 14.10.2014.

ALBERT SCHWEITZER ZIEKENHUIS, 'Albert Schweitzer Ziekenhuis en Rivas Zorggroep zien af van fusie, geen hoger beroep' ('Albert Schweitzer Hospital and Rivas Care Group will not merge – no further appeal'), Press Release, 10.11.2016, <https://www.asz.nl/nieuws/nieuwsberichten/2016/11/21396/> accessed 24.06.2018.

ALDWYCH PARTNERS, 'Benefits from mergers: lessons from recent NHS transactions', <https://improvement.nhs.uk/resources/how-make-nhs-mergers-work-better-patients/> accessed 24.06.2018.

ALINPOUR, M., Loyens & Loeff response to consultation 21.08.2017, <https://www.internetconsultatie.nl/zorgconcentraties/reactie/d41ac314-818a-4e1c-8b39-c89a6787038d> accessed 24.06.2018.

ANDERSSON ELFFERS FELIX (AEF) (in samenwerking met Radicand Economics and Tilburg Law and Economics Center (TILEC)), 'Ordening en Toezicht in de zorg: Evaluatie van de Wet marktordening gezondheidszorg (Wmg) en de Nederlandse Zorgautoriteit (NZa)' (AEF in cooperation with Radicand Economics and TILEC, 'Oversight and regulation in healthcare: Assessment of the Wmg and the NZa'), September 2014.

ANDREANGELI, A., 'Healthcare Services, the EU Single Market and Beyond: Meeting Local Needs in an Open Economy – How Much Market or How Little Market?' (2016) 43(2) *Legal Issues of Economic Integration* 145.

ARORA, S., CHARLESWORTH, A., KELLY, E. and STOYE, G., 'Public payment and private provision – the changing landscape of health care in the 2000s', *Institute for Fiscal Studies / Nuffield Trust Research Report*, May 2013.

ARROW, K., 'Uncertainty and the Welfare Economics of Medical Care' (1963) 53 *American Economics Review* 941.

AUTORITEIT CONSUMENT EN MARKT – AUTHORITY FOR CONSUMERS AND MARKETS (ACM), *Jaarverslag 2017* (Annual Report 2017).

—— 'Prijs- en volume-effecten van ziekenhuisfusies – Onderzoek naar effecten van ziekenhuisfusies 2007–2014' ('Price and volume effects of hospital mergers – investigation into the effects of hospital mergers 2007–2014'), Zaaknummer (Reference) ACM/17/009041, 05.12.2017.

—— Jaarverslag 2016 (ACM Annual Report 2016), <https://jaarverslag.acm.nl/jaarverslag-2016/concentratietoezicht> accessed 24.06.2018.

—— *Jaarverslag 2016 – concurrentie zorgverzekeringsmarkt* (Annual Report 2016 – Competition in the health insurance market), <https://jaarverslag.acm.nl/jaarverslag-2016/concurrentie-zorgverzekeringsmarkt> accessed 24.06.2018.

—— 'Uitgangspunten toezicht ACM op zorgaanbieders in de eerste lijn' ('Starting points for ACM oversight of primary care providers'), 19.09.2015.

—— 'ACM prohibits proposed merger between two Dutch hospital groups', Press Release, 15.07.2015, <https://www.acm.nl/en/publications/publication/14503/ACM-prohibits-proposed-merger-between-two-Dutch-hospital-groups> accessed 24.06.2018.

—— 'Position paper Autoriteit Consument en Markt. Rondetafelgesprek fusietoets zorginstellingen', ('ACM Position Paper on the roundtable discussion of the healthcare institution merger test'), 29.06.2015.

—— Spreekpunten Henk Don bij rondetafelgesprek 'kwaliteit loont' in de Tweede Kamer op 17.04.2015 ('Points for discussion by Henk Don at the "Quality Pays" round table discussion in the Second Chamber 17.04.2015').

—— 'Position Paper Autoriteit Consument en Markt Rondetafelgesprek "Kwaliteit loont"' ('ACM Position Paper on the "Quality Pays" roundtable discussion'), 17.04.2015, <https://www.zorgkennis.net/downloads/kennisbank/ZK-kennisbank-Position-paper-AC&M-Kwalitieit-loont-3147.pdf> accessed 24.06.2018.

—— 'Further investigation needed into merger between hospitals', Press Release, 18.03.2014, <https://www.acm.nl/en/publications/publication/12845/Further-investigation-needed-into-merger-between-hospitals> accessed 24.06.2018.

—— 'Assessing mergers and collaborations in hospital care', 27.09.2013.

—— 'ACM-lijn maatschappen en ziekenhuizen' ('ACM Guidance on Partnerships and Hospitals'), 06.06.2013.

—— 'Regierol zorgverzekeraar crucial bij toestaan ziekenhuisfusies' ('Leading role of health insurers critical in approving hospital mergers'), 07.12.2012.

—— *Richtsnoeren voor de zorgsector* (Guidelines for the Healthcare Sector), March 2010.

—— *Richtsnoeren Remedies 2007* (Remedies Guidelines 2007) 21.09.2007.

ACM, 'Organogram', <https://www.acm.nl/nl/organisatie/organisatie/organogram> accessed 24.06.2018.

ACM Website, 'Denk mee met ACM in de zorg' ('join the ACM's conversation about healthcare'), <https://denkmee.acm.nl/thema/gezonde-samenwerking-de-zorg-2016-2017?status=inactief> accessed 24.06.2018; <https://jaarverslag.acm.nl/sites/default/files/acm-jaarverslag-2017.pdf> accessed 24.06.2018.

—— 'Wat doet de ACM in de zorgsector?' ('What does the ACM do in the healthcare sector?'), <https://www.acm.nl/nl/onderwerpen/zorg/wat-doet-de-acm-in-de-zorgsector> accessed 24.06.2018.

—— 'Samenwerken in de zorg' ('Collaboration in healthcare'), <https://www.acm.nl/nl/onderwerpen/zorg/samenwerking-in-de-zorg/samenwerking-in-de-zorg> accessed 24.06.2018.

—— 'Informatiekaart – ACM beoordeling fuseren of samenwerken in ziekenhuiszorg' ('Information Map – ACM assessment of mergers and collaborative working in hospital care'), <https://www.acm.nl/sites/default/files/old_publication/publicaties/12562_informatiekaart-acm-beoordeling-fuseren-of-samenwerken-in-ziekenhuiszorg.pdf> accessed 24.06.2018.

—— 'Samenwerking kankerzorg drie ziekenhuizen Utrecht goed voor patient' ('Collaborative working in cancer care by three hospitals in the Utrecht region is good for patients'), 25.08.2016, <https://www.acm.nl/nl/publicaties/publicatie/16190/Samenwerking-kankerzorg-drie-ziekenhuizen-regio-Utrecht-goed-voor-patient> accessed 24.06.2018.

—— 'Samenwerking in de geboortezorg' ('Collaborative working in obstetrics'), <https://www.acm.nl/nl/onderwerpen/zorg/samenwerking-in-de-zorg/samenwerking-tussen-aanbieders-van-geboortezorg> accessed 24.06.2018.

ACM and NEDERLANDSE ZORGAUTORITEIT (ACM/NZA), *Samenwerkingsprotocol Autoriteit Consument en Markt en Nederlandse Zorgautoriteit* (ACM and NZa Cooperation Protocol), December 2014.

ACM and NEDERLANDSE ZORGAUTORITEIT (NZa), 'Echte keuze op de polismarkt?' ('Real choice in the health insurance market?'), 01.12.2017. <https://www.acm.nl/nl/publicaties/consultatie-echte-keuze-op-de-polismarkt> accessed 25.08.2018.

BAARSMA, B. and SNOEP, M., 'Voeg toezichthouders NMa, OPTA, NZa en Consumentenautoriteit samen' ('Merge the NMa, OPTA, NZa and the Consumer Authority'), *MeJudice – Economen in debat*, 22.10.2010, <http://www.mejudice.nl/artikelen/detail/voeg-toezichthouders-nma-opta-nza-en-consumentenautoriteit-samen> accessed 24.06.2018.

BAINES, D., 'Improvements suggested by Enthoven and Maynard' (2014) 25(12) *Prescriber* 33.

BAQUERO CRUZ, J., 'Beyond Competition: Services of General Interest and European Community Law' in DE BÚRCA, G. (ed.), *EU Law and the Welfare State: In Search of Solidarity*, Oxford University Press, Oxford 2005.

BARNES, F., 'Competition law and patient choice in the NHS: help or hindrance?' *Oxera Agenda*, January 2014, <https://www.oxera.com/Latest-Thinking/Agenda/2014/Competition-law-and-patient-choice-in-the-NHS-help.aspx> accessed 24.06.2018.

BARTLETT, W. and LE GRAND, J., 'The Theory of Quasi-Markets' in LE GRAND, J. and BARTLETT, W. (eds.), *Quasi-Markets and Social Policy*, Macmillan, London 1993.

BELHAJ, S. and VAN DE GRONDEN, J.W., 'Some room for competition does not make a sickness fund an undertaking. Is EC competition law applicable to the health care sector? (Joined cases C-264/01, C-306/01, C-453/01 and C-355/01 AOK)' (2004) 25(11) *European Competition Law Review* 682.

BENNETT, D., 'Monitor's plan for a better merger regime', *Health Service Journal*, 23.01.2014.

BEVAN, A., 'A Free Health Service' in BEVAN, A., *In Place of Fear*, Quartet Books, London 1978.

BIJKERK, J. and SAUTER, W., 'Een nieuwe mededingingsbevoegdheid voor de NZa? Artikel 45 Wmg over ingrijpen in de voorwaarden en de wijze van totstandkomen van overeenkomsten met betrekking tot zorg of tarieven' ('A new competition power for the NZa? Article 45 Wmg and intervention in the conditions and formulation of agreements relating to healthcare or tariffs') (2010) *Markt & Mededinging*, 4, 145.

BORSTLAP, H., VAN DER MEER MOHR, P.F.M. and SMITS, L.J.E., 'Het rapport van de onderzoekscommissie intern functioneren NZa', 02.09.2014 ('Report of the investigation committee on the internal operation of the NZa'), 02.09.2014.

BN DE STEM 'Zorg en kabel-tv: ze lijken op elkaar' ('Healthcare and Cable TV are similar'), Interview with Marcel Canoy and Wolf Sauter, 07.02.2009.

BOER & CROON, 'Fusies en overnames in de gezondheidszorg: onderzoek 2018'. Executive summary – maart 2018, Amsterdam ('Mergers and takeovers in healthcare: 2018 Investigation'), <https://bccf.nl/wp-content/uploads/2018/03/Fusies-en-overnames-in-de-gezondheidszorg_onderzoek-2018-1.pdf> accessed 24.06.2018.

—— 'Fusies en overnames in de gezondheidszorg: onderzoek 2017'. Executive summary – maart 2017, Amsterdam ('Mergers and takeovers in healthcare: 2017 Investigation'), <https://bccf.nl/wp-content/uploads/2017/04/BCCF-Healthcare-Onderzoek-maart-2017.pdf> accessed 24.06.2018.

—— *Evaluatie CVZ en NZa* ('Assessment of the Dutch Healthcare Insurance Board (*College voor Zorgverzekeringen* CVZ) and NZa'), 25.09.2009.

BOEGER, N., 'Solidarity and EC competition law' [2007] *European Law Review*, 32, 319.

BOEGER, N. and PROSSER, T., 'United Kingdom' in M. KRAJEWSKI, U. NEERGAARD and J.W. VAN DE GRONDEN (eds.), *The Changing Legal Framework for Services of General Interest in Europe – Between Competition and Solidarity*, TMC Asser Press, The Hague 2009.

BOJAKOWSKI, S., 'Market power: a PCT acting as a monopsony' [2012] *British Journal of Healthcare Management*, 18(2).

CABINET OFFICE, Press Release, 'Opening Up Public Services', 11.07.2011, <https://www.gov.uk/government/news/opening-up-public-services> accessed 24.06.2018.

CALKIN, S., 'CMA warning over public sector bid rigging', *Health Service Journal*, 21.06.2016.

CAMPBELL, D., 'May to give NHS 'significant' cash boost, Jeremy Hunt reveals', The Guardian, 06.06.2018.

CANOY, M. and SAUTER, W., 'De recidivist onder het mes: NMa beboet de Landelijke Huisartsenvereniging' ('Repeat offender under the knife: the NMa fines the Dutch GPs' Association') (2012) *Markt & Mededinging* 15, 92.

—— 'Out of control? Hospital mergers in the Netherlands and the public interest', [2010] *European Competition Law Review*, 31(9), 377.

CARE QUALITY COMMISSION (CQC), 'CQC consults on plans to evolve regulation of independent healthcare services in England', 26.01.2018, <https://www.cqc.org.uk/news/releases/cqc-consults-plans-evolve-regulation-independent-healthcare-services-england> accessed 24.06.2018.

CASS BUSINESS SCHOOL, CITY UNIVERSITY LONDON AND NHS IMPROVEMENT, 'Mergers in the NHS: lessons learnt and recommendations – Summary', May 2016, <https://improvement.nhs.uk/resources/how-make-nhs-mergers-work-better-patients/> accessed 24.06.2018.

—— 'Mergers in the NHS: Lessons Learnt and Recommendations – Update 2017', <https://improvement.nhs.uk/resources/how-make-nhs-mergers-work-better-patients/> accessed 24.06.2018.

CERESTE, M., DOHERTY, N. and TRAVERS, C., 'An investigation into the level and impact of merger activity amongst hospitals in the UK's National Health Service' (2003) 17(1) *Journal of Health Organization and Management* 6.

CHARLESWORTH, A., 'Size may not be everything: reviewing hospital mergers', *Nuffield Trust Blog Post*, 24.02.2012, <https://www.nuffieldtrust.org.uk/news-item/size-may-not-be-everything-reviewing-hospital-mergers> accessed 24.06.2018.

CLAASSEN, R. and GERBRANDY, A., 'Rethinking European Competition Law: From a Consumer Welfare to a Capability Approach' (2016) 12(1) *Utrecht Law Review* 1.

COLLINS, B., 'Procurement and Competition Rules – Can the NHS be exempted?', *The King's Fund Briefing*, London March 2015, <https://www.kingsfund.org.uk/sites/default/files/field/field_publication_file/procurement-competition-rules-kings-fund-mar-2015.pdf> accessed 24.06.2018.

COMPETITION COMMISSION, *National Tariff Methodology Reference Rules under the Health and Social Care Act 2012: Guide*, February 2014, CC22.

COMPETITION AND MARKETS AUTHORITY (CMA), 'Annual Report on Concurrency 2018', 30.04.2018, CMA79.

—— 'News Story: CMA puts vulnerable consumers at the heart of its annual plan', 29.03.2018, <https://www.gov.uk/government/news/cma-puts-vulnerable-consumers-at-the-heart-of-its-annual-plan> accessed 24.06.2018.

—— 'CMA requires sale of East Midlands adult mental health hospital', Press Release, 16.10.2017, <https://www.gov.uk/government/news/cma-requires-sale-of-east-midlands-adult-mental-health-hospital> accessed 24.06.2018.

—— Press Release, 'CMA demands action from hospitals on private healthcare information', 31.08.2017, <https://www.gov.uk/government/news/cma-demands-action-from-hospitals-on-private-healthcare-information> accessed 24.06.2018.

—— Private Healthcare Market Investigation, last updated 28.04.2017, <https://www.gov.uk/cma-cases/private-healthcare-market-investigation> accessed 24.06.2018.

—— 'Annual Report on Concurrency 2017', 28.04.2017, CMA63.

—— News Story, 'Manchester hospitals trust request fast track merger reference', 09.02.2017, <https://www.gov.uk/government/news/manchester-hospital-trusts-request-fast-track-merger-reference> accessed 24.06.2018.

—— 'Annual Report on Concurrency 2016', 28.04.2016, CMA54.

——'60-second summary – Private medical practitioners: information on competition law', 03.12.2015.

—— 'Guidance: Private Medical Practitioners: Guidance on Competition Law', 03.12.2015.

—— 'Guidance: Competition Law for Private Medical Practitioners: Cans, Can'ts, and Maybes', 03.12.2015.

—— 'Guidance – Private medical practitioners: information about fees', 03.12.2015.

—— 'Annual Report on Concurrency 2015', 01.04.2015, CMA43.

—— Press Release, 'Better information for private patients moves closer', 01.12.2014.

—— 'Private Healthcare Market Investigation – Explanatory Note to accompany the Private Healthcare Market Investigation Order 2014', 01.10.2014.

—— *Private Healthcare Market Investigation Final Order*, 01.10.2014.

—— *CMA guidance on the review of NHS mergers*, 31.07.2014, CMA29.

—— *Private Healthcare Market Investigation Final Report*, CMA25, 02.04.2014.

—— '"Baseline" annual report on concurrency – 2014', 01.04.2014, CMA24.

—— Guidance on concurrent application of competition law to regulated industries, CMA10, 29.03.2014.

—— *Merger Assessment Guidelines*, CC2 (Revised) OFT1254.

—— *Mergers: Guidance on the CMA's jurisdiction and procedure*, January 2014, CMA2.

—— 'Network launched to help drive competition in regulated sectors', Press Release, 03.12.2013.

COMPETITION AND MARKETS AUTHORITY (CMA) AND NHS IMPROVEMENT, *Memorandum of Understanding between the Competition and Markets Authority and NHS Improvement*, 01.04.2016.

CONSUMENTENBOND, 'Premieoverzicht basiszorgverzekeringen', 03.05.2018, <https://www.consumentenbond.nl/zorgverzekering/premieoverzicht-zorgverzekering> accessed 24.06.2018.

CORRIGAN, P. and TAYLOR, A., 'The CMA can improve the NHS merger regime: here's how', *Health Service Journal*, 26.03.2014.
CSERES, K., 'The Controversies of the Consumer Welfare Standard' (2007) 3(2) *Competition Law Review* 121.
CURRAN, R. and ALBERT, S., 'It seemed like a good idea at the time: the application of competition law to the health sector in England' (2014) 35(9) *European Competition Law Review* 419.
DABBAH, M.M., 'The Relationship between Competition Authorities and Sector Regulators' (2011) 70(1) *Cambridge Law Journal* 113.
DALTON, D., *Examining new options and opportunities for providers of NHS care*, December 2014.
DASKALOVA, V., 'Consumer Welfare in EU Competition Law: What Is It (Not) About?' (2015) 11(1) *Competition Law Review* 133.
DAVIES, A.C.L., 'This Time, It's For Real' (2013) 76(3) *Modern Law Review* 564.
—— 'Foundation Hospitals: a new approach to accountability and autonomy in the public services?' [Winter 2004] *Public Law* 808.
DAWSON, D., 'Regulating competition in the NHS. The Department of Health guide on mergers and anti-competitive behaviour', University of York Centre for Health Economics Discussion Paper 131, March 1995.
DE BOER, C.J., Van Doorne Advocaten, Notarissen, Fiscalisten, response to consultation, 10.08.2017, <https://www.internetconsultatie.nl/zorgconcentraties/reactie/79ec6634-6385-464a-941b-f6425f4ed80f> accessed 24.06.2018.
DEKKER, C.T. and SIJMONS, J.G., 'Continuïteit van zorg en zorgspecifieke fusietoetsing' ('Continuity of healthcare and healthcare-specific merger assessment') (2013) *Tijdschrift voor Gezondheidsrecht*, (37)2, 136.
DEN EXTER, A.P. and GUY, M.J., 'Market Competition in Health Care Markets in The Netherlands: Some Lessons for England?' (2014) 22(2) *Medical Law Review* 255.
DEPARTMENT OF HEALTH, 'The Government's Revised Mandate to NHS England for 2017–18', March 2018.
—— 'The Mandate – A Mandate from the Government to the NHS England: April 2015–March 2016', December 2015.
—— 'The Mandate – A Mandate from the Government to the NHS Commissioning Board: April 2013–March 2015', November 2013.
—— 'Sector Regulation – a short guide to the Health and Social Care Bill. What you need to know as a provider of NHS services', 23.02.2012, <https://www.gov.uk/government/publications/sector-regulation-a-short-guide-to-the-health-and-social-care-bill> accessed 24.06.2018.
—— 'Protecting and Promoting Patients' Interests: the role of Sector Regulation', Department of Health, London, 01.12.2011.
—— 'Government response to the NHS Future Forum report', Cm 8113, June 2011.
—— 'Equity and Excellence: Liberating the NHS', Cm 7881, July 2010.
—— 'Principles and Rules for Cooperation and Competition', 30.07.2010, <https://www.gov.uk/government/publications/principles-and-rules-for-cooperation-and-competition> accessed 24.06.2018.
—— 'Guidance on NHS patients who wish to pay for additional private care', Department of Health, London, 2009.

—— *A Guide to NHS Foundation Trusts*, Department of Health, London December 2002.

—— *The NHS Plan – A Plan for Investment, A Plan for Reform*, 01.07.2000, Cm 4818-I July 2000.

DESAI, K., 'Public hospital mergers: a case for broader considerations than competition law?' (2013) 34 (12) *European Competition Law Review* 646.

DIXON, A., HARRISON, T. and MUNDLE, C., 'Economic regulation in healthcare – what can we learn from other regulators?', The King's Fund, London 2011.

DIXON, A. and ROBERTSON, R., 'Patient Choice of Hospital' in MAYS, N., DIXON, A. and JONES, L., (eds.), *Understanding New Labour's Market Reforms of the English NHS*, The King's Fund, London 2011.

DOWLER, C., 'Exclusive Hunt Interview: CQC ratings have replaced Foundation Trust status as a definition of success', *Health Service Journal*, 09.09.2015.

—— 'Bennett calls for freeze of Foundation Trust pipeline', *Health Service Journal*, 05.11.2015.

DUNNE, N., 'Recasting Competition Concurrency under the Enterprise and Regulatory Reform Act 2013', (2014) *Modern Law Review*, 77(2), 254.

—— 'Knowing when to see it: state activities, economic activities, and the concept of undertaking' (2010) 16(3) *Columbia Journal of European Law* 427.

ELLIOTT, L., 'Run the NHS and social care like John Lewis, says Frank Field', *The Guardian*, 02.12.2016, <https://www.theguardian.com/society/2016/dec/02/run-the-nhs-and-social-care-like-john-lewis-says-frank-field> accessed 24.06.2018.

ENTHOVEN, A.C., 'Introduction' in ENTHOVEN, A.C., *Health Care, the Market and Consumer Choice*, Edward Elgar, Cheltenham 2012.

—— 'A Living Model of Managed Competition: A Conversation with Dutch Health Minister Ab Klink' (2008) 27(3) *Health Affairs* 196.

—— 'The History and Principles of Managed Competition' (1993) 12(1) *Health Affairs* 24.

—— 'Internal Market Reform of the British National Health Service' (1991) 10(3) *Health Affairs* 60.

—— *Reflections on the management of the National Health Service – An American looks at incentives to efficiency in health services management in the UK*, The Nuffield Trust, London, 04.10.1985.

—— 'Consumer-Choice Health Plan – A National-Health-Insurance Proposal Based on Regulated Competition in the Private Sector' (1978) 298(13) *New England Journal of Medicine* 709.

—— 'Consumer-Choice Health Plan – Inflation and Inequity in Health Care Today: Alternatives for Cost Control and an Analysis of Proposals for National Health Insurance' (1978) 298(12) *New England Journal of Medicine* 650.

ENTHOVEN, A.C. and VAN DE VEN, W.P.M.M., 'Going Dutch? Managed Competition Health Insurance in the Netherlands' (2007) 357(24) *New England Journal of Medicine* 2421.

EUOBSERVER, 'Dutch PM misses EU summit to save coalition', 18.12.2014, <https://euobserver.com/news/126994> accessed 24.06.2018.

EUROPEAN COMMISSION, 'What is competition policy?', <http://ec.europa.eu/competition/consumers/what_en.html> accessed 24.06.2018.

EUROPEAN COMMISSION, EXPERT PANEL ON EFFECTIVE WAYS OF INVESTING IN HEALTH (EXPH), 'Competition among health care providers in the European Union – Investigating Policy Options', 17.02.2015.

FAULL, J., and NIKPAY, A., *The EU Law of Competition*, 3rd edn., Oxford University Press, Oxford 2014.

FERNÁNDEZ-GUTIÉRREZ, M., JAMES, O. and JILKE, S., 'Competition and switching in public service markets: Can they reduce inequalities?' (2017) 11 *Regulation and Governance* 41.

FONTEIJN, C., 'Netherlands: Authority for Consumers and Markets', *The European, Middle Eastern and African Antitrust Review 2017*, 22.07.2016, <https://globalcompetitionreview.com/insight/the-european-middle-eastern-and-african-antitrust-review-2017/1067851/netherlands-authority-for-consumers-and-markets> accessed 24.06.2018.

—— Letter of 22 May 2015 to the Minister for Health, Wellbeing and Sport, <https://www.eerstekamer.nl/overig/20161107/uitvoerbaarheids_en/meta> accessed 24.06.2018.

FRIELE, R.D., *Evaluatie Wet marktordening gezondheidszorg* (Assessment of the Wmg), ZonMw, Den Haag 2009.

GASH, T. and ROOS, T., 'Choice and competition in public services: learning from history', *Institute for Government*, August 2012.

GAYNOR, M., 'Competition in Hospital Services', OECD Directorate for Financial and Enterprise Affairs Competition Committee, Working Party No. 2 on Competition and Regulation, DAF/COMP/WP2(2012)3, 06.02.2012.

GAYNOR, M., LAUDICELLA, M. and PROPPER, C., 'Can governments do it better? Merger mania and hospital outcomes in the English NHS' (2012) 31(3) *Journal of Health Economics* 528.

GAYNOR, M. and TOWN, R.J., 'Competition in Health Care Markets' in PAULY, M. et al. (eds.), *Handbook of Health Economics, Part 2*, Elsevier, North-Holland Elsevier 2012.

GEELHOED, W.S. and LEEFLANG, F.J., 'NMa-richtsnoeren voor de zorgsector nader beschouwd' ('A closer examination of the NMa Guidelines for the Healthcare Sector') (2008) *Markt & Mededinging*, 4, 115.

GLAS, L., LOOIJESTIJN, A., and VAN DE GRONDEN, J.W., 'Advies 2: Beoordeling van verschillende voorgenomen zorgmaatregelen in het licht van het EU-recht en het EVRM. Avies in opdracht van VGZ en Zilveren Kruis' ('Opinion 2: Assessment of different proposals for healthcare measures in light of EU law and the European Convention on Human Rights. Opinion commissioned by VGZ and Zilveren Kruis').

GOULDING, L., 'Is the NHS subject to competition law?', *eutopia law*, 19.07.2013, <https://eutopialaw.com/tag/health/> accessed 24.06.2018.

GOVERNMENT OF THE NETHERLANDS, 'Health Insurance', <https://www.government.nl/topics/health-insurance> accessed 24.06.2018.

—— 'Standard Health Insurance', <https://www.government.nl/topics/health-insurance/contents/standard-health-insurance> accessed 24.06.2018.

GRAHAM, C., 'UK: The Concurrent Enforcement by Regulators of Competition Law and Sector-Specific Regulation' (2016) 7(6) *Journal of European Competition Law & Practice* 407–13.

GREENER, I., 'Towards a history of choice in UK health policy' (2009) 31(3) *Sociology of Health & Illness* 309.

GUPTA STRATEGISTS, 'Het Bedrijfsmodel van zorgverzekeraars – Mogelijkheden om te concurreren' ('Health insurer business model – options for competition'), Amsterdam, 24.12.2015.

GUY, M., 'Competition and Sectoral Regulation in Dutch and English Healthcare: Factors shaping the competition focus of the new healthcare regulators and their relationship with the competition authorities' (2017) 2 *Ius Publicum Network Review*, ISSN 2039 2540.

—— 'Book Review: The Affordable Care Act and Medicare in Comparative Context' (2017) 25(4) *Medical Law Review* 684.

—— 'What could repeal of the Health and Social Care Act 2012 mean for the application of competition law and the English NHS?', *Competition Policy Blog*, 05.05.2015, <https://competitionpolicy.wordpress.com/2015/05/05/what-could-repeal-of-the-health-and-social-care-act-2012-mean-for-the-application-of-competition-law-and-the-english-nhs/> accessed 24.06.2018.

—— 'Monitor's Advice to the OFT and the New Healthcare Regulation', *Competition Policy Blog*, 20.03.2013, <https://competitionpolicy.wordpress.com/2013/02/20/monitors-advice-to-the-oft-and-the-new-healthcare-regulation/> accessed 24.06.2018.

—— 'The Meaning of "Relevant Customer Benefits" in the Context of Health Care: Monitor's Advice and the Competition Commission's Response', *Competition Policy Blog*, 28.10.2013, <https://competitionpolicy.wordpress.com/2013/10/28/the-meaning-of-relevant-customer-benefits-in-the-context-of-health-care-monitors-advice-and-the-competition-commissions-response/> accessed 24.06.2018.

HALBERSMA, R., VAN MANEN, J. and SAUTER, W., 'De verzekeraars als motor van het zorgstelsel' ('Health insurers as motor of the healthcare system') (2012) *Zorg en Financiering*, 11(10), 10.

HAM, C., 'Simon Stevens' vision for the NHS: welcome but challenging to deliver', *The King's Fund blog*, 14.10.2015, <https://www.kingsfund.org.uk/blog/2015/10/simon-stevens-vision-nhs-welcome-challenging-deliver> accessed 24.06.2018.

HANCHER, L. and SAUTER, W., *EU Competition and Internal Market Law in the Health Care Sector*, Oxford University Press, Oxford 2012.

HANRATTY, G., 'Heatherwood-Frimley Park shows the way through merger process', *Health Service Journal*, 26.06.2014.

HARKER, M., 'EU competition law as a tool for dealing with regulatory failure: the broadband margin squeeze cases' [2013] *Journal of Business Law* 817.

HEALTH FOUNDATION, 'The Principles and Rules for Cooperation and Competition (2007)', *Policy Navigator*, <https://navigator.health.org.uk/content/principles-and-rules-cooperation-and-competition-prcc-2007> accessed 24.06.2018.

HERVEY, T.K., 'Public Health Services and EU Law' in CREMONA, M. (eds.), *Market Integration and Public Services in the European Union*, Oxford University Press, Oxford 2011.

HERVEY, T.K. and MCHALE, J.V., *European Union Health Law: Themes and Implications*, Cambridge University Press, Cambridge 2015.

HERVEY, T.K., STARK, A., DAWSON, A., FERNANDEZ, J.-L., MATOSEVIC, T. and MCDAID, D., 'Long-term care for older people and EU Law: the position in England and Scotland' (2012) 34(1) *Journal of Social Welfare and Family Law* 105.

'HET ROER MOET OM' ('We Must Change Course'), <http://www.hetroermoetom.nu/> accessed 24.06.2018.

HM GOVERNMENT, 'Open Public Services White Paper', Cm 8145, July 2011.

HM TREASURY, 'Autumn Budget', HC 587, November 2017.

—— 'Spending Review and Autumn Statement 2015', Cm 9162, November 2015.

HOUSE OF COMMONS HEALTH COMMITTEE, *Independent Sector Treatment Centres*, Fourth Report of Session 2005–2006, Volume I.

HOUSE OF COMMONS HEALTH AND SOCIAL CARE COMMITTEE, *Integrated care: organizations, partnerships and systems*, Seventh Report of Session 2017–19, 11.06.2018.

HOUSE OF LORDS SELECT COMMITTEE ON THE LONG-TERM SUSTAINABILITY OF THE NHS. Report of Session 2016–17, 'The Long-term Sustainability of the NHS and Adult Social Care', 05.04.2017.

HVIID, M., 'Procurement By Dominant Buyers', *CCP Research Bulletin*, May 2011, <http://competitionpolicy.ac.uk/documents/8158338/8193544/CCP-Research-Bulletin_May_2011.pdf/2b0743e2-db4d-49e8-9829-dddeb85002be> accessed 24.06.2018.

JANSEN, R.J.P., 'Samenwerken of fuseren in de zorg?' ('Collaborating or merging in healthcare?') (2013) *Markt & Mededinging*, 2, 77.

KEMP, R., LEIJH-SMIT, M.-L. and SCHEP, K., 'Concentratietoezicht ACM in de ziekenhuissector – Inzicht in en reflectie op de praktijk' ('ACM merger control in the hospital sector – insights into, and reflections on practice') (2015) *Markt en Mededinging*, 3, 103.

KIERS, B., 'Kleine zorgverzekeraar ontloopt prijsstijging bij ziekenhuisfusie' ('Small health insurers avoid price increases in hospital mergers'), *Zorgvisie*, 08.06.2018, <https://www.zorgvisie.nl/kleine-verzekeraar-ontloopt-prijsstijging-bij-ziekenhuisfusie/> accessed 24.06.2018.

KING'S FUND, 'The Health and Social Care Act: the tale in a timeline', <http://www.kingsfund.org.uk/topics/nhs-reform/health-and-social-care-act-2012-timeline> accessed 20.05.2018.

KINGSTON, S., *Greening EU competition law and policy*, Cambridge University Press, Cambridge 2012.

KPMG PLEXUS, *Evaluatie Zorgverzekeringswet – Eindrapportage*, September 2014, <http://docplayer.nl/5145339-Evaluatie-zorgverzekeringswet-eindrapportage-september-2014.html> accessed 24.06.2018.

KRAJEWSKI, M. and FARLEY, M., 'Non-economic activities in upstream and downstream markets and the scope of competition law after *FENIN*' (2007) 32(1) *European Law Review* 111.

KRAJEWSKI, M., NEERGAARD, U. and VAN DE GRONDEN, J.W., (eds.), *The Changing Legal Framework for Services of General Interest in Europe – Between Competition and Solidarity*, TMC Asser Press, The Hague 2009.

KÜÇÜK, E., 'Solidarity in EU Law – An Elusive Political Statement or a Legal Principle with Substance?' (2016) 23(6) *Maastricht Journal of European and Comparative Law* 965.

LAFOND, S., ARORA, S., CHARLESWORTH, A., and MCKEON, A., 'Into the red? The state of the NHS' finances – An Analysis of NHS Expenditure between 2010 and 2014', Nuffield Trust Research Report, July 2014.

LEAR, J., MOSSIALOS, E. and KARL, B., 'EU competition law and health policy' in MOSSIALOS, E., PERMANAND, G., BAETEN, R. and HERVEY, T.K, (eds.), *Health Systems Governance in Europe: The Role of European Union Law and Policy*, Cambridge University Press, Cambridge 2010.

LE GRAND, J., *The Other Invisible Hand – Delivering Public Services Through Choice and Competition*, Princeton University Press, Oxford 2007.

—— 'Quasi-Markets: the answer to market failure in health care?' in DAY, P., FOX, D.M., MAXWELL, R. and SCRIVENS, E. (eds.), *The State, Politics and Health: Essays for Rudolf Klein*, Blackwell, Oxford 1996.

LEYS, C., 'Treating private patients in NHS hospitals – benefit or cost?', *Health Service Journal*, 13.03.2018.

LIANOS, I., 'Toward a Bureaucracy-Centred Theory of the Interaction between Competition Law and State Activities' in CHENG, T.K., LIANOS, I. and SOKOL D.D. (eds.), *Competition and the State*, Stanford University Press, Stanford 2014.

—— 'Some reflections on the goals of EU competition law' in LIANOS, I. and GERADIN, D. (eds.), *Handbook in EU Competition Law: Substantive Aspects*. Edward Elgar, Cheltenham 2013.

LITTLECHILD, S., *Regulation of British Telecommunications' Profitability*, Department of Trade and Industry, London 1984.

LOOZEN, E.M.H., 'Public healthcare interests require strict competition enforcement' (2015) 119(7) *Health Policy* 882.

—— 'ACM en ziekenhuisfusies: hoeder van het publiek belang?' (Hospital mergers and the ACM: guardian of the public interest?') (2015) *Markt en Mededinging*, 5, 178.

—— 'Inrichting van meervoudig toezicht op marktwerking' ('Introduction of multisector regulation of competition') (2013) *RegelMaat*, (28) 2, 105.

—— 'Mededingingstoezicht op maatschappen van zorgaanbieders: welke rol is weggelegd voor ACM respectievelijk NZa?' ('Competition regulation of healthcare provider partnerships: what roles do the ACM and NZa play?') (2013) *Tijdschrift voor Gezondheidsrecht*, 7(37), 622.

—— 'NMa en NZa: houd je bij je leest! Een analyse van de mededingingsbevoegdheden van beide toezichthouders aan de hand van het Samenwerkingsprotocol NMa-NZa 2010' ('NMa and NZa, stick to what you're good at! An analysis of the competition powers of both agencies in light of the NMa-NZa Cooperation Protocol 2010') (2011) *Tijdschrift voor Toezicht*, 4, 25.

LOOZEN, E.M.H., VARKEVISSER, M. and SCHUT, E., 'Beoordeling ziekenhuisfusies door ACM: staat de consument wel echt centraal?' ('Are consumers really at the centre of the ACM's hospital merger decisions?') (2014) *Markt & Mededinging*, 1, 5.

—— 'Dutch Authority for Consumers and Markets fails to meet the standard of proof in recent hospital merger decisions' (2014) 35(1) *European Competition Law Review* 16.

LOUISSE, M.L. and WIGGERS, M., 'Toezicht' ('Regulation') in M. WIGGERS and OOSTWOUDER, W. *Handboek compliance in de zorg* ('Compliance in Healthcare Handbook'), Uitgerverij Paris, Zutphen 2017.

LYONS, B., READER, D. and STEPHAN, A., 'UK competition policy post-Brexit: taking back control while resisting siren calls' (2017) 5 *Journal of Antitrust Enforcement* 347.

MAARSE, H., JEURISSEN, P. and RUWAARD, D., 'Results of the market-oriented reform in the Netherlands: a review' (2016) 11 *Health Economics, Policy and Law* 161.

MAASDAM, Y. and SLUIJS, J.-K., 'Wie van de drie is de echte marktmeester in de zorg: de IGZ, de NMa of toch de NZa?' ('Who is the real market umpire in healthcare? The IGZ, the NMa or actually the NZa?') (2009) *Actualiteiten Mededingingsrecht*, 5, 103, <https://www.legaltree.nl/site_media/uploads/Wie_van_de_drie_is_de_echte_marktmeester_in_de_zorg.pdf> accessed 24.06.2018.

MAVERICK LAW, 'Druk NZa en ACM bij Zorg en Farma neemt toe' ('Increasing pressure on the NZa and ACM in healthcare and pharma'), 05.03.2018, <https://www.maverick-law.com/nl/blogs/druk-nza-en-acm-bij-zorg-en-farma-neemt-toe.html> accessed 24.06.2018.

MEIJER, C.C., 'Beleidsregel AMM in de zorg – een groeimodel' ('Policy Rule SMP in Healthcare – a Growth Model') (2007) *Markt & Mededinging*, 8, 219.

MINISTRY OF HEALTH, WELLBEING AND SPORT, 'Healthcare in the Netherlands', 09.02.2016, <https://www.government.nl/topics/health-insurance/documents/leaflets/2016/02/09/healthcare-in-the-netherlands> accessed 24.06.2018.

MONITOR, 'Patients in South Devon set to get integrated care after hospital acquisition', Press Release, 01.10.2015, <https://www.gov.uk/government/news/patients-in-south-devon-set-to-get-integrated-care-after-hospital-acquisition> accessed 24.06.2018.

—— Supporting NHS Providers: Guidance on merger benefits, 26.08.2015.

—— *Functional conflicts and balancing competing regulatory interests policy*, 02.07.2015, <https://www.gov.uk/government/publications/functional-conflicts-and-balancing-competing-regulatory-interests-policy> accessed 24.06.2018.

——'Improving GP services: commissioners and patient choice', 01.06.2015.

—— 'Choice and competition toolkit: scenarios for GPs working together', 01.06.2015.

—— 'Supporting NHS Providers: Guidance on Transactions for NHS Foundation Trusts – Updated March 2015'.

—— 'Choice and competition: hypothetical scenarios for NHS healthcare providers', 12.09.2014.

—— 'Choice and competition licence conditions: guidance for providers of NHS-funded services', 12.09.2014.

—— 'Monitor's Strategy 2014–2017 – Helping to redesign healthcare provision in England', 10.04.2014.

—— 'The application of the Competition Act 1998 in the healthcare sector', 12.09.2014.

—— 'Substantive Guidance on the Procurement, Patient Choice and Competition Regulations', London, December 2013.

—— Briefing Note 'The respective roles of Monitor, the Office of Fair Trading and the Competition Commission in relation to mergers involving NHS trusts and NHS foundation trusts', 17.10.2013.

—— 'The New NHS Provider Licence – Monitor's response to the statutory consultation on the new NHS provider licence', 14.02.2013.

—— NHS Provider Licence Annex: Standard Conditions, Condition C2, 'Competition Oversight', <https://assets.publishing.service.gov.uk/government/uploads/system/uploads/attachment_data/file/285009/Annex_NHS_provider_licence_conditions_-_20120207.pdf> accessed 24.06.2018.

MONITOR and NHS ENGLAND, NHS National Tariff Payment System 2015–2016 Engagement Documents, <https://www.gov.uk/government/consultations/nhs-national-tariff-payment-system-201516-engagement-documents> accessed 24.06.2018.

MOTTA, M., *Competition Policy – Theory and Practice*, Cambridge University Press, Cambridge 2004.

NATIONAL AUDIT OFFICE, 'Department of Health – Achievement of Foundation Trust status by NHS hospital trusts', Report by the Comptroller and Auditor General, HC 1516, Session 2010–12, 13.10.2011.

NAYLOR, C. and GREGORY, S., 'Briefing - Independent Sector Treatment Centres', The King's Fund, London, October 2009.

NEDERLANDSE MEDEDINGINGSAUTORITEIT - Dutch Competition Authority (NMA), *Richtsnoeren voor de zorgsector* (Guidelines for the Healthcare Sector), 2007.

—— 'Concurrentie in de ziekenhuissector', Visiedocument 3128/55, Den Haag, januari 2004 ('Competition in the hospital sector', Vision Document 3128/55, The Hague, January 2004).

—— *Richtsnoeren voor de zorgsector* (Guidelines for the Healthcare Sector), 2002.

NEDERLANDSE MEDEDINGINGSAUTORITEIT and NEDERLANDSE ZORGAUTORITEIT (NMA/NZA), *Samenwerkingsprotocol NMa-NZa* ('NMa-NZa Cooperation Protocol'), December 2010.

—— Position Paper 'Werking van het zorgstelsel' ('Operation of the Healthcare System'), April 2015.

—— *Protocol tussen de Nederlandse Mededingingsautoriteit en de Nederlandse Zorgautoriteit over de wijze van samenwerking bij aangelegenheden van wederzijds belang* (Protocol signed by the Dutch Competition Authority and the Dutch Healthcare Authority regarding cooperation in matters of mutual interest), October 2006.

—— *Richtsnoeren Zorggroepen* (Guidelines for Healthcare Groups), August 2010.

NEDERLANDSE ZORGAUTORITEIT (Dutch Healthcare Authority (NZa)), *Stand van de zorgmarkten 2017* (2017 Annual Report), <http://www.standvandezorgmarkten.nl/> accessed 24.06.2018.

—— *Stand van de zorgmarkten 2016* (2016 Annual Report), <https://puc.overheid.nl/nza/doc/PUC_3496_22/1/> accessed 24.06.2018.

—— *Stand van de zorgmarkten 2015* (Annual Report 2015), <https://puc.overheid.nl/nza/doc/PUC_3352_22/1/> accessed 24.06.2018.

—— 'Toelichting op de beleidsregel Aanmerkelijke Marktmacht in de Zorg' ('Explanatory Notes to the Policy Rule Significant Market Power in Healthcare'), September 2010.

—— 'Toelichting Toepassing artikel 45 Wmg' ('Explanatory Notes regarding the application of Art. 45 Wmg'), December 2009.

—— 'Visiedocument: (In) het belang van de consument' ('Vision Document: (In) the general consumer interest') (November 2007).

NEWDICK, C., 'The Organisation of Healthcare' in A. GRUBB (ed.), *Principles of Medical Law*, 2nd edn., Oxford University Press, Oxford 2004.

NHS COMMISSIONING BOARD (now NHS England), 'Commissioning Policy: Defining the boundaries between NHS and Private Healthcare', April 2013, Ref: NHSCB/CP/12.

NHS CONFEDERATION, 'NHS statistics, facts and figures', 14.07.2017, <http://www.nhsconfed.org/resources/key-statistics-on-the-nhs> accessed 24.06.2018.

NHS COOPERATION AND COMPETITION PANEL (NHS CCP), <http://ccpanel.org.uk/cases/index.html> accessed 24.06.2018.

—— 'The Implications of Competition Rules for the Unilateral Conduct of Providers of NHS-funded Services', 22.03.2013.

—— 'The Implications of Competition Rules for Agreements Involving Providers of NHS-Funded Healthcare Services', 22.03.2013.

—— 'The Implications of Competition Rules for Clinical Networks', 22.03.2012.

—— 'The Implications of Competition Rules for the Delivery of Integrated Care', 14.12.2012.

—— 'Merger Guidelines', 25.10.2010, <http://www.ccpanel.org.uk/reports-and-guidance/index.html> accessed 24.06.2018.

—— 'Response to Consultation Document', 04.10.2010.

NHS ENGLAND, 'Five Year Forward View – The Success Regime: A whole systems intervention', <https://www.gov.uk/government/publications/five-year-forward-view-the-success-regime-a-whole-systems-intervention> accessed 24.06.2018.

—— 'Local Partnerships to Improve Health and Care – Sustainability and Transformation Partnerships (STPs) and Accountable Care Organisations (ACOs)', <https://www.england.nhs.uk/systemchange/> accessed 24.06.2018.

—— 'Integrated Care', <https://www.england.nhs.uk/integratedcare/> accessed 24.06.2018.

—— 'Personal Health Budgets', <https://www.england.nhs.uk/personal-health-budgets/> accessed 24.06.2018.

—— 'Five Year Forward View', <https://www.england.nhs.uk/five-year-forward-view/> accessed 24.06.2018.

—— 'About NHS England', <https://www.england.nhs.uk/about/about-nhs-england/> accessed 24.06.2018.

—— 'Understanding the New NHS – A guide for everyone working and training within the NHS'.

—— 'Friends and Family Test', <http://www.nhs.uk/NHSEngland/AboutNHSservices/Pages/nhs-friends-and-family-test.aspx>, accessed 24.06.2018.

—— 'NHS England frees up millions of pounds which could be used for frontline services', News, <https://www.england.nhs.uk/2018/03/nhs-england-frees-up-millions-of-pounds-which-could-be-used-for-frontline-services/> accessed 24.06.2018.

NHS EXECUTIVE, 'The Operation of the NHS Internal Market: Local Freedoms, National Responsibilities', Department of Health, December 1994.

NHS FUTURE FORUM, *Choice and Competition – Delivering Real Choice. A report from the NHS Future Forum*. NHS Future Forum, London 2011.

NHS IMPROVEMENT, 'Who We Are', <https://improvement.nhs.uk/about-us/who-we-are/> accessed 24.06.2018.

—— 'NHS Foundation Trust Directory – Related Documents', <https://improvement.nhs.uk/resources/nhs-foundation-trust-directory-and-register-licensed-healthcare-providers/> accessed 24.06.2018.

NHS IMPROVEMENT, 'National Tariff Payment System 2017/18 and 2018/19: a consultation notice', 22.12.2016, <https://improvement.nhs.uk/resources/national-tariff-1719-consultation/> accessed 24.06.2018.

—— 'National Tariff Payment System 2017/18 and 2018/19', 23.02.2018, <https://improvement.nhs.uk/resources/national-tariff-1719/> accessed 24.06.2018.

—— 'Regulatory Action: licensed independent healthcare providers', 16.06.2017, <https://improvement.nhs.uk/about-us/corporate-publications/publications/regulatory-action-licensed-independent-healthcare-providers/> accessed 24.06.2018.

—— *Transactions Guidance – for Trusts undertaking transactions, including mergers and acquisitions*, November 2017.

—— 'National Tariff Payment System 2017/18 and 2018/19: a consultation notice', 22.12.2016, <https://improvement.nhs.uk/resources/national-tariff-1719-consultation/> accessed 24.06.2018.

—— 'Single Oversight Framework for NHS Providers', 30.09.2016, <https://improvement.nhs.uk/resources/single-oversight-framework/> accessed 24.06.2018.

—— 'Making Mergers Work: Improvements NHS providers have achieved through merger', May 2016, <https://improvement.nhs.uk/resources/how-make-nhs-mergers-work-better-patients/> accessed 24.06.2018.

NHS PARTNERS NETWORK / NHS CONFEDERATION, 'Working together since 1948: celebrating 70 years of partnership between the NHS and independent sector', June 2018.

—— '15 Years of Concordat: reflection and renewal', June 2015.

NHS TRUST DEVELOPMENT AUTHORITY (NHS TDA), National Health Service Trust Development Authority Directions, <https://www.gov.uk/government/uploads/system/uploads/attachment_data/file/175350/NTDA_Directions_2013.pdf> accessed 24.06.2018.

—— 'Delivering High Quality Care for Patients – The Accountability Framework for NHS Trust Boards', April 2013.

—— 'Delivering for Patients – The 2014/15 Accountability Framework for NHS Trust Boards', 31.03.2014.

—— 'Delivering for Patients – The 2015/16 Accountability Framework for NHS Trust Boards', 02.04.2015.

NICOLAIDES, P., 'Non-Economic Activities', *Stateaidhub.eu* blog, 10.03.2015, <http://stateaidhub.eu/blogs/stateaiduncovered/post/1707> accessed 24.06.2018.

NISTOR, L., *Public Services and the European Union: Healthcare, Health Insurance and Education Services*, TMC Asser Press, The Hague 2011.

ODUDU, O., 'Competition law and the welfare state', forthcoming in GALLOWAY, J. (ed.), *Intersections of Antitrust: Policy and Regulations*, Oxford University Press, Oxford, <https://papers.ssrn.com/sol3/papers.cfm?abstract_id=3160784> accessed 24.06.2018.

—— 'Why it matters – Selling competition law in the new frontier' (2013) *Competition Law Insight*, 10.12.2013.

—— 'Competition Law and the National Health Service' (*Competition Bulletin: Competition Law Views from Blackstone Chambers*, 08.10.2012), <https://competitionbulletin.com/2012/10/08/competition-law-and-the-national-health-service/> accessed 24.06.2018.

—— 'Are State Owned Healthcare Providers That Are Funded By General Taxation Undertakings Subject To Competition Law?' (2011) 32(5) *European Competition Law Review* 231.

OFFICE OF FAIR TRADING (OFT), 'OFT welcomes action by NHS trusts to ensure compliance with competition law', OFT Press Release 71/12, 16.08.2012.

—— 'Developing public service markets – Insights for regulators, commissioners and policy makers', OFT1497.

—— 'Orderly Exit – Designing continuity regimes in public markets', OFT1468.

—— *Private Healthcare Market Study*, OFT1396.

—— 'Competition Law and Public Bodies', OFT1389.

—— 'Commissioning and Competition in the Public Sector', OFT1314.

—— 'Empowering Consumers of Public Services through Choice-Tools', OFT1321.

—— 'Competition in Mixed Markets: Ensuring Competitive Neutrality', OFT 1242.

—— 'Choice and Competition in Public Services', OFT 1214.

—— 'Government in Markets – Why competition matters – a guide for policymakers', OFT1113.

—— 'Guidance on how to assess the competition effects of subsidies', OFT829.

—— 'Assessing the impact of public sector procurement on competition', OFT742a.

—— 'Competition Act 1998 and public bodies', 2004 OFT443.

OFFICE OF HEALTH ECONOMICS (OHE), *Competition in the NHS*, OHE, London 2012.

OFWAT, 'Ofwat's approach to mergers and statement of methods', October 2015.

OTTOW, A., *Market & Competition Authorities – Good Agency Principles*, Oxford University Press, Oxford 2015.

PIKE, C., 'CCP Working Paper 2: An Empirical Analysis of the Effects of GP Competition', 2010.

—— 'Inside the Black Box: How competition between hospitals improves quality and integration of services', *NHS CCP Working Paper Series*, Volume 1, Number 5, July 2012.

PLAYER, S. and LEYS, C., *Confuse and Conceal: The NHS and Independent Sector Treatment Centres*, Merlin Press, London 2008.

PROPPER, C., 'Competition in health care: lessons from the English experience' (May 2018) *Health Economics, Policy and Law* 1 (online).

PROSSER, T., 'Monitor, the Independent Regulator of NHS Foundation Trusts' in PROSSER, T., *The Regulatory Enterprise: Government, Regulation, and Legitimacy*, Oxford University Press, Oxford 2010.

—— 'EU competition law and public services' in MOSSIALOS, E., PERMANAND, G., BAETEN, R. and HERVEY, T.K. (eds.), *Health Systems Governance in Europe: The Role of European Union Law and Policy*, Cambridge University Press, Cambridge 2010.

—— 'Regulation and Social Solidarity' (2006) 33(3) *Journal of Law and Society* 364.

—— *The Limits of Competition Law*, Oxford University Press, Oxford 2005.

—— 'Public Service Law – Privatization's unexpected offspring' (2000) 63(4) Law and Contemporary Problems 63.

—— 'Competition, Regulators and Public Service' in RODGER, B. and MACCULLOCH, A., *The UK Competition Act – A New Era for UK Competition Law*, Hart Publishing, Oxford 2000.

—— 'Theorising Utility Regulation' (1999) 62(2) *Modern Law Review* 196.

RAPTOPOULOU, K., *EU Law and Healthcare Services – Normative Approaches to Public Health Systems*, Wolters Kluwer, Alphen aan den Rijn 2015.

READER, D., 'Accommodating Public Interest Considerations in Domestic Merger Control: Empirical Insights', *CCP Working Paper* 16-3.

REYNOLDS, L. and MCKEE, M., 'Opening the oyster: the 2010–11 NHS reforms in England' [2012] *Clinical Medicine*, 12(2), 128.

RIJKSOVERHEID (Government of the Netherlands), 'Wat verandert er in het basispakket van de zorgverzekering in 2018?' ('What's changing in the basic package of health insurance in 2018?'), <https://www.rijksoverheid.nl/onderwerpen/zorgverzekering/vraag-en-antwoord/veranderingen-basispakket-zorgverzekering-2018> accessed 24.06.2018.

—— 'Wat is het eigen risico van mijn zorgverzekerring en wanneer betaal ik dat?' ('What is the mandatory excess in my health insurance and when do I pay it?'), <https://www.rijksoverheid.nl/onderwerpen/zorgverzekering/vraag-en-antwoord/eigen-risico-zorgverzekering> accessed 24.06.2018.

—— 'Wanneer betaal ik een eigen bijdrage voor zorg?' ('When do I pay a personal contribution for healthcare?'), <https://www.rijksoverheid.nl/onderwerpen/zorgverzekering/vraag-en-antwoord/wanneer-eigen-bijdrage-zorgverzekering> accessed 24.06.2018.

RODGER, B.J., 'The Competition Act 1998 and State Entities as Undertakings: promises to be an interesting debate', *CLaSF Working Paper Number 1 2003.*

ROYAL SURREY COUNTY HOSPITAL NHS FOUNDATION TRUST, 'Update on proposed hospital merger', <http://www.royalsurrey.nhs.uk/update-on-proposed-hospital-merger/> accessed 24.06.2018.

SÁNCHEZ GRAELLS, A., 'New rules for health care procurement in the UK: a critical assessment from the perspective of EU economic law' (2015) 1 *Public Procurement Law Review* 16.

—— 'Monitor and the Competition and Markets Authority' (2014) *University of Leicester School of Law Research Paper*, No. 14-32.

—— 'Why are NHS Commissioners "undertakings" and, consequently, subject to competition law?' *How to crack a nut*, 02.06.2014, <http://www.howtocrackanut.com/blog/2014/06/why-are-nhs-commissioners-undertakings.html?rq=%E2%80%98Why%20are%20NHS%20Commissioners%20%E2%80%98undertakings%E2%80%99%20and%2C%20consequently%2C%20subject%20to%20competition%20law%3F%E2%80%99> accessed 24.06.2018.

SANDERSON, M., ALLEN, P. and OSIPOVIC, D., 'The regulation of competition in the National Health Service (NHS): what difference has the Health and Social Care Act 2012 made?' (2017) 12 *Health Economics, Policy and Law* 1.

—— *Public Procurement and the EU Competition Rules*, 2nd edn., Hart Publishing, Oxford 2015.

SAUTER, W., *Coherence in EU Competition Law*, Oxford University Press, Oxford 2016.

—— *Public Services in EU Law*, Cambridge University Press, Cambridge 2015.

—— 'The balance between competition law and regulation in Dutch healthcare markets' (2014) *TILEC Discussion Paper* DP 2014-41.

—— 'The Impact of EU Competition Law on National Healthcare Systems' (2013) 38(4) *European Law Review* 457.

—— 'Sectorspecifiek mededingingsrecht en fusietoetsing' ('Sector-specific competition law and merger control') (2013) *RegelMaat*, (28) 2, 77.

—— 'Experiences from the Netherlands: The Application of Competition Rules in Health Care' in VAN DE GRONDEN, J.W., SZYSZCZAK, E., NEERGAARD, U. and KRAJEWSKI, M. (eds.), *Health Care and EU Law*, TMC Asser Press, The Hague 2011.

—— 'Is the general consumer interest a source of legitimacy for healthcare regulation? An analysis of the Dutch experience' (2009) 2–3 *European Journal of Consumer Law* 419.

—— 'Diensten van algemeen economisch belang en universele dienstverplichtingen in de gezondheidszorg' ('Services of General Economic Interest and Universal Service Obligations in Healthcare') (2008) *Markt & Mededinging*, 1, 4.

—— 'Services of General Economic Interest and Universal Service Obligations as an EU Law Framework for Curative Healthcare' (2007) *TILEC Discussion Paper* 29.

SCHIPPERS, E., 'Kwaliteit loont' ('Quality Pays'), Letter from the Minister for Health, Wellbeing and Sport to the Chairman of the Second Chamber, 06.02.2015.

—— *Kabinetsreactie rapport commissie Borstlap en evaluatie Wmg en NZa*, (Cabinet response to the Borstlap and AEF reports, Letter from the Minister for Health, Wellbeing and Sport to the Chairman of the First Chamber), 02.04.2015.

SCHRIJVERSHOF, D.W.L.A., Maverick Advocaten response to consultation, 08.08.2017, <https://www.internetconsultatie.nl/zorgconcentraties/reactie/f30a08d1-3a15-418e-ae17-553246839253> accessed 24.06.2018.

—— 'Kostbare zorgfusietoetsing en lage ACM-drempels' ('Expensive healthcare merger assessment and low ACM thresholds'), *Zorgvisie*, 19.07.2017, <https://www.zorgvisie.nl/zorgfusietoetsing-en-de-acm-drempels/> accessed 24.06.2018.

SCHRIJVERSHOF, D.W.L.A. and PLETTENBURG, J.C., 'Toetsing van zorgfusies en toezicht in de zorg door ACM: hoe nu verder?' ('Healthcare merger assessment and regulation of healthcare by the ACM: where now?') (2016) *Tijdschrift Mededingingsrecht in de praktijk*, 3, 21.

SCHUT, F.T. and VARKEVISSER, M., 'Competition policy for health care provision in the Netherlands' (2017) 121(2) *Health Policy* 126.

SCOTT, A., STEVENSON, T. and CHUA, V., 'The profitability of private patients', *Health Service Journal* 27.09.2012.

SENGERS, I.H.E., Federatie Medisch Specialisten, response to consultation, 20.08.2017, <https://www.internetconsultatie.nl/zorgconcentraties/reactie/c8bfdf1f-dfbe-4f16-818a-8d83512f5542> accessed 24.06.2018.

SHEPPARD, M.K., 'Fallacy or Functionality: Law and Policy of Patient Treatment Choice in the NHS' (2016) 24 *Health Care Analysis* 279.

SICILIANI, L., CHALKLEY, M. and GRAVELLE, H., 'Competition policy in five European countries – What can be learned for health policy in England?', *The Health Foundation Working Paper Number 1*, July 2017.

SINCLAIR, D., '"Undertakings" in competition law at the public-private interface – an unhealthy situation' (2014) 35(4) *European Competition Law Review* 167.

SKILBECK, J., 'Just when is a public body an 'undertaking'? *Fenin* and *BetterCare* compared' (2003) 4 *Public Procurement Law Review* 75.

SMITH, S., HEARD, E. and BEVAN, D., 'New procurement legislation for English healthcare bodies – the National Health Service (Procurement, Patient Choice and Competition) (No. 2) Regulations 2013' (2013) 4 *Public Procurement Law Review* 109.

SMYTH, C., 'Gas and power markets are a model for the health service', *The Times*, 25.02.2011.

SOUTH KENT COAST CLINICAL COMMISSIONING GROUP, 'French elective care contracts', News article, 08.09.2015, <http://www.southkentcoastccg.nhs.uk/news/news-articles/?blogpost=7639> accessed 24.06.2018.

SPENCELAYH, E. and DIXON, J., 'Mergers in the NHS – Lessons from the decision to block the proposed merger of hospitals in Bournemouth and Poole', *The Health Foundation Policy Analysis*, December 2014.

STEVENS, S. and BENNETT, D., Letter to Chief Executives of providers of NHS-funded care, 18.02.2015, <https://www.england.nhs.uk/wp-content/uploads/2015/02/tariff-arrangmnts-2015-16nhs-activity.pdf>, accessed 24.06.2018.

STIRTON, L., 'Back to the Future? Lessons on the Pro-Competitive Regulation of Health Services' (2014) 22(2) *Medical Law Review* 180.

STOLTZFUS JOST, T., DAWSON, D. and DEN EXTER, A., 'The Role of Competition in Health Care: A Western European Perspective' (2006) 31(3) *Journal of Health Politics, Policy and Law* 687.

STREET, A., 'Overview' in CHARLESWORTH, A. and KELLY, E. (eds.), *Competition in UK health care – Reflections from an expert workshop*, Nuffield Trust and Institute for Fiscal Studies, London 2013.

SZYSZCZAK, E., 'Modernising Healthcare: Pilgrimage for the Holy Grail?' in KRAJEWSKI, M., NEERGAARD, U. and VAN DE GRONDEN, J.W. (eds.), *The Changing Legal Framework for Services of General Interest in Europe – Between Competition and Solidarity*, TMC Asser Press, The Hague 2009.

TAYLOR, A., 'Unintended effects of limiting out-of-area placements?', *Aldwych Partners blog*, 13.11.2017, <http://aldwychpartners.co.uk/unintended-effects-of-limiting-out-of-area-placements/> accessed 24.06.2018.

—— 'Making NHS mergers more successful', *Aldwych Partners blog*, 22.09.2017, <http://aldwychpartners.co.uk/making-more-nhs-mergers-more-successful/> accessed 24.06.2018.

—— 'Competing over health – What's next for the National Health Service in England?', *Competition Law Insight*, 16.02.2016.

—— 'Using patient referrals to analyse hospital competition', *Aldwych Partners blog*, 26.11.2015, <http://aldwychpartners.co.uk/using-patient-referrals-to-analyse-hospital-competition/> accessed 24.06.2018.

—— 'Is clearance for hospital mergers about to get easier?' *Nuffield Trust Blog*, 10.09.2015, <https://www.nuffieldtrust.org.uk/news-item/is-clearance-for-hospital-mergers-about-to-get-easier> accessed 24.06.2018.

—— 'When does an alliance become a merger?', *Aldwych Partners blog*, 14.07.2015, <http://aldwychpartners.co.uk/when-does-an-alliance-become-a-merger/> accessed 24.06.2018.

—— 'Has patient choice made it harder for mental health trusts to merge?', *NHS Competition Regulation*, 15.05.2015.

TEMPLE LANG, J., 'Privatisation of Social Welfare: EU Competition Law Rules' in DOUGAN, M. and SPAVENTA, E. (eds.) *Social Welfare and EU Law*, Hart Publishing, Oxford 2005.

THOMAS, R. and WEST, D., 'STPs will end the purchaser-provider split, says Stevens', *Health Service Journal*, 27.02.2017.

THOMSON, S. and MOSSIALOS, E., 'Private health insurance and the internal market' in MOSSIALOS, E., PERMANAND, G., BAETEN, R., and HERVEY, T.K. (eds.), *Health Systems Governance in Europe: The Role of European Union Law and Policy*, Cambridge University Press, Cambridge 2010.

TIMMINS, N., *The Five Giants – A Biography of the Welfare State*, 3rd edn., William Collins, London 2017.

—— *Never Again? The Story of the Health and Social Care Act 2012 – A Study in Coalition Government and Policy Making*, The King's Fund and Institute for Government, London 2012.

TRITTER, J., KOIVUSALO, M., OLLILA, E., and DORFMAN, P., *Globalisation, Markets and Health Policy – Redrawing the Patient as Consumer*, Routledge, Abingdon 2010.

VAN DE GRONDEN, J.W., 'Services of General Interest and the Concept of Undertaking: Does EU Competition Law Apply?' (2018) 41(2) *World Competition* 197.

—— *Mededingingsrecht in de EU en Nederland* (Competition Law in the EU and the Netherlands), Uitgeverij Paris, Zutphen 2017.

—— 'The Treaty Provisions on Competition and Health Care' in VAN DE GRONDEN, J.W., SZYSZCZAK, E., NEERGAARD, U., and KRAJEWSKI, M. (eds.), *Health Care and EU Law*, TMC Asser Press, The Hague 2011.

—— 'Een upgrade van het zorgbeleid van de NMa: de derde versie van de Richtsnoeren voor de zorgsector' ('Upgrade of the NMa's healthcare policy: the third edition of the Guidelines for the Healthcare Sector') (2010) *Markt & Mededinging*, 6, 195.

—— 'Purchasing care: economic activity or service of general (economic) interest?' (2004) 25(2) *European Competition Law Review* 87.

—— 'Richtsnoeren voor de zorgsector: codificatie van de NMa-beleidspraktijk' ('Guidelines for the healthcare sector: codification of the NMa's policy practice') (2003) *Markt & Mededinging*, 2, 36.

—— 'Toezichthouders in de zorg en de NMa: conflicterende bevoegdheden?' ('Healthcare regulators and the NMa: conflicting competences?') (2002) *Tijdschrift voor Gezondheidsrecht*, 5, 323.

—— 'Mededingingsrecht en gezondheidszorg' ('Competition law and Healthcare') (2001) *Markt & Mededinging*, 8, 267.

VAN DE GRONDEN, J.W. and RUSU, C.S., 'EU competition law and policy and health systems', Chapter 11 in HERVEY, T.K., YOUNG, C.A., and BISHOP, L.E. (eds.), *Research Handbook on EU Health Law and Policy*, Edward Elgar, Cheltenham 2017.

VAN DE GRONDEN, J.W. and SZYSZCZAK, E., 'Introducing Competition Principles Into Health Care Through EU Law and Policy: A Case Study of the Netherlands' (2014) 22(2) *Medical Law Review* 238.

—— 'Conclusions: Constructing a "Solid" Multi-Layered Health Care Edifice' in VAN DE GRONDEN, J.W., SZYSZCZAK, E., NEERGAARD, U. and KRAJEWSKI, M. (eds.), *Health Care and EU Law*, TMC Asser Press, The Hague 2011.

VAN DE GRONDEN, J.W. and DE VRIES, S.A., 'Independent competition authorities in the EU' (2006) 2(1) *Utrecht Law Review* 32.

VAN DER HEUL, S. 'Wetsvoorstel voor overheveling zorgspecifieke fusietoets en het toezicht op Aanmerkelijke Marktmacht in de zorg' ('Legislative proposal for transferring the healthcare-specific merger test and SMP oversight in healthcare'), 18.04.2016, <https://www.dirkzwager.nl/kennis/artikelen/wetsvoorstel-voor-overheveling-zorgspecifieke-fusietoets-en-het-toezicht-op-aanmerkelijke-marktmacht-in-de-zorg/> accessed 24.06.2018.

VAN DER HEUL, S. and CORNELISSEN, F., 'Markttoezicht in de gezondheidszorg na wijziging Wmg' ('Market regulation in healthcare after Wmg amendments') (2016) *Markt & Mededinging*, 5, 175.

VAN DER WOLK, A.P.E., 'Nieuw samenwerkingsprotocol ACM & NZa' ('New ACM/NZa Cooperation Protocol'), Banning publicaties, 16.01.2015, <https://www.banning.nl/publicaties/nieuw-samenwerkingsprotocol-acm-nza/> accessed 24.06.2018.

VARKEVISSER, M. et al., 'Instellingsoverstijgende maatschappen: Huidige ontwikkelingen, mogelijke gevolgen en de aanpak van eventuele mededingingsproblemen. Eindrapport', Maart 2013 ('Cross-institution partnerships: current developments, possible consequences and managing potential competition problems. Final Report', March 2013).

VARKEVISSER, M., CAPPS, C., and SCHUT, F., 'Defining Hospital Markets for Antitrust Enforcement: New Approaches and their Applicability to the Netherlands' (2008) 3(1) *Health Economics, Policy and Law* 7.

VARKEVISSER, M., and SCHUT, F., 'The Impact of Geographic Market Definition on the Stringency of Hospital Merger Control in Germany and the Netherlands' (2012) 7 *Health Economics, Policy and Law* 363.

VERLOREN VAN THEMAAT, W. and BOSCH, M., 'De uitgangspunten toezicht eerstelijnszorg in een context' ('The starting-points for oversight of primary care providers in context') (2016) *Markt en Mededinging*, 1, 31.

VONK, R.A.A. and SCHUT, F.T., 'Can universal access be achieved in a voluntary private health insurance market? Dutch private insurers caught between competing logics' (May 2018) *Health Economics, Policy and Law* 1 (online).

VVD, CDA, D66 EN CHRISTENUNIE, *Regeerakkoord 2017–2021 'Vertrouwen in de toekomst'* ('Trust in the Future'), 10.10.2017, <https://www.rijksoverheid.nl/regering/regeerakkoord-vertrouwen-in-de-toekomst/1.-investeren-voor-iedereen/1.4-zorg> accessed 24.06.2018.

WALSHE, K., 'Queen's Speech: We can't avoid legislation for ever', *Health Service Journal*, 28.05.2015.

WIGGERS, M., *De NMa en de NZa in de curatieve zorgsector – Een toetsing aan het Europees mededingingsrecht* (The NMa and the NZa in the curative healthcare sector – an assessment against EU competition law), Kluwer, Deventer 2013.

WIGGERS, M. and DIBBITS, J., 'Twintig jaar karteltoezicht in de zorg – A bumpy ride' ('Twenty years of regulating anticompetitive agreements in healthcare – a bumpy ride') (2018) *Tijdschrift Zorg & Recht in Praktijk*, 1, 13.

WIGGERS, M. and SLUIJS, J.J.M., 'CBb-trilogie: Apotheek Van Dalen – NZa (en Menzis)' ('Dutch Trade and Industry Appeals Tribunal (CBb) Trilogy: Van Dalen Pharmacy v NZa (and Menzis)'), (2012) *Markt en Mededinging*, 6, 213.

—— 'Menzis – Apotheek Van Dalen' ('Menzis v Van Dalen Pharmacy'), (2011) *Markt en Mededinging*, 4, 145.

—— 'Menzis – Apotheek J.D. van Dalen' ('Menzis v Van Dalen Pharmacy'), (2010) *Markt en Mededinging*, 3, 114.

WIGGERS, M., STRUIJLAART, R., and RUIGEWAARD, J., 'Landelijke Huisartsen Vereniging – Annotatie van de uitspraak van de Rechtbank Rotterdam van 17 december 2015' ('Dutch GPs' Association – Case Comment on the judgment of the Rotterdam District Court of 17 December 2015') (2016) *Markt en Mededinging*, 4, 160.

—— 'Landelijke Huisartsen Vereniging ('Dutch GPs' Association') (2014) *Markt & Mededinging*, 4, 160.

WOLTERS KLUWER, Juridisch-Economisch Lexicon – The Legal and Economic Lexicon, Online edition.

ZORGWIJZER, 'Hoe kom ik aanmerking voor het PGB?' ('How do I qualify for the Personal Healthcare Budget?'), <https://www.zorgwijzer.nl/faq/hoe-kom-ik-aanmerking-voor-het-pgb> accessed 24.06.2018.

ZUIDERANT-JERAK, T., GRIT, K. and VAN DER GRINTEN, T., 'Markets and Public Values in Healthcare', *iBMG Working Paper* W2010.01.

ZWART, F.S.A., Nederlandse Vereniging van Participatiemaatschappijen (NVP) response to consultation, 18.08.2017, <https://www.internetconsultatie.nl/zorgconcentraties/reactie/219f2288-46f8-4a10-a556-c05f6972f994> accessed 24.06.2018.

# INDEX

# ABOUT THE AUTHOR

Dr Mary Guy is a Lecturer in Law at Lancaster Law School and is directing the law component of a British Academy/Leverhulme Trust–funded interdisciplinary project on 'EU Health Policy and Law – Shaping a Future Research Agenda' in 2018–2020. She is a member of the European Association of Health Law, the Society of Legal Scholars, the Socio-Legal Studies Association, the British Association of Comparative Law and the Chartered Institute of Linguists Educational Trust.

www.ingramcontent.com/pod-product-compliance
Ingram Content Group UK Ltd.
Pitfield, Milton Keynes, MK11 3LW, UK
UKHW051847100926
8556IPUK00005B/493

9 781780 6864